Indians & Energy

This School for Advanced Research advanced seminar book is published in cooperation with the William P. Clements Center for Southwest Studies, Southern Methodist University.

Publication of this book and the SAR seminar from which it resulted were made possible with the generous support of the Annenberg Conversations Endowment and The Brown Foundation, Inc., of Houston, Texas.

School for Advanced Research
Advanced Seminar Series

James F. Brooks
General Editor

Indians & Energy

Contributors

Benedict J. Colombi
School of Anthropology and School of Natural Resources and the Environment, University of Arizona

Susan Dawson
Department of Sociology, Social Work, and Anthropology, Utah State University–Logan

Donald L. Fixico (Shawnee, Sac & Fox, Muscogee Creek, and Seminole)
Department of History, Arizona State University

Brian Frehner
Department of History, Oklahoma State University

Leah S. Glaser
Department of History, Central Connecticut State University

Barbara Rose Johnston
Center for Political Ecology, Santa Cruz

Dáilan J. Long (Diné)
Diné Citizens Against Ruining Our Environment

Gary Madsen
Department of Sociology, Social Work, and Anthropology, Utah State University–Logan

Andrew Needham
Department of History, New York University

Colleen O'Neill
Department of History, Utah State University

Dana E. Powell
Department of Anthropology, University of North Carolina–Chapel Hill

Sherry L. Smith
Department of History, Southern Methodist University
Clements Center for Southwest Studies

Rebecca Tsosie (Yaqui)
Sandra Day O'Connor College of Law, Arizona State University

Garrit Voggesser
Tribal Lands Conservation Program, National Wildlife Federation

Indians & Energy

Exploitation and Opportunity in the American Southwest

Edited by Sherry L. Smith and Brian Frehner

School for Advanced Research Press
Santa Fe

School for Advanced Research Press
Post Office Box 2188
Santa Fe, New Mexico 87504-2188
www.sarpress.sarweb.org

Managing Editor: Lisa Pacheco
Editorial Assistant: Ellen Goldberg
Designer and Production Manager: Cynthia Dyer
Manuscript Editor: Kate Whelan
Proofreader: Mary June-el Piper
Indexer: Margaret Moore Booker
Printer: Cushing-Malloy, Inc.

Library of Congress Cataloging-in-Publication Data

Indians & energy : exploitation and opportunity in the American Southwest / edited by Sherry L. Smith and Brian Frehner. — 1st ed.
p. cm. — (School for Advanced Research advanced seminar series)
Includes bibliographical references and index.
ISBN 978-1-934691-15-1 (alk. paper)
1. Indians of North America—Southwest, New—Land tenure. 2. Indians of North America—Southwest, New—Economic conditions. 3. Energy development—Southwest, New. 4. Renewable energy sources—Southwest, New. 5. Mines and mineral resources—Southwest, New. I. Smith, Sherry L. (Sherry Lynn), 1951- II. Frehner, Brian. III. Title: Indians and energy.
E98.L3I535 2010
333.7908997'079—dc22

2010008829

Manufactured in the United States of America.
Library of Congress Catalog Card Number 2010008829
International Standard Book Number 978-1-934691-15-1
First edition 2010.

This book was printed on paper containing 30% PCR.

Cover illustration: *Natural Resource Management*, 92 x 54 inches, acrylic on canvas, © 2004 Bunky Echo-Hawk (Pawnee/Yakama).

For David J. Weber, whose dedication, example, and guidance have inspired a generation of scholars.

Contents

Figures

Acknowledgments

Many people made this volume possible, and we would like to extend our gratitude for their efforts, contributions, and participation. This project originated from a discussion between Brian Frehner and David J. Weber at Southern Methodist University (SMU). David expressed his enthusiastic support from the outset and marshaled the resources of the Clements Center for Southwest Studies to provide financial and administrative aid. The Clements Center arranged for all authors to convene in Dallas, where they discussed and critiqued their essays and identified key themes at the center of this book. The authors then presented their papers at a public symposium on SMU's campus in March 2008. David played a vital role as well by reaching out to James F. Brooks, president and chief executive officer of the School for Advanced Research (SAR), and asking him to participate. James also invited all the volume's authors to SAR's beautiful campus in Santa Fe, New Mexico, where they read one another's initial drafts, offered suggestions, and enjoyed one of the most beautiful locations for scholars in the American Southwest. We would also like to thank others at SAR who helped with this project, including Lynn Baca, director of SAR Press; Catherine Cocks, who initially oversaw the editorial process; Nancy Owen Lewis, director of scholar programs; and Leslie Shipman, guest services manager, who graciously welcomed us into SAR's comfortable housing facilities and accommodated us throughout our stay.

We also extend our gratitude to William P. Clements Jr., whose generosity makes possible so many activities at the Clements Center. Anyone familiar with the center knows that much of what happens there occurs because of the energy, enthusiasm, and intelligence of Andrea Boardman, associate director, and we appreciate all that she does. We also thank Ruth Ann Elmore, who performed many of the administrative and organizational activities associated with this project and graciously hosted a dinner at her home for the authors after our Dallas symposium. Aiding in the smooth functioning of the symposium were Anna Banhegyi and Jenna Valadez, two of SMU's best and brightest graduate students, and we appreciate their efforts. We also appreciate the assistance of Steve Denson (Chickasaw), who is director of diversity at SMU's Cox School of Business and helped publicize the symposium and book. Krys Boyd's informed and probing questions also publicized the project during an interview on her program "Think," which aired on the Dallas public radio station KERA.

Indians & Energy

1

Introduction

Sherry L. Smith and Brian Frehner

In 1969 the Bureau of Reclamation commissioned artist Norman Rockwell to produce a painting commemorating the completion of Glen Canyon Dam. Located just south of the Utah/Arizona border, the dam is a central feature of the Colorado River Storage Project. Its waters generate electricity and irrigate the desert Southwest, and its structure provides flood control. Glen Canyon Dam sits on the Navajo reservation, but its proponents were, and its primary beneficiaries remain, non-Indian people. Upon visiting the site with Bureau of Reclamation employees, Rockwell, best known for sentimental images of Anglo-Americans that appeared on the cover of *The Saturday Evening Post,* announced that he painted people, not objects. A painting of the dam alone would be nothing more than "a mechanical drawing." Scrambling to provide the human element, W. L. Rusho, Regional Public Affairs officer for the federal agency, asked a local Navajo family to pose for the artist. They are the figures in the foreground of the final canvas, looking down at the colossal dam and its power lines (figure 1.1). Rockwell's wife photographed the family in various poses outside their home, and the artist, working in his Stockbridge, Massachusetts, studio, later superimposed them onto the scene. In the process, Rockwell created an arresting image of Native Americans and energy.[1]

FIGURE 1.1

Norman Rockwell painting of Glen Canyon Dam with a Navajo family in the foreground. Image courtesy of the Bureau of Reclamation.

The family's reaction to Glen Canyon Dam is difficult to discern. The man and boy, wearing contemporary dress, stand with their backs to the viewer, making it impossible to gauge their feelings (though the boy's fists are clenched). The woman, dressed in a long skirt and velvet blouse and perched on an apparently relaxed horse, is in profile and also difficult to read. Only the dog looks stressed—albeit worried more about the cliff than the technological behemoth in the background. Soaring overhead are a bald eagle and a hawk, patriotic symbols more concerned with each other than with the people or the dam. The image blends the old and the new, the human and the technological, the wild and the manmade. The message, perhaps not surprising, given the client, was clear: dams nestled nicely into the landscape and attracted rather than repelled wildlife. As for the Navajos, does their demeanor suggest acceptance? Resignation? What *is* the implication about the relationship between Indians and energy production? This is ambiguous. In some respects, Rockwell linked these people to premodern life through the woman's dress and transportation. He presented them as culturally—and physically—separate from modernity, not a part of the industrial age. They seemingly had no role in the creation of the dam—as owners, workers, or consumers of the electric power it would produce. They were merely colorful onlookers, powerless observers of the new world arriving in their lands. Their future remained unclear. Would they benefit from this icon of industrial life or remain apart from it?

Such an image of Native Americans was not unusual in the 1960s. At a historical moment when many policymakers considered Indians and tribes as anachronistic and Congress moved to extinguish tribes as legal entities through the Termination policy, many non-Indians assumed that Indians' only options were to assimilate and acculturate. It was impossible, they believed, to be modern and Native American simultaneously. Even today, in the wake of the Red Power movement, with the revitalization of tribal politics and cultures and the reassertion of tribal sovereignty and treaty rights, many non-Indians continue to assume that American Indians live only in the past. The chapters in this book, through the prism of energy, challenge such simplistic notions. They explain how, from the beginning of energy development on Indian lands, Indian people have been actively engaged: as owners and lessees of resources, workers in the industries, consumers of electricity and gasoline, and developers of tribal energy companies, as well as environmentalists who sometimes challenge these enterprises. The story of the relationship between Indians and energy, in other words, is much more complicated than Rockwell's painting suggests. And it is a story that will continue to have relevance, for Indians and non-Indians, well into the twenty-first century and beyond.

As of 2005, there were 561 federally recognized tribes and communities in the United States, with more than 350 of them in the "lower forty-eight states." According to the 2000 census, 4.1 million people self-identified as American Indian or Alaska Native, and 2.5 million of those people identified as single-race Native American. Tribes own 2 percent of the nation's land base, with reservation lands totaling 72 million acres. Considerable energy resources rest in those lands, particularly in the West. To be sure, not all tribes have energy resources. Still, 30 percent of the known coal reserves in the United States are in Indian Country. Tribes own 37 percent of the country's uranium, 3 percent of its oil and gas, and 10 percent of its onshore natural gas deposits. One-third of the nation's reservations have high potential for wind energy production, and more than one hundred reservations have high biomass potential. In 2004, Indian oil and gas production generated more than $245 million in royalty revenues, suggesting that Indian-owned oil and gas resources yielded more than $2 billion in output. Their undeveloped resources may be even more valuable. More than 2 million acres of land have been actively mined for coal, gas, and oil;

another 15 million have potential for such development. The only other mineral-property owners with holdings as large as the tribes' are the railroads (beneficiaries of generous construction land subsidies from the federal government in the nineteenth century) and the US government. Historically, tribes have contributed enormously to energy development, including $15.3 billion in oil, $10 billion in coal, and about $8 billion in natural gas, although they have often been grossly underpaid for these resources. In sum, as one source put it, Native Americans represent 1 percent of the US population but hold 10 percent of the nation's energy reserves.[2]

Clearly, American Indians play an important role in the United States' energy development. This matters, of course, to tribes and their members. But it also matters to all who consume these resources. At a moment when oil prices are volatile and the United States largely depends on foreign sources of petroleum, the place of Native Americans in the nation's energy future is critical. As the Southwest continues to grow, sources for its electricity (hydropower, coal-fired plants, uranium, wind farms) will certainly include those based in Indian Country. The central questions this book addresses are these: What has been the meaning of energy development on Native American lands in the American Southwest, particularly for American Indian people? Is this a story of exploitation or of opportunity? And how does our understanding of past patterns guide policies and decisions—tribal, state, federal, corporate, and individual—that will affect all of us in the future? The authors here reveal answers that are far from simple.

As journalist Marjane Ambler discovered nearly twenty years ago when she wrote about Indians and energy, it is impossible to generalize about the topic.[3] Still, patterns emerge in this volume even if they are, at times, contradictory. As Leah Glaser shows in chapter 8, "An Absolute Paragon of Paradoxes," Native people have been victimized by energy developers, but they have also taken advantage of opportunities to bring energy to their communities. Similarly, Ben Colombi's chapter 5 highlights the "paradox" of hydroelectric energy generated by dams on tribal lands that improved Indians' lives but inflicted serious environmental damage. The diversity of tribes and individuals, experiences, and attitudes further complicates the story. Brian Frehner's chapter 3 discusses Charles Curtis, vice president under Herbert Hoover, who, though identified strongly with his Native ancestry, profited from his efforts to provide non-Indian oil companies access to lands in Indian Territory. And in chapter 4, Garrit Voggesser charts how, in the course of generating power (whether through water, oil, gas, uranium, or coal), a variety of tribes and Indian people gradually came to exercise greater political and economic control over their own resources and, consequently, their lives. By contributing to the nation's energy sources, they have fueled tribal economic development; this, in turn, has strengthened their political, cultural, and social positions.

Perhaps no example better demonstrates the opportunities energy development can provide than that of the Southern Ute. Their 700,000-acre reservation in Colorado's San Juan Basin contains one of the world's richest deposits of methane found in coal seams. Consequently, the Southern Utes control the distribution of approximately 1 percent of the nation's natural gas supply, making the tribe's holdings worth about $4 billion. Things were not always so. One of seven bands of Utes, who occupied one-third of Colorado when the United States took over that territory, the Southern Utes ended up with a reservation reduced to a fraction of their lands. After allotment, their land base became even smaller with a checkerboard of Southern Ute and non-Indian ownership. In fact, today 9,500 non-Indians live on the reservation, compared with 1,000 Southern Utes and 433 American Indians of other tribes. Energy companies began drilling for natural gas in the 1950s. Reflecting the politics of the time, the tribe had little power over this development and received meager royalties, distributed to members as per capita payments. In the 1970s, tribal chairman Leonard Burch, a navy veteran who served as chair almost continuously for thirty-six years, began to change the dynamics of Southern Ute energy policies. He put a stop to per capita payments, sending lease revenues to the tribal government. Burch and the tribal council declared a moratorium on new mineral leases until the tribe could build its management capabilities. They enacted a severance tax in the 1980s as the energy boom went into full swing. Still, in 1990 the Southern Utes were not prospering, even though sixty-three oil and gas companies operated on the reservation.[4]

By this time, Burch and the Southern Utes had begun to realize that the real profits came not in royalties, but in ownership of production. They took action to become producers with the aid of business executive Bob Zahradnik, a former Exxon employee who began working for the Utes in 1988, monitoring companies' compliance with leases and strengthening the Utes' negotiating power. Zahradnik wrote up a business plan for one of the first tribe-owned energy companies in the nation, Red Willow Production Company. With $8 million in seed capital, it began buying back wells and leases. Red Willow now has interests in more than 1,000 wells, operates 450 on the reservation (second only to British Petroleum), and is the thirteenth largest privately held energy company in the nation. The tribe also created the Red Cedar Gathering Company to transport the natural gas. It owns 3,000 miles of pipelines, processes natural gas, and delivers it to transmission. Altogether, by 2008 the Southern Ute Tribe employed more than six hundred people in several states.[5]

At the beginning of the twenty-first century, Red Willow's and Red Cedar's net revenues totaled about $100 million. To offset the day when natural gas prices will decline or the resource itself disappears, the Southern Utes established the Permanent Fund, a conservatively invested endowment, to cover tribal government costs and services. In 2005 the fund's worth approximated $650 million. The tribe also created the Growth Fund to manage tribal businesses and develop new ventures, with Zahradnik as the operating director and a Southern Ute, Bruce Valdez, as the executive director. The vast majority of the Growth Fund's assets are in energy, but its directors also have expanded non-energy investments, including real estate in Colorado, New Mexico, Texas, and Missouri. So successful have the tribe's enterprises been, its bonds received the highest AAA Fitch rating in 2001 and again in 2007. Some Utes complain that the tribe relies too much on non-Indians to run its businesses. Some non-Utes in the area remain wary and suspicious of the tribe's new economic power. One local commented, "You'll hear some people say they liked the tribe better when it was poor."[6] But the Southern Utes' economic success has served as one example of how self-determination and control of one's own energy resources can dramatically turn things around for American Indians.[7]

Of course, gaining such control has not been easy. In the mid-twentieth century, as the Southern Ute case attests, most energy tribes (defined as those that receive a significant portion of their income from energy minerals or that own significant undeveloped reserves) fell far short of realizing their economic potential. Hamstrung by a federal government that assumed paternalistic control of Native Americans, the latter had to fight both government and corporations to secure a place "at the table." From the outset, conflicts arose over ownership of the mineral resources: did these belong to the tribes or to the federal government? By the end of the 1950s, tribes finally established their rights to both ownership and consent authority—that is, deciding whether resources could be developed. Development was not necessarily a given. High unemployment and poverty rates on reservations certainly encouraged it, but Native American conceptions about their relationship to land did not. And the fact that they could not relocate if mining ended up in environmental disaster underscored their potential vulnerability. Also, royalty rates, hammered out in consultations between the Bureau of Indian Affairs and corporations, fell far below market value, cheating tribes (and individual allottees) of their fair share of profits.[8] The advantages and disadvantages of energy development led to debates within tribes. For some, developing coal and other energy resources seemed to violate their sacred responsibilities to the land. Others privileged the economic opportunities that might result from mining or other mineral extraction.[9] Clearly, energy development offered no perfect panacea.

Meanwhile, some energy tribes learned how to fight back and gradually transformed their role from passive recipients of under-market royalty payments to active partners in decision making and profit taking. They moved away from simply leasing to contracts that gave them ownership options, joint management, and fair profit sharing. Creation of the Council of Energy Resource Tribes (CERT) in 1975, a pan-Indian organization designed to share information, obtain scientific expertise, and increase political clout, further signaled this new determination to ensure fair royalties and increase tribal control. By the 1990s, legal and legislative victories acknowledged Native American tribes' authority to tax mineral producers, enforce royalty regulations, impose air and water quality standards, issue tax-free bonds, and negotiate with industry to develop tribal resources.[10]

When one adds Native American workers to the equation, the narrative of Indians and energy turns, again, toward exploitation. Energy development on the Navajo reservation brought jobs to Indian people, but workers had to fight to secure such employment, as Colleen O'Neill's chapter 7 demonstrates. These jobs often paid well. But they also carried enormous costs. For example, of the 150 Navajo uranium miners who worked at the Kerr-McGee mine in Shiprock, New Mexico, until 1970, 133 succumbed to lung cancer or forms of fibrosis by 1980.[11] Chapter 6, by Barbara Rose Johnston, Susan Dawson, and Gary Madsen, speaks to the devastating impact of this industry on workers' health. Mining and refining minerals is never a clean industry. The health and environmental costs of such development fall heaviest on those who toil in the industry or live in its vicinity.

This was apparent from the outset. The uranium ore extracted from southwestern Indian lands was destined for the Manhattan Project, which developed the world's first atomic bomb, and then for the nation's Cold War era stockpile of nuclear weapons. When the United States stopped purchasing ore for weapons in 1971, the commercial nuclear energy market stepped in as the primary consumer until the early 1980s. Throughout these decades, private companies mined the ore, even when the US government was the sole purchaser. Scientists knew that uranium workers were at higher risk for lung cancer and other deadly respiratory diseases, but the miners (about 25 percent of whom were Native American—Laguna, Hopi,

Zuni, Ute, and Navajo) did not. They remained uninformed about the hazards of their jobs, received no protective equipment, and often labored in mines with no ventilation.[12] Even those who did not work in the uranium mines suffered health consequences. Workers' clothes, which they wore home, were coated in toxic dust. When the industry came to a standstill, more than a thousand mines and four processing mills on tribal lands closed, leaving behind radioactive waste piles, open tunnels, and pits. Navajo reservation inhabitants, in particular, breathed in radioactive dust, drank contaminated water from abandoned pit mines and holding tanks, played in mill tailings, and constructed dwellings with radioactive debris. Fifty years ago, cancer rates on the Navajo reservation were so low, one medical journal described it as a place where people seemed immune to cancer. Between the early 1970s and the late 1990s, the cancer death rate doubled. Exposure to mining by-products in the air, water, and soil, according to one source, "almost certainly contributed to the increase in Navajo cancer mortality."[13]

Starting in the 1970s, grassroots organizations such as the Red Mesa/Mexican Water Four Corners Uranium Committee and the Uranium Radiation Victims Committee sought compensation for this environmental and health disaster. They found an ally in former Secretary of the Interior Stewart Udall. But in 1979 their lawsuits against the uranium companies and the US Department of Energy failed. The court held that the government was immune from such suits and that the Indians' only redress could come from legislation. In 1990 Congress passed the Radiation Exposure Contamination Act, acknowledging the US government's responsibility for mistreatment of uranium miners and millers and providing compensation to those with diseases related to mining. In 2000 Congress passed amendments to the original law, and by mid-2005, 3,415 miners, 550 millers, and 112 ore transporters had received compensation totaling $407 million. Money, of course, could not bring back the lives of those who had died or the health of those permanently disabled. But such trouble mobilized people to fight back.

> The one bright spot in this history is the view it affords of communities and labor organizations that identified problems, organized themselves to learn about them, and formed alliances to address them. In the future, government bureaucracies and scientific communities should listen to the representatives of these constituencies and respond appropriately in a timely fashion.[14]

As for those who did not work in the mines but simply lived—and grew up—near contaminated sites, no redress exists. But the legacy of uranium mining and its presumed health costs had such an enormous emotional impact, the Navajo Nation banned uranium mining altogether in 2005, even as the price of the ore rose.[15]

The Southern Utes' phenomenal economic success and the uranium workers' tragic health legacy bookend the tribal and individual experiences of American Indians with energy development. Perhaps no people demonstrate more clearly the shades of gray, the in-between, the complexities, than the Navajos. Their story is emblematic of the larger narrative arc that many Native Americans have experienced: the early exploitation by the federal government and corporations, the rise of nationalism and consequent increased control over their resources (as Andrew Needham's chapter 9 demonstrates), the devastation of workers' health and the growing determination to prevent future abuses, the realization that coal-fired power plants and strip mines carry heavy environmental costs for local people, who do not benefit from the power these produce, and the growing resistance to such developments at the grassroots level within the tribe itself. As people of the twenty-first century, some Navajos express deep concerns about climate change and global warming, generating in the process a "homegrown version of the global debate on slowing climate change."[16] These critics point their fingers not solely at the Bureau of Indian Affairs or the corporations that hope to continue mining Navajo coal and producing electric power on the reservation, but also at their own tribal council, which initiated such economic activities.

The modern Navajo Tribal Council had its genesis in the 1920s, created in part to expedite leasing of the reservation's minerals to non-Indians. Energy demands of the 1960s, ramped up by the spectacular growth of the urban Southwest in the years following World War II, led western states and energy companies to lean on Congress to pass "a Christmas tree bill of dams, power plants, highways and transmission lines in the interior West."[17] The centerpiece was the Central Arizona Project, a huge aqueduct that would funnel water from the Colorado River to Phoenix and Tucson. To push this water (literally) to its thirsty consumers, developers needed power. They decided to mine Black Mesa coal—on the Hopi and Navajo reservations—and build coal-fired power plants to generate the electricity for this project and other Southwestern urban needs.[18] Neither the Hopi nor the Navajo tribal council had sufficient expertise or knowledge to negotiate in their people's best interests. They did not know the value of their coal, the environmental impacts of mining and generating electricity, or the alternatives to coal. They also kept many of the project details secret from tribal members. In 1966 Peabody Coal (at the time, a subsidiary of Kennecott Copper Corporation) signed two leases with the tribes for 40,000 acres on Black Mesa, in the Joint Use Area, a controversial space shared by both tribes. Eventually, Black Mesa became the most notorious mine in the nation, a symbol of Indian exploitation. To make matters worse, the Hopi tribal attorney, John S. Boyden, who encouraged the project, also represented Peabody Coal—a blatant conflict of interest.[19]

In the face of federal and tribal council unresponsiveness, Hopi and Navajo dissidents found allies in the American Indian Movement (AIM) and environmental groups. The Black Mesa Defense Fund convinced the Senate to investigate plans for energy development in the Southwest, and Black Mesa became a rallying cry for environmentalists all across the country. Such actions did not stop the mining at Black Mesa but did increase awareness of the potential for exploitation. Eventually, the Hopi and Navajo renegotiated their Black Mesa contracts, and federal and tribal regulations regarding mineral leasing underwent reform. The publicity given to the abuses, in other words, improved the processes and results of mineral leasing thereafter.[20]

As Hopi and Navajo energy development have changed from exploitation to opportunity, however, controversies have continued to swirl around coal mining at Black Mesa. On January 1, 2006, the Mohave Generating Station in Laughlin, Nevada, shut down rather than pay $1 billion for environmental upgrades. So, too, did the Black Mesa Mine, because its sole purpose was to deliver coal to Mohave. A lawsuit that the Grand Canyon Trust and other environmental groups filed against Southern California Edison, the major owner of Mohave, for violation of the Clean Air Act was partly responsible. Other factors included water and market concerns. Since the 1960s, Hopi and Navajo critics had worried about Peabody's pumping and depleting the Navajo Aquifer to deliver coal to Mohave through a 273-mile slurry pipeline. Southern California Edison, meanwhile, feared that natural gas–fired plants would render coal plants obsolete and therefore no longer profitable.[21]

Closing the generating station and the mine represented an environmental victory for some, but it had serious economic consequences for Native Americans. The Black Mesa Mine shutdown cost the Navajos 15 percent of their tribal revenues and the Hopi 33 percent. Today approximately half of the Navajos on the reservation remain unemployed, and per capita income is only slightly more than $8,000 a year. So it is not surprising that tribal leaders continue to pursue energy projects. In 2003 the Navajo tribal council invited Sithe Global Power, with offices in Houston and New York, to build a $3 billion, 1,500-megawatt power plant with the Navajo-owned Diné Power Authority. Navajo president Joe Shirley Jr. argued that the power plant would bring hundreds of jobs, higher incomes, and better lives for Navajos. He expected the plant, named Desert Rock, to bring in $50 million a year in taxes, royalties, and other income by selling the power to Phoenix and Las Vegas. Shirley also claimed that the project would include a power line to send electricity to twenty thousand remote homes on the reservation. One-third of the reservation's residences lacked electricity.[22]

The project has elicited a firestorm of protest because the Desert Rock Energy Project would be the third coal-fired plant in the Four Corners region. The two existing plants emit noxious fumes and rate the area the worst in New Mexico, for instance, for air quality. At the forefront of opposition are Navajo people themselves, particularly those who live in the vicinity of Burnham, the projected location for Desert Rock. Dana Powell and Dáilan Long's chapter 10 explains that the protest started with Navajo women who sat vigil on the dusty expanse of the site, hoping to block the project. Resistance grew. At ten public hearings on the environmental impact statement, hundreds of Navajos protested Desert Rock, voicing concerns about air pollution, large-scale water consumption, and loss of grazing land. Worries about air quality and health, in particular, tap into the lingering anxieties about previous energy development on tribal lands, particularly uranium. Several groups formed, including Dooda Desert Rock (Navajo for "No to Desert Rock") and Diné CARE (Citizens Against Ruining Our Environment), to organize the opposition, generate publicity, and offer alternatives. Diné CARE, concerned about global warming, urged the council to reject coal in favor of solar, wind, and natural gas.[23] In fact, the Navajo Nation has contemplated harnessing wind energy by partnering with Citizens Energy Corporation, a Boston company chaired by Joseph P. Kennedy II, through the Diné Wind Project, located about fifty miles north of Flagstaff. If it materializes, this will be the first commercial wind farm in Arizona and among the largest wind-power installations in the nation, with approximately three hundred wind turbines generating 500 megawatts of electricity capacity, enough to service 100,000 households. Navajos will have significant ownership in the project, earning $60 to $100 million over the project's lifetime, according to a tribal news release.[24] But this project is intended to supplement, not replace, the proposed coal-fired power plant.

The Desert Rock controversy encapsulates the complexities of energy on southwestern Indian reservations, which policymakers originally carved out of deserts they assumed had little value. That such lands proved to contain enormous mineral wealth is a delicious irony. So how can tribes with energy resources decline the opportunity to contribute millions of dollars to tribal coffers, provide well-paying jobs, and ultimately use the profits to diversify tribal economic investment? On one hand, as consumers of energy and potential consumers, do they not benefit from these resources too? And some might ask, do they not have an obligation to produce resources that will make all Americans less dependent on foreign sources? On the other hand, what about the environmental and health risks associated with energy development? Why should Native Americans pay the greatest costs as the vast majority of benefits accrue to non-Indians in far-off cities? Where is the justice in this? And should American Indian people, who often see themselves as having a special relationship to the earth (as Don Fixico's chapter 2 demonstrates), contribute to climate change and global warming? Should they—of all people—not lead the nation in alternatives that make use of wind and sun to provide cleaner energy? Finally, who should decide the answers to these questions? To the extent that the story of energy development in Indian Country is partly one of evolution from exploitation to opportunity, surely the reemergence of tribal sovereignty in the late twentieth century is a critical factor. But several forms of sovereignty are at stake—one at the tribal and the other at the grassroots level. The Bureau of Indian Affairs' and corporations' colonial relationship with the tribes has transformed. Today more "energy tribes" operate on a government-to-government basis with states and the federal government. Corporations understand that they must work with tribes as powerful stakeholders in energy enterprises. But internal struggles remain, pitting reservation residents of development sites against their own tribal councils. Who is the exploiter now? How will these conflicts be resolved?

The chapters here provide historical context to help address these questions. Together, they present bedrock themes of Native identity and tribal sovereignty, tradition and modernity, the devastating legacies of colonialism, grassroots efforts by Native people to craft sustainable alternatives to traditional energy resources, environmental politics in a time of global warming, and political, legal, and organizational empowerment. They demonstrate divisions within and among tribes. They address tensions between traditionalist and conservationist values and the need for economic development. They speak to the possibilities for enormous opportunity and the potentially devastating environmental and health costs that accompany it. And finally, as noted above, these chapters reveal that the topic of Indians and energy does not lend itself to a single or simple narrative. Rather, this volume presents a mosaic of many stories revealing energy as an issue that historically has divided not only Natives and non-Natives but also Native people among themselves. At the same time, the history of Indians and energy offers glimpses into how people have sometimes collaborated, cooperated, and negotiated to meet society's growing energy needs in a way that minimizes the negative effects on people and environments.

The book begins with two chapters that address ways of conceptualizing the problem at the heart of the volume. Don Fixico (chapter 2) provides an overview of how various southwestern Native Americans perceive the earth and discusses the people for whom energy development poses particular problems. Brian Frehner (chapter 3) cautions readers to view Indians who participated in energy development as complicated people who defy easy categorization. Regarding Indians' relationship to energy development as a product of their "traditional" or "progressive" orientation or as a result of their "full-blood" or "mixed-blood" ancestry reinforces stereotypical representations of Indian people and robs them of their ability to act as individuals, whose decisions do not always conform to prescribed norms. The contrasting viewpoints of Fixico and Frehner are implicit in Garrit Voggesser's chapter 4, which surveys the evolution of federal Indian energy policy and tells a story in which some Native people successfully used federal courts to control their energy resources, most notably, the Jicarilla Apaches.

Less sanguine portraits of Indians and energy emerge in the two chapters that follow. Benedict J. Colombi (chapter 5) examines hydroelectric dams on the Colorado River within the context of a capital-intensive political economy in which indigenous people bore the brunt of energy development's social and ecological costs while government agencies and non-Native participants empowered and enriched themselves. Barbara Rose Johnston, Susan Dawson, and Gary Madsen (chapter 6) document a story of environmental racism in which Navajo uranium miners and mill workers suffered adverse health effects when the federal government withheld safety information and later failed to compensate them or their families for exposure to radioactivity.

As Native people began empowering themselves legally, politically, and economically to gain control over energy development, their active roles in asserting, contesting, and redefining issues such as sovereignty, identity, and nationalism influenced how they functioned as consumers and producers of energy. For example, Colleen O'Neill's chapter 7 argues that Native people's demand for (and acquisition of) jobs created by energy industries constitutes one of the many ways Indians have redefined sovereignty. Leah Glaser's chapter 8 maintains that federal programs to assimilate Native people conditioned them to function as consumers of electricity but that Arizona Indians joined regional power grids and incorporated electrical technologies according to their existing traditions and cultures. Thus, Indians did not participate in a zero sum game in which their cultures deteriorated as a result of economic betterment offered by energy development.

In some cases, intense disagreements among Indians over the best methods to control and profit from energy resources reinforced their culture, identity, and nationalism. Andrew Needham's chapter 9 asserts that energy development served as the central issue around which Navajos debated, and often disagreed vehemently over, "self determination," "nationalism," and "decolonization." Authors Dana Powell and Dáilan Long (chapter 10) also examine the ongoing debates and cleavages among Navajos, concentrating on grassroots opposition to the proposed Desert Rock Energy Project, and argue that rural place-based communities have responded with alternative energy technologies that grew out of the communities' "changing expressions of indigeneity." Summarizing and pulling together the volume's central themes, Rebecca Tsosie's chapter 11 articulates how the issue of energy development fundamentally links Native and non-Native people to the global community through the issue of climate change. She illustrates how multiple histories in this volume might serve as lessons from the past to guide future policymakers toward a sustainable future, providing a roadmap for the difficult moral choices that Native and non-Native people alike must make as they continue to produce and consume energy.

To be sure, this book is not comprehensive in its coverage. First, it focuses on the Southwest instead of the entire span of Indian Country. We chose to concentrate on this region because the Southwest is particularly well suited for exploring how people have transformed the region's resources into fuel supplies for human consumption. Not only do Native Americans possess a large percentage of the region's total acreage, but also on their lands reside much of the nation's coal, oil, and uranium resources. Regional weather and climate patterns have enabled Native people to take advantage of solar and wind power as sources of energy. But issues related to energy and Indians transcend the region—and the nation. Clearly, we believe that the lessons of the Southwest illuminate broader trends in other places. Still, much more work needs to be done on tribes in the Southwest and elsewhere who are not covered here and on issues that we do not address (reservations as nuclear waste sites, for instance).

Our purpose is not to end the conversation, but to join it—and encourage others to do the same. Forty years ago, Norman Rockwell participated in this conversation through his Glen Canyon Dam painting, which so strikingly juxtaposed Native people and energy development. His work perpetuated the mistaken notion that Indians' lives intersect with energy development only in distant and unfortunate, even tragic, ways. Although exploitation undoubtedly has a role in this narrative, ever since Rockwell put paintbrush to canvas, Native Americans have been altering the picture by creating significant opportunities for themselves in a world with ravenous energy appetites. His image remains compelling, however, because it suggests that he wondered, as do all the authors in this book, what *is* the relationship between Indians and energy? The authors provide varied and, at times, contradictory answers. Collectively, they conclude that this is not a simple story of evolution from exploitation to opportunity. Rather, these exist in tension with each other in Indian Country—as they do for all of us who consume energy and cope with its environmental costs.

Notes

1. W. L. Rusho, personal communication June 2, 2008. Rusho found the family living in a hogan near Page, Arizona. They agreed to pose when they learned that Norman Rockwell was the artist. The dog was apparently Rockwell's invention. The Bureau of Reclamation arranged for various painters to depict its projects across the country. Artists donated the paintings to the Bureau of Reclamation and received a tax deduction for their value. Rockwell's Glen Canyon Dam painting, which remains to this day on display at the dam, was part of this program.

2. Ambler 1990:29, 86; The Harvard Project on American Indian Economic Development 2008:161–162; Kathy Helms, "Tribal Energy Drive Touted," *The Gallup Independent*, July 20, 2007. The Fish and Wildlife Service says that American Indian lands in the lower forty-eight comprise 45 million acres of reserved lands and an additional 10 million in individual allotments, as well as 40 million acres of Native lands in Alaska. The 95 million acres figure for tribal lands comes from http://www.fws.endangered/tribal.index.html (accessed June 2008). The Harvard Project (2008) puts the total at 72 million acres. Donald Fixico (1998:143–144) reports that "twenty-five to forty percent of America's uranium, one-third of its coal, and approximately five percent of its oil and gas are on Indian reservations in the West."

3. Ambler 1990:xiv.

4. Susan Moran, "Indian Tribe Becomes Force in West's Energy Boom," *New York Times*, July 24, 2007; Wilkinson 2005:245–246. Although Don Fixico does not write about the Southern Ute case in chapter 2, he sees their situation as reflective of his

broader thesis regarding pressures from federal policies and American capitalists to seek out and grow wealthy from Indians' natural resources. He argues that "American capitalism...has continued through the twentieth century to exploit tribal nations for their natural resources, thus forcing Indian leadership to adopt modern corporate strategies to ensure the survival of their nations and people" (Fixico 1998:ix–x).

5. Susan Moran, "Indian Tribe Becomes Force in West's Energy Boom," *New York Times*, July 24, 2007.

6. Quoted in Susan Moran, "Indian Tribe Becomes Force in West's Energy Boom," *New York Times*, July 24, 2007.

7. Susan Moran, "Indian Tribe Becomes Force in West's Energy Boom," *New York Times*, July 24, 2007; Wilkinson 2005:347.

8. Utah International, for example, paid the Navajo Tribe between $.15 and $.20 per ton of coal in a lease signed in 1957. Arizona Public Service paid Utah International $6 per ton for the same coal (Fixico 1998:169).

9. For more on these debates, see Fixico 1998:144–146.

10. Ambler 1990:3, 30, 32, 54, 85–86, 91–114, 202, 261; Fixico 1998:159–175. For more information on CERT, see its Web site at www.cert.com. See also Ambler 1984a; LaDuke 1984.

11. Ali 2003:xx. See also Johnston and Madsen 2007:117–144; Eichstaedt 1994.

12. Brugge and Goble 2006:25–26.

13. Judy Pasternak, "Blighted Homeland: A Peril That Dwelt among the Navajos," November 19, 2006, and "Blighted Homeland: Navajos' Desert Cleanup No More Than a Mirage," November 21, 2006, *Los Angeles Times*, http://www.latimes.com/news/nationworld.nation/la-na-navajo (accessed November 2006), and "Navajos Still Await Toxics Cleanup Plan. EPA Testing Will Resume, but a Coordinated Federal Strategy Is Still Lacking, Lawmakers Told," *Los Angeles Times*, December 7, 2007; Florence Williams, "On Cancer's Trail: The Women in Stefanie Raymond-Whish's Family Have a History of Breast Cancer. Now the Young Navajo Biologist Is Asking Why," *High Country News*, May 26, 2008. Our thanks to Edward Countryman and Colleen O'Neill for bringing these articles to our attention.

14. Brugge and Goble 2006:43; see also Dawson, Charley, and Harrison Jr. 2006.

15. Florence Williams, "On Cancer's Trail: The Women in Stefanie Raymond-Whish's Family Have a History of Breast Cancer. Now the Young Navajo Biologist Is Asking Why," *High Country News*, May 26, 2008.

16. Felicity Barringer, "Navajos and Environmentalists Split on Power Plant," *New York Times*, July 27, 2007.

17. Wilkinson 2005:306.

18. Ibid.

19. Ambler 1990:59; Wilkinson 2005:306–310.

20. Ambler 1990:59–60.

21. Daniel Kraker, "The End of an Era on the Colorado Plateau," *High Country News*, January 23, 2006.

22. Felicity Barringer, "Navajos and Environmentalists Split on Power Plant," *New York Times*, July 27, 2007; see also Ryan Randazzo, "For Navajos, Coal Means Survival," *The Arizona Republic*, April 13, 2008.

23. Jason Begay,"Desert Rock Critics Flood Final Hearing," *Navajo Times*, July 26, 2007; Felicity Barringer, "Navajos and Environmentalists Split on Power Plant," *New York Times*, July 27, 2007; Susan Montoya Bryan, "BIA Criticized for Handling of Navajo Power Plant," August 16, 2007, and "Navajo Group Offers Alternatives to Coal-Fired Power Plant," January 18, 2008, The Associated Press State and Local Wire; Randazzo 2008. For an account of the Diné Power Authority general manager's testimony on Navajo energy development plans, see "Diné Power Authority General Manager Begay Testifies on Indian Energy Development before Senate Panel," *US Federal News*, May 1, 2008.

24. "Navajos Set to Tap Power of the Wind," *National Wind Watch*, March 28, 2008, http://www.wind-watch.org/news (accessed April 2008). For more information on renewable energy projects in Indian Country, see "New Era of Energy for Tribes," *Indian Country Today*, November 25, 2005, http://www.indiancountry.com (accessed January 2006); Hanna 2007; "Renewable Energy Development on Tribal Lands" and "Tribal Energy Project" on the US Department of Energy Office of Energy Efficiency and Renewable Energy Web site, http://www.eere.energy.gov/tribalenergy/ (accessed June 2008). See also the winter 2005 issue of *The Tribal College Journal of American Indian College Education* for articles about sustainability and designing tribal colleges to be "green."

2

Understanding the Earth and the Demand on Energy Tribes

Donald L. Fixico

The Southwest is undergoing considerable growth. Phoenix has become the fifth largest city in the United States. Driving across Arizona, one can see power lines stretching across reservations of Indian tribes. The Native people of the region have shared in some of the economic growth, but tribal communities are still struggling to do better. One would think that every household in a modern America would have running water and electricity, but this is not the case. In too many situations, not enough change has occurred. About twenty-five years ago, a young Hopi boy was asked about the energy crisis. Feeling frustrated and angry, he retorted, "Don't tell me about an energy crisis. I don't even have electricity in my village."[1]

As the United States continues its dependence on fossil fuels to support an automobile culture and continues to fuel electric power plants, the demand on tribes with natural resources increases in the American market economy. This demand began spiraling upwards in the 1970s, and little has changed since then. With many of the needed natural resources like timber, coal, uranium, and oil located on Indian lands, tribes face difficult decisions about whether to mine their resources to benefit their own peoples and the rest of America.

This chapter is about that dilemma. If tribes accelerate energy development, what will be the impact on their cultural and spiritual lives and on their centuries-old homelands? What kind of new culture will manifest because of the catalyst of energy demand? Will it become an agent for permanent change among these tribes? This chapter asks the reader to try to understand the Earth as Indian people do, what it means to them, and the contradiction between mining natural resources and honoring traditional beliefs.

The Southwest is mostly a desert region. If you come to it from elsewhere, your first encounter removes your points of reference, and new ones need to be discovered. The barrenness strangely distracts you from the comfort of the green, eastern half of the continent. Yet, in their own way, desert shades of brown, red, pink, and touches of green ring with their own beauty. George Lee, a Navajo, described his homeland of the Four Corners area this way:

> My spiritual eyes are taught while gazing upon the vastness of the endless desert vision. So unending is the vista that the supple curve of Mother Earth's horizon heals the hungering heart. Always, as far as memory goes, this land has been one of everlasting enchantment. This is our home, the land of the Navajos. My own heart can be found enwrapped with the same beauty. And my people, the same goes for them. This land is our destiny and our being; it is our soul, for we are known as Dineh, the People.[2]

What, to some, appears as emptiness becomes endless space. Distortion occurs, and you have to understand Nature's way in the Southwest, where water is precious to the living.[3] Green is alien to most of the Southwest, except for the lush pine forests climbing and resting on mountain sides. Noted Laguna writer Leslie Silko described the area from the viewpoint of one of her characters in her renowned novel, *Ceremony*. She wrote:

> "This is where we come from. This sand, this stone, these trees, the vines, all the wildflowers. This earth keeps us going." He took off his hat and wiped his forehead on his shirt. "These dry years you hear some people complaining, you know, about the dust and the wind, and how dry it is. But the wind and the dust, they are part of life too, like the sun and the sky. You don't swear at them. It's people, see. They're the ones. The old people used to

> say that droughts happen when people forget, when people misbehave."[4]

The Earth becomes a teacher, a harsh one that instructs human beings and other life in lessons of survival. One might call this a difficult love, a love for such a land.

Tribal love for the Earth is strong, and it is the fiber of the souls of the Native peoples. We are of the Earth. George Lee stated:

> This seemingly barren and forlorn place even today is the home of my heart, the sweetness of my youth. As one drives north on US Highway 666 from Shiprock, New Mexico, toward Cortez, Colorado, the terrain, although hilly and with broken mesas, is virtually treeless. But it is not without life, for the abundance, the thriving life of the living desert, surrounds the periphery of human view. Only the distant mountain ranges far to the north and the tops of the higher eastern mesas are forested.[5]

In this Earth's region, there is no escape from the elements. One learns to cope with only periodic rains that bring the danger of flashfloods, winter's cold temperatures at night, and the almost unbearable heat of summer days.

The desert Southwest is a place of extreme heat and vast distances. Summer temperatures average 100 degrees Fahrenheit and can reach up to 115 degrees or more. Like an oven, the sun cooks everything—living and nonliving. Rain in the desert is precious when it falls. Rain's importance comes through in many Native ceremonies. The Navajos say that praying under a rainbow gives a person "strength and force" and that person will be fortunate and strong at what he or she does.[6]

The Navajos and other tribes of the Southwest are people of the Earth. In Leslie Silko's novel, *Ceremony*, she describes the years of World War II and the impact on the Native world in the Southwest as its contact with the outside world increased. The war brought many changes, including automobiles and pickup trucks, to Native homelands. But the land endured all change. Tayo's aunt, in Silko's book, symbolizes this endurance. Silko writes:

> An old sensitivity had descended in her [the aunt], surviving thousands of years from the oldest times, when the people shared a single clan name and they told each other who they were; they recounted the actions and words each of their clan had taken, and would take; from before they were born and long

> after they died, the people shared the same consciousness. The people had known, with the simple certainty of the world they saw, how everything should be.
>
> But the fifth world had become entangled with European names: the names of the rivers, the hills, the names of the animals and plants—all creation suddenly had two names: an Indian name and a white name.[7]

The land, the water, and the Earth had become shared, by friends and enemies.

Long before this time, Hopi prophecy foretold of the day coming when Indians would share the Earth with the white race. Dan Katchongva, in his eighties at the time, repeated this prophecy in 1955, more than half a century ago:

> In ancient times it was prophesied by our forefathers that this land would be occupied by the Indian people and then from somewhere a White Man would come.... We knew that this land beneath us was composed of many things that we might want to use later, such as mineral resources. We knew that this is the wealthiest part of this continent, because it is here the Great Spirit lives. We knew that the White Man will search for the things that look good to him, that he will use many good ideas in order to obtain his heart's desire, and we knew that if he had strayed from the Great Spirit, he would use any means to get what he wants. These things we were warned to watch, and we today know that those prophecies were true because we can see how many new and selfish ideas and plans are being put before us. We know that if we accept these things, we will lose our land and give up our very lives.[8]

Various tribes of the Southwest believe that their people came from the Earth. Their ancestors lived in stone dwellings in the sides of mountains and in pit houses dug into the Earth. They were of the Earth. Even the traditional hogan of the Navajo is designed with an earthen floor to remind the people from where they come. Navajo poet and writer Luci Tapahonso described the connection of the hogan to her people and the Earth, in her story "Starlore":

> On this June night, we gather at our parents' home and leave in a caravan of nine cars, a string of headlights across the flat desert

> to the home of the man who will listen and help us. It is almost midnight when we park outside his hooghan, the round ceremonial house. We enter slowly, clockwise, then sit on the smooth, cool ground. Above the flickering fire in the center of the hooghan, we see clouds rushing by through the chimney hole. The wind whistles through the opening. It makes us hope for rain. The family has filled the hooghan. We whisper among ourselves until he arrives—the one who knows the precise songs, the long, rhythmic prayers that will restore the world for us.[9]

The Diné believe in a supreme Earth Mother called Changing Woman, who created their people, according to Diné mythology. Changing Woman created the four original clans, and she was the first to be honored with Kinaalda, a girl's puberty ceremony. Changing Woman was the mother of "hero twins," who saved the world from monsters. She symbolizes the four seasons of the year by representing the young girl changing from youth to age and returning to youth. Called the Earth Mother, Changing Woman represented the gift of life and its phases.[10] Changing Woman gave other important things to the Diné. To women, the Earth Mother gave the responsibility of protecting the Earth Bundle. Soil from four or six sacred mountains, along with its power of renewal, was contained in the bundle. The power of rendering life came from within the Earth Bundle, and the Diné used the bundle in their most important ceremony, the Blessingway.[11] The Diné believe the Earth to be a female deity that serves as a host to other metaphysical powers.

In the beginning, the Diné say, there were four worlds their ancestors passed through. Like hemispheres, these were piled on top of one another and pillars of precious stone in striking colors—red, blue, yellow, and black and white. In George Lee's autobiography, he wrote:

> We came to the surface of the land from several levels far beneath the earth's surface. Just thinking of the earth caused me to watch the deft hand strokes of the medicine man as he made sand images upon the earthen floor. The bright array of colors connected in my conscious thought. Black, red, blue, and now this world, yellow, representing the levels Diné, my people, had passed through to arrive upon the earth's surface. My father's interpretation of the legend was that the five-fingered people (earth people) came from beneath the earth through much water. The medicine man was using three promising colors in

> the sand painting on the floor. This sacred sing was for me, for something in the outside world had brought a terrible sickness upon me. This was the way of my people. And I believed it.[12]

One must believe, if things good are to happen. The Navajo believe that the Earth holds power, not human beings. Even medicine makers like Annie Kahn said, "We really don't have any power at all to heal anybody. It's the natural power that the Earth has that heals."[13]

Finally, the Diné made their way into the fifth world or level. First Man and First Woman created the Sun and the Moon.[14] It is here that

> the gods laid one buckskin on the ground with the head to the west, and on this they placed the two ears of corn with their tips to the east. Under the white ear they put the feather of a white eagle, under the yellow ear the feather of a yellow eagle. Then, they told the people to stand back and allow the wind to enter. Between the skins the white wind was blowing, eight of the gods, the Mirage People, came and walked around the objects on the ground four times. As they walked, the eagle feathers, whose tips protruded from the buckskins, were seen to move. When the Mirage People had finished their walk, the upper buckskin was lifted. The ears of corn had disappeared; a man and a woman lay in their place. The white ear of corn had become the man, the yellow ear the woman, First Man and First Woman. It was the wind that gave them life, and it is the wind that comes out of our mouths now that gives us life. When this ceases to blow, we die.[15]

The sacred mountains upheld the universe of the Diné, and the people held women's responsibility for life in high regard. The Diné have Mount Blanca to the east, and Mount Taylor stands in the south. To the west, the San Francisco Peaks stand. To the north, La Plata Mountains rise skyward.[16]

For other Indian groups, special places on the landscape were empowered, and these sites helped the people. Throughout the Southwest and the rest of Indian Country, there are hundreds of sacred and empowered places. Taos Blue Lake among the Pueblo people of New Mexico, San Francisco Peaks in Arizona, and other spiritual sites dot the landscape in this region. Ironically, sacred Indian land has not always been protected. It has a long history of exploitation, control by non-Indians, and denial to Native peoples.

To understand the Earth is to know that it has power. Many kinds of power come from the Earth in various forms that manifest in storms, creation, rain, wind, and other kinds of energy. Carl Gorman, renowned Navajo artist, recalled what his father said: "When I was very young, my father used to say there was a power in me, an energy that comes from the Earth and the Sun, from the lightning and the many colors of the rainbow."[17] As a young man, he learned about music from his mother, who encouraged his art. His father taught him about his heritage and the culture of their people. From these influences, Carl Gorman learned to "walk in beauty." He learned about the Navajos' four sacred mountains and how the ancestors of his people brought them to the fifth world.[18]

Oliver LaFarge, a non-Indian anthropologist and writer, described this feeling of beauty in the opening of his Pulitzer Prize–winning novel, *Laughing Boy*. LaFarge describes Laughing Boy this way:

> The sun was hot and his belly was empty, but life moved in rhythm with his pony loping steadily as an engine down the miles. He was lax in the saddle, leaning back, arm swinging the rope's end in time to the horse's lope. His new red headband was a bright colour among the embers of the sun-struck desert, undulating like a moving graph of the pony's lope, or the music of his song—
>
> "Nashdui bik'e dinni, eya-a, eyo-o…
>
> Wildcat's feet hurt, eya-a, eyo-o…"
>
> Rope's end, shoulders, song, all moved together, and life flowed in one stream. He threw his head back to sing louder, and listened to the echo from the cliffs on his right. He was thinking about a bracelet he should make, with four smooth bars running together, and a turquoise in the middle—if he could get the silver. He wished he could work while riding; everything was so perfect then, like the prayers, hosoji nashad, traveling in beauty. His hands, his feet, his head, his insides, all were hozoji, all were very much alive.[19]

"Walking in beauty" is walking with the Earth, feeling it and feeling that it is a part of you. Listening for and hearing the many sounds of the Earth and understanding them are what will keep one safe from harm. The sounds of Earth include the sounds of the many animals that also live. One Navajo man talked to the animals where he lived on the reservation. Indian people have become fond of talking to plants and animals. Navajo surgeon Lori Alvord described her father's relationship with animals and how he communicated with them:

> Almost everywhere we went, on the reservation or off, he knew the dogs, and they recognized him and came running. Rez dogs. Chocolate and black-splotched or the color of coyote and mesa and riverbed mud. One blue eye, one brown, or two piercing green. They were everywhere on the reservation, used to watch the sheep or guard the Hogan, and when you arrive, they appear magically, just like those annoying friends who materialize at mealtime. My father knew them. Crows also seemed to gather in groups or come and stand on a fence post whenever my father was around. Sometimes I'd turn a corner and find my father standing deep in a philosophical discussion with a crow.[20]

In Luci Tapahonso's book *Sáanii Dahataal: The Women Are Singing*, she described the important relationship between dogs and Navajo families:

> They say that Navajo shouldn't buy or sell dogs because they are considered family members. This means, too, that dogs are expected to be responsible and to possess some degree of intelligence. At times, my father owned dogs who understood only Navajo and would extend their right paw when someone said "Ya'at'eeh" to them. We told my father that, rather than dog obedience school, his dogs would have to enroll in bilingual education classes so [that] they could learn English, too. Sometimes people criticize pets, saying, "I don't know what's wrong with that dog. He has no respect! Doesn't even listen! Just runs into the house all the time!" Likewise, a well-behaved dog earns affection and respect quickly. Generally, dogs are valued as sheepherders, watch dogs, and playmates for the children.[21]

All the years I have known Luci and her husband, Bob Martin, they have always had a dog.

In this way, Native people humanize animals and everything else. Native people talk to, think, and try to understand responses from things. Explaining the Earth's past is essential for the present needs of people. All things can be human-like. Tapahonso wrote, "Before the world existed, the holy people made themselves visible by becoming the clouds, sun, moon, trees, bodies of water, thunder, rain, snow, and other aspects of this world we live in. That way, they said, we would never be alone. So it is possible to talk to them and pray, no matter where we are and how we feel. Biyazhi daniidli, we are their little ones."[22]

The Hopi, a Pueblo tribe, have lived for centuries in the Southwest. In their Uto-Aztecan language, the Hopi call themselves Hopituh, which means "the peaceful ones." Still, today, they cultivate fields of corn, squash, beans, and melons using a planting stick, which is a method their ancestors have used since as long ago as 300 BC. Old Oraibi remains the oldest continuing community north of the Rio Grande. (Some say that Acoma Pueblo is the oldest community.) Located on Third Mesa, Old Oraibi dates back to AD 1100. The majority of the Hopi people live in the twelve villages atop the three mesas on the reservation.[23]

The Hopi Indians maintain that in the beginning there was only Tokpela, Endless Space. Somehow in this endless space a spark of consciousness was struck. The Hopi named this Tawa, the Sun Spirit. Tawa created the first world. It was a cavern of a kind, with nothing but insects in it. The insects disappointed him. Tawa sent Spider Grandmother down to them as a messenger. She said, "Tawa, the Sun Spirit who made you is unhappy because you do not understand the meaning of life. Therefore, he has commanded me to lead you from this first world to a second one." The journey upward to the second world proved very arduous and long. Then Tawa sent Spider Grandmother to lead the animals upward until they reached a third world, which was somewhat lighter and less forbidding. On that new and extremely difficult journey, some of the animals became people. Then Spider Grandmother taught the people how to weave cloth to keep their bodies warm and how to make pots for storing food and water. Men and women began to have some glimmering, after a time, of the meaning of life. But certain *powaka* (sorcerers) distorted this intuitive knowledge. People began to feel that they had created themselves.

Once more, Spider Grandmother appeared. She spoke only to a few, saying, "The Sun Spirit is displeased with what he has created. The powaka have made you forget what you should have remembered. Therefore, you ought to get away." This time, however, Spider Grandmother made no offer to lead the faithful remnant into a new world. They had to find the way by themselves, somehow or other. They decided to send a catbird to see how things were up there, up through the Sipapuni, or Hole in the Sky. The catbird flew through the new world until it came to a place much like the Arizona desert. There stood a stone hut beside an irrigated patch of Earth where squash, melons, and maize were growing. A person sat between the house and the garden whom the catbird recognized as death. The catbird said, "I have come on behalf of people in the world below this one. They would like to share this country with you. Would that be possible?" Death, whom the Hopi called Masuwu, thought for a while, gloomily. Then he said, "You see how it is in this place. If the people wish to come, then let them come." Spider Grandmother commanded that a bamboo be planted in a village square. She taught the people how to sing it up into the sky by the power of music alone. Each time they stopped for breath, the bamboo stopped growing. Spider Grandmother was dancing silently back and forth to help the people sing the bamboo straight into the sky. Just at sunset, she cried out, "It is finished! The bamboo tip has passed through the Sipapuni!" Now the people had a very long climb to make. Soon the entire bamboo was covered with figures struggling upward into the sky.

As the people emerged through the Sipapuni and set their feet upon the firm ground of the upper world, Yawpa the Mockingbird greeted each one. "You shall be a Hopi and speak the Hopi language," she would sing, or "You shall be a Navaho and speak the Navaho language." In the same way, she assigned the Apache tongue, and so on, through the Indian tribes. As the magical bamboo crumpled, thousands of doomed human beings toppled like seeds from its tottering and falling stalk, down into the darkness of the world below.

The instinct for human beings is to search for something that is valued. The need for important things drives the human spirit to locate or seek these valued things. These myths (above) speak to the issue of finding a homeland. In them, the search seems endless for an environment that will furnish food, shelter, and security. In the Hopi oral tradition, "if surviving myths and legends are listened to with care, they may tell us that these restless ancestors were also in search for places of spiritual harmony with nature."[24] Such a quest is always based on the need of the people, compelling human beings to migrate to new home areas. Constructing stone houses in clusters among cliffs, the ancestors of the Hopi were likely driven to their current homeland by drought. One migration led to the Rio Grande Valley along the river, enabling Pueblo communities to thrive.[25] The Hopi found their new home on the land below and atop three mesas in northeast Arizona.

The land is the home to various tribes, with each possessing its own viewpoint about it. The region is demanding, and its inhabitants have learned this lesson. You cannot permanently control the land, for its elements of climate and terrain are too powerful. One Navajo person, Freddy Big Bead of Little Bluff on the Navajo reservation, stated, "You don't own the land. You just use it. Some people have a small patch. They plant melons and corn. If the crop fails, they go hungry. They live the best they know how."[26] The solution to living here is to learn about the environment and adapt to it.

Native peoples of the Southwest must also deal with the white man. The history of Indian–white relations has not always been pleasant. It has been a story of conflict over control of Native people's homeland ever since the Spanish arrived in the region in 1541. More recently, the issue of control has turned to energy development. Leslie Silko describes the impact of mining on her main character, Tayo, in *Ceremony*:

> Waves of the heat caught him [Tayo], and his legs and lungs were vapor without sensation; only his memory or running and breathing kept him moving and alive. He stumbled and ran behind the sun, not following, but dragged with it across arroyos, over mesas and hills. At sundown he was lying on the sand at the bottom of the long mesa, feeling the heat recede from the air and from his body into the earth. The wind came up and he shivered. He crawled through the strands of barbed wire. Twilight was giving way to darkness. He scooped water off the top of thick green moss that clogged the steel water trough under the windmill. The water was still warm from the sun and it tasted bitter. He sat on the edge of the trough and looked across the wide canyon at the dark mine shaft. Maybe the uranium made the water taste that way.[27]

With all of this said, what have we learned from the Earth, and what do we understand? George Lee's wise Navajo father said to him:

> Our people began to covet what the white man had. The white man is learned, but his knowledge has not brought him to understand the Mother Earth. He may own the land and be in control, but only we have the power to understand the spirits within the land. So, on a higher level, it is yet ours. Only an Indian has the power to understand the spirits within Mother Earth and all creations.[28]

In 1992 Hopi elder Thomas Banyaca gave this testimony to a World Uranium Hearing in Salzburg, Austria. He used a map, describing his homeland of the Four Corners. He shared the Hopi prophecy with these words:

> This white part is on the rock near my home in Oraibi. The Great Spirit laid this path for us to follow. There's no end to this work, none to the circle, there's no end to that as long as we follow instructions. The white brother came. Instead of bringing

> this circle, he brought this cross. And we let him go on up the road. We refer to that materialistic path, inventing of many things, powerful things that are supposed to help. They go side by side—First, Second, Third World, First World War, Second World War and this...on the upper line, to the Hopi, is beginning a Third World War, the Persian Gulf, but it stopped. So it gave us people to correct, to change, to stop this thing we were talking about.
>
> Uranium mining is a dangerous thing—we know that now. Are we going to continue to develop that? Are we going to continue to mine them? We know it's dangerous and we test out many things like the Nevada testing area—some day, we're going to burn ourselves up. So many things known to the Hopi tell the world not to do that any more. Stop uranium mining, testing. Stop everything. So I hope we will correct this and whoever comes out will meet the Great Spirit on the other end again. "I'm the first, I'm the last and I will welcome those that survive and we will have beautiful, clean life again, everything will become new again." These are some of the things that are mentioned, that we as human beings [are] like these flowers here—they are beautiful flowers, and they form a circle. And outside there are many kinds of flowers. We, the people, are like that. We will no longer have any discrimination against black, white, red and yellow. We are going to be one human being. We are brothers and sisters, and we are going to help to protect this Mother Earth for the next generations, and then we will have a good life again. So this symbol represents male, this one represents female, and this sun symbol represents also the power. If we do not correct this ourselves—we're talking about peace—if we do not correct this thing, those with that symbol will have to purify this with the power that the Great Bear [Spirit] will give them. These are some of the things known.[29]

What is the response to the prophecy? What is to be done? Who will make the right decision? Perhaps the answers to such questions are in the Earth itself. Annie Kahn, a Navajo medicine woman, said to ask the Earth: "Everything one wants to know is in these [sacred] mountains. To test our beliefs, they remain quiet. They're so old. They've witnessed so much."[30]

We must be patient and alert to hear the Earth. Tribal ways are of wisdom, but such wisdom derives from the source called Earth.

Native people know the past through stories passed from one generation to the next one. Knowledge helps us to understand. Peterson Zah, former tribal chairman of the Navajo and special advisor to the president of Arizona State University, wrote, "Our stories teach us where we come from and who we are. They say we arrive here in this, the Fifth World, after dwelling in four lower worlds below....We are called the Earth-Surface people because of our ancestral resistance in other worlds."[31] It is on the Earth's surface that the politics are waged over what is below. This story of energy demands for tribal lands will become a part of the stories told about the white man. The story will be one of how Native people like the Navajo and Hopi see their side of the story in this shared experience with white-owned energy companies. This is not a new story of how Indians and whites fought for the Earth. It will not be the last one.

The situation for energy tribes has not changed significantly in regard to the demand for their natural resources. As Americans remain committed to their automobile culture, the demands on the energy tribes increase as well. And, of course, Indian people use cars. The vastness of the Southwest compels Native peoples like the Navajo and other tribes to drive considerable distances. Many prefer trucks to cars—Fords, Chevys, and Dodge. The terrain dictates a changing culture among Indian people who have quickly adopted the automobile and pickup, especially since World War II.

All of this places more pressure on tribal leaders to decide whether to mine and develop their tribal resources. This situation has put more of their traditional cultures at risk. Although all living cultures change and go through transitions, traditionalists in the energy tribes find themselves in an ever-smaller minority than before. Of utmost importance, to understand the Earth, you must "see" this dilemma of whether to mine from the perspective of the tribe(s) involved.[32] Out of this Native ethos, Indian people are trying to do what they think is right.

Notes

1. Harris and Harris 1974:25.
2. Lee 1987:xii.
3. Crapanzano 2003[1972]:25.
4. Silko 1977:47.
5. Lee 1987:10.
6. Crapanzano 2003[1972]:45.

7. Silko 1977:70.

8. Katchongva 1992:6–7.

9. Tapahonso 1997:15.

10. Shepardson 1995:160. For information on Navajo religion, see Reichard 1963.

11. Shepardson 1995:172.

12. Lee 1987:29.

13. Kahn 1990:132.

14. Crapanzano 2003[1972]:3.

15. Matthews 1984:40.

16. Coffer 1982:126–127.

17. Greenberg and Greenberg 1996:25.

18. Ibid., 25–27.

19. LaFarge 1929:11.

20. Alvord and Van Pelt 1999:84; see also Shepard 1978.

21. Tapahonso 1993:29.

22. Ibid., 19.

23. Coffer 1982:70–73.

24. Courlander 1971:9.

25. Ibid., 10–11.

26. Crapanzano 2003[1972]:34–35.

27. Silko 1977:236.

28. Lee 1987:47.

29. Poison Fire, Sacred Earth: Testimonies, Lectures, Conclusions. The World Uranium Hearing, Salzburg, 1992, pp. 32–36, http://www.ratical.org/radiation/WorldUraniumHearing/ThomasBanyacya.html (accessed August 2007).

30. Kahn 1990:128.

31. Zah 2001:2.

32. See Young Bear and Theisz 1994; Fixico 2003.

3

Oil, Indians, and Angie Debo

Representations of Energy Development on Tribal Lands

Brian Frehner

Historian Angie Debo once described Indian Territory's transition to statehood as an "orgy of exploitation." As she saw it, primarily white settlers and some mixed-blood Indians stripped predominantly full-blood Indians of their land and mineral holdings and in the process consolidated enormous wealth.[1] Some state and local officials attempted to protect the Indians, but in general, "the entire Five Tribes area was dominated by a vast criminal conspiracy to wrest a great and rich domain from its owners."[2] Debo maintained this perspective throughout her long life, describing the subject of her book as "a criminal conspiracy to cheat these Indians out of their land."[3] Debo's allegation of a "conspiracy," however, fails to account for the chaotic, improvisational, and contingent character of the oil industry throughout much of its early history and oversimplifies the people who profited from oil as villains motivated solely by profit, greed, and duplicity. Furthermore, this Manichaean perspective prevented Debo from understanding how some Native people also profited from oil resources. She mistakenly assumed a relationship between blood quantum and Native people's willingness and ability to engage in capitalism.

Historians like Debo have often characterized the activities of Native people through a variety of categories such as premodern, modern, traditional, progressive, and dependent, which oversimplify and obscure behavior. Such categories place Indians outside mainstream society economically and culturally.[4] There exists a growing body of scholarship, however, that challenges such concepts.[5] Increasingly, historians are recognizing the need to cast Native Americans as historical actors who actively participated in shaping their economic worlds and engaged in capitalism on their own terms.[6] Collectively, this work calls for transcending static categories that perpetuate images of Indians as people defined by ideologies and ideas and, instead, casting them as individuals who participated in the market whenever and however they chose. Ideologies can and do influence identity, but the process by which ideologies are constructed at the national level and filtered to the local level provides many opportunities for people to internalize, reproduce, manipulate, and resist them.[7] Thus, categories historians use to document Native American history can prove useful but limited; definitions remain constantly in flux.

Categories based upon "blood quantum" (the quantity of Indian blood an individual possesses) further complicate the effort to write about Indians who participated in capitalist economies without surrendering their culture. Researchers who sought to understand and explain Native American behavior have long linked behavior with race. For example, historians have applied the terms *mixed-blood* and *full-blood* to describe Indian people, labels loaded with meaning and implications about an individual or group's cultural status relative to a supposedly "modern," non-Indian society. Racial designations meant to characterize a person's blood quantum function as more than merely neutral descriptors and carry political meanings with important implications for Indians and non-Indians. Designations referring to "blood" emerge from sociohistorical and sociopolitical contexts. Thus, blood quantum functions as both a measure of and a metaphor for Indian identity situated within a variety of contexts.[8]

In order to take seriously the prospect of Native American agency within capitalist economies, this chapter explores how Angie Debo's historical writings established a pattern for understanding how Indian people of various blood quanta related to the oil industry in Indian Territory and Oklahoma. Debo's use of categories as static descriptors perpetuated stereotypes of capitalist conspirators and innocent, defenseless full-bloods. Such ideas not only are historically inaccurate but also undermine our ability to see how Indians have acted in politically and economically sophisticated and thoughtful ways. Indians with oil interests did not always prevail, nor did all Indian people share identical values or similar goals.

Contemporary analysts of energy production and indigenous people would do well to see these complexities more clearly than did Debo.

OKLAHOMA STATEHOOD

According to the front page of *The Daily Oklahoman* on November 17, 1907, the state's governor had just blocked a conspiracy of vast proportions. It explained how the Standard Oil Company conspired to build a pipeline unlawfully into the newly created state, formerly dubbed "Indian Territory." Beneath the headline, which declared "Oklahoma Becomes State," the paper claimed that Governor Thomas L. Haskell exposed the oil company's "ruse."[9] Standard had acquired oil and natural gas interests and built a refinery in Kansas. The company then tried to build a pipeline into Indian Territory to siphon off oil resources. To achieve this end, Standard orchestrated a "ruse" to take advantage of Indian Territory's transition to Oklahoma statehood by building the pipeline before government officials could thwart the plot. Standard underestimated Haskell, however, who secretly took the oath of office two hours before the public ceremony and worked with a county judge and attorney to issue an injunction preventing the pipeline, which had encroached within 200 feet of Oklahoma's state line. Haskell ordered a local sheriff to cooperate with Indian police to arrest and jail anyone constructing the pipeline on Oklahoma soil. The governor declared, "I told the Standard Oil Company and kindred monopolies before election that if they did not lick me at the polls, I would lick them every day that I was governor until they decided to abide by the law."[10]

The governor's willingness to exercise state power to thwart a monopolistic oil company's attempt to acquire energy resources contrasts starkly with Debo's interpretation of Oklahoma statehood. At the dawn of the twentieth century, approximately seventy thousand Indians owned territory in the eastern half of present-day Oklahoma, a locale Debo described as "immensely wealthy in farmland and forest and coal mines, and with untapped oil pools of incalculable value."[11] There ensued an "orgy of exploitation" in which primarily white settlers and some mixed-bloods stripped Indians of their land and mineral holdings.[12] Debo wrote graphically and passionately about "the grafters" who conspired to acquire Indians' wealth by devious methods that included intermarriage, guardianship, undue influence of the legislature and courts, and often outright deceit. Debo did not define the term *grafter* in absolute terms but said that dealers in Indian land and wealth applied it routinely to themselves and, apparently, never considered it offensive.[13] The grafters she identified included some of the most prominent Oklahomans, including Governor Haskell and Senator Robert L. Owen, as well as the family members of prominent legislators, lawyers, judges, and businesspeople.[14] The blatant nature of their crimes and the unsavory behavior of the criminals motivated Debo to record this previously untold history. As she combed through voluminous research materials, past injustices stood out unequivocally on the pages: "I'd pick up a newspaper and here would be on the front page...the prominent names of people who had attained their power and prominence by robbing the Indians, and this was criminal too. A criminal conspiracy."[15] Debo believed that she had found clear and convincing evidence to explain how land and resources in Indian Territory transferred from Native people to Euroamericans.

Given the enormous profits Native people potentially could have derived from resources beneath their land, the lessons of socially conscious historians resonate all the more powerfully for present-day Native people who sit atop vast stores of energy resources. Debo remains central to our understanding of energy development on Native lands, in part, because she wrote about an area that contained the largest stores of energy reserves on tribal lands in the nation. Within the lands designated as Indian Territory sat huge deposits of coal, oil, and natural gas. Particularly noteworthy is that after statehood was established, Oklahoma became the only state with a constitution mandating creation of a geological survey, an entity that greatly facilitated locating and mapping energy resources. Debo revealed her understanding of the linkage between energy resources and statehood when she observed that "the plunder of Indians was so closely joined with pride in the creation of a great new commonwealth that it received little condemnation."[16] Furthermore, she explained, "after statehood," the half of Oklahoma that had been Indian Territory "dominated state politics, and to a certain extent it dominated the economic situation because the oil fields were in the eastern half, and they were spectacular oil fields."[17] At the heart of this story sat the "guardians of a few oil rich Indians," but she had no idea of the "explosive character" of what she was about to "uncover." Willing and eager to condemn the linkage between oil and statehood, she pulled no punches in identifying the plunderers.

Although Indians possessed various forms of material wealth, oil resources particularly made the Osages vulnerable to outside fortune hunters. People trying to acquire headrights on tribal lands murdered approximately twenty-three Osages. Debo admonished, "Historians have been inclined to pussyfoot in this field of Indian exploitation, but nobody who ignores it can understand Oklahoma politics."[18] Far from pussyfooting, Debo boldly named the people who had exploited Indians, described their methods, and consequently alienated many prominent Oklahomans.

Recounting the experience of researching *And Still the Waters Run*, Debo presented herself as a Sam Spade–like detective. She believed that she approached her research subjects in an entirely disinterested manner and contended frequently that her lack of knowledge about a topic before research began enhanced her objectivity. To support her contention that she wrote with no particular agenda, she explained, "I just took something that I didn't know a thing about and it seems as though something had happened and I had wanted to know what happened."[19] Growing up in the small north-central Oklahoma town of Marshall, she had little knowledge of the eastern half of the state, where most Indians resided, for "there were two separate halves of Oklahoma that didn't know each other very well."[20] She knew so little about the land and its people to the east, they held an exotic appeal. The land of the Five Tribes "was far away as, oh farther away than Cambodia is now, from our thoughts and everything."[21] She had no knowledge about how the federal government liquidated Indian Territory's tribal governments or how allotment paved the way for Indians to lose their land after statehood had been established in 1907: "I didn't know of this criminal conspiracy. I just thought that it would be a story of how the land was divided and things like that."[22]

Debo may have known little about her subject, but she was not as objective as she thought. She acknowledged the contested nature of the term *objectivity* but dismissed any suggestion she had written anything less than an accurate representation of the past. She was eighty-six years old when she observed in 1976, "It is fashionable just now to assert that no scholar can be objective, that he slants his findings according to his own bias," but she would have none of it: "I do not admit this."[23] Rather than provide readers with a historical context in which to view past events, Debo believed that she could locate a clear, identifiable, and verifiable truth and document it through her research.[24] She said, "I simply want to dig out the truth and record it," but conceded, "Sometimes I find all the truth on one side of an issue."[25] Her contention that truth lay "on one side of an issue" influenced her perspective in *And Still the Waters Run* and led her to invoke a narrative in which greedy oil industry capitalists conspired to rob helpless full-blood Indians.[26]

To be sure, the people primarily responsible for pushing Indians from their lands were white Americans of European descent in search of material betterment and political opportunities. From the Curtis Act in 1898, which abolished Indians' tribal status, to the creation of Oklahoma statehood in

1907, most of the Indians' wealth passed into outsiders' hands.[27] Debo only rarely identified the "grafters" solely on the basis of race but clearly saw white people as the greedy culprits. Restlessness and opportunities for adventure in developing a frontier attracted thousands of young white Americans to Indian territory.[28] A frenzy of development ensued as the white population mushroomed from approximately 340,000 in 1890 to 529,000 in 1907.[29] They arrived with "no knowledge of Indian tradition, no respect for Indian institutions," but instead were guided to discover oil fields, build cities, and plow land by a philosophy that commingled greed and public spirit.[30]

Not all of the greedy grafters were white people, however, and Debo explained that some Indians at times participated in the disenfranchisement of their own people. Although some served unwittingly as grafters' dupes, other Indians "were the grafters' willing tools."[31] They relied upon their cultural affiliations to secure names and signatures of tribal members as part of the grafters' efforts to defraud Native people of their wealth. Some Indians who aided grafters may not have realized the extent of their betrayal, she says, "but too often they were educated Indians who absorbed too much of the white man's acquisitiveness."[32] One group of real estate speculators employed "usually young Indians who could speak English to make a house-to-house canvass of the fullblood settlements" for the purpose of securing guardianship over their children.[33] Debo all too often invoked "the language of blood" to account for the actions of Native people.[34] By emphasizing how "educated" Indians "who could speak English" targeted "fullblood" settlements, she casts Native people within a dichotomous framework of traditional full-bloods, on the one hand, and assimilationist mixed-bloods, on the other.

The "progressive–traditional" dichotomy Debo employs obscures the complexity of individual Native people's motivations, fails to explain tribal factionalism fully, and discounts the role of individual Native people who acted as cultural middlemen. Scholars of Native American history have long perpetuated static categories of "traditional" and "progressive" to explain social, economic, and political dimensions to tribal factionalism.[35] Euroamericans too readily dubbed Native people who achieved material success, spoke English, or chose non-Native clothing styles as "progressives."[36] When individuals made choices more consistent with Native American cultural practices, Euroamericans considered them "traditional." But Native people behaved in ways that defied categorization under either of these labels.

Throughout *And Still the Waters Run*, however, Debo adopts an inconsistent position regarding blood quantum as a determining factor in Native people's actions. She explains that blood quantum played a relatively small role in how Native people behaved. She argues that large numbers of Indians adapted to white society but notes that "adaptability was not entirely a matter of blood," because some "fullblood families" had always possessed wealth.[37] Again, she contends that Indians who asserted themselves, "whether mixed-bloods or full-bloods," claimed positions of leadership in the state.[38] But elsewhere she interprets the actions of "mixed-blood" Indians within the context of their "progressive" outlook.[39] Whether consciously or not, Debo subscribed to the progressive–traditional dichotomy and considered blood quantum part of a formula that informed her interpretations.

THE CONSPIRACY NARRATIVE

Debo's influential scholarship shaped her readers' perceptions of the relationships between Indians and the oil industry. Other writers, however, shaped Debo's conspiratorial view of the oil business. Many people sought to acquire oil in Indian Territory and elsewhere. The term *conspiracy*, however, fails to account for the diverse, complex, and highly competitive motives that characterized oil producers before and after Oklahoma statehood. Oil producers have been embroiled in political battles at the local, state, and federal levels throughout the history of their industry. They have competed fiercely with one another to consolidate control over this resource. Often, the losers in these battles see the victors as conspirators. So the notion of a "conspiracy" among oil producers has a long history and accurately describes the motivations of some within the industry at certain times and places. But conspiracy theories can greatly obscure and oversimplify the economics, politics, and history of energy production.

The oil industry began in Pennsylvania in 1859 when Captain Edwin Drake drilled the first commercial well. Pennsylvania led US oil production every year of the nineteenth century until 1895, when Ohio produced about one million barrels more. Oil production climbed steadily throughout the 1880s and 1890s and gradually moved west. By the turn of the century, the total annual yield in states east of the Mississippi River began to decline, and western states such as Kansas, Oklahoma, Texas, and California took the lead in production.[40] From its inception, the oil industry was a boom-or-bust endeavor. So much oil sprang from the bowels of the earth and flooded its surface in the early stages of production that too few markets existed to absorb it all. When prospectors found oil, they raced to extract it from the ground. Derricks sprouted overnight, and the consequent contest for profits began to drain as much oil as possible before one's competitors

FIGURE 3.1

Udo Keppler's Standard Oil "octopus." Courtesy of Library of Congress.

could acquire it. The problem of overproduction plagued the oil industry from its inception until well into the twentieth century.

John D. Rockefeller's genius for addressing these problems earned him a vast fortune, as well as infamy within the oil industry and in the annals of American history. Rockefeller was the most important figure to shape the early oil industry, and perhaps no other person did more to shape industrial development or the modern corporation.[41] Just as Rockefeller played a primary role in shaping the oil industry and modern business practices, so too did his actions prompt harsh critiques from muckraking journalists. Rockefeller and his critics loom large in American history, and together they have particularly shaped the public's perception of the oil industry, past and present. In fact, the muckraking movement in American journalism started, in large part, because of Rockefeller and his oil business dealings. To appreciate the power of Rockefeller's critics, one need only consider the 1904 political cartoon of the Standard Oil "octopus" published in *Puck* magazine (figure 3.1). Udo Keppler depicted a huge octopus that has a refinery tank for its head, labeled "Standard Oil," its tentacles reaching ravenously to squash the US capitol building, the White House, and anyone within its grasp.[42]

Rockefeller orchestrated a revolution in business practices that pushed smaller oil producers out of the industry because they lacked the capital to compete. This practice in particular evoked the wrath of muckraking journalists.[43] For example, Ida Tarbell's perception that Rockefeller had victimized her father motivated her to allege a conspiracy in 1904—using the word *conspiracy* thirty times in her famous two-volume muckraking tract, *The History of Standard Oil Company*. Born in 1857, two years before Edwin Drake drilled the first commercial oil well and thirty miles from the site, Tarbell grew up around oil derricks, pipelines, and refineries.[44] She recounted in her memoirs that as an impressionable fifteen-year-old, she witnessed her father's personality transform when he and other independent producers failed to compete with Standard Oil. Whereas her father had once sung songs and told funny stories, he grew into a "silent and stern" man.[45] This lasting impression would influence her later interpretation of Standard Oil, giving rise to a conspiratorial narrative in her classic, muckraking work.

The conspiracy narrative that muckrakers fashioned to elucidate how the Standard Oil octopus squeezed independent producers continued to shape how people understood the motivations of oilmen who sought access to Indian Territory. The reach of Standard's tentacles extended well beyond Pennsylvania, into the Southern Plains states of Kansas, Oklahoma, and Texas. Not surprisingly, independent producers interested in acquiring oil in Indian Territory expressed animosity toward Standard Oil Company, which they viewed as a monopoly undermining their own ability to compete. Lewis Emery spoke for a group of independent oil producers when he testified at a 1906 hearing on oil-leasing practices.[46] Emery wanted investigators to understand that not all oilmen operated in the same manner and that they often held different and competing interests. He explained that neither he nor the independent producers he represented operated in the manner of the Standard Oil Company, maintaining that they had "fought the octopus since its origin."[47] Far from being "tainted with anything that pertains to monopoly," independent producers actively opposed monopolistic control. Henry Demarest Lloyd testified that they sought "in every way [they could] to shut out the Standard Oil Company from grasping up the oil lands."[48] Emery and producers like him simply wanted equal access to Indian Territory's oil, and this meant exempting them from a law that limited leases to 4,800 acres or less.[49]

Emery conceded that in some isolated instances, his associates may have violated the Department of the Interior's rulings governing production but that they generally tried to follow the law and the advice of their attorneys. In fact, existing laws and rules proved so effective, these prevented independent oil producers from competing on an even footing with Standard. What Indian Territory needed in order to maximize profitability for Native people, according to Emery, were laws and rules that gave independent oilmen greater access. Open access was in everyone's best interest, he argued: "You must have competition there if you would get for your wards what belongs to them."[50]

This was the context of the oil industry at the time people and companies poured into Indian Territory, and much of the consequent chaos and disorder influenced Debo's perspective and interpretation of the situation. The scramble to acquire and control oil in Indian Territory is a convoluted story and often difficult to comprehend. She acknowledged that the Interior department's "regulations aimed to prevent monopoly control" but concluded that "apparently the industry was not seriously retarded."[51] Rather, the industry blossomed because "oil men complained loudly of the delay occasioned by Departmental 'red tape'" in securing leases and proved "eminently successful" in gaining access to Indians' lands.[52] Competition reigned supreme, and "as a result the oil industry was a free-for-all scramble, with the great Mellon and Standard interests, the young oil worker who could scrape together enough money to drill a well of his own, and the gambler who must try one more 'sure thing,' all entering into the most unrestricted rivalry."[53] The "unrestricted rivalry" had characterized and plagued the oil industry since its inception, creating winners and losers along the way. Some, like Rockefeller, played the game well, but others, like Tarbell and her father, felt victimized by its unpredictable nature. These qualities only reinforced in Debo's mind how "the wild, speculative, active spirit of the oil field gave a lurid phase to the early development of the Indian Territory."[54]

This "lurid phase," she argued, constituted only one part of a much larger story of capitalists' amoral confrontation with and colonization and conquest of Native people. Debo saw the process by which Indians lost much of their land and oil to speculators and capitalists as an "age of economic absorption" that succeeded an age of military conquest, in which the frontiersman's long rifle was "displaced by the legislative enactment and court decree of the legal exploiter, by the lease, mortgage, and deed of the land shark."[55] Private industry merely perpetuated conquest, but in a new form, by co-opting state and local government throughout Oklahoma. Certainly, corruption existed, and Debo accurately recorded numerous instances in which people manipulated the legal system to acquire guardianship over Indian children and steal their resources. At what point corruption qualified as a "vast conspiracy," however, remains less certain.

In addition to corruption at the state and local levels, Debo contended that the federal government participated in the conspiracy that unfolded in Indian Territory. Initially, Indian Territory's Five Tribes avoided the negative impacts of the Dawes Act, which exempted them from dissolution of communally held tribal lands and of tribal governments. A subsequent federal law, the Curtis Act of 1898, however, dissolved communal ownership and tribal sovereignty among the Five Tribes too. Whereas the Dawes Act mandated the terms of allotment, the Curtis Act allowed Five Tribes members to negotiate the terms by which they allotted their lands by participating in bilateral agreements.[56] Furthermore, the Curtis Act abrogated tribal courts and laws and implemented federal authority over all residents of Indian Territory regardless of race.[57] It constituted the "death knell" of the Five Tribes' sovereignty.[58] The law designated that the Interior department serve as the entity to award or deny mineral leases on tribal land.[59] Debo's interpretation of the corruption that plagued Indian Territory and paved the way for Oklahoma statehood hinged upon this act. Within a month of its passage, "the most feverish activity was displayed all over the Territory in seizing lots and erecting 'improvements.'"[60] Because of the act, anyone who improved a lot earned the right to purchase it at half its appraised value. During the ten years between the Curtis Act and Oklahoma statehood, "the bulk of the landed wealth of the Indians passed into individual hands."[61]

CHARLES CURTIS

Given Debo's emphasis on the Curtis Act as the legislation that most facilitated an "orgy of exploitation," it is ironic that the author of the law was a Native American. Charles Curtis was a Kansas senator and served under Herbert Hoover as the thirty-first vice president of the United States. Born in 1860, Curtis was a Native American whose mother was a member of the Kansa (later Kaw) Tribe and whose father was French. Curtis spent part of his early childhood on the Kaw reservation in central Kansas. A field officer of the Indian Office dropped Curtis from the tribal roll in 1878 for failing to take up residence on a Kaw reservation established in Indian Territory.[62] Curtis began to learn at an early age that people felt justified in assessing his identity as an Indian.

Curtis's Indianness contrasted sharply with Debo's definition of an Indian. For Curtis, being Indian had less to do with blood quantum and more to do with ensuring that Indians retained property in order to assimilate economically into mainstream society. To some, the idea of simultaneously assimilating *and* retaining a distinct Indian identity may sound anomalous. But Curtis valued both of these goals. His Indian identity emerged from experiences related specifically to his mixed racial background. For example, he grew up at a time when Kansa of mixed racial backgrounds faced questions as to the legality of their tribal membership and whether they owned fee-simple title to lands granted them by treaty. These unresolved issues left Curtis and the growing number of Kansa with mixed ancestry vulnerable to land speculators. As a result, when Curtis gained power, he felt particularly committed to defending the property, honor, and character of other people with mixed ancestry. Curtis fought as a congressman to ensure that children of white men and Indian women retained the same property and annuity rights as other tribal members.[63] Being cast off the tribal roll as a child directly impacted his life and livelihood and galvanized him to protect others marginalized by their mixed racial ancestry. The legislation he advocated eventually failed to win passage, and this defeat must have particularly stung when the bill's primary opponent declared to Curtis that US citizens will support Indians "but draw a line as to who are to be considered Indians."[64] To Curtis, the message was nothing new. Powerful people believed that Indians looked and behaved in obvious and recognizable ways, and these people used their authority to determine what constituted Indianness.

Another irony in Curtis's authoring legislation that, according to Debo, allowed grafters to steal Indians' wealth was that he profited significantly from the oil industry. Curtis used his political power to further his private interests, and he helped some of the most important oilmen in the industry to access Indian Territory. His cozy relationship with oil interests gained national attention when *The Nation* reported on his longtime friendship with oilman Harry Sinclair and noted: "[Curtis] for many years has ridden into office on money furnished by the oil owner."[65] Curtis also worked closely with Theodore N. Barnsdall, who held a lease on the Osage reservation for just under 56,000 acres and who, many believed, worked for Standard Oil.[66] As chairman of the House Committee on Indian Affairs, Curtis wrote a clause attached to an Indian appropriations bill that relinquished leases to the Indian Territory to Illuminating Oil Company, which, in turn, subleased to Barnsdall, James F. Guffey, and J. Paul Getty.[67] Curtis's political connections put him in contact with other oilmen, who consulted him on legal matters relating to leases, leading him to recall, "I soon had quite a business from Tulsa, Bartlesville, and other towns in Oklahoma."[68] Curtis used his ethnicity to amass political and economic power. Increasingly, congressional colleagues deferred to him on matters relating to Indians, and he leveraged their attentive ears, according to historian William Unrau, into "sheer political power, conceived and nurtured by an ambitious mixed-blood who was determined to prove the truth of the assimilationists' dream."[69] For Curtis, making money from the oil industry did not dilute his Indianness.

Debo's failure to mention Curtis's Indian heritage or his relationship to the oil industry reflected a tendency throughout *And Still the Waters Run* to privilege some manifestations of Indian identity as authentic and others as less so. Americans have long attempted to understand Indian people through the prisms of value-laden categories such as primitive, technologically incompetent, physical isolated, or culturally different. Curtis defied these categories, and as a result, Debo failed to acknowledge his Indian ancestry or interpret his actions as those of an Indian. Expectations of how Indians should or should not behave reveal social, political, legal, and economic power imbalances in society. These expectations function as products of domination but can also serve as tools of domination.[70] Debo, although she documented the economic domination of Indians, failed to recognize the cultural domination in her own work. She expected "real" Indians to exist only outside the oil industry.

Indians failed to participate in the oil industry because their racial background demarcated them, in Debo's mind, as noncapitalists. Her book centers on the idea that racial difference resulted in the disempowerment of Native people by circumscribing their range of economic opportunities. She perpetuates, however, the image of Indians as noncapitalists by characterizing oil development, urban growth, and farming as activities solely the domain of "white people" who rushed into Indian Territory from 1890 to 1900:

> Most of this [population] increase was the result of the immigration of the young, restless, adventurous element naturally attracted to a developing frontier. These newcomers had no knowledge of Indian tradition, no respect for Indian institutions. In the excitement of discovering oil fields, building cities, and placing rich land under the plow, they created a philosophy in which personal greed and public spirit were inextricably joined. If they could build their personal fortunes and create a great state by destroying the Indian, they would destroy him in the name of all that was selfish and all that was holy.[71]

Debo spelled out that "greed" and "personal fortunes" associated with oil and other industries trumped Indian tradition and institutions, even if it meant "destroying the Indian." Oddly, she frequently painted a different picture toward the end of her book. She contended that the "controversies" and "stormy conflicts" documented in preceding chapters "were in a manner settled and a working basis was reached during the first few years of statehood. The white people soon accepted the unusual situation [of an Indian presence] as a permanent feature of Oklahoma life."[72] One paragraph later, Debo described Oklahoma's territorial seal, in which Lady Justice stands poised, with her scales, between a frontiersman and an Indian who are shaking hands. Any failure to realize this ideal, she explained, "was due to the individual greed of the white man and the individual ineptitude of the red rather than to any general racial discrimination."[73] At a minimum, she expressed confused reasoning but most often revealed inconsistent and contradictory notions of Indian people and their economic motivations. Debo expected Indians to behave in "traditional" ways consistent with their "institutions," and the oil industry clashed with her notions of Indianness.

Despite these shortcomings, perhaps one reason Debo's reputation as a pioneering historian of Indian people persists stems from the similarities between the subtext of her life and the Native people about whom she wrote. Both stories involve people who confronted significant obstacles, behaved with dignity and character, and eventually triumphed through their own gumption, perseverance, and tenacity. One version of Debo's personal history particularly serves as a corollary to her histories documenting the exploitation of Oklahoma Indians. Debo was born in 1890 and arrived at the age of nine in a covered wagon in Marshall, Oklahoma Territory, after her father purchased land in what had formerly been Indian Territory.[74] Although educational opportunities proved elusive in this frontier community, Debo, who loved reading, persevered in her studies and eventually received a PhD from the University of Oklahoma. She encountered obstacles to employment as a professor because of sexual discrimination but wrote prolifically, producing nine books over the course of her life, some of which remain classics in Native American history.

Debo was not encumbered by racial prejudice, but rather by gender prejudice. This version of her life possesses a trajectory that parallels her story of the vast conspiracy she alleges involving the oil industry and Native people living in Indian Territory. The people who made up the Five Civilized Tribes began arriving in Indian Territory in the early nineteenth century. Despite their long-established ties to the land in the southeastern United States, the federal government relocated them to the west. In addition to the injustice of forced removal, many died along the way, and those who lived endured significant cultural dislocation that greatly disrupted but did not destroy their societies. Other tribes eventually followed. Toward the end of the nineteenth and early into the twentieth century, Native and non-Native people began to realize that valuable stores of energy resources, especially petroleum, sat beneath the lands. A minority of Native people in Oklahoma, such as the Osages, experienced unprecedented wealth for a short time, but most of them unjustly lost control of their mineral resources because of the duplicity of outsiders. Like Debo, Oklahoma's Native people experienced great obstacles throughout their lives, endured hardships and challenges, but ultimately persevered with dignity and self-respect.

Determining where to place Debo on a moral spectrum proves a tricky but necessary task, given the influential nature of *And Still the Waters Run*, her condemnation of the grafters, and her avowal "to establish justice" for Native people. When the oil industry arrived in Oklahoma, Debo hoped to share in the profits coming to so many of her neighbors. Just as towns throughout Oklahoma boomed upon discovery of oil, Debo's hometown of Marshall bustled with new inhabitants and thriving businesses when oil was discovered nearby in 1927. Eleven years previously, the Debos had sold their farm, so they were disappointed when prospectors found oil at that site.[75] The onslaught of new residents created a housing shortage, and Debo "caught the speculative fever," purchased a downtown lot, and her brother began building a house she planned to rent for extra income.[76] Debo's speculative venture proved a bust, however, when wells quickly dried up and the town's population decreased, leading her to turn the house over to her parents, who assumed the loan. What does this incident reveal, if anything, about Debo's moral culpability in profiting, albeit indirectly, from resources that had previously belonged to Osages and, later, Cherokees? It is important to recall the proximity of her life to the nation's frontier past in assessing Debo's moral culpability.[77] Her failed efforts at speculating in real estate development reveal most clearly that if judged by her own standards, she, too, participated in the process (she would say "imperialism") that disenfranchised Native people.

Debo struggled to reconcile her understandings of the oil industry and what it meant to be an Indian in the twentieth century. Oil connoted modernity, a natural resource that fueled internal combustion engines in an industrializing and urbanizing country. It also connoted wealth, power, and privilege. None of its connotations, in her mind, applied to Native people. Rather, given its symbolic resonance to Debo and muckrakers who preceded her, oil and the people who produced it bore a large share of the blame for the victimization of Oklahoma's Native people.

Debo's work remains important and continues to inspire many. But it was a product of her time and place, thus influencing her interpretations. Her commitment, diligence, and professionalism enabled her to document legitimate instances of corruption, graft, and greed. Her argument—that the oil industry contributed to a vast conspiracy designed to steal resources from Indians—overstates the case, however. Contemporary analysts of energy production would do well to consider the complexities of the relationship between Native people and their energy resources. Historical narratives that tell only stories of exploitation run the risk of ignoring Native people who recognized economic opportunities in developing energy resources and participated in capitalism on terms they defined. Now more than ever, as the energy demands of industrializing societies increasingly influence our daily lives and decisions, we need histories of Indians and energy production that present the complexities of these interactions.

Notes

1. Debo 1968[1940]:x.
2. Ibid., 196–197.
3. Angie Debo, Interviews by Gloria Valencia-Webber and Glenna Matthews, 1981 to 1984, Box 2, Folder 4, pp. 7, 8; Folder 8, pp. 8, 9; Folder 12, p. 6; Folder 16, p. 38; Folder 18, p. 2, Special Collections and University Archives, Oklahoma State University, Stillwater (hereafter cited as *Debo Interviews*).
4. Some accounts of capitalism's impact on Native people in Indian Territory do well in documenting the many injustices that occurred but do not typically present Indians with much choice in the economic activities they confronted (see Fixico 1998:x; Miner 1976). For an account that demonstrates how Indians exercised significant choice when faced with new economic activities, see Colleen O'Neill 2005:144: "American Indians have crafted alternative pathways of economic development that transcend linear analytical categories."
5. Deloria 2004; Harmon 1995:430; Lewis 1991; Hosmer 1999.
6. Harmon 2003; see also O'Neill's edited collection with Brian Hosmer (2004).
7. Sturm 2002:2.
8. Perdue 2003:70–71; Sturm 2002:2; Harmon 2001.
9. "Blocks Ruse of Big Oil Company," *The Daily Oklahoman*, November 17, 1907.
10. Ibid., 3.
11. Debo 1968[1940]:ix.
12. Ibid., x.
13. Ibid., 92.

14. Leckie 2000:66.

15. Debo Interviews, Box 2, Folder 4, p. 8.

16. Debo 1968[1940]:92.

17. Debo Interviews, Box 2, Folder 18, p. 2.

18. Debo 1949:43, 1968[1940]:viii; McIntosh 1988:175.

19. Throughout the oral interviews conducted for the documentary, Debo repeatedly states that she knew nothing about her subjects before research began (Debo Interviews, September 24, 1993, Folder 4, p. 7; see also Box 2, Folder 18, p. 2).

20. Debo Interviews, Box 2, Folder 12, p. 6.

21. Ibid., Box 2, Folder 16, p. 39.

22. Ibid., September 24, 1993, Box 2, Folder 4, p. 7.

23. Debo 1976:405.

24. Ibid.

25. Ibid. Elsewhere, Debo (1988:2) described her goal in writing history: "to discover truth and publish it."

26. Debo Interviews, Box 2, Folder 16, p. 38.

27. Debo 1968[1940]:92.

28. Ibid., 93.

29. Ibid., 92.

30. Ibid., 93.

31. Debo 1968[1940].

32. Ibid., 94.

33. Ibid., 106.

34. Perdue 2003:98.

35. Lewis 1991:125.

36. Perdue (2003:91) explains the irrelevance of so-called markers such as clothing because both mixed- and full-blood Indians expressed themselves through garments.

37. Debo 1968[1940]:126.

38. Ibid., 293.

39. For a few examples of Debo's use of the term *progressive*, see Debo 1968[1940]:80, 165. Perdue (2003:99) cites Debo as one of several historians who associated cultural change with mixed ancestry.

40. For oil production statistics by these and other states, see the appendices in Rister 1949 and the epilogue in Franks and Lambert 1985.

41. Yergin 1991:36; Chernow 1998:xvi.

42. *Puck* 1436:56 (September 7, 1904). For other versions of the image, see "The Image of the Octopus: Six Cartoons, 1889–1902," National Humanities Center Web

site, http://nationalhumanitiescenter.org/pds/gilded/power/text1/octopusimages.pdf (accessed December 2009).

43. Henry Demarest Lloyd (1881) initiated these attacks with his "Story of a Great Monopoly," published in March 1881 in *Atlantic Monthly*.

44. Chernow 1998:435.

45. Tarbell 1939:203, quoted in Chernow 1998:436.

46. US Department of the Interior 1972:21.

47. Ibid., 22.

48. Ibid.

49. The Curtis Act of 1898 forbade leases larger than 4,800 acres in Indian Territory except on Osage lands (Oklahoma Heritage Association 1993:82).

50. US Department of the Interior 1972:22.

51. Ibid., 89.

52. Debo 1968[1940].

53. Ibid.

54. Ibid.

55. Debo 1968[1940]:ix.

56. Thorne 2003:29–30. Each of the Five Tribes negotiated individual agreements subsequent to passage of the act. Debo concluded that these agreements revealed a change of "Indian thought" from 1896 to 1902. Originally, the Curtis Act provided for the retention of mineral rights by the tribes, but Creeks and Cherokees repealed this provision, choosing to allot minerals with individual parcels of land (Debo 1968[1940]:35).

57. Unrau 1989:122–123.

58. Thorne 2003:29–30.

59. Ibid., 119.

60. Debo 1968[1940]:120.

61. Ibid., 92.

62. Unrau 1989:9, 4.

63. Ibid., 5, 54, 7, 1.

64. Congressional Record, 54th Cong., 1st sess., February 24, 1896, vol. 28, p. 2079.

65. Babcock 1928:288.

66. Unrau 1989:114.

67. Ibid.

68. Quoted in Charles Curtis, "Autobiography," William P. Colvin copy, typed copy in the possession of Tom Dennison, Ponca City, OK.

69. Ibid.

70. Deloria 2004:4.

71. Debo 1968[1940]:93.

72. Ibid., 291.

73. Ibid., 292.

74. Debo Interviews, Box 2, Folder 17, p. 1; Debo 1985.

75. Leckie 2000:43.

76. Debo Interviews, Folder 15, pp. 5–6.

77. Hurtado 2001:419.

4

The Evolution of Federal Energy Policy for Tribal Lands and the Renewable Energy Future

Garrit Voggesser

Examination of federal energy policy for tribal lands reveals the evolution of federal–tribal relations and the federal trust responsibility to tribes. More important, this examination reveals the key relationship between Indian energy development and the rise of tribal sovereignty and empowerment in energy resource management. Energy development on Indian reservations has proven a mixed blessing for tribes. Federal decision makers failed in their role as trustees for tribes and also brokered energy deals that made non-Indian developers rich at the expense of tribes. Some tribes received considerable income, but the economic benefits did not always outweigh the negative impacts on tribal communities, natural resources, and culture. In the past few decades, tribes have seized opportunities for greater authority over tribal energy resource development and have displayed significant flexibility and ingenuity in seeking more diverse economic growth through renewable energy projects.

This chapter offers a historical overview of federal policy related to Indian energy development. The chapter concludes with the Jicarilla Apache Tribe as a compelling case study of how tribes have increased their control over energy resource development by exercising their sovereign power, increasing their technical capacity, and using the courts to shape federal policy. Federal policy for and supervision of tribal energy resources inflicted incredible damage on Indian lands and communities. But the most enduring legacy of Indian energy development is the remarkable success of tribes in combating external forces, reinforcing self-determination, and securing control of their own natural resources for the future of their people.

THE EARLY YEARS

In 1891 Congress enacted the first legislation for leasing minerals on tribal lands, authorizing ten-year mineral leases of "bought and paid for" land (reservation lands set aside by treaty or agreement) not needed for agriculture or allotments. The leases required the approval of the secretary of the Interior and the consent of the tribe. Unfortunately, the stipulation for tribal consent meant very little because tribes frequently lacked the knowledge and experience to make informed decisions about leasing. Also, their development decisions were made under pressure from economic hardship and external forces.[1]

In 1924 Congress passed an act to lengthen oil and gas leases on treaty reservations to a term of ten years *or* for as long as oil or gas "produced in paying quantities." The act called for lease sales by competitive bidding at public auction. In 1927 Congress passed similar legislation that applied to reservations created by executive order. Both the 1924 and 1927 acts permitted states to tax oil and gas production on tribal lands.[2]

For years to come, disputes created by the 1924 and 1927 acts would have serious ramifications for tribal energy resource development. Questions of ownership—of the land, not the minerals—threatened tribal rights. In the early 1920s, Interior secretary Albert B. Fall argued that mineral leasing laws for public lands applied to executive order reservations because these lands had merely been "withdrawn" and could be restored to public access. Fall's misguided interpretation posed a threat to Indian interests; more than half of Indian lands had been created by executive order. Fall's ambitions quickly unwound with his departure from federal employment after the Teapot Dome Scandal. In 1924 Attorney General Harlan Stone ruled that the public land leasing laws did not apply to executive order lands and that these lands should be treated the same as treaty lands. The conflict, however, paved the way for the state taxation provisions in the 1924 and 1927 acts. Taxation became compensation for the purported loss of public revenue from executive order lands and would ultimately result in tribal antagonism in the 1970s and 1980s.[3]

The early years of federal policy for tribal energy resources set the stage for decades of tumult. Not only did the lack of continuity and clarity in Indian energy policy threaten Indian rights to and profit from the energy resources they owned, but it also contributed to a protracted battle over who should control tribal energy development.

THE INDIAN MINERAL LEASING ACT OF 1938

The unease of the 1930s led to a reassessment of federal Indian administration programs. During the Great Depression, the federal government faced self-inflicted hurdles in managing Indian affairs, in particular, tribal sovereignty and economic development. The Osage and other tribes in Oklahoma had experienced an economic boom from oil. But Assistant Commissioner for Indian Affairs Edgar B. Meritt explained, "We should not get the impression that all Indians are well to do. We have a large number of Indians who are exceedingly poor and need every assistance possible from the Government."[4]

In 1934, to remedy the problems of Indian administration, Congress passed the Indian Reorganization Act (IRA). The IRA promoted tribal sovereignty and self-governance, theoretically giving Indians more control over their natural resources. Despite provisions for tribal consent in Indian energy law, the Bureau of Indian Affairs (BIA) almost wholly directed oil and gas leasing on tribal lands. Tribes organized under the IRA gained new authority over energy development, but there were many energy tribes not organized under the IRA. Simultaneously, the existing statutes on Indian mineral leasing could not be applied with consistency to all the energy tribes.[5]

In 1938 Congress passed the Omnibus Indian Mineral Leasing Act (IMLA), which would regulate the management of Indian minerals and fuels for the next forty-four years. Congress intended the IMLA to bring consistency to mineral leasing on tribal lands, by providing a "repealer clause" for the contradictions in past legislation. Congress also expected the IMLA to support the IRA's objectives of tribal self-government and greater control over tribal resources. Many tribes, however, did not utilize specific IRA provisions for controlling mineral leases. Finally, Congress intended the IMLA to encourage tribes to take full advantage of their economic development opportunities and to increase mineral leasing profits.[6]

The IMLA streamlined Indian mineral leasing. Leases now required competitive bidding, tribal consent, and approval by the Interior secretary; the lease term was ten years or as long as oil, gas, and minerals "produced in paying quantities." To ensure honest bidding and the integrity of lessees, the act also required a bonus payment upon lease approval. If the bids did not reflect the value of the energy resource, the Interior secretary could initiate private negotiations to secure an economically acceptable offer. Though the language regarding tribal consent remained similar to that of past legislation, the IMLA's leasing authority constituted a significant step forward in empowering tribes in energy development decisions.[7]

Despite the IMLA's advances in leasing clarity, tribal self-government, and tribal economic development, the act left out many important considerations. Tribes had limited authority to cancel leases and to seek redress if lessees did not live up to lease terms, and the IMLA did not address such issues as cultural and natural resource preservation. In a period of general economic depression, coupled with the long-term poverty in Indian communities, the environmental impacts of energy development were not a priority. The focus on economic development also ignored tribal ecological beliefs. Nonetheless, the 1938 IMLA should be recognized for the impetus it gave to tribal sovereignty, a momentum that would propel major advances for tribes in the final thirty years of the twentieth century.[8]

THE CALM BEFORE THE STORM

As the United States transitioned from the depression years to World War II and then into the postwar economic boom, both the government and industry focused on Indian energy resource development. Tribal energy, like other western natural resources, became a means for building American economic might. "Our prospective energy requirements are a reflection of our economic goals; and our ability to attain these goals is a reflection of the availability of energy," Secretary of the Interior Julius Albert Krug proclaimed in 1948. "These goals may never be realized if energy is not available in quantities and at a cost appropriate to meet the demands."[9] Krug's declaration echoed BIA policy for Indian energy development. "The policy...is to encourage industry to intensify exploration activities and develop new techniques," asserted G. M. Paulus, chief of the BIA's Mineral Section. "The Indian Service has endorsed that policy and has indicated that it will cooperate to keep reservations open to exploration and production."[10] These declarations foreshadowed the intensification of tribal energy development and an associated increase in conflict.

As development intensified, tribes fought for control of their resources. The IMLA standardized a lease and royalty method for Indian energy resources, in which tribes had little control or supervision over how companies developed tribal resources or the amount of royalties tribes received for those resources. In the 1950s, in the termination era, the federal government sought to terminate tribal land rights, trust rights to mineral and energy resources, and energy and mineral rights on allotted lands.

The termination era has a dark legacy, and the assault on Indian resources highlights its most disturbing implications. Presented as a means by which Indians could enjoy equal rights with other American citizens, termination was actually a direct attempt to seize the natural resource wealth on tribal lands. The attacks on Indian ownership generated tribal factionalism and weakened the authority of tribal councils. Although the threats of termination gave way after the 1950s, this era left an indelible mark on the minds of tribal leaders seeking greater control for their people.[11]

In the aftermath of termination, the federal government's trust responsibility to tribes became central to federal energy policy for tribal lands. The nature and requirements of the trust relationship influenced all aspects of Indian energy development, from economic issues to environmental protection. The passage of the National Environmental Policy Act (NEPA) in 1969 came on a wave of public demand for the protection of the nation's natural resources and for public involvement in major federal actions, such as energy development, that affected the quality of the environment, human health, and cultural sites. Although tribes and tribal resources are not explicitly addressed in NEPA, the federal government's trust responsibility to tribes established obligations to tribes under NEPA. Moreover, court cases confirmed that NEPA applied to tribes if there was no legislative language to the contrary. In Indian energy development, the Interior secretary's approval authority made NEPA applicable and required the secretary to consider the environmental impacts of energy development when approving leases.[12]

RED POWER RISING

In the late 1960s and 1970s, Indian attitudes about energy resource development shifted. A surge in Indian nationalism shook the halls of Congress, courtroom chambers, and fields of the energy industry. The 1938 IMLA aimed to bring consistency to Indian leasing, foster tribal sovereignty and self-government, and bolster Indian economies. The act's failure, not its success, catalyzed the tribal self-government and sovereignty movement and the exposure of the federal government's gross financial mismanagement. Numerous government studies from the late 1950s to the early 1980s highlighted the inefficiency and inadequacy of federal energy policy for tribal lands, the paltry income generated for many tribes, and the negative cultural, environmental, and other effects of energy development on tribal communities. Federal Indian policy, particularly on energy development, wrote Arizona congressman Morris K. Udall, could be termed nothing more than a "general failure."[13] Good intentions or not, federal decision makers were failing their Indian trustees. Indian energy resources had certainly generated economic returns, but the lion's share had not flowed to tribes. "If we have benefited from mineral development," Navajo chairman Peter MacDonald pointed out, "the rest of the United States has certainly benefited much more."[14] Along with the rise of Red Power, the swelling movement for tribal control of natural resource development and for federal accountability would reshape the Indian energy industry.

The impact of energy development on tribal communities and their lands had largely been ignored for more than seventy years. Now, tribal communities were experiencing the long-term effects of resource extraction. NEPA required a review of environmental, cultural, and other effects of Indian energy leasing so that the Department of the Interior and tribes could make informed decisions about development. The department's dual role, however, as a representative of the federal government and as a trustee for tribes, raised questions about its objectivity. In whose interest was the Interior secretary acting? Moreover, did the large role played by the federal government in lease approval and environmental review encroach upon tribal sovereignty? In addition, many tribal leaders were dubious about the effectiveness of NEPA. While striving to prevent or lessen environmental impacts, it caused delays in project approval. Most, if not all, tribes wanted to protect their other natural resources while developing oil and gas, but they also wanted to generate income. The problem with federal involvement was not environmental protection; rather, it was the obstruction of tribal control and decision-making authority, making energy development inefficient.[15]

The economic focus of federal Indian energy policy negated tribal sovereignty and threatened the future of Indian communities. By the mid-1970s many had charged that the Department of the Interior was blatantly ignoring the many harmful effects of energy leasing and development. Reid Peyton Chambers, associate Interior solicitor for the Bureau of Indian Affairs, went so far as to say, "[The secretary of the Interior's] principal view of Indian trust land is as a resource to be used singularly for the production of income in the form of lease revenues." Energy development triggered large migrations of non-Indians to reservations, posing threats to cultural survival and tribal member employment. State governments frequently did not recognize the sovereign status of tribes and consistently sought ways to cash in on Indian energy development. Despite the concentration on income generation, tribes usually did not receive the highest returns from their mineral leases. In fact, Chambers pointed out, if maximizing lease revenue constituted the ultimate goal, then the Interior secretary was guilty of breaching his trust responsibility. Alternatively, if tribes and their federal trustee had multiple goals for tribal natural resources, then the Interior secretary needed to exercise lease approval authority within a broader framework. Lease income alone did not resolve the many problems facing tribal leaders. Rather, tribes needed to prioritize income, jobs, environmental and cultural preservation, community health, and more diverse economic development plans. Also, the Interior secretary needed to respect tribal priorities and use these to guide decision making.[1]

The record profits for energy companies and the minimal returns for tribes became the predominant theme of conflict over Indian energy resource development in the 1970s. Federal energy policy for tribal lands sanctioned substandard leases that prevented tribes from getting fair returns on their energy resources. The Department of the Interior approved Indian energy leases that essentially wrote off most of the profit for tribes. Charles Lipton, a renowned advisor on energy negotiations, charged that the standard lease "passed control over to the lessee, the company—a total surrender of any control whatsoever—and in return the Tribe got the absolute, bare rock-bottom price."[17]

In 1981 Interior secretary James Watt appointed a commission led by David Linowes to investigate royalty management and accounting on Indian and federal energy leases. The Linowes Commission found "serious inadequacies" in federal oversight of royalty accounting and a general failure to identify and handle royalty underpayments. For decades, energy companies had been shorting royalty payments on tribal and federal leases by as much as 10 percent, and the federal government had done nothing to correct this. More disturbing, these were not new insights into the inadequacy of federal energy policy for tribal lands. In 1976, three years after calling for the formation of the American Indian Policy Review Commission (AIPRC), Senator James Abourezk of South Dakota finally won enough support to create the commission. In its final report, the AIPRC described Indian energy leases as "inequitable agreements," with revenues to tribes being "only a fraction of what they should be." The AIPRC summarized, "The leases negotiated on behalf of Indians are among the poorest agreements ever made."[18]

Even though royalty underpayment was a serious problem, low and fixed royalties were an even greater one. In fact, royalties, as well as bonus and rent payments, typically did not reflect market conditions nor parallel the rising oil prices in the 1970s. Indian leases often fixed royalty rates "in dollars per unit," such as per barrel of oil or gallon of gas, disregarding increases in energy resource value over time. The AIPRC concluded, "As a general principle…in a time of anticipated inflation, a fixed-price contract for a commodity is…a poor contract." Five years later, the Linowes Commission argued that fair market value dictated Indian royalties in theory but that the meaning of this value had "a wide latitude for differing interpretations." The federal government allowed energy companies to set the value of the resources for which they paid royalties, but many companies were vertically integrated and sold the resources to their own divisions for processing and distribution. In the early 1970s the Jicarilla Apache Tribe requested that the federal government conduct a comprehensive audit of the companies that leased natural gas from the tribe. When the government balked at the tribe's request, citing lack of capacity and manpower to do the audit, the tribe sued the companies and the Department of the Interior. The Jicarilla's challenge not only reflected tribes' greater capacity to deal with the complexities of the energy industry and valuation of their resources but also heralded the growing movement for tribal sovereignty and control. In the coming years, as tribes such as the Jicarilla Apache took a hands-on approach to managing their energy resources, federal energy policy for tribal lands would be radically redrawn.[19]

As attention intensified on the inequity of Indian energy leasing, tribal criticism also turned to lease terms. In retrospect, the 1938 IMLA contained an incomprehensible stipulation that the term of Indian leases would not exceed ten years or "as long thereafter as minerals produced in paying quantities"; the indefinite extension contradicted the ten-year term. The larger the oil or gas play, or the more valuable the energy resource, the more likely the indefinite term would apply. A company could speculate on energy resources simply by keeping at least one well producing while the company waited for prices to rise before developing its entire lease. This strategy increased profits by playing the market and maintaining low royalty rates fixed by the lease. Lease terms indefinitely extended low revenues for tribes from their energy resources.[20]

Energy companies may have been unscrupulous in developing accounting procedures for Indian energy leases, but the federal government, which was supposed to protect and guide the tribes, was complicit in this deceit. For many tribal leaders, the Linowes Commission's statement that the "federal government share[d] the concerns of Indian landowners in the prudent management of their energy resources" seemed facetious at best. In 1977 Senator Edward Kennedy charged that the federal agencies "responsible for effectuating the trusteeship role [were] hopelessly compromised by pervasive conflicts of interest." Kennedy's accusation was credible and warranted, but tribes had been speaking out about the problems with Indian energy development for years and no one seemed to be listening. Many legislators and federal agencies displayed a distinct lack of historical awareness of the problem. Before the AIPRC findings in 1977, the Senate Indian Affairs Committee had conducted field investigations into the problems of Indian administration in 1974. At a hearing in New Mexico, Jicarilla Apache chairman Hubert Velarde told senators that Jicarilla energy resources had been exploited for decades and all along "at the mercy of [the federal] trustee," who should have guaranteed proper supervision and technical assistance. Enough was enough, Velarde informed them, and his tribe was investigating whether its trustee had "again failed to respond to his trust obligation" and whether the tribe had been "the foil of the oil and gas industry."[21]

Tribal voices rising against the federal government's Indian energy policy in the 1970s and early 1980s brought the issue of tribal sovereignty to the fore. The rebirth of tribal nationalism in the 1960s and 1970s had its roots in the congressional effort to terminate tribes in the mid-1950s. The energy crisis of the 1970s, however, focused attention on the production of domestic oil and gas resources and, in particular, the vast energy resource wealth underneath tribal lands. These resources did not go unnoticed in previous decades, yet tribal leaders now found, and helped to create, a broader platform for voicing their concerns about and rights to energy revenue.[22]

Tribal leaders testified before the various federal commissions and congressional hearings, and tribal sovereignty, in the context of the federal trustee's failures, was the overarching theme in their litany of complaints. As Navajo chairman Peter MacDonald explained, tribes contributed natural resources to meet the "needs of the nation" and "to provide a better life for most Americans." MacDonald concluded, "[But] most Indians live in poverty without such 'luxuries' as running water and electricity that most other Americans regard as the barest necessities of life."[23] Not only did the benefits of energy resources flow away from reservations, but also the federal government provided little or no assistance to tribes for managing the resources that benefited the American public. The Jicarilla Apache, for example, had asked the BIA to examine energy companies' exploration activities and revenue accounting, but the tribe received little help because the BIA lacked the funds, staff, and expertise. Even more unconscionable, the Jicarilla provided funds to the BIA to employ personnel to assist the tribe with energy assessment—a clear violation, even mockery, of trustee responsibilities. "[We] have told this story time and again," Jicarilla chairman Velarde told the Senate Indian Affairs Committee, "and our problems today are no different from those that we related to your predecessors in years past." There was one solution: tribes themselves needed to play a much larger role in defining the leasing of their energy resources and in directing federal funds earmarked for tribal programs.[24]

Underpayments, inequitable royalties, and, in 1980, the discovery of oil theft on the Wind River Reservation in Wyoming highlighted the shortcomings of federal agency oversight of Indian energy development.[25] A 1976 study by the General Accounting Office (GAO) found that the majority of BIA agencies on reservations had inadequate mineral expertise: "Minerals management is...carried out by staff without formal minerals training."[26] Likewise, the AIPRC found that the BIA and the US Geological Survey (USGS), in charge of accounting for Indian leases, failed to examine energy companies' statements on production volume to determine whether tribes were receiving all the royalties they were owed. "Information is power" in energy development, the AIPRC argued, and energy corporations had larger pocketbooks to access information than did tribes. Corporations knew how to work the system, and because of poor federal oversight, many tribes received payment from lessees as many as eighteen months late. Without accurate information, the BIA was operating in a vacuum, leaving tribes without key financial and production data to make wise management decisions, "thus failing to discharge the federal government's trust responsibility." Because the BIA did not acquire and assess information to guide its decisions about Indian energy resources, tribes had little chance to weigh the "true value and dangers" of energy development. Moreover, the USGS's lack of attention to data analysis and coordination with the BIA amplified the problems.[27]

Inflexibility lay at the heart of Indian leasing problems. The standard lease method, managed by the BIA and USGS with minimal tribal involvement, excluded approaches that would involve tribes more fully and ensure better returns to them. Rather than work with tribes to explore options and protect tribal interests, the BIA arranged leases to major energy corporations, frequently at "questionable rates," making the lessee, instead of the lessor (the tribe), the primary beneficiary. Although leases contained stipulations requiring energy companies to share production data, the tribes did not obtain this information because the USGS and the BIA failed in this responsibility as well. Consequently, many tribes did not know the true value of their energy resources and could not determine whether leases contained equitable royalty rates. Many leases contained preference rights for tribal member employment, but companies seldom honored these and the agencies rarely enforced them. Moreover, the

Interior secretary's authority over lease approval stifled tribal initiatives to develop leases directly with energy companies. Even if tribes received initial endorsements for leases with preference stipulations and requirements, the lengthy approval process often hampered tribally supported development. Energy companies could bank on the government's non-enforcement of stipulations that would improve Indian employment, provide accurate and timely data, and prevent environmental degradation.[28]

The shortcomings of federal energy policy put the onus on tribes to prioritize their objectives and take control of their energy resources. Moving forward, tribes had to do something about their "weakness in bargaining strength." Task Force Seven of the AIPRC, composed almost entirely of tribal members, isolated three major goals of tribal energy development: protecting and strengthening tribal sovereignty; increasing income and making revenue equitable; and minimizing the negative impacts on environmental, cultural, and other values. These goals were not mutually exclusive. Each tribe might prioritize the goals in different ways, but weighing these considerations would help tribes develop their own principles for energy development. "A tribe with secure sovereignty, a high revenue, and with few imposed environmental or cultural costs," the Task Force explained, "can go about welfare maximization with few constraints, whatever the particular meaning of welfare to its members." Tribal bargaining power would rise commensurately with goal prioritization and planning on the part of tribes. This would, in turn, foster tribal authority over energy resource development. Tribes would thus achieve their "paramount goal," Navajo Chairman MacDonald informed the US Senate: "tribal utilization and development of tribal natural resources, and tribal control over business activities on the reservations."[29]

States long sought a means to generate revenue from Indian energy, but the 1938 IMLA did not authorize states to tax mineral or energy production on tribal lands. Nevertheless, many states taxed leases over the next forty years. State taxation raised questions about tribal sovereignty, and the right of tribes to tax non-Indians for energy resource development elicited even greater debate.[30]

The rationale for state taxation of Indian energy production is no less sordid than the other inequities of federal energy policy for tribal lands. The AIPRC found that Congress may not have acted to prevent state taxation because of the "favorable economic position" of some tribes that quickly reaped big profits from energy development. As more tribes began to develop their energy resources, this argument gained in influence. States also put great pressure on the federal government for their share of energy revenues. State taxation became more ingrained in the 1950s, during the termination era, when many saw state taxation as a means of assimilation. By the 1970s the repercussions of state taxation had become increasingly clear. Task Force Seven reported that one state's taxation of a tribe's oil lease generated as much as three times the revenue for the state as the tribe earned in royalties. When states taxed energy companies, the companies passed on the costs to tribes by deducting the taxes from the tribes' profit figures. As the AIPRC put it, "the larger the tax, the smaller the royalty" for a tribe. Because state taxation subjugated tribal authority and control over energy development, it contradicted stated federal goals for tribal sovereignty and economic development.[31]

In the growing movement for tribal sovereignty and control of energy resource development, tribal leaders sought strength and unity in numbers. In 1974 twenty-six Northern Plains tribes formed the Native American Natural Resources Development Federation (NANRDF) to share information and expertise and protect tribal rights to natural resources. NANRDF leaders quickly recognized that the challenges facing energy tribes required broader collaboration, so tribal leaders from the Northern Plains and Southwest began reaching out to each other. In 1975 they formed the Council of Energy Resource Tribes (CERT), uniting tribes west of the Mississippi River to defend Indian mineral and energy resources.

To rectify the problems created by the federal government's historic neglect of tribal interests, CERT assertively fought for tribal economic interests and to establish a stronger bargaining position in energy negotiations. Over the years, CERT provided critical support for tribes so that they could assess the quantity and value of their energy resources and learn about development, technology, accounting, and other related subjects. To build long-term capacity for tribes, CERT also helped train tribal members for energy-related jobs and promoted natural resource and energy-related college education for tribal youth. Although CERT had its critics, including some tribal members, it provided a timely and strong alliance against the exploitation of tribes.[32]

THE INDIAN MINERAL DEVELOPMENT ACT

More than a decade of conflict culminated in a late 1981 push to rewrite federal policy governing tribal energy development. The many problems afflicting Indian energy leasing can be summarized in five categories: (1) inadequate tribal control and poor trust management; (2) inequitable revenues and deficient accounting; (3) lack of alternatives to the standard lease and inflexibility of lease terms; (4) lack of employment for tribal members;

and (5) weak protection for environmental and cultural resources. The 1982 passage of the Indian Mineral Development Act (IMDA) offered great hope that tribes would truly govern their energy resources and determine the future well-being of their people and homelands.[33]

Introduced by Senator John Melcher of Montana, the IMDA's primary goals seemed not all that different from those of the 1938 IMLA. The IMDA aimed to protect and enhance tribal sovereignty and maximize tribal revenues from energy development. Congress, however, intended the IMDA to broaden tribes' ability to negotiate more favorable energy development agreements. To counteract the poor revenues from low offers in the competitive bidding process under the standard lease procedure, the IMDA authorized tribes, subject to the secretary of the Interior's approval, to develop joint ventures; service contracts; or operating, production sharing, managerial, lease, or other agreements for energy development. The IMDA required the Interior secretary to ensure that each agreement was in the best interest of the tribe by considering potential cultural, environmental, social, and other effects on the tribe and its resources. In short, the IMDA extended much greater control to tribes and significantly changed the status quo.[34]

The IMDA offered tribes new advantages and also risks. Tribes could negotiate alternative agreements, royalty rates, and other financial provisions; acquire an ownership interest in energy development; and incorporate provisions for environmental protection, tribal member employment, site reclamation, and lease term limitations. More control, however, introduced potential drawbacks. Agreements could place tribes at greater financial risk, so tribes needed proper internal expertise or outside assistance to make the complex financial, geological, and environmental decisions related to energy development. The IMDA, as Marjane Ambler argued, posed a risk for tribes by "dramatically limiting the role of the federal government in protecting them." Nevertheless, this risk seemed minimal compared with the federal "protection" tribes had received for the preceding forty-four years.[35]

FOGRMA

Correcting the deficiencies in federal energy policy for tribal lands required going beyond restructuring the leasing or agreement process addressed by the IMDA. In 1982 the Linowes Commission also documented the "gross underpayment, under-reporting, and even outright theft" of oil and gas.[36] The federal government had allowed energy companies "to operate essentially on an honor system" for accounting and reporting of energy production and profits, with millions of dollars of revenue hanging in the balance. The commission found the record-keeping system for energy royalties in "complete disarray" and so severely lacking that the federal government could not accurately estimate the amount of underpayments to tribes. Following the scandal, the Department of the Interior created the Minerals Management Service (MMS) to take over royalty management from the US Geological Survey.[37]

In 1983 Congress followed up by passing the Federal Oil and Gas Royalty Management Act (FOGRMA). Congress intended FOGRMA to meet the federal government's trust responsibility to tribes and "improve royalty collection, management, and enforcement." FOGRMA required the Interior secretary to account fully for the production of Indian energy resources and track the collection and remittance of royalties and other payments owed to tribes. FOGRMA also established a process by which the Interior secretary could form cooperative agreements with tribes to supply them with royalty data and empower them to conduct investigations, audits, and inspections to enforce lease provisions and prompt revenue payment.[38]

Predictably, FOGRMA did little to improve the system. Problems with accounting and royalty collection continued, and the Department of the Interior implemented only a few cooperative agreements with tribes. Only one year later, a presidential commission on reservation economies found that federal agencies, particularly the BIA, continued to lack the ability to assist tribes with economic development. Moreover, the BIA did not have the flexibility to adapt to changing economic conditions or the needs of tribes. Not only did the government fail to meet its trust responsibility, but also it frequently failed to yield to tribal sovereignty. "The system is designed for paternalistic control," the commission reported, "and it thrives on the failure of Indian tribes." Within a few years, despite adding staff, the Department of the Interior still could not meet its obligation to inspect all high-priority leases as required by FOGRMA, conducting annual inspections of only 62 percent of total oil and gas wells on tribal lands. Some tribes managed to form cooperative agreements for accounting and auditing, but FOGRMA made them responsible for 50 percent of the cost, even though the federal government paid the entire cost when states took over such responsibilities. Nevertheless, because of FOGRMA's mandate, tribes were able to collect millions of dollars in late payments and lost royalties. More important, both the IMDA and FOGRMA advanced the efforts tribes initiated in the 1970s to build their capacity to manage energy resource development.[39]

THE INDIAN ENERGY RESOURCES ACT

In the years following the passage of FOGRMA, tribes quickly discovered that the creation of a new agency, the MMS (Minerals Management Service), would not solve the energy accounting and auditing problems. MMS failed to account for financial variations in tribal leases and produce accurate enough data for the Department of the Interior to meet its obligations under FOGRMA. The Jicarilla Apache Tribe, for instance, pointed out the Interior secretary's inability to account for nearly $500 billion in Indian and federal royalties for oil and gas production. In 1987 MMS proposed new royalty valuation regulations that tribes feared would result in millions of dollars in lost revenue. MMS officials countered that its methods were "revenue neutral." Four years later, MMS admitted that what it had meant by "revenue neutral" was "that the potential gains in offshore royalty collections by implementing the new regulations would offset the royalty losses that Indian lessors would suffer." The federal government's royalties would increase at the cost of the tribes. A year later, Congress concluded that FOGRMA had failed to improve royalty management and accounting.[40]

In 1992, as part of the Energy Policy Act, Congress passed the Indian Energy Resources Act (IERA) with ostensibly the same objective as that of the IMDA: to increase tribal control of energy development and promote economic self-sufficiency through energy development. The IERA directed the Interior secretary to assist tribes with the "development of a vertically integrated energy industry on Indian reservations." The IERA also authorized the secretary to make grants for implementing energy development and enforcement and to establish the Indian Energy Resource Commission to address energy resource issues. Unfortunately, Congress never funded this, and the Department of the Interior never appointed the commission. In addition, it became increasingly clear that federal policies contributed to tribal economic dependence on energy resource revenue. In 1982, tribal income from oil and gas production hit the high point of $198 million but within four years plummeted as much as 60 percent. This reinforced the tribes' need to get the full, equitable value of their energy resources. Despite good intentions, failed federal policy also made it clear that tribes needed to develop expertise in managing energy development without expecting the government to follow through on its promises. As one observer pointed out, tribal self-determination had increased significantly, but it was quite possible that the "colonial past of mineral development on Indian lands [may have] set up permanent inequities for reservation economies."[41]

THE ENERGY POLICY ACT OF 2005

After 1992, congressional legislation including provisions for Indian energy development primarily provided clarification to the IMDA, similar to the provisions of the 1992 IERA. In 1994 and 2003 Congress supplied further guidance for approving energy development agreements, particularly emphasizing methods for ensuring environmental protection and revenue generation. For example, the Indian Energy Title of the Energy Policy Act of 2003 authorized grants, low-interest loans, and technical assistance for developing energy resources, building tribal technical and managerial capacity, and improving the energy efficiency of reservation homes and buildings. The provisions in these bills evidenced an evolution in federal energy policy for tribal lands that was years in the making—the federal government increasingly aimed to withdraw from Indian energy development, aside from providing funding and assistance for tribes themselves to control energy development. In a press release, the US Senate proclaimed that the Indian Energy Title allowed tribes to develop their energy resources "just as any other American citizen…or corporation would be allowed to do."[42]

As part of the 2005 Energy Policy Act, Congress passed Title V, the Indian Tribal Energy and Development and Self-Determination Act of 2005, again to encourage energy and mineral resource development on tribal lands and promote self-determination. The act established the Office of Indian Energy Policy and Programs (IEPP) to coordinate the promotion of energy development, efficiency, and use; assist with the stabilization and reduction of energy costs; build and increase tribal capacity in energy development; and improve access to electricity on Indian reservations. Title V directed the Interior secretary to provide grants and low-interest loans to tribes to build technical capacity for the development of energy resources (both nonrenewable and renewable), manage and account for energy production revenue, and promote energy development and the integration of energy resources. Title V authorized the IEPP's director to establish education programs for energy-related issues, including development, efficiency, conservation, and transmission.[43]

Title V's section on tribal energy resource agreements (TERAs) proved the most controversial. A TERA established an arrangement between a tribe and the Department of the Interior in which the tribe could negotiate leases and other types of agreements for energy resource development without the secretary of the Interior's approval. A TERA served as a master agreement outlining the methods and mechanisms a tribe would use in developing all individual agreements for energy development. Congress believed that TERAs would bring efficiency to tribal energy development by removing the federal government middleman from the process, allowing tribes to work directly with energy companies. Tribes executing a TERA could enter into leases of no longer than thirty years. Oil and gas leases replicated the terms of past policy—ten years or as long as oil and gas are produced in paying quantities—but now tribes could choose to execute a shorter lease term. TERAs had to address lease terms; the economic return to the tribe; methods for environmental review and compliance with federal environmental laws; technical requirements; public notification of final agreement approvals; a process to consult with states on off-reservation impacts; remedies for breach of agreements; inclusion of all applicable tribal laws; and any financial assistance needed from the Department of the Interior for implementing a TERA. For a tribe to establish a TERA, the Interior secretary had to determine whether the tribe had "sufficient capacity to regulate the development of energy resources of the Indian tribe." The act required the secretary to review a TERA annually for three years to ensure that no threats to trust assets existed. Upon approval of a TERA, the federal government no longer had a role in the development of agreements for energy development.[44]

Of any federal energy policy for tribal lands, Title V gave tribes the most control. Tribes could more easily make decisions about energy development based on the values and interests of their community. In particular, Congress believed that TERAs, by empowering tribes, would streamline the process and guarantee more certainty. TERAs provided a flexible mechanism for handling a variety of energy resources, whether oil, gas, or wind power. By eliminating federal review, a tribe and an energy company could negotiate and proceed to development more efficiently. Finally, TERAs gave more assurance that tribes would receive greater revenue.[45]

Nonetheless, Title V had its detractors. Although it required the Interior secretary to ensure that a tribe has "sufficient capacity" to obtain a TERA, the act did not define the meaning of "sufficient capacity." Removing the federal role also removed the applicability of NEPA and the National Historic Preservation Act (NHPA), so tribes had to assume full responsibility for environmental and cultural resource protection. Removing NEPA and NHPA could make Indian energy resources more vulnerable to outside interests. Title V increased the likelihood of conflict between tribal members in favor of energy development and those opposed. Some also worried that Title V threatened to erode the federal government's trust responsibility. Some tribes may have the experience and capacity to negotiate energy development agreements, conduct accounting, and inspect development to ensure compliance with agreements, but many tribes may not. The act specifically upheld the trust responsibility but greatly minimized the federal government's role. Consequently, the government could pay less attention to the impacts of energy development on tribes. Title V had the potential for both positive and negative outcomes. Tribes had made great advances and fought hard to manage energy resource development and secure tribal sovereignty. Although they were not completely on their own, Title V helped to put the future of energy development on tribal lands in their hands.[46]

RENEWABLE ENERGY: A NEW "LEASE" ON TRIBAL ENERGY DEVELOPMENT?

The federal government created many reservations out of what it considered to be barren wastelands and outposts on the frontier. In this light, tribal lands offer one of the finest ironies in American history. If one were to overlay a national map of coal deposits on a map of Indian reservations, one would see that Indian reservations contain a large proportion of the nation's coal (figure 4.1). If one were to overlay that second map with yet another, one would discover that tribal lands are located in the best wind energy–generating locations in the United States (see figure 4.1). At the dawn of the twenty-first century, Americans are facing what has been termed an "energy crisis." Rising fuel costs, international consumption, and the global threat of energy scarcity have propelled a rush toward energy development and have again put tribal resources in the crosshairs of exploitation. Yet, renewable energy can meet many of the energy and economic development needs in Indian Country and throughout the United States with less harm to the environment, cultural resources, and community health.[47] Looking beyond oil, gas, and other traditional energy resources, many tribes are headed toward a renewable energy future.

Since passage of the 1992 IERA, congressional legislation on Indian energy has contained provisions related to renewable energy. In the mid-1990s, tribes began to capitalize on these opportunities. Between 1994 and 1999, the Department of Energy (DOE) gave grants to thirty-eight tribes for energy projects, including renewable energy assessment, planning, and development. The DOE also created the Tribal Energy Program to offer technical and financial assistance to tribes. Between 2002 and 2006 the program awarded grants totaling $12.4 million to seventy-six tribes. With this funding, tribes have determined their renewable energy options and then planned and implemented wind, biomass, solar, and geothermal energy projects (figure 4.2).[48]

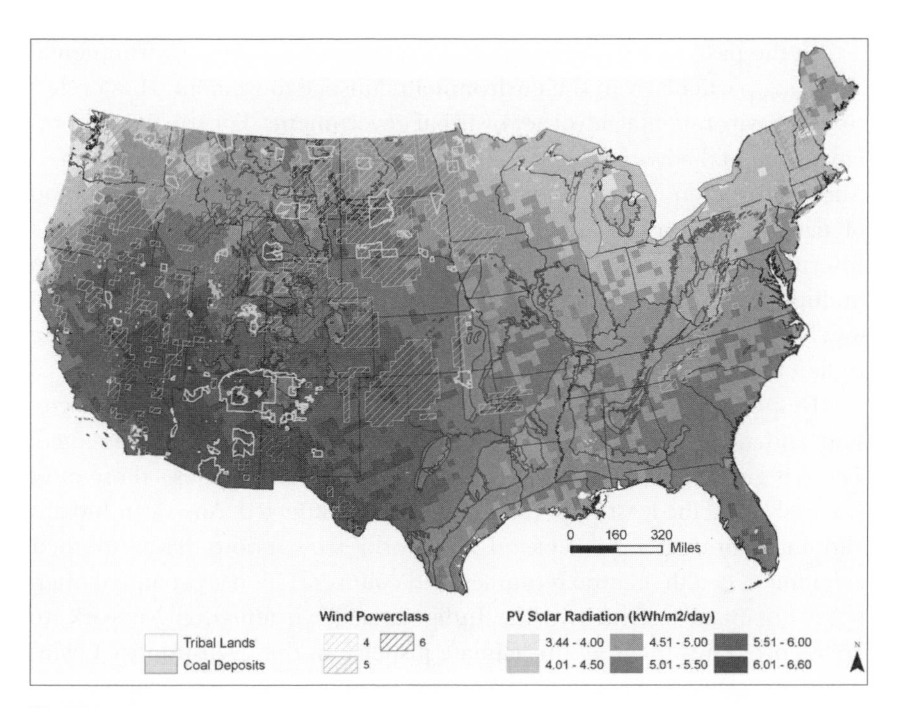

FIGURE 4.1

Tribal lands' energy potential for wind, solar, and coal.

FIGURE 4.2

Wind turbines on the Campo Kumeyaay reservation east of San Diego, California.Photo by Garrit Voggesser.

In the past decade, tribes began to participate more in environmental advocacy, particularly in the environmental justice movement. (I am referring to environmental advocacy by tribal governments. For tribal grassroots environmental advocacy, see chapter 10 by Powell and Long, this volume.) American Indian history contains numerous examples of the exploitation of tribal communities and natural resources. As Robert Gough of the Intertribal Council on Utility Policy has pointed out, tribes "can point to multiple cases of environmental injustice all along America's energy pathway."[49] Energy resource development has damaged the environment on Indian reservations across the United States.

Despite warnings as far back as the 1950s and 1960s, worldwide discussion and understanding of climate change have only recently emerged. There is growing consensus that global warming discriminates—those most vulnerable are the least responsible yet the most affected. American Indians and indigenous peoples around the world face serious harm to their economies, health, natural resources, and cultures. This has prompted intertribal organizations, such as the Indigenous Environmental Network, to create programs focusing on "climate justice." In the 1970s Amory Lovins proposed a shift from hard to soft energy technologies, from unsustainable energy technologies detrimental to the environment to sustainable, flexible, and more environmentally friendly energy development approaches. Fifteen years ago, Dean Suagee, an environmental attorney and a member of the Cherokee Tribe, wrote, "The time has come for political leaders to realize that soft energy paths are...the key to dealing with global warming." Moreover, Suagee concluded, soft paths such as renewable energy give tribes a sustainable approach to economic development.[50]

Tribal lands contain many of the nation's renewable energy resources. Reservations in the West, particularly the Southwest, have the most direct solar radiation. Northern Plains reservations contain significant wind energy potential, and many western reservations have geothermal energy. Reservations across the nation contain biomass resources. Wind energy potential on tribal lands alone can meet at least 15–20 percent of the nation's energy needs, and solar electric potential on tribal lands is 4.5 times greater than the total US electrical generation in 2004. Advocates argue that renewable energy can partly atone for the legacy of natural resource injustice to tribes. In addition to the economic and environmental benefits, Suagee has noted, renewable energy can honor the values held "by many Indian people to balance relationships among the natural world and human beings."[51]

In the past ten years, many tribes took advantage of this opportunity to benefit their communities. For instance, the Citizen Potawatomi Band developed geothermal power to heat tribal enterprises. The Assiniboine and Sioux, Northern Cheyenne, and Rosebud Sioux tribes developed wind energy. The Ramona Band of Cahuilla Indians developed ecotourism facilities powered by multiple renewable energy sources. Many tribes in the Southwest developed solar energy projects, and dozens of tribes throughout the West conducted assessments of their renewable energy resources and implemented energy efficiency projects.[52] Meanwhile, tribal colleges across the West—such as Turtle Mountain Community College in North Dakota, the Crownpoint Institute for Technology in New Mexico, and the Blackfeet Community College in Montana—installed geothermal heat pumps to heat and cool their campuses and wind turbines to meet energy needs. The Blackfeet Community College became the first to utilize wind power, in 1996, and the Turtle Mountain College became the first college anywhere to be completely powered by renewable energy. Many of these colleges developed a curriculum to teach students about renewable energy methods, build tribal capacity, and arm tribes with the knowledge to make informed decisions regarding energy development. These projects demonstrate that renewable energy offered tribes a path to self-determination and alternative options for economic growth so that tribes could truly make their own decisions about what future energy development means to their communities.[53]

THE JICARILLA APACHE TRIBE

The trajectory and vicissitudes of Indian energy development are explicit in the case of the Jicarilla Apache Tribe. The large energy resource holdings of the Jicarilla Apache compelled them to play a major role in transforming federal energy policy for tribal lands and gaining tribal control over energy resource development. Located in the San Juan Basin of northern New Mexico, the 850,000-acre Jicarilla Apache Reservation contains rugged, forested mesas, piñon pine and juniper woodlands, and sagebrush plains with abundant big game and other wildlife. Former Jicarilla Apache chairman Hubert Velarde explained, "Our most valuable natural resource is our oil and gas deposits with which nature blessed our reservation." The Jicarilla Apache became one of the largest natural gas and oil–producing tribes in the nation. The tribe exemplifies the travails of Indian energy development, and Jicarilla Apache history affords us an important glimpse into the evolution of federal policy, conflicts over energy leasing and revenues, and the power of tribes to protect the well-being of their people.[54]

When oil and gas exploration began on the Jicarilla Apache Reservation in the early 1920s, drought and the Great Depression limited exploration. Yet, top BIA officials believed that the Jicarilla reservation contained valuable energy resources, and three oil domes were discovered in the late 1930s. Meanwhile, the BIA superintendent worked with Jicarilla leaders to form a tribal government under the mandate of the 1934 Indian Reorganization Act (IRA). The confluence of the IRA and the 1938 Indian Mineral Leasing Act opened the way to maximum energy development.[55]

During World War II and the postwar economic boom, government and industry put more and more pressure on tribes to give them access to Indian energy resources. Developers such as the Continental Oil Company began leasing Jicarilla lands. BIA policy encouraged "industry to intensify exploration activities" and maintained full access to Indian lands for development. By 1950 more than a hundred tracts had been leased for oil and gas exploration, and in March alone the Jicarilla received nearly $350,000 in revenue (figure 4.3). Beginning in the late 1940s, the San Juan Basin, adjacent to the reservation's western side, rapidly became a focal point for exploration. Speculation rose so much that one company requested a two-year exploration permit for 750,000 acres on the reservation.[56]

Oil discoveries in the basin brought new and larger requests for development on Jicarilla lands. By the end of 1950, four big companies had leased more than 133,000 reservation acres. "The Jicarilla Reservation stole the oil-news spotlight in the southern Rocky Mountain area," an oil trade magazine reported in 1954. Production tests run by Phillips Petroleum indicated the largest potential recorded to date in the basin, catapulting leasing on Jicarilla lands. From 1952 to 1958 the tribe struck leases for nearly 300,000 acres, and revenue from oil and gas leasing equaled about $1 million annually (figure 4.4). Each tribal member received annual per capita payments averaging $500, composing 60 percent of total individual income. In 1959 the royalty rate for the Jicarilla Apache rose to 16.66 percent, generating millions of dollars in new income for the tribe. Energy development provided much needed support and outweighed any other economic activity on the reservation.[57]

The rapid pace and success of energy development on the Jicarilla reservation concealed growing problems with federal energy policy for the Jicarilla and other tribes. Companies were increasingly delinquent on their payments to the Jicarilla. BIA and Interior officials did not entirely ignore this predicament, but their inattentiveness contributed to its worsening. Officials failed to notice not only the magnitude of delinquent payments but also the growing crisis in accounting for all energy leasing revenue. As

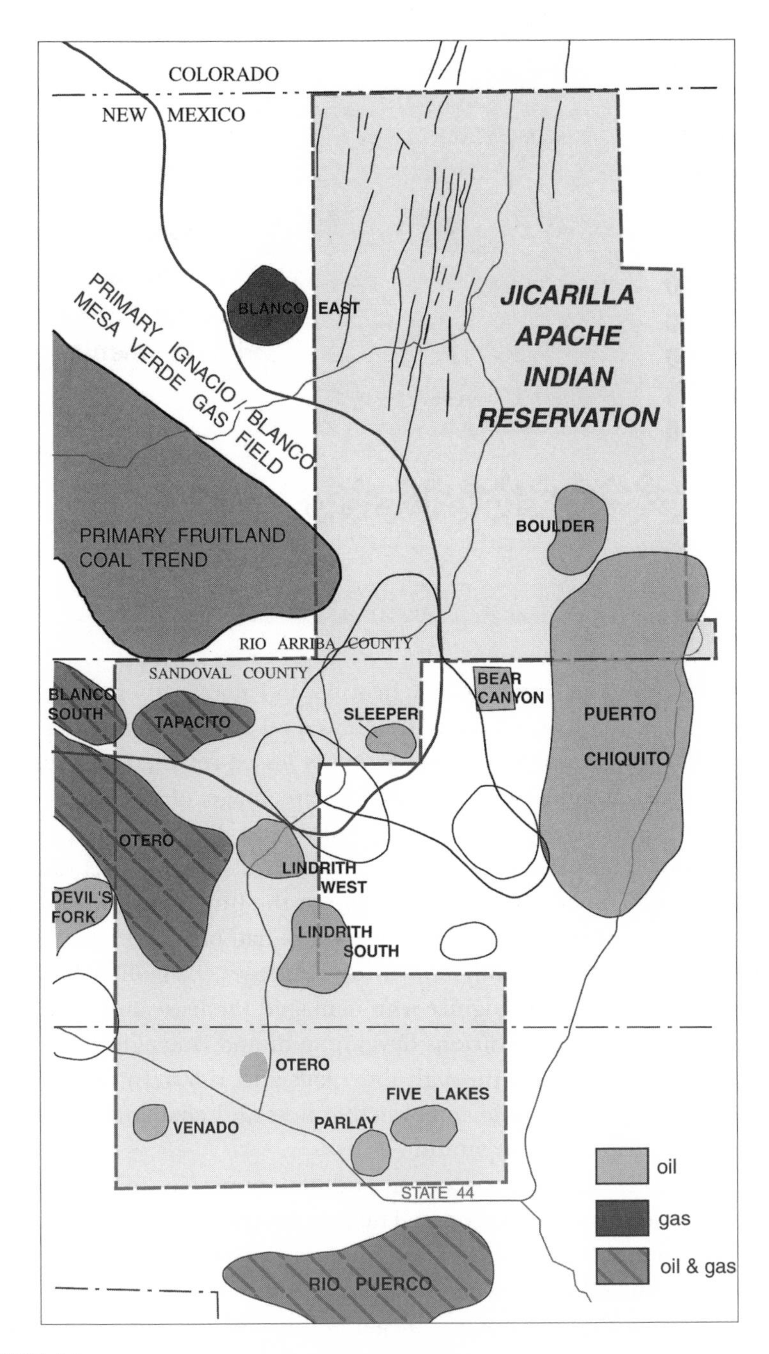

FIGURE 4.3

Oil and gas fields on and near the Jicarilla Apache reservation, 1998. Reproduced from US Bureau of Indian Affairs, "Atlas of Oil and Gas Plays on American Indian Lands."

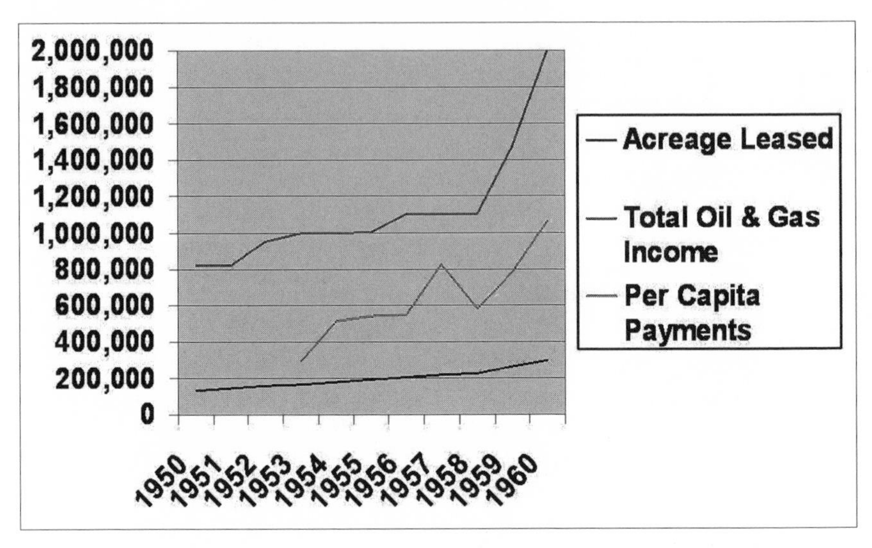

FIGURE 4.4

Leased and oil and gas income on the Jicarilla Apache reservation, 1950–1960.

energy development expanded at Jicarilla and many other reservations, USGS and BIA employees frequently allowed oil and gas companies to subdivide their interests in leases. The primary lessee retained an overriding royalty, but each sublessee obtained a percentage of the royalty. This occurred dozens if not hundreds of times on Jicarilla energy leases. Nevertheless, multiple letters between USGS and BIA officials stated, "It has not been the policy of the Department or the Bureau to approve agreements creating overriding royalties," but there had been "some exceptions to the policy." By continually approving subleases, BIA officials made it increasingly difficult to recognize who managed the lease and which party had responsibility for the various development and oversight procedures. These problems escalated through the 1950s and 1960s. In the 1970s the Jicarilla Apache Tribe would uncover the mess and challenge the federal government head-on for reparation.[58]

The Jicarilla Apache took on oil and gas companies in 1976 by instituting an oil and gas severance tax. The Jicarilla used their authority under the IRA to counteract the underpayments and low revenues partially by levying a tax on any oil and gas removed from their lands. Energy companies balked, arguing that the tax was illegal because of the significant federal presence in Indian energy leasing and because the leases did not sanction the additional economic burden. Nonetheless, in *Merrion v. Jicarilla Apache Tribe* (1982), the Supreme Court ruled in favor of the Jicarilla, concluding that tribal sovereignty granted inherent power to tribes for taxation. The Jicarilla tribe's defense of tribal sovereignty generated strong support and respect for the tribe in Indian Country. Seven years later, in *Cotton Petroleum v. New Mexico,* the Supreme Court decreed that the State of New Mexico also had the authority to impose taxes on energy and mineral resources removed from the Jicarilla reservation. The double taxation—6 percent for the tribe and 8 percent for the state—struck a serious blow to tribal economic development. Nevertheless, the *Merrion* decision cleared the way for tribes to assert authority over their resources.[59]

Tribal taxation was only one of the multiple problems with Indian energy leasing and development that came to a head in the 1970s and early 1980s. Before the development and passage of the 1982 IMDA, Senator John Melcher conducted a series of Senate Indian Affairs hearings. The Jicarilla Apache played a large role in highlighting the legacy of federal energy policy for tribal lands and the impact on tribal communities. The tribe supplied oral testimony, as well as hundreds of letters and other documents confirming the experiences of the Jicarilla. In a letter to the Interior solicitor, the Jicarilla declared, "[The department] in its supervision of oil and gas leasing, exploration, development and royalty accounting, has been guilty of inexcusable neglect and failure to fulfill trust responsibilities."[60]

The Jicarilla argued that energy companies had speculated on Jicarilla energy development and the federal government had simply ignored this. As early as 1973, the tribe had informed Interior secretary Rogers C. B. Morton that lessees failed to diligently drill and operate oil and gas wells, which was required by the lease provisions for wells that contained oil or gas in paying quantities. Regulations directed the secretary to impose penalties or cancel leases if lessees failed to comply with lease provisions. In 1976 the tribe had informed the solicitor of the Department of the Interior that Southern Union Company had not developed more than one hundred wells. The Interior department's failure to compel drilling sanctioned Southern Union's attempts to postpone well development until upswings in market prices and to extend leases and thereby fix royalty rates. The department's repeated evasion of tribal requests for lease enforcement lost the tribe revenue and violated the trust responsibility.[61]

The Jicarilla Apache also argued that the federal government did not properly manage leases. The tribe discovered that oil and gas lessees circumvented regulations meant to prevent lease assignments. Since the 1950s, lessees had entered into subleases so that they could maintain only a "passive interest or even only a royalty interest," yet the lessee's name continued to be listed as the responsible party in the BIA records. The tribe pointed out, "Many Jicarilla oil and gas leases have been subdivided horizontally...to the point that many oil and gas operators are involved in one lease but no one is responsible for the entire lease." By farming out leases to other companies to do such things as on-the-ground development, the lessee significantly limited its risk in exchange for a small fee or percentage of the profit to the sublessee. Without the ability to identify the party responsible for the lease, federal agencies could not enforce lease provisions or federal energy regulations for tribal lands.[62]

Lack of capacity and accountability created a wide array of problems with Indian energy leases. The GAO noted a significant lack of energy development experience in the BIA. For instance, in the mid-1970s the BIA employed two staff members to supervise oil and gas activities on the Jicarilla Apache Reservation, which was producing more than $2 million annually in revenue for the tribe. The BIA, however, assigned nine staff members to supervise forestry activities that generated $258 and eight staff members to rangeland work that produced $498,000. Moreover, the GAO found that almost 50 percent of lessees were late on royalty payments to the tribe and that regulations did not require penalties for past-due royalties. In March 1973 the Jicarilla Apache reported that lessees owed past-due amounts of more than $400,000. Over a fourteen-month period in 1974 to 1975, lessees made payments totaling more than $270,000 as many as eleven months late. When the USGS reported that it did not have the staff to follow up on late payments and made "no special effort to collect the amounts due," the tribe demanded that the Department of the Interior institute late fees. The failure of the department to "enforce the leases by reason of lack of manpower," tribal leaders argued, constituted "no excuse in law for failure to fulfill its trust responsibilities."[63]

Poor production accounting and underpayments generated far more trouble than late payments. Since Jicarilla oil and gas administrator Thurman Velarde's entry into the energy field, one question had been foremost in his mind: "How accurate is USGS's accounting of full oil production on Indian lands?" No system existed for the BIA and USGS to make reports to the tribe on oil and gas production. When the tribe sought information directly from the agencies, it "met with resistance and apprehension." The agencies had total control over supervising energy production and minimized tribal participation. To determine the appropriate value of oil and gas to set royalty rates, as required by regulations, the USGS used energy company figures even when these did not match market value. From 1970 to 1976, the USGS utilized Federal Power

Commission rates as the minimum price to set royalty rates but did not adjust the price of oil and gas produced on the Jicarilla Apache Reservation for inflation. Moreover, the USGS failed to account for liquid by-products of gas, a loophole that enabled company lessees to reap even greater profit at the expense of the tribe. The Jicarilla chose to take a large amount of its royalties in kind (as oil or gas), tribal vice president Richard Tecube reported, because the Jicarilla "felt that the tribe was not getting proper accounting help on the producers' royalties."[64]

Receiving little or no support from the federal government, the Jicarilla Apache took the case to the courts. Beginning in 1974, the tribe filed suit against Secretary of the Interior Morton and a number of companies producing oil and gas from the reservation.[65] The Jicarilla charged that royalties paid by the companies did not reflect the actual value of the resources and that the companies conspired to keep royalties artificially low. The tribe also argued that the Interior secretary "failed to fulfill his fiduciary duty" as trustee for the tribe and neglected to properly supervise royalty accounting. The Department of the Interior "maintained an adverse posture" in these suits and denied all of the tribe's allegations.

Rather than go to trial, the El Paso Natural Gas Company settled in less than nine months time, agreeing to increase royalties by more than one-third, pay several hundred thousand dollars in damages, and exercise due diligence in drilling. Seven months later, several companies named in a suit against the Southern Union Company reached a settlement agreement with the tribe to raise royalty rates, as much as 8 to 13 percent on some leases, pay the tribe damages of several hundred thousand dollars, and return to the tribe some leases that had not been developed. The Jicarilla Apache also settled with several other companies, receiving more than a million dollars in damages. "We have never believed that the concessions our producers and purchasers offered us in settlement came out of the goodness of their hearts," Jicarilla president Rodger Vicenti later concluded. "Rather, we are convinced that our underlying claims were meritorious and that we had been very significantly underpaid for many years." The tribe's victories not only restored decades of lost energy revenue but also heralded the power of tribal sovereignty and control of natural resources for tribes across the country.[66]

The Jicarilla Apache also built their capacity to control energy development. The most direct way to combat federal ineffectiveness and industry abuse, Tecube concluded, was for the Jicarilla to "take it upon themselves" to develop and monitor energy production. In 1980 the Jicarilla became the first tribe to control all aspects of energy development directly, including production, monitoring, inspections, and accounting. The tribe developed the Jicarilla Energy Company and initiated two joint ventures to carry out oil and gas production. It built a twelve-person staff for its energy company and reached out to nontribal experts for information on the reservation's production potential and revenue projections. By building its capacity, the tribe could more effectively acquire the information it needed from government agencies rather than rely on them.[67]

While improving their ability to control development and maximize revenue, the Jicarilla Apache also assessed the environmental and cultural impacts of energy production. Since the Jicarilla first chartered their tribal government in the 1930s, their tribal code had included stipulations on environmental protection from development. In 1976 the tribe filed suit against the Department of the Interior in *Jicarilla v. Andrus* to cancel leases on more than 276,000 acres because of the BIA's failure to comply with lease bidding procedures and NEPA. BIA policy called for environmental review of individual well sites but did not consider the cumulative effects of all oil and gas development on the reservation. In the 1980s the tribal council, energy company, and natural resource and wildlife departments established a rigorous environmental review process for oil and gas production. Energy leases contained provisions concerning site reclamation and lessee liability for environmental damage.[68]

The Jicarilla Apache have continued to build their expertise and broaden their horizons in energy development. In the past decade, oil production has accounted for 25 percent of energy revenue, and natural gas for 75 percent. Next to the federal government, the Jicarilla is the largest mineral and energy resource owner in the San Juan Basin. Since 1999, however, the tribe also has been exploring its renewable energy opportunities and has found good potential for solar and wind energy projects. In 1999 the Jicarilla installed a solar photovoltaic system at the tribal high school, reducing the school's reliance on nonrenewable electricity while providing a teaching tool to educate community members and other New Mexico tribes about the environmental impacts of energy use and how even modest renewable projects make a difference in energy efficiency. In 2005 the tribe conducted an assessment of energy supply and demand on the reservation and in the surrounding communities. As a result, in 2008 the Jicarilla finalized a strategic plan to implement a reservation-wide energy efficiency program. Subsequently, the tribe will develop solar and biomass renewable energy projects. The Jicarilla Apache Tribe's venture into renewable energy reflects the enormous strides it has made in controlling its energy resources and utilizing adaptation and innovation to secure its economic and energy future.[69]

TRIBAL POWER OVER INDIAN ENERGY

Federal policy and management shaped the contours of tribal energy development in ways detrimental to the economic, political, and social well-being of tribes. The federal government mismanaged tribal leasing and failed to compensate tribes for the resulting loss of energy revenues. Nonetheless, the mess created by the federal government provided a catalyst to the growing movement for tribal sovereignty and self-determination. Indian law and cultural resources expert Rebecca Tsosie has argued that tribal natural resource management is not a choice "between preserving the past or ensuring economic development for the future" but requires tribes to do both.[70] Tribal control has generated benefits beyond energy development. Since the first half of the twentieth century, many tribes have built their capacity and expertise in managing all of their natural resources and have strategically designed plans for economic development that integrate cultural and environmental values, community health, and sustainability for future generations.

Tribal perseverance and insistence on control have reshaped federal energy policy for tribal lands. Yet, obstacles remain. The focus on Indian energy resources will continue because of rising energy demands and threats of scarcity. Tribes such as the Jicarilla Apache will continue to face difficult decisions involving negotiations between tribal members who advocate and those who oppose oil, gas, and other energy development. Tribes will have to navigate the complex dilemmas of energy resource development versus natural resource preservation. But by taking the reins of control, tribes crossed a huge divide between the federal fetters of the past and the tribal energy sovereignty of today.

Notes

1. Cohen 2005:para. 17.03; Fox 1982:35; Ambler 1990:37.

2. In 1926 Congress passed legislation making existing mineral leasing regulations applicable to reservation lands reserved for agency and school purposes. The act reserved one-eighth of lease proceeds for Congress to appropriate for Indian education and agency administration (Fox 1982:36–37; Cohen 2005:para. 17.03).

3. Ambler 1990:40–42; Fox 1982:27.

4. Edgar B. Meritt, "The American Indian and Government Indian Administration," Bulletin 12 (Washington, DC: GPO, 1926), Box 6, Folder 011—

Publications, Indian Office 1929–1951, RG 75, Bureau of Indian Affairs, Jicarilla Agency, General Correspondence Decimal File 1911–1950 (National Archives, Denver, Colorado) (hereafter cited as *RG 75, 1911–1950).*

5. Tsosie 1996–1997:301; Ambler 1990:52; Cohen 2005:para. 17.03.

6. Fox 1982:411; Cohen 2005:para. 17.03.

7. Ibid.

8. Cohen 2005:para. 17.03; Tsosie 1996–1997:301–302; Ambler 1990:53.

9. Address by Secretary of the Interior J. A. Krug, "Our National Energy Program," The University of Wisconsin Dinner of the American Society of Mechanical Engineers, Milwaukee, WI, June 4, 1948, Box 8, Folder 012—Publications—Interior Dept., RG 75, 1911–1950.

10. G. M. Paulus, Address to the Conference of the Regional Counsels of the Bureau of Indian Affairs, Washington, DC, New Interior Building, May 10–12, 1948, Box 11, Folder 112—Indian Circulars, RG 75, 1911–1950.

11. Charles Lipton, "Indian Energy Resource Development: The Legal and Economic Considerations," Speech presented at the Conference on Energy Resource Development and Indian Lands, Billings, MT, September 28–29, 1977 (NARF, Native American Rights Fund); Ambler 1990:53–54.

12. Miles 2005–2006:466; Fox 1982:54; *Davis v. Morton,* 10 CIR 378 (1972); *Federal Power Commission v. Tuscarora Indian Nation,* 362 US 99 (1960).

13. Fox 1982:57; US Senate 1980:957.

14. MacDonald 1976:1–5.

15. Gross 1981:320; Miles 2005–2006:467–468; Task Force Seven 1976:49.

16. Chambers and Price 1973–1974:1063, 1065.

17. Fox 1982:1; Lipton.

18. Commission on Fiscal Accountability of the Nation's Energy Resources (hereafter cited as *Linowes Report*) 1982:11; Cohen 2005:para. 17.03; Prucha 1984:1162–1170; AIPRC 1977:339.

19. Cohen 2005:para. 17.03; AIPRC 1977:339–340; Task Force Seven 1976:141; Linowes Report 1982:23, 122; Fixico 1998:160.

20. AIPRC 1977:342; Task Force Seven 1976:141; Cohen 2005:para. 17.03; Linowes Report 1982:23–24.

21. Linowes Report 1982:6; Gross 1981:318; US Senate 1974:572.

22. Israel 1976:621; Gross 1981:318; Linowes Report 1982:121.

23. MacDonald 1976:1–5.

24. US Senate 1980:957, 1974:572–573, 576.

25. Swimmer 1981–1982:525; Ambler 1990:118–120.

26. GAO 1976:11.

27. GAO 1976:32; AIPRC 1977:341; Task Force Seven 1976:22, 47, 49–50, 139.

28. Fox 1982:1; Task Force Seven 1976:22, 49, 139–140; AIPRC 1977:346.

29. Task Force Seven 1976:137; AIPRC 1977:307, 346; US Senate 1980:957.

30. Cohen 2005:para. 17.03; Gross 1981:318–319.

31. AIPRC 1977:174–175, 343–344; Task Force Seven 1976:48.

32. Fixico 1998:150, 160–163; Ambler 1990:92–99.

33. Task Force Seven 1976:47; Swimmer 1981–1982:511, 521–522.

34. Cohen 2005:para. 17.03; Swimmer 1981–1982:510–511; Fixico 1998:149; Shipps 1992:5.

35. Cohen 2005:para. 17.03; Ambler 1990:237–241; Swimmer 1981–1982:523–524.

36. Alan Taradash, Prepared Statement on Behalf of the Jicarilla Apache Tribe in the Oversight Hearing on Oil Royalty Valuation, US House of Representatives, Subcommittee on Government Reform, Government Management, Information and Technology, 106th Cong., 1st sess., May 19, 1999.

37. Taradash, Prepared Statement; Cohen 2005:para. 17.03.

38. Ibid.

39. Cohen 2005:para. 17.03; Presidential Commission on Indian Reservation Economies 1984:31; Ambler 1990:132–133, 136–137, 140, 143.

40. Taradash, Prepared Statement; Cohen 2005:para. 17.03.

41. Public Law Number 102-486; Cohen 2005:para. 17.03; Ambler 1990:118–119; Tsosie 1996–1997:303.

42. Miles 2005–2006:464–465; Title III, Indian Energy, Energy Policy Act of 2003, http://energy.senate.gov (accessed July 2007); US Senate, Highlights of the Energy Policy Act of 2003 and the Energy Tax Incentives Act of 2003, Committee on Energy and Natural Resources, press release, May 1, 2003, http://energy.senate.gov/news/rep_release.cfm?id=203374 (accessed July 2007).

43. Indian Tribal Energy and Development and Self-Determination Act of 2005, Title V, Energy Policy Act of 2005 (42 USC 15801), 519–536; Miles 2005–2006:462, 468.

44. Indian Tribal Energy and Development and Self-Determination Act of 2005, 536–559; Miles 2005–2006:463, 468–470; Shipps 2007.

45. Miles 2005–2006:463, 474.

46. Miles 2005–2006:463, 470–473; Natural Resources Defense Council 2005; Tom Goldtooth, Indigenous Environmental Network, to Darryl Francois, Department of the Interior, Office of Indian Energy and Economic Development, February 10, 2006 (copy in author's possession).

47. Gough 2001b:18.

48. Cohen 2005:para. 17.03; DOE 2006.

49. Gough 2001a:22.

50. Gough 2002:1, 4; Indigenous Environmental Network, www.ienearth.org (accessed August 2007); Suagee 1992:730; Lovins 1977.

51. Suagee 1998:3, 5; Gough 2001a, 2001b, 2002; personal communication with Roger Taylor, Tribal Program Manager, Department of Energy, January 17, 2007.

52. All these projects and many more can be found on DOE's Tribal Energy Program Web site, www.eere.energy.gov/tribalenergy/ (accessed August 2007).

53. Ambler 2005; *Tribal College Journal* 2004, 2005a:41, 2005b; Hawpetoss 2007:42; Stevenson 2005.

54. Jicarilla Apache Nation, http://www.jicarillaonline.com/ (accessed August 2007); US Senate, "New Mexico Indian Oversight Hearings," 572; GAO 1976:149.

55. C. E. Faris, Superintendent, Jicarilla Agency, to the Commissioner of Indian Affairs, January 8, 1920, and E. B Meritt, Assistant Commissioner, to C. E. Faris, Superintendent, Jicarilla Agency, January 17, 1920, Box 31, Folder 2588-20-322, Jicarilla, RG 75, Central Classified Files, 1907–1939, Jicarilla (National Archives, Washington, DC) (hereafter cited as *Jicarilla NARA DC I*); E. B. Meritt, Assistant Commissioner, to Messrs. Pilcher and Woodard, February 25, 1920, C. E. Faris to the Commissioner of Indian Affairs, March 31, 1920, and C. E. Faris, Superintendent, Jicarilla Agency, to the Commissioner of Indian Affairs, May 10, 1920, Box 31, Folder 13643-20-322, Jicarilla NARA DC I; A. E. Stover to the Commissioner of Indian Affairs, October 20, 1936, Box 2, Folder 004—Letters to Commissioner, 1/7/36–12/28/36, RG 75, 1911–1950; A. E. Stover to the Commissioner of Indian Affairs, February 25, 1938, A. E. Stover to the Commissioner of Indian Affairs, August 22, 1938, and A. E. Stover to the Commissioner of Indian Affairs, October 4, 1938, Box 1, Folder 004—Letters to Commissioner, 1/5/38–12/20/38, RG 75, 1911–1950; Ambler 1990:10–13; Prucha 1984:886–887; McDonnell 1991:38–42.

56. Paulus, Address, 18 (see note 10); Wilson and Wolfe 1961:589; Guy Hobgood to Karla Vicenti, March 21, 1950, Box 11, Folder 112—Indian Circulars, RG 75, 1911–1950; Foster Morrell, Supervisor, Oil and Gas Operations, US Geological Survey, to James H. Hyde, September 25, 1946, Box 18, Folder 111857-47, Jicarilla, 322, RG 75, Central Classified Files, 1940–1957, Jicarilla (National Archives, Washington, DC) (hereafter cited as *Jicarilla NARA DC II*).

57. Guy Hobgood to the Commissioner of Indian Affairs, May 19, 1950, Box 6, Folder 005—Letters to Others, 5/1/50–6/30/50, RG 75, 1911–1950; Guy Hobgood to Foster Morrell, July 12, 1950, Guy Hobgood to L. N. Whealton, July 26, 1950, and Guy Hobgood to Eric T. Hagberg, December 1, 1950, Box 6, Folder 005—Letters to Others, 7/5/50–12/28/50, RG 75, 1911–1950; Guy Hobgood to the Commissioner of Indian Affairs, January 30, 1950, and Guy Hobgood to the Commissioner of Indian Affairs, February 20, 1950, Box 7, Folder 004—Letters to the Commissioner, Jan–May

1950, RG 75, 1911–1950; Wilson and Wolfe 1961:589–591; Frank J. Gardner, "San Juan Strides Eastward," May 31, 1954, Box 17, Folder 4353-1947, Jicarilla, Part 2, 322, Jicarilla NARA DC II; Guy Robertson to the Commissioner of Indian Affairs, May 10, 1957, John B. Keliiaa to the Commissioner of Indian Affairs, June 20, 1958, Commissioner of Indian Affairs to William Wade Head, July 29, 1959, Melvin Helander to the Commissioner of Indian Affairs, September 30, 1959, Melvin Helander to the Commissioner of Indian Affairs, July 28, 1960, and Graham Holmes to the Commissioner of Indian Affairs, May 25, 1961, Box 28, Folder 7097-57, Jicarilla, 322, Jicarilla NARA DC II.

58. Glen L. Emmons, Commissioner, to the Secretary of the Interior, December 19, 1955, Glen L. Emmons, Commissioner, to William Wade Head, December 6, 1956, W. Barton Greenwood, Deputy Commissioner, to William Wade Head, February 4, 1957, Fred H. Massey, Commissioner, to W. Wade Head, August 8, 1958, Franklin C. Salisbury, Assistant Solicitor, Indian Legal Activities, to the Commissioner of Indian Affairs, August 13, 1958, Box 297, 2-2, Bureau of Indian Affairs (Indian Affairs–Great Lakes to Indian Affairs–Klamath Agency), File "Indian Affairs–Jicarilla Agency," RG 48, Records of the Department of the Interior, Central Classified Files, 1954–1958 (National Archives, College Park, MD).

59. Shipps 1992:5; Gross 1981:318–319; Royster 1997:484–485; Fixico 1998:170; Murphy 1990:CRS-14; Ambler 1990:196–197, 200.

60. Senate Select Committee on Indian Affairs 1980:245.

61. Ibid., 149, 241, 243.

62. Ibid., 162.

63. GAO 1976:27, 47–48; Senate Select Committee on Indian Affairs 1980:240.

64. Senate Select Committee on Indian Affairs 1980:142, 144–145, 150–151, 156.

65. The lawsuits included the following: *Jicarilla Apache Tribe v. El Paso Natural Gas Company, Northwest Production Company, Northwest Pipeline Corporation* (filed March 4, 1974); *Jicarilla Apache Tribe v. Southern Union Gas Company, Southern Union Production Company (Supron Energy Company), Aztec Oil and Gas Company, Exxon Corporation, Southern Union Gathering Company and the Secretary of the Interior* (filed May 7, 1975); and *Jicarilla Apache Tribe v. Continental Oil Company, Atlantic Richfield Company, Tenneco Oil Company, Amoco Oil Company, Exxon Corporation, and Secretary of the Interior* (filed July 29, 1976).

66. US House of Representatives, Subcommittee on Energy and Mineral Resources, Testimony of Rodger Vicenti, Acting President, Jicarilla Apache Tribe on H.R. 3334: A Bill to Provide Certainty for Federal Royalty Collection, 105th Cong., 2d sess., May 21, 1998; Senate Select Committee on Indian Affairs 1980:151, 158, 236–238.

67. Senate Select Committee on Indian Affairs 1980:141, 161; Jorgensen 1984a:38; Ernst and Ernst, Analysis of Legal Constraints of Energy Management

Activities of the Jicarilla Apache and the Pueblo of Laguna, Report for the Department of Energy (July 1978), I-3; Ambler 1990:254–255; Velarde Tiller 1996:445.

68. Jicarilla Apache Nation 2006:640–645, 650–651, 662–666, 678; Guy Hobgood to W. M. Reed, Continental Oil Company, March 18, 1949, Box 5, Folder 005—Letters to Others, 1/4/49–3/31/49, and Guy Hobgood to L. D. Kempton, February 9, 1950, Box 5, Folder 005—Letters to Others, 1/3/50–4/28/50, RG 75, 1911–1950; Senate Select Committee on Indian Affairs 1980:150, 153–155; Fox 1982:56.

69. Velarde Tiller 1996:445; John D. Jones Engineering, Inc., "Feasibility Study for a Petroleum Refinery for the Jicarilla Apache Tribe," report prepared for the US Department of Energy (2004); Advanced Resources International and Jicarilla Apache Oil and Gas Administration, "Application of Advanced Exploration Technologies for the Development of Mancos Formation Oil Reservoirs, Jicarilla Apache Indian Nation, San Juan Basin, New Mexico," report prepared for the US Department of Energy (2002); Jicarilla Apache Nation, "Photovoltaic Demonstration Project on Dulce High School" and "Renewable Energy and Energy Efficiency Strategic Planning," http://www.eere.energy.gov/tribalenergy/publications.cfm (accessed August 2007); Karl R. Rabago, "Jicarilla Apache Nation Utility Authority: Strategic Plan for Energy Efficiency and Renewable Energy Development" (Dulce, NM: Jicarilla Apache Nation Utility Authority, June 28, 2008), iii, chap. 9, 3.

70. Tsosie 1996–1997:226.

APPENDIX

Acronyms

AIPRC—American Indian Policy Review Commission
BIA—Bureau of Indian Affairs
CERT—Council of Energy Resource Tribes
DOE—Department of Energy
FOGRMA—Federal Oil and Gas Royalty Management Act (1983)
GAO—Government Accounting Office
IEPP—Office of Indian Energy Policy and Programs
IERA—Indian Energy Resources Act (1992)
IMDA—Indian Mineral Development Act (1982)
IMLA—Indian Mineral Leasing Act (1938)
IRA—Indian Reorganization Act (1934)
MMS—Minerals Management Service
NANRDF—Native American Natural Resources Development Federation
NEPA—National Environmental Policy Act (1969)
NHPA—National Historic Preservation Act (1966)
TERA—Tribal Energy Resource Agreement
USGS—United States Geological Survey

5

Indigenous Peoples, Large Dams, and Capital-Intensive Energy Development

A View from the Lower Colorado River

Benedict J. Colombi

The Western Area Power Administration transmits huge amounts of hydroelectric energy from three large dams on the Lower Colorado River—the Hoover, Parker, and Davis dams—to consumers in Nevada, California, and Arizona. The federal system utilizes more than 3,000 miles of high voltage lines and produces roughly 3,000 megawatts of electricity, enough energy to power more than two million homes for a year or more. Utility companies profit from the more than 9.5 billion kilowatt-hours of Colorado River hydroelectric energy they produce each year, resulting in annual revenues to the US Treasury of roughly $140 million.[1] This chapter takes a probing look at the relationship of indigenous peoples to large dams and capital-intensive energy development on the Lower Colorado River and asks the questions, where are we going, and at what price?

Hydroelectric energy from dams and irrigated water on Indian lands have improved many lives, but at enormous ecological costs. Hydroelectric development on the Lower Colorado River is a story full of great tensions between patterns of exploitation and opportunity. The larger question, then, is whether dams and other hydraulic projects *ultimately* ensure the sustainability of an entire region. The present century marks a period of prolonged drought, global climate change, and increased population pressures. In this context, how well do these technologies function, and will human intervention solve the social and environmental problems of our time?

For the past 150 years, capital-intensive development on the Lower Colorado River has taken the form of energy-producing dams, irrigation projects, and storage reservoirs on Indian lands in the extreme deserts of the Southwest. This chapter documents indigenous histories of exploitation, paternalism, and dependency and shows how some indigenous peoples broke free from the hardships of colonial life and gained social, economic, and political empowerment. This chapter highlights two comparative case studies: (1) the transformation of indigenous Colorado River floodwater farming traditions and the Bureau of Reclamation matrix (upper sub-basin) and (2) the transformation of the Colorado River Delta and its impact on the Cucapá Indians of northern Mexico (lower sub-basin).

The large-scale energy development on Indian lands and the transformation of floodwater-farming indigenous communities on the Lower Colorado River have not occurred in a simple historical process. Edward Spicer, in *Cycles of Conquest,* describes Southwest indigenous peoples' encounter with colonization not as "an even and progressive replacement of Indian with European customs and ways of thought. On the contrary, as in the wake of other conquests, there were many different trends and counter-trends with respect to the acceptance and rejection of what the conquerors offered as a new and superior way of life."[2] The development of the Colorado River and the role of indigenous people in this development exist within a set of complex national and global policies. Anthropologist Eric Wolf suggests that we look at the "world as a whole" and consider how "people of diverse origins and social makeup were driven to take part in the construction of a common world."[3] The central purpose of this chapter, then, is to explore capital-intensive development as a cultural process of historically changing, unbounded patterns.

THE COLORADO RIVER TRIBES AND THE BUREAU OF RECLAMATION MATRIX

The Bureau of Reclamation took control of the Colorado River through the Newlands Reclamation Act of June 17, 1902. This act provided funding for the federal government to build large dams and large-scale irrigation works and to reserve lands reclaimed by irrigation for non-Indian settlers. As a result, energy-producing dams, storage lakes, canals, and reservoirs have transformed the Colorado River in an age of increasing uncertainty and drought. Because rainfall and snow pack in the Colorado River drainage are neither predictable nor consistent, regulation and development cannot ensure water. Precipitation comes only a few months of the year, followed by long dry seasons and droughts that may last for years or decades. A recent editorial in *High Country News* warned that "Arizona's looming water problems are not the stuff of disaster movies. In this engineered age, drought is not a tsunami that will crush civilization overnight. Instead, it's a slow-motion landslide, gradually toppling the best-laid plans of the visionaries who built the Southwest as we know it."[4]

The Colorado River originates in the Rocky Mountains, fed by many tributaries in a drainage system of nearly 250,000 square miles. These tributary streams flow out of the Rocky Mountains and join to become the Little Colorado and Gila rivers. The Lower Colorado River valley is a region of mild winters, hot summers, and very low annual precipitation. It extends through three American states (California, Nevada, and Arizona), with a delta in the Mexican states of Baja California and Sonora. Deserts rise on both sides of the river as it flows through narrow bottomlands bordered by sandy stretches, high mesa rims, and barren mountains. It winds out of the Grand Canyon, snakes around a bend at the present boundary between Arizona and Nevada, and turns south through narrow canyons and floodplains across the US-Mexican border and down into the Sea of Cortez.

The Yuman-speaking Colorado River tribes are the Mojave, Quechan, and Cocopa. They originated in First Times at Avikwame, their sacred mountain (figure 5.1), where Mutavilya, the First God, built his Sacred House.[5] The Chemehuevi do not share this origin, being a small Paiute band that came to the river from the Mojave Desert in a time of serious drought. They are speakers of one of the many Uto-Aztecan languages. The Mojave allowed them to settle on the river, where they began to practice the floodwater farming methods of their new neighbors.

Before the nineteenth century, indigenous communities settled largely on the east side of the river, where most of the fertile bottomlands were located. Cottonwoods and black willows covered the lower portions of the bottomland, and indigenous farmers planted their crops in clearings among the trees. The fields were dependent on floodwater irrigation and annual overflow from the Colorado River.[6] In the years when the river flooded, its waters irrigated the fields and fertilized them with silt. There were years, however, when the floods never arrived and the people relied on the gathering of wild foods for sustenance. When the floodwaters came, the farmers planted their crops in the moist silt, using any vacant land for cultivation. The amount of the annual flooding was variable and not always enough for crop production to furnish the estimated 30–50 percent of their food supply.[7]

FIGURE 5.1
Avikwame Mountain from the south, on the east side of the Čolorado River, 1953. Courtesy of The Phoebe A. Hearst Museum of Anthropology, University of California at Berkeley.

Colorado River indigenous floodwater farmers planted several varieties of corn, tepary beans, pumpkins, and melons and several varieties of seeds, which were unimproved or wild seeds that grew in the wet mud (semidomesticate).[8] Additional plants produced edible seeds and grew without cultivation in the river silt, including Mexican panicgrass, a wild grass that resembles millet. In the sixteenth century, when contact with the Spanish had been established, many Colorado River indigenous farmers planted wheat from the food plants that the Spanish brought to their settlements. Wheat, the indigenous farmers observed, would also grow and mature on their floodwater farms.

What did their fields look like?[9] Men and women worked in the fields of melons and corn, with men chopping the weeds with wooden hoes and women gathering beans in flood patches on the far sides of the river. Cornstalks grew in irregular bunches of three and four, and scattered among them were watermelon vines, including both small and big melons. During cultivation, in the hot mornings one could hear the sounds of men with their hoes, women in the bean patches, and an occasional dove cooing in the distance. It is important to note that the food produced from these floodwater farms furnished the Colorado River tribes with half of their subsistence.[10] Fishing supplied the principal flesh food, and wild mesquite beans and other undomesticated plant foods supplied the rest. Because of the scarcity of large animals, hunting was less important; deer, rabbits, and other small animals only supplemented the diet.

The first plants began ripening in August, and harvest began in late September and continued through October. The women husked the corn in the fields, and the portion of the crop not roasted and eaten was dried in the sun on the roofs of ramadas. The corn was then stored in large granary baskets made of woven arrowweed branches and resembling large birds' nests.[11] All lived principally on cultivated crops and gathered wild plant foods. There was some game to hunt, and fish, such as the Colorado pikeminnow, was an important food source. According to the ethnobiologists Castetter and Bell, these fish were "soft and unpalatable to the white men, but the several tribes relished and ate them in large quantity."[12]

The fields of the indigenous floodwater farmers yielded crops several times a year. In February, the farmers planted maize and melons, which did not need the annual flooding in order to grow. Before the annual floods arrived, the main farming began with the clearing of brush from the fields. After the floods receded, the farmers planted seeds in the silt drying in the midsummer sun. During the frequent times of drought or massive flooding, the farmers relied exclusively on wild foods. Mesquite and screwbean were of great importance. The farmers used screwbeans for their pods, as a food staple, and the wood of the plant for fishhooks; they used the mesquite pods as food or fermented them into a desirable beverage. Also, the wood of the mesquite trees served a variety of utilitarian purposes, such as arrow foreshafts, planting sticks, and branches for dwellings.

By the mid-nineteenth century, however, the Mojave, Chemehuevi, Quechan, and Cocopa had their homelands divided when the United States and Mexico redefined their territories and Euroamericans settled in the Colorado River valley. Over time, reservations and tribes, through the alchemy of the US Bureau of Indian Affairs and the federal courts, merged into federally recognized legal and political entities. They became treaty tribes whose homelands the United States acquired after the Treaty of Guadalupe Hidalgo of 1848 (which ended the war between the United States and Mexico) and the Gadsden Purchase of 1854. Mexico had not established a governmental presence on the Colorado River before either of these events but did retain title downriver, south of the present US-Mexican border, on the lowest portion of the Colorado River leading to the

Sea of Cortez. After the United States assumed control of the Colorado River valley, the US Army established Fort Mojave in 1859 following several skirmishes with the Mojaves. In 1865 the federal government established the Colorado River Indian reservation and then expanded the reservation size through the accretion of several parcels of land by Executive Order in 1873 and in 1876.[13]

The indigenous methods of floodwater farming had worked for centuries along the Colorado River, so the Indian Service superintendents met with little success when they pushed subsistence farmers to become commercial farmers. In the nineteenth century, with the establishment of the riverine reservation, the Mojave, Chemehuevi, Quechan, and Cocopa encountered two difficulties in farming the arid region: dependency on federally controlled water and federal oversight. Reservation officials did not allow subsistence floodwater farming, enforcing instead a system of modern commercial farming using the latest hydraulic technology. They also introduced crops such as cotton and sugar and a capital-intensive market exchange.

In 1902 Congress passed the Newlands Reclamation Act, placing the US Reclamation Service in charge of developing water projects in the arid West. The service became the US Bureau of Reclamation in 1923. The bureau, as Leah Glaser's chapter 8, this volume, demonstrates, manages the construction and operation of hydroelectric dams, canals, and other capital-intensive technological interventions involving water, including irrigation for reservation land. In 1904, following the design and intent of the General Allotment Act of 1887, Congress authorized the secretary of the Interior to divide Indian lands within the Colorado River Indian reservation into 5-acre tracts. In 1911 the allotment size increased to 10 acres, and the abundant "surplus" lands were then opened to purchase by non-Indian farmers. The farms of white settlers varied in size from 40 to 100 acres and eventually surrounded the Colorado River tribes.[14] The white settlers wanted more Indian land and demanded more water for irrigation and agricultural production.

The Colorado River has become one of the most engineered rivers in the world, with large dams and canals regulating its water flow for a variety of capital-intensive endeavors. In fact, the sustainability of the entire Southwest depends on the Colorado River. Energy development on Indian lands intensified with the completion of Hoover Dam in 1936. The dam provides hydroelectricity and irrigation water to the people of the greater Southwest, but mostly to non-Indian consumers and farmers in California, Arizona, and Nevada. Eventually, the Bureau of Reclamation also constructed Parker,

Davis, Imperial, Laguna, and Glen Canyon dams on the Colorado. Morelos Dam, built in 1950, is the farthest downstream dam on the Colorado River, in the northern Mexican state of Baja California. Roughly 117 impoundments on the tributaries of the Colorado River and more than 40 diversion systems export Colorado River water to adjacent basins. As a result, dams and storage reservoirs on the Colorado River have the capacity each year to control about four times the mean annual flow of the river.

Glen Canyon Dam, for instance, lies on the edge of the Navajo reservation in northern Arizona near the Grand Canyon. Completed in 1964, it provides more storage water than all other reservoirs combined in Colorado, Utah, Wyoming, New Mexico, and Arizona. Glen Canyon Dam generates enough electricity to supply 650,000 persons in the greater Southwest with power. In total, nearly 85 percent of the water stored behind Glen Canyon Dam is used for irrigation farming; the remainder goes to adjacent municipalities in Arizona, New Mexico, and Utah.

The Colorado River then flows into Lake Mead, on the border between Arizona and Nevada, and is impounded by Hoover Dam, also known as Boulder Dam. Completed in 1936 and located in the Black Canyon of the Colorado River, Hoover Dam remains one of the world's top-forty hydroelectric-generating stations. The majority of its hydroelectricity goes to residential and commercial consumers in California, Nevada, and Arizona. In fact, as Andrew Needham's chapter 9 indicates, the Metropolitan Water District of southern California alone consumes nearly 30 percent of the energy generated from Hoover Dam. Moreover, roughly 88 percent of southern Nevada's water, including water for Nevada's fastest-growing city, Las Vegas, comes from the Colorado River. Las Vegas is the highest per capita consumer of water in the world, using 47 percent of the total water diverted from Lake Mead for urban irrigation use, including golf courses, residential lawns, cooling misters, and decorative fountains, ponds, and lakes.[15]

From Hoover Dam, the river flows south to Lake Mohave and Davis Dam, which was built after World War II and completed in 1953. Davis Dam produces significant amounts of hydroelectric energy, but its primary purpose is to control water releases from Hoover Dam and store and release them to Mexico. The water, however, must first travel south to Parker Dam. The deepest dam in the world, Parker Dam rises only 320 feet above the river's surface but descends 235 feet below it. Behind Parker Dam is Lake Havasu, a reservoir with the capacity to store about 210 billion gallons of water each year. Nearly half the electricity generated by Parker Dam is used to pump river water through the massive Colorado River Aqueduct, which delivers water to southern California's large metropolitan areas, Los Angeles and San Diego, and to the rapidly growing cities of Phoenix and Tucson in southern Arizona. Moreover, farmers in central and southern Arizona and adjacent regions in California use the aqueduct for large-scale irrigation. The dam's surplus energy is sold to utilities in Arizona, Nevada, and California. Without the massive Colorado River Aqueduct, recent population growth in the desert regions of the greater Southwest would have been impossible.

Located 20 miles northeast of the US-Mexican border, in Yuma, Arizona, is the Imperial Dam, built in the 1930s. It diverts water into the All-American Canal, which takes water to commercial farmers in California's Imperial Valley. Water from the All-American Canal also goes to the Gila River and Yuma Project aqueducts in Arizona. In sum, roughly 90 percent of all US Colorado River water never reaches Mexico. For years, when the All-American Canal lost water because of seepage problems, Mexican farmers just south of the US-Mexican border were able to irrigate their fields with well water. In 2003, however, US state and federal authorities obtained rights to place an impermeable lining along the entire length of the All-American Canal. The canal lining benefits large commercial farming operations in the Imperial Valley and urban entities such as Los Angeles and San Diego at the expense of local communities and farmers in rural Mexico.[16]

Indian economies in the Colorado River valley must deal with a number of political systems beyond their own and the Bureau of Reclamation. According to the anthropologist James Greenberg, the Colorado River is "divided among a hierarchy of territorial entities from local communities to nation states, and among a variety of local, state, and federal agencies."[17] For Colorado River tribes, this political hierarchy has meant land loss, dependency, exploitation, paternalism, and all the hardships of colonialism.

At the international level, agreements between the United States and Mexico address the management of the Colorado River on Indian lands in the greater Southwest and beyond the confines of the United States. A 1944 treaty commits the United States to ensure the flow of Colorado River water into Mexico at an average of 1.2 million acre-feet per year and 1.7 million acre-feet in surplus years. Under the 1944 treaty, little water enters Mexico's Sea of Cortez; in most years, it amounts to only 10 percent of the mean annual flow of the Colorado River. Many legal and political disputes involving local, state, and national bureaucracies resulted in a 1973 addendum to the treaty that provided some solution to the water quality problem by limiting the salinity of water reaching Mexico each year.[18]

At the federal level, the social and environmental problems affecting the Colorado River are the responsibility of the Department of the Interior, divided among the Bureau of Reclamation, Bureau of Land Management, National Park Service, Environmental Protection Agency, Fish and Wildlife Service, and Bureau of Indian Affairs, which regulates Indian water rights and reservation programs, and the US Forest Service, under the Department of Agriculture. At the state level, there is a similar crowd of agencies. At the local level, there are counties, municipalities, irrigation districts, and power companies. Mexico has an equally complex water-management structure, with four federal secretarias involved, not counting local and state governments.

The following section examines how the upstream control of Colorado River water has negatively impacted the health of the Colorado River Delta and the farming and foraging traditions of the Cucapá Indians of northern Mexico.

CUCAPÁ IDENTITY AND THE POLITICAL ECOLOGY OF THE COLORADO RIVER DELTA

The Cucapá Indians originated in the Colorado River Delta long before the arrival of the Spanish in the sixteenth century. At the time of contact, population estimates of nearly eight thousand Cucapá Indians reveal how successfully they had maintained themselves for hundreds of generations in the arid mountains and brackish wetlands located at the end of the Colorado River.[19] Now, about nine hundred Cocopah live north of the US-Mexican border in Somerton, Arizona, on several small Indian reservations.[20] In Mexico, self-identifying Cucapá Indians total about two hundred individuals. They live in the small rural villages of El Mayor Indigena Cucapá, Campo Flores, and Pozas de Arvizu and in the urban areas of Mexicali and San Luis Rio Colorado in the northern Mexican states of Baja California and Sonora, respectively.

Drastic reductions in Cucapá population occurred after contact with Europeans, Mexicans, and Americans, as a result of the colonial strategies of invading non-Indian settlers from the sixteenth to nineteenth centuries. Tuberculosis, smallpox, and other foreign diseases decimated Cucapá communities literally overnight. Colonial histories of disease and hardship on the Lower Colorado River are found in the accounts of early Spanish explorers and missionaries, such as Hernando de Alarcón and Melchior Díaz in 1540, Juan de Oñate in 1605, Father Eusebio Francisco Kino in 1702, and Father Francisco Garces in 1776.[21]

The Colorado River Delta is a downstream ecosystem supported by upstream river water. The area originally encompassed more than 2 million acres of brackish wetlands and extreme desert. Shortly after the completion of Glen Canyon Dam in 1963, however, the Colorado River Delta dried up. North America's largest desert estuary, a wetland roughly the size of Rhode Island, was reduced to 10 percent of its original size.[22] Aldo Leopold, in his famous essay, "The Green Lagoons," described the environment after his canoe trip through the Colorado River Delta in 1922, before the completion of all the major upstream dams:

> All this wealth of fowl and fish was not for delectation alone. Often we came upon a bobcat, flattened to some half-immersed driftwood log, paw poised for mullet. Families of raccoons waded the shallows, munching water beetles. Coyotes watched us from inland knolls, waiting to resume their breakfast of mesquite beans, varied, I suppose, by an occasional crippled shore bird, duck, or quail. At every shallow ford were tracks of burro deer. We always examined these deer trails, hoping to find signs of the despot of the Delta, the great jaguar, *el tigre*.[23]

Before the dams, the delta environment was rich in ecological diversity. Another early-twentieth-century author noted that "the delta area was a country of abundant food supplies, and even with a non-agricultural people would have supported a large population. There is no indication that the Cocopa were ever visited by famine."[24]

Each year, the lower half of the Colorado River valley flooded with rain and melting snow pack, and annual peak flows occurred from May to July. The Colorado River was the lowest during the winter, and gentle winter rains and summer monsoons allowed for mild and abrupt fluctuations, respectively. The annual flooding of the Colorado River deposited vast amounts of exceptionally fertile sediments, free from alkaline salts.[25] The fertilizing sediments contained nitrogen, phosphorus, and potassium, which enriched the soil each year and increased the reliability and productivity of floodwater farming traditions on the Lower Colorado River.

Freshwater floods also fostered critical spawning and nursery habitats for important Colorado River fish and other aquatic life. With the fluctuating river, saltwater fish species migrated to the delta's extensive brackish wetlands and vast estuaries to spawn and rear their young. The silvery totoaba, one of the largest fish in the Colorado River Delta, with reported maximum lengths of 70 inches and exceeding 300 pounds in weight, spawned in great numbers. Other important aquatic species included the Gulf corvina fish, a type of sea bass; the harbor porpoise, or vaquita; and various mollusks and shellfish, including endemic clams. All depended on the mixture of freshwater and saltwater for survival and reproduction.

It is important to note here that the Cucapá Indians differed significantly from other Colorado River tribes because of their long history in the Colorado River Delta. Instead of relying on domesticated, floodwater-farmed foods, the Cucapá chose from a wide array of delta wild foods.[26] Native fauna included deer, rabbit, duck, quail, and other small birds and animals. Hardy desert plants, such as the agave, were gathered on mountainous slopes bordering the delta and baked in the hot sun. In late summer, the Cucapá moved downstream to large islands near the mouth of the Colorado River to collect seeds of water grasses, including wild rice. The extent to which the Cucapá consumed fish or other aquatic foods is uncertain.

Since the construction of the major upstream dams, of which all but one are located in the United States, the Mexican delta has suffered devastation due to reduced flows and a declining fishery. According to William H. Kelly, a well-known Cucapá ethnographer who conducted fieldwork from 1940 to 1952, "fish was not an important source of food. Every Cucapá family in Mexico possessed fishing nets but used them only rarely. Only two of the poorest families, both living near water, usually had fish in camp when we visited them."[27] The Cucapá, however, had previously maintained their indigenous culture and economic well-being through totoaba fishing. This had declined before the 1920s, when there was a high market demand in China and California for totoaba air bladders, called *bauche* by the Mexicans, for use in soups and chop suey.[28] To meet the demand, non-indigenous delta fishermen overharvested, leaving large numbers of totoaba wasting on the beach while the bauche retailed for several dollars or more per pound in distant markets.

During the mid 1950s, the shrimp trawling industry began in the delta and the upper Sea of Cortez, replacing commercial totoaba catches with more-profitable shrimp. Again, market forces were responsible for the shift. Totoaba fishery declined to alarming levels in 1975 as upstream dams and other capital-intensive endeavors destroyed totoaba habitats. Fertilizers, pesticides, sewage, and salts leached from agricultural lands in the United States and Mexico caused further destruction. Each market turn and resulting decline prevented Cucapá fisherman from actively fishing. Furthermore, several times in the 1970s, Mexican officials closed the commercial fishery and prohibited all sport fishing activities. The totoaba became a protected species under Mexican law. In spite of these measures, Cucapá fisherman continued fishing, and the demand for the totoaba persisted in US markets and abroad.

In 1979 the preservation of totoaba became a binational interest, and officials for the US Fish and Wildlife listed totoaba under the Endangered Species Act to thwart imports and reduce overfishing and demand. The illegal fishing of totoaba continued throughout the delta, and juvenile totoaba composed a significant portion of the by-catch in the nets of commercial shrimp trawlers. In June 1993 the Mexican government enacted stricter regulations and greatly enlarged the Delta Biosphere Reserve to protect totoaba and the endangered vaquita porpoises. But as the numbers of protected totoaba increased, more vaquita porpoises died in the nets set by commercial fisherman and shrimp trawlers.

CUCAPÁ CULTURAL GENOCIDE AND THE MEXICAN DELTA BIOSPHERE RESERVE

The collapse of the delta fishery has driven many Cucapá into a state of absolute poverty and criminalization.[29] Nevertheless, after years of engagement with the Mexican government, the Mexican Cucapá retained legal rights to communal ownership of 375,500 acres of traditional lands. The reserved land is principally desert and too salty for the cultivation of traditional foods or even modern crops. Furthermore, enormous environmental degradation encouraged the Mexican government and nongovernmental environmental officials to impose stricter regulations within the protected area of the Cucapá homeland and Colorado River Delta. The stricter regulations, in turn, denied the Cucapá access to traditional fishing places within the safeguarded area.

Cucapá leaders and human rights lawyers responded by declaring that the increased fishing restrictions in the Mexican delta were violating basic subsistence rights and long-standing connections to indigenous identity. Environmentalists and bureaucrats from Mexico's Commission for Indigenous Development (CDI) argued against Cucapá claims to the fishery in the established biosphere reserve and protected areas. The controversy involved the following three questions about Cucapá fishing rights: Is fishing a traditional Cucapá custom? Are the protected fishing grounds a traditional Cucapá place? Are modern Cucapá fishing techniques indigenous in character?[30]

Mexican federal laws specifically acknowledge indigenous rights to resources and communal lands and protect indigenous peoples' rights to collective use of waters, forests, and lands. The Political Constitution of the United Mexican States of 1917 and the Agrarian and the Forestry Laws of 1992 affirmed the rights of collective indigenous use of natural resources.[31] Under particular conditions, the Mexican government gives officials greater jurisdiction and control over indigenous natural resources for the purposes of protection and, in some instances, economic development.

Specific omissions in Delta Biosphere Reserve policy prevented the Cucapá from fishing in their traditional homeland—this included fishing in protected areas and for protected fish. Delta-related resources were maldistributed along lines of social and political power. Environmentalists, transnational nongovernmental organizations, and Mexican governmental officials utilized self-serving strategies in the preservation of delta species, sacrificing traditional Cucapá culture to "save" the delta. The preservation of declining plant and animal species did not depend on denying Cucapá their legal access to the delta, but ultimately, strategies of exclusion impeded Cucapá political and economic autonomy and contributed to the forced destruction of a millennia-old cultural system.

In the end, the Mexican courts rejected Cucapá fishing rights on the grounds that these were both "un-sustainable" and "un-indigenous."[32] The courts contended that Cucapá contemporary fishing strategies, which included the use of large nets and fishing boats outfitted with outboard motors, did not conform to traditional Cucapa fishing methods and negated the legitimacy of their rights to delta-related resources. Ironically, several studies demonstrated that annual Cucapá fish yields accounted for less than 3 percent of the total fish harvested in the zone.[33] In this unjust political ecology, differential fishing rights negated the constitutional guarantee of Mexican indigenous rights to communal lands and natural resources.

CUMULATIVE IMPACTS OF UPSTREAM DAMS ON THE COLORADO RIVER DELTA

In 1930, before the capital-intensive development of the Colorado River, the delta's total size was approximately 1,930,000 acres (475 square miles). Since then, the Colorado River has diminished each year, and is now roughly 10 percent of its original size.[34] Disproportionate water reductions in twenty-four of the past forty years directly contribute to this ecological catastrophe: less than 10 percent of the Colorado River's estimated annual flows reaches the delta annually.[35] The delta's wetlands, estuaries, and shallow coastal marine areas, in sum, are 5 percent of their original extent.[36] Non-endemic plant species, better adapted to hypersaline, low-water conditions, have replaced native forests of willows and cottonwoods and continue to challenge the biological integrity of the region.

Moreover, the loss of annual flows from the Colorado River has diminished species diversity. The entire list of lost terrestrial and aquatic species is too exhaustive to be covered here, but the impact on Cucapá cultural autonomy is acute. Six factors have reduced water in the Lower Colorado River: dams, drought, climate change, industrial agriculture, urban growth, and politics, on both sides of the border.[37]

Ten upstream US dams located on the main-stem Colorado River and more than eighty water-diversion projects divert or waste the river water for the following three reasons: irrigation for industrial agriculture in the United States and Mexico; evaporative loss of surface water in storage reservoirs and diversion canals; and transfer of water to more than thirty million people in urban centers in Arizona (Phoenix and Tucson), California (Los Angeles and San Diego), Nevada (Las Vegas), and northern Mexico (Mexicali).

As a result, the capital-intensive development of the Colorado River on Indian lands has enabled a modern global economy to emerge, as Andrew Needham's chapter 9 stresses, in the greater Southwest and beyond. But energy-producing dams and their negative effects on the environment have reduced ecological sustainability and challenged the resiliency of Mexican Cucapá communities and other Colorado River tribes dependent on a free-flowing river and native plant and animal species. Currently listed as threatened, endangered, or of concern by US and Mexican authorities are the following delta species: Mexican long-tongued bat, vaquita porpoise, jaguar, blue whale, fin whale, California gray whale, great blue heron, California brown pelican, reddish egret, brant, bald eagle, Harris's hawk, American peregrine falcon, Yuma clapper rail, mountain plover, Hermann's gull, elegant tern, blue-footed booby, southwestern willow flycatcher, northern mockingbird, large-billed savannah sparrow, house finch, desert tortoise, flat-tailed horned lizard, lowland leopard frog, Colorado pikeminnow, bonytail chub, humpback chub, razorback sucker, desert pupfish, and totoaba.

THE UPSTREAM COCOPAH: A DIFFERENT SET OF CULTURAL ADAPTATIONS

As one heads north and away from the abject poverty of the Mexican Cucapá, a very different set of cultural adaptations persists across the US-Mexican border. Before the 1980s the Cocopah Nation had few tribal businesses and lived on very remote tracts of desert land, located on three reservations in Arizona's Yuma County. Since gaining federal recognition in 1917 under Executive Order by President Woodrow Wilson, the US Cocopah were forced by the US government to sever all formal ties with Cucapá communities living in northern Mexico.[38] The Executive Order reserved about 2,300 acres of land for the Cocopah, and in 1985 President

Ronald Reagan passed the Cocopah Land Acquisition Bill, which provided an additional 4,200 acres of land. Located on the east side of the Lower Colorado River, the Cocopah reservations are mostly fertile bottomland.[39]

To generate adequate income, several Cocopah farmers in the second half of the twentieth century began leasing individually owned tribal farmland to non-Indian farmers and large agribusinesses. Today's non-Indian agribusinesses in Yuma County produce 90 percent of all domestically grown winter vegetables consumed in Canada and the United States, as well as 98 percent of all iceberg lettuce.[40] The lettuce growers rely on large amounts of irrigated Colorado River water and available Cocopah land. It takes roughly 3 gallons of water to produce a 1-cup serving of lettuce, and 24 gallons to produce about 1 pound.[41] Annual rainfall in the extremes of southwestern Arizona amounts to roughly 3.5 inches, and the region remains frost-free for 350–365 days per year. Of the 2.8 million acre-feet of Colorado River water allotted for Arizona, Yuma County irrigation consumes more than one-third.[42] Additional water-intensive crops on the Lower Colorado River include cotton, alfalfa hay, wheat, lemons, oranges, and tangerines. Yuma County food commodities, with the exception of local varieties of melons and corn, were first cultivated in agricultural regions located outside the Americas. Spanish and later Mexican and American immigrants brought them to the Southwest.

Energy-intensive, contemporary farming practices for the Mojave, Chemehuevi, and Quechan generally mirror the modern agriculture on Cocopah lands. Most Indian landowners lease farmland to non-Indian agribusinesses. Throughout the Colorado River valley, important commercial crops of cotton, alfalfa, wheat, onions, lettuce, cauliflower, broccoli, cantaloupes, honeydews, and watermelons all rely on much needed water from diversion canals and storage reservoirs along the Lower Colorado River. The Colorado River Indian Tribes, located outside Parker, Arizona, is an amalgamation of several indigenous nations. Comprising nearly 3,500 active members with Mojave, Chemehuevi, Hopi, and Navajo tribal affiliations, the Colorado River Indian Tribes manages Indian and non-Indian farming through leases of approximately 85,000 acres of cotton, wheat, alfalfa, and several other staple crops cultivated on fertile river bottomland. Moreover, the Colorado River Indian Tribes has senior water rights to about one-third of all Colorado River water allocated to the state of Arizona, totaling about 717,000 acre-feet of water each year.[43] Twenty-first-century tribal reliance on large dams to control water for purposes of storage, irrigation, and hydroelectricity complicates the relationships among indigenous peoples, large dams, and capital-intensive energy development on the Lower Colorado River and returns us to the questions, where are we going, and at what price?

In the present global economy, Colorado River indigenous communities are diversifying business opportunities and attracting non-Indians to several development efforts on Indian lands. In the late 1990s the Colorado River Indian Tribes invested $52 million in the Blue Water Resort and Casino, a Las Vegas–style gaming operation with fine dining, an indoor water park, and live entertainment. It also built a large conference center and an exercise facility, miniature golf, and several retail shops. In 1987 the Cocopah opened a tribal gas station, smoke shop, and bingo hall and currently own and operate several business enterprises in Somerton, Arizona. A large gaming casino with a nearby golf and recreational vehicle park caters to non-Indian tourists and retirees. The Cocopah participate in a growing leisure industry, offering residences on an eighteen-hole golf course, walking paths, bicycle paths, and a shaded swimming pool in the warm southern Arizona sun.

All of these tribally owned enterprises rely on the energy and water from dams, storage reservoirs, and irrigation projects on the Lower Colorado River. And recreation and gaming are not the only tribally managed economic activities. For the Colorado River tribes, recent economic development efforts have brought rapid growth in real estate ventures. The tribes are strategically located along major interstates that connect the greater Southwest. Reservation-based land development includes a 140-acre industrial park, community residential and commercial development, and a planned Wal-Mart retail center along the highway in Parker, Arizona. Colorado River indigenous communities are constructing "a common world" within the larger political economy. This demands that we rethink what it means to be "indigenous" and "traditional" in the context of energy development in the greater Southwest.

CONCLUSION

Indigenous communities are historically changing, unbounded societies. Floodwater-farming indigenous communities have responded in novel ways to the land and water development in the Colorado River valley. The twenty-first-century pattern reflects indigenous social and economic adaptations to the global economy, instead of the "bounded" reservation development and federal paternalism of the late nineteenth and twentieth centuries. Reservation planning in the paternalistic tradition usually championed the interests of non-Indian settlers and ignored or thwarted the well-being and economic opportunities of indigenous peoples. In the age of Native Nation-building and indigenous self-governance, individual tribal nations make their own decisions and retain greater power while reinterpreting the meaning of "sovereignty."

Even though most American Indian tribes in the desert Southwest are experiencing a period of economic renaissance and Native Nation-building, water crises and the effects of global climate change, as Dana Powell and Dáilan Long's chapter 10 (this volume) demonstrates, are everyday reality. Continued drought conditions will resurrect tribal negotiations concerning reserved water rights and will strengthen tribal sovereignty. For roughly a century, indigenous communities along the Lower Colorado River lacked the political and economic might to reclaim reserved rights to much of the river; the great centers of the Southwest economy, such as Las Vegas, Phoenix, Tucson, and Los Angeles, now have "the worst water-rights priorities on the river."[44] This means that non-Indian citizens, municipalities, and corporations hold junior water rights and soon will have to answer to the tribes for the use of Colorado River water.

In terms of global climate change, recent studies by Tim Barnett and colleagues in the journal *Science* link human activities to a fifty-year decline in the West's water.[45] In fact, the researchers suggest that human-caused warming is responsible for the major reductions in winter snowpack, downward trends in total river flow, and earlier spring runoff occurring from 1950 to 1999. Previous work by Barnett on water resources in western North America projects significant physical changes to the Colorado River system by the mid-twenty-first century:

> [The reservoir system on the Colorado River] will not be able to meet all of the demands placed on it, including water supply for Southern California and the inland Southwest, since reservoirs levels will be reduced by over one-third and releases reduced by as much as 17%. The greatest effects will be on lower Colorado River Basin states. All users of Colorado River hydroelectric power will be affected by lower reservoir levels and flows, which will result in reductions in hydropower generation by as much as 40%. Basically, we found the fully allocated Colorado system to be at the brink of failure, wherein virtually any reduction in precipitation over the Basin, either natural or anthropogenic, will lead to the failure to meet mandated allocations.[46]

Rapid growth in the greater Southwest, in sum, is using most if not all of the available water. Continued growth in residential and commercial real estate and in global agricultural commodities on the Lower Colorado River "foretells of water shortages, lack of storage capability to meet seasonally changing river flow, [and] transfers of water from agriculture to urban uses and other critical impacts."[47] This does not bode well for indigenous Southwest communities and others living in the desert Southwest in an age of prolonged drought and global climate change.

Meanwhile, in the current political ecology, capital-intensive energy development on the Lower Colorado River continues to threaten ancient species and indigenous cultures. For three days in March 2008, the Bureau of Reclamation flooded the Grand Canyon, releasing at a massive rate roughly 300,000 gallons of water every second from Glen Canyon Dam.[48] The large-scale experiment was meant to mimic spring flooding on the pre-dam Colorado River. Before the dams, the Grand Canyon was muddy and warm, and the annual floods built up sandbars throughout the river. Today, 98 percent of the sediment formerly carried by a free-flowing Colorado River has been lost behind the large dams. US Secretary of the Interior Dirk Kempthorne explained, "We're here to set the river free once again. And through this experiment, we hope to enhance the habitat in the canyon and its wildlife and learn more about these complex natural systems."[49]

The complexity of these systems consists of biotic relationships and deeply rooted political and economic relationships. What seems rational for one resource policy may harm another. Colorado River indigenous communities with floodwater farming traditions of great antiquity have been transformed by the greater political power of corporate actors operating through congressional influence on federal agencies in five reservations: the Fort Mojave, Chemehuevi, Colorado River Indian Tribes, Quechan, and Cocopah. Except for the Chemehuevi, all continue to live on portions of ancestral homelands. In Mexico, the Cucapá Indians are embedded in hierarchies that more often privilege the rich and powerful, and multinational interest groups vie for control (and gain power) over the Cucapá and the Colorado River Delta.

We can no longer think of large dams, storage lakes, canals, and reservoirs as existing separately from the larger political economy based on the manipulation of the West's greatest river. Indigenous Colorado River communities, corporate actors, and political agencies continue to divide the physical landscape among local, state, and national entities and nonterritorial entities such as world markets. Add to this picture the droughts and water shortages that may extend across years and decades. In this "engineered age" of regulated water, drought may not destroy overnight the greater Southwest built by "the visionaries." Rather, Indian and energy development in the context of hydroelectricity and large storage dams is about the technological control of water in an era of unprecedented growth, increasing uncertainty, and constant change.

Notes

1. "Parker Dam and Power Plant," US Bureau of Reclamation Lower Colorado River Region, June 6, 2008, http://www.usbr.gov/lc/region/pao/brochures/parker.html (accessed June 2008).

2. Spicer 1962:1.

3. Wolf 1982:385.

4. Greg Hanscom, "The Best-Laid Plans," *High Country News*, March 21, 2005, http://www.hcn.org/servlets/hcn.Article?article_id=15362 (accessed November 2008).

5. Kroeber 1925:770–771; Stewart 1983:65–66.

6. Colorado River tribes did not have the large population numbers necessary to construct the massive hand-made and hand-dug irrigation canals like those of other Southwest peoples, such as the Hohokam on the Gila River in central Arizona.

7. Driver 1957:175.

8. Castetter and Bell 1951:166–178.

9. Charles McNichols gives ample descriptions of Colorado River indigenous floodwater farming in his book, *Crazy Weather* (1944).

10. Kroeber 1925:735.

11. Stewart 1983:58.

12. Castetter and Bell 1951:218.

13. Spicer 1962:262–275.

14. Caylor 2000:202; Fontana 1963:168; Pisani 2002:159–160.

15. High Plains Regional Climate Center, "The Southwestern US Drought of 2003, Some Hydrological Impacts," University of Nebraska–Lincoln, http://www.hprcc.unl.edu/nebraska/sw-drought-2003.html (accessed October 2008).

16. Matt Jenkins, "The Efficiency of Paradox," *High Country News*, February 5, 2007.

17. Greenberg 1998:134.

18. Glenn et al. 1995; Glennon and Culp 2001; Spiegel 2005.

19. Kelly 1944, 1977; Kniffen 1931:50–52.

20. *Cocopah* is what the Cocopa north of the US-Mexican border call themselves. *Cucapá* is what the Mexican Cocopa call themselves. The most widely used name in the ethnographic literature is *Cocopa*.

21. Kroeber 1920:485.

22. Frank Clifford, "In Colorado River Delta, Water—and Prospects—Are Drying

Up," *Los Angeles Times*, May 25, 2008, http://articles.latimes.com/2008/may/25/local/me-newcolorado25 (accessed January 2009).

23. Leopold 1949:141–149; also, for general discussions on the natural history of the Colorado River Delta before completion of major upstream US dams on the Colorado River, see MacDougal 1906; Sykes 1937.

24. Kniffen 1931:55.

25. Castetter and Bell 1951:5–14.

26. For a discussion on Cocopa ethnography and subsistence patterns and Lower Colorado River and Colorado River Delta ethnobiology, see Castetter and Bell 1951; Driver 1957; Kelly 1977; Kniffen 1931; Kroeber 1920.

27. Kelly 1977:44.

28. Bahre 1967:91–95; Craig 1926.

29. Muehlmann 2009.

30. Ibid., 472.

31. Anaya and Williams 2001:63.

32. Muehlmann 2009:472.

33. Ibid.

34. Pitt et al. 2000:820.

35. Pitt et al. 2000:824.

36. Glenn et al. 1995:1178–1184.

37. Frank Clifford, "In Colorado River Delta" (see note 22).

38. Cocopah Indian Tribe, "Overview," on the official tribal Web site, http://www.cocopah.com/docs/overview.html (accessed March 2008).

39. Tisdale 1997.

40. Daniel Gonzalez, "Shortage of Workers Imperils Yuma Crops," *The Arizona Republic*, November 21, 2006, http://www.azcentral.com/arizonarepublic/news/articles/1121yumalabor1121.html (accessed January 2009).

41. Kreith 1991:26–30.

42. Barry Bequette, Barry Tickes, and Mohammed Zerkoune, "Yuma County Agricultural Statistics," University of Arizona, Cooperative Extension, 2001, http://cals.arizona.edu/crop/counties/yuma/agstats2001.html (accessed August 2008).

43. Colorado River Indian Tribes, "Business Opportunities," http://critonline.com/index.shtml (accessed March 2008); Inter Tribe Council of Arizona, "Colorado River Indian Tribes," http://www.itcaonline.com/tribes_colriver.html (accessed March 2008).

44. Matt Jenkins, "Seeking the Jackpot," *High Country News*, March 17, 2008.

45. Barnett et al. 2008.

46. Barnett et al. 2004:7.

47. Barnett et al. 2008:1083.

48. For a discussion of the most recent artificial flood on the Colorado River, see Chris Ayers, "Grand Canyon Is Flooded to Save a Rare Fish," *Times* Online, March 7, http://www.timesonline.co.uk/tol/news/environment/article3495956.ece (accessed March 2008); Amanda Lee Myers, "Three-Day Grand Canyon Flood Aims to Restore Ecosystem," *National Geographic News,* March 6, 2008, http://news.nationalgeographic.com/news/2008/03/080306-AP-grand-canyo.html (accessed March 2008); Jerd Smith, "Grand Canyon Flood, Mud to Boost Lifeblood," *Rocky Mountain News,* March 4, 2008, http://www.rockymountainnews.com/news/2008/mar/04/flood-mud-to-boost-lifeblood/ (accessed March 2008).

49. US Department of the Interior, "Remarks as Prepared for Delivery for the Honorable Dirk Kempthorne, Secretary of the Interior, Glen Canyon Dam," http://www.doi.gov/secretary/speeches/080305_speech.html (accessed March 2008).

6

Uranium Mining and Milling

Navajo Experiences in the American Southwest

Barbara Rose Johnston, Susan Dawson, and Gary Madsen

Today the Navajo Nation is experiencing a health crisis of epidemic proportions, which many believe to be the result of uranium mining and milling operations and the failure of the federal government to protect its citizens. This chapter explores legacies of uranium mining and milling, with a focus on the human costs of producing yellowcake on Navajo lands in the American Southwest, arguing that the US government failed to meet its legal and moral obligations to miners and millworkers in three ways. First, while the government was aware of uranium exposure health risks and provided occupational safety information and measures to atomic scientists and some workers, it failed to provide the same information to Navajo and other American Indian workers, and when uranium-related health problems were documented by government scientists, this personal health information was withheld from sick workers. Second, the government failed to provide compensation to the workers and their families for the deaths and illnesses resulting from uranium exposure. And third, the ecological damage created by uranium mining and milling processes was not addressed for an extended period of time, creating further health hazards.

To a very limited degree, federal legislation now addresses these historical grievances. The provisions of the 1990 Radiation Exposure

Compensation Act (RECA) and its amendments authorize compassionate payment for Navajo underground uranium miners or their widows, as well as residents exposed to downwind radiation from nuclear weapons testing. However, the compensation for costs of treatment and the pain and suffering of radiation-related disease offer, at best, an imperfect remedy. Furthermore, few Navajo workers and residents have been recognized as meeting the standards of exposure: reportedly, only one in four workers (or their survivors) who developed radiogenic disease has been awarded compensation under RECA.

It is our argument that the historic context of environmental racism—withholding basic health and safety information from Navajo workers, their families, and residents and neglecting to take protective measures—prevented the Navajo from making informed decisions regarding their health and employment. Combating the consequences of this history has required government transparency, access to key environmental health data, and enhanced civic and scientific participation in monitoring and remediation. Such efforts suggest that a transformation in the loci of power with regards to uranium mining decisions on Navajo lands is well underway.[1]

URANIUM—A "STRATEGIC" RESOURCE

Uranium is found in trace quantities everywhere on earth. Rock containing uranium is mined, crushed, and processed in a mill, where it is then leached, generally using an acidic or alkaline leach, dried, and barreled. The resulting uranium oxide powder is typically yellow in color, and when this "yellowcake" is further processed and enriched, it is used to fuel nuclear power plants. With additional processing, the highly enriched fuel can serve as the fissile core of a nuclear bomb.

The element uranium was discovered in 1789 by a chemist analyzing the components of pitchblende ore from a German mine. A French scientist first isolated pure uranium in 1841. In the United States, uranium was first mined as a component of pitchblende ore in 1871, when 200 pounds of ore from a Denver, Colorado, mine were sent to London for research on possible industrial applications. In 1898 French scientists Pierre and Marie Curie isolated radium from pitchblende, describing it as a daughter of uranium decay. That same year, low-grade uranium, vanadium, and radium were found in carnotite, a mineral containing red and yellow ores used as body paint by early Navajo and Ute Indians on the Colorado Plateau. These discoveries triggered a prospecting boom in southeastern Utah, whose radium mines became a major source of ore for the Curies.[2]

Outside of research, medical treatments, and luminous paint, demand for radium proved over time to be limited, and when high-grade ores were located and developed in the Belgian Congo in the 1920s, the market price for radium plummeted, prompting abandonment of many US mines. Canadian production at Great Bear Lake began in the mid-1930s, and when production outstripped market demand in 1937, the Belgian Congo mines were closed. One year later, US researchers discovered a military weapons application for vanadium: it adds tensile strength and elasticity to molten steel. This discovery prompted remining of tailings piles near abandoned radium mines, the reopening of a vanadium mine in southeastern Utah in 1938, and, beginning in 1939, renewed exploration of the Navajo reservation.[3]

When German physicists Otto Hahn and Fritz Strassmann successfully demonstrated a technique to split the uranium atom and generate energy in 1938, the scientific and military establishment took note. By 1939–1940, uranium weapons research was being conducted in Germany, the Soviet Union, France, Canada, Great Britain, Japan, and the United States, through its radiological warfare program in the Chemical Warfare Department and its Manhattan Project.[4]

In the United States, uranium was scarce and limited to materials in tailings piles and the small amount mined on the Colorado Plateau. Thus, 90 percent of the uranium eventually used in the Manhattan Project was imported from Canada and the Belgian Congo, with smaller amounts obtained from mines in South Africa. Recognizing the urgent need to develop a national supply of uranium, the government established a covert program to mine uranium from vanadium dumps and to survey the Colorado Plateau in search of new lodes. In late 1940, shortly after Germany began its occupation of Belgium, the twenty-year stockpile was transferred from the Congo to the United States and stored in a warehouse on Staten Island. In 1942 this stockpile of 1,200 tons of uranium was turned over to the US Army and processed at the Canadian Chalk River facility. In late 1942 the US Geological Survey completed its classified survey of the Colorado Plateau, and from 1943 to 1945 approximately 76,000 pounds of uranium oxide for the Manhattan Project were secretly recovered from tailings piles on the Navajo reservation. In 1944–1945, following a uranium mining agreement negotiated by the British with the South African government, some 40,000 tons of uranium oxide were imported to the United States from South Africa.[5]

Germany also made great efforts to locate and protect uranium stocks, advancing into Czechoslovakian Sudetenland and in 1938 taking control of the Joachimstal uranium mines, the world's first known source of uranium. The Germans used slave labor to work these mines, and the German firm Auerwerke used slave labor from the Sachsenhausen concentration camp to process uranium at the Oranienburg works near Berlin. Slave labor from Ravensbrück, a concentration camp for women located about 50 miles north of Berlin, was also reportedly used.[6]

The use of slave labor to mine uranium was not limited to World War II. After the war, German POWs were forced to work in the Czechoslovokian mines under the terms of the Czechoslovak–Soviet Agreement of 1945, until late 1949, when the Czech government was forced by the terms of the agreement to return them to Germany. Thereafter, labor for the mines was provided by political prisoners and others interned by representatives of the communist government. Prison labor was used in these and other uranium mines in the region until they closed in 1961. Forced labor to mine and process uranium occurred elsewhere in the former Soviet Union as well. In Sillamäe, an Estonian town on the Gulf of Finland, the Soviet Union established a uranium processing facility and mined uranium shale deposits using forced labor. By the late 1940s, some "16,000 prisoners and convicts, and a 10,000 man forced-labor unit consisting mainly of Baltic conscripts who had served in the German army" worked there. Of this number, an estimated 79 percent were prisoners of war and criminal convicts, 19 percent were soldiers serving various kinds of punishment, and 2 percent were free labor.[7]

The first known use of uranium on the battlefield occurred in 1943, when munitions minister Albert Speer addressed a shortage of wolframite with the order to use Germany's stockpiled supply of uranium, some 1,200 metric tons, to produce fuel cores for solid-core ammunition. By this point in the war, Germany was unable to sustain its atomic weapons research program and ended up using its stockpile of uranium as presumably an inadvertent, rather than overt, radiogenic weapon.[8]

In the same year, 1943, the United States established a radiological warfare unit to explore the use of dirty bombs (mixing radioactive material with explosives, creating a "terrain contaminant"), develop uranium as a gas warfare instrument, and conduct field trials to ensure

> that the United States should be ready to use radioactive weapons in case the enemy started it first.... The material would be ground into particles of microscopic size and would be distributed in the form of a dust or smoke or dissolved in liquid, by ground-fired projectiles, land vehicles, airplanes, or aerial bombs.... Areas so contaminated by radioactive dusts and

> smokes, would be dangerous as long as a high enough concentration of material could be maintained. In these forms, the materials take on the characteristics of a quickly dissipating gas and it is improbable that heavy concentrations could be maintained for more than a few minutes time over a given area. However, they can be stirred up as a fine dust from the terrain by winds, movement of vehicles or troops, etc., and would remain a potential hazard for a long time. These materials may also be so disposed as to be taken into the body by ingestion instead of inhalation. Reservoirs or wells would be contaminated or food poisoned with an effect similar to that resulting from inhalation of dust or smoke. Four days production could contaminate a million gallons of water to an extent that a quart drunk in one day would probably result in complete incapacitation or death in about a month's time.[9]

After World War II, the US Congress approved the Atomic Energy Act of 1946, establishing the Atomic Energy Commission (AEC). In 1947 the AEC opened offices in Colorado, New Mexico, and Utah, publishing advice on uranium prospecting and offering a $10,000 discovery bonus for high-grade deposits. In the decade that followed, "uranium fever" swept the United States. In 1953 alone, Americans bought thirty-five thousand Geiger counters. Finding uranium, according to Gordon Dean, chairman of the AEC from 1950 to 1953, became a patriotic duty:

> The security of the free world may depend upon such a simple thing as people keeping their eyes open. Every American oil man looking for "black gold" in a foreign jungle is derelict in his duty to his country if he hasn't at least mastered the basic information on the geology of uranium. And the same applies to every mountain climber, every big game hunter, and for that matter, every butterfly catcher.[10]

By 1958 there were 7,500 reports of uranium finds in the United States, with 850 underground and 200 open-pit mines producing uranium.[11]

URANIUM AND THE NAVAJO

With their intimate knowledge of the land, Native Americans played a significant role in locating uranium sources in the American Southwest. Shown samples of numerous types of uranium-bearing ore, many Native

Americans were able to lead miners to areas where years before they had seen similar rocks. Significant deposits were found in the Colorado Plateau, a 120,000-square-mile region known as the Four Corners (where Colorado, Utah, Arizona, and New Mexico come together) and home to the largest concentration of Native Americans remaining in North America: Navajo, Southern Ute, Ute Mountain Ute, Hopi, Zuni, Laguna, Acoma, and several other Pueblo nations. This chapter focuses on the Navajo people, who live on 26,110 square miles of land and number approximately two hundred and seventy thousand residents who played host to more than a thousand mines. Some 40 million tons of uranium were extracted between 1946 and the late 1970s. For every 4 pounds of uranium extracted, some 996 pounds of radioactive waste was left behind in mine tailings.[12]

In late 1949 and early 1950, Henry Doyle, a US Public Health Service (USPHS) sanitary engineer, conducted the earliest study of uranium miners on the Navajo Nation. This exploratory study examined working conditions and radiation exposures in several mines leased by the Vanadium Corporation of America (VCA). According to Doyle:

> In general, standard mining practices were being used at these properties and all drilling was being done wet. There was no source of water in the immediate vicinity of these mines. Water for the drills was being hauled by a truck from a spring approximately three miles away. No change house, toilets, showers, or drinking water was available to the workers at these mines. It is my understanding that the US Bureau of Mines made a safety inspection in June 1949 and recommended that change houses and basic sanitation facilities be made available at these sites. No action on this recommendation has been taken by the Vanadium Corporation of America and it is my understanding that they have doubts that the facilities would be used by the Indians if they were provided.[13]

Furthermore, Doyle found that the Navajo workers were not given preemployment examinations and there was no medical program for the miners. Doyle also assessed working conditions in radium mines. None of the mines had mechanical ventilation or even crosscuts in the mineshafts providing limited natural ventilation. In addition, radon samples from these mines identified concentrations 4 to 750 times the accepted maximum allowable concentration of 10^{-8} curies per cubic meter.[14]

While the ore was on Native American lands, the rights to exploit and profit from this scarce and rare mineral were granted by the US federal government to private commercial operators. For example, in 1952 the Department of the Interior's Bureau of Indian Affairs awarded a uranium mining contract to Kerr-McGee Corporation. The contract was negotiated by federal agents and then presented as a job-creating initiative to the Navajo Tribal Council. The council, without receiving information on the nature of uranium mining or its known dangers, endorsed the contract, and Kerr-McGee hired one hundred Navajo miners to work at two-thirds the off-reservation pay scale. An additional three hundred to five hundred miners were employed in "independent mining" operations supported by the Small Business Administration. These workers mined shallow (50 feet or less) deposits of rich uranium ore, which was sold in small lots to the AEC buying station located behind the Kerr-McGee milling facility.[15]

Under the 1946 Atomic Energy Act, the AEC controlled the uranium industry. No one else was permitted to own uranium; all that was mined had to be sold to the AEC, and the AEC declared itself not responsible for protecting the health of miners. Despite government awareness that uranium mining was a dangerous business that posed a high degree of health risk for workers and area residents, this information was not communicated to workers or residents. Thus, in the AEC's 1951 *Prospecting for Uranium*, there is no reference to radiation except to say that "the radioactivity contained in rocks is not dangerous to humans unless such rocks are held in close contact with the skin for very long periods of time."[16]

At the end of the 1950s, the government ended the uranium-prospecting boom, announcing that it would buy uranium only from existing deposits. By that time, Kerr-McGee had rights to about one-quarter of the known US reserves. The AEC continued to purchase uranium up until the late 1960s, when it decided it had enough to meet weapons development needs. The US federal government continued to purchase uranium for nuclear fuel needs until 1971, when the commercial nuclear industry was able to directly acquire its fuel source.[17]

DIRTY BUSINESS

The nuclear fuel cycle involves four different industrial processes: mining, milling (producing uranium oxides commonly called yellowcake), enrichment, and fuel fabrication. These industrial processes all generate hazardous by-products, in the form of radon gas and radioactive dust. The human health risks associated with these hazardous by-products have been known for a long time.

As early as 1546, miners of uranium-bearing pitchblende in the Erzgebirge Mountains of central Europe were reported to have an unusually high incidence of fatal lung disease. Cases of lung cancer in uranium miners were first clinically and anatomically diagnosed in Germany in 1879. In 1824 Christian Gmelin published findings from his research on the acute and chronic health effects of uranyl nitrate, chloride, and sulphate in dogs and rabbits. By the early 1900s, uranium had been shown to increase glucose secretion (this property of uranium was also thought to be therapeutic and was being administered as a treatment for diabetes). In 1913 a study reported that of the 665 uranium miners who worked at the Schneeberg mines in the Erzgebirge Mountains in southern Germany and died between 1876 and 1912, 40 percent had died of lung cancer. Because there was little silicosis in these cases, investigators concluded that the most probable cause of the lung cancer was radiation from radon and its daughters.[18]

Studies of Czechoslovakian uranium miners found, in addition to fatal lung disease, significant increases in the rate of miscarriage, cleft palate, and other birth defects. These studies suggested a simple and cheap way to reduce the danger by installing adequate mine ventilation, which by the 1930s was required by the Czechoslovakian government. By 1942, with additional studies documenting the relationship between radiation exposure and lung cancer among pitchblende miners, the French had begun installing ventilation systems in their uranium mines.[19]

The health risks associated with uranium mining and the causal relationship between mining and lung cancer were known and cited in Manhattan Project studies on the biomedical effects of radiation. In 1942 Wilhelm C. Hueper published a review of the literature on the European miners, suggesting that radon gas was implicated in causing lung cancer. When the US Advisory Committee on Human Radiation Experiments (ACHRE) reviewed the case of radiation experimentation involving uranium miners in its 1994 report, it noted:

> At the time its own program began, the AEC had many reasons for concern that the experience of the Czech and German miners portended excess lung cancer deaths for uranium miners in the United States. The factors included the following: (1) No respected scientist challenged the finding that the Czech and German miners had an elevated rate of lung cancer; (2) these findings were well known to the American decision makers; (3) as Hueper points out, genetic and nonoccupational factors could be rejected; and (4) radon standards existed for other

FIGURE 6.1

As illustrated in this 1947 "health physics" poster produced by Oak Ridge National Laboratory, efforts were made to educate and protect the scientists, engineers, and technicians who refined uranium and developed the fuel for reactors and bombs. Photo courtesy of Oak Ridge Associated Universities.

> industries, and there was no reason to think that conditions in mines ruled out the need for such standards.[20]

Not only was the AEC aware that uranium mining posed significant health risks (figure 6.1), with the assistance of the United States Public

Health Service (USPHS), it was actively monitoring radon levels in the mines, finding higher levels than those reported in the European mines. In 1952 a federal mine inspector at the Shiprock, New Mexico, facility discovered that the ventilation fans in the mine's primary shaft were not working. Returning in 1955, the same inspector noted that the fans ran out of fuel during his visit. By 1959 USPHS monitors documented radiation levels in the Shiprock facility at an estimated ninety to one hundred times the permissible limits for worker safety.[21]

Navajo miners in the 1950s and 1960s worked in dusty mine shafts, eating their lunch there, drinking water from sources inside the mine, and returning home to their families wearing dust-covered radioactive clothing. According to testimony by George Kelly, a Navajo miner who spoke in 1979 to a US Senate committee:

> Inside the interior of the mine was a nasty area, smoky, especially after the dynamite explodes. We run out of the mine and spend five minutes here and there and were chased back in to remove the dirt by hand in little train carts.... The water inside the mine was used as drinking water, no air ventilators, however. The air ventilators were used only when the mine inspectors came and after the mine inspectors leave, the air ventilators were shut off.[22]

Another Navajo miner, Phillip Harrison, stated: "When I went to work [in 1969], I was never told anything inside the mine would be hazardous to my health later. It really surprised us to find out after so many years that it would turn out like this, that it would kill a lot of people. They said nothing about radiations or safety, things like that. We had no idea at all."[23]

Beginning in 1949, the USPHS monitored the health of uranium miners, conducting epidemiologic studies to determine the health effects of radiation. In exchange for the mining company's list of miners' names, the USPHS agreed that its doctors would not divulge the potential health hazards to the workers, nor would they inform those who became ill that their illnesses were radiation related. In reviewing the available evidence in 1994, ACHRE concluded "that an insufficient effort was made by the federal government to mitigate the hazard to uranium miners through early ventilation of the mines, and that as a result miners died."[24]

Since 1940 more than fifteen thousand people have worked in the mines or processing mills in the Southwest. They include an estimated three thousand Navajo who worked, at one point or another, in the approximately twelve hundred mines scattered across the Four Corners region. Many more thousands of Navajo and Pueblo Indian families lived near uranium mine and mill operations and tailings and have been exposed to contaminated water, dust, and radon gas. Many developed radiation-related diseases.[25]

Epidemiologic studies of uranium miners over the years have demonstrated a number of harsh facts. Of the 150 or so Navajo miners who worked at the Shiprock facility, 18 had died of radiation-induced cancer by 1975, an additional 20 were dead by 1980 of the same disease, and another 95 had contracted serious respiratory ailments and cancers.[26]

Epidemiological studies have also identified miscarriages, cleft palates, and other birth defects as health effects related to uranium mining and exposure to contaminated environs. For example, a review of medical records for 13,329 Navajo born in the Shiprock, New Mexico, area (1964–1981) determined statistically significant associations between uranium exposure and unfavorable birth outcomes when (a) the mother lived near tailings or mine dumps, (b) the father had a lengthy work tenure, and (c) either parent worked in the Shiprock electronics assembly plant. In addition to the association between uranium exposure and birth defects, this study raises important questions concerning the role of cumulative exposure to radiogenic substances and the possibility of synergistic effects.[27]

Because underground uranium miners were considered to have greater risks associated with their employment than other workers, including surface miners, millers, and ore transporters, those employed in the aboveground occupations did not receive similar attention. Consequently, there were no long-term studies of the surface miners and ore transporters. A few epidemiologic studies have been conducted on uranium millers, and several health problems associated with the milling process have been identified. Findings include statistically significant elevations of certain nonmalignant respiratory diseases, lymphatic and hematopoietic cancers other than leukemia, and nonsignificant elevations (meaning increased incidence at slightly less than the threshold for statistical significance) of lung cancer and chronic renal disease. These diseases were identified with exposures to uranium, silica, and vanadium dusts and chemicals used in the processing of the ore.[28]

None of the epidemiologic studies of uranium millers focused explicitly on American Indian populations. This has been a significant omission, since several tribes have uranium mills on or near their lands, and many American Indians were employed in milling operations. More than forty uranium mills operated in the western United States from the late 1940s through the 1980s, generally employing 100 to 150 workers at any one time. On the Navajo Nation, there were four privately owned mill companies, which operated during the 1950s and 1960s and employed primarily

Navajo workers. While precise figures are unknown, the total number of Navajo and other American Indian uranium millworkers, both on and off the reservations, probably numbered in the thousands.

In addition to hazards and exposures within the milling process, each mill produced a significant amount of tailings—the by-product of refining the ore. Such tailings have provided an additional source of radioactive exposure to workers, community members, and the larger environment through contamination of the air, groundwater, streams, and soil.

Many southwestern uranium deposits were played out by 1970. Other mining operations were abandoned because the market for uranium oxide was at an all-time low and extraction costs exceeded the market return. When Kerr-McGee closed its Shiprock mill operation and pulled out of the community, it left behind some 70 acres of raw uranium tailings containing approximately 80 percent of the original radioactivity found in uranium ore. These tailings were piled in huge mounds less than 60 feet from the San Juan River—the only significant surface water for some fifteen thousand people in the Shiprock area. The tailings pile was also within a mile of a day care center, public schools, the Shiprock business district, and cultivated farmlands.[29]

Furthermore, in July 1979, the United Nuclear Corporation's mill tailings dam near Church Rock, New Mexico, broke under pressure and released more than 93 million gallons of radioactive water and 1,000 tons of contaminated sediment into the Río Puerco. Outside of the nuclear weapons testing program, the Church Rock disaster is the largest release of radioactive materials in the continental United States.[30]

According to a US congressional investigation, United Nuclear had known of cracks in the dam structure at least two months before the break but had made no effort to make repairs. About seventeen hundred Navajo were immediately affected, and their single water source was severely contaminated. Sheep and other livestock were found to be heavily contaminated with higher-than-normal levels of lead-210, polonium-210, thorium-230, and radium-236. Indian Health Service area director William Mohler advised Native Americans to continue to eat their livestock but to avoid consuming organ tissues, where radioactive toxins were expected to lodge most heavily. Three years later, Church Rock sheepherders were still having difficulty locating commercial markets for their mutton: the animals were deemed safe by the government for Native American consumption but unsafe for non-Indians in New York and London. United Nuclear refused to supply emergency food and water to the community and argued for more than a year before agreeing to pay a minimal out-of-court settlement.[31]

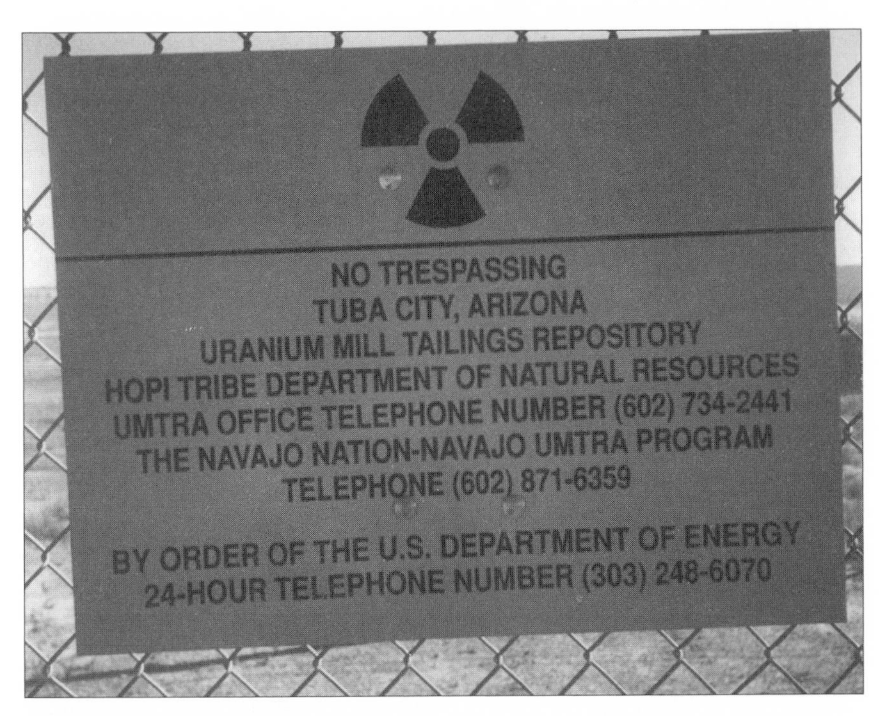

FIGURE 6.2
Reclaimed mill site at Rare Metals, Tuba City, Arizona, Diné Nation. Photo by Gary Madsen.

The mill was closed in 1982, and due to seepage from the tailings and off-site migration of radiological and chemical contaminants in groundwater, the site was placed on the Superfund National Priorities List in 1983. Groundwater remediation efforts began in 1989, and while mine tailings have been stabilized, cleanup has not proceeded to the point where the site can be removed from the list. In 2003 the Navajo Nation Environmental Protection Agency conducted assessments of soil, water, and air contamination at the Church Rock site and in the homes and surrounding region. It found radiological contaminants in water, soil, and some homes built with rocks from the tailings piles.[32] (See figure 6.2).

Some of the consequences of federal failures to protect the health of uranium workers, their families, and residents were explored in anthropological fieldwork conducted by Susan Dawson on the Navajo reservation in 1989. Some fifty-five Navajo households and thirty-three key informants were interviewed over a four-month period to determine the psychological and financial needs of Navajo families with uncompensated occupational illnesses. Dawson identified whether or not the families had applied for workers' compensation or filed lawsuits; documented whether or not the families had applied to entitlement programs; determined the extent to which the families' needs were being met through compensation; and tried to understand the day-to-day lifestyle of Navajo families that had experienced occupational illness.[33]

The respondents in this study provided consistent descriptions of working conditions from the 1940s through the 1970s. A number of problems were identified, including the lack of engineering controls (for example, mine ventilation), personal protective equipment, and worker-safety education and training. Several miners explained that they were forced to enter the mines directly after blasting, when the mines were filled with smoke and dust. White workers were not forced to do so, according to the respondents. All workers reported that at no time during their employment were they informed of the dangers of radiation, nor were they informed of their rights under state workers' compensation laws when they became ill. The respondents also indicated that workers were not even aware that radiation existed. The workers spoke little or no English and believed that the uranium companies had their best interests in mind. One Navajo supervisor, who spoke at a reservation chapter meeting, said he had been trained for his role as foreman with one of the mining companies. He was informed explicitly about the dangers of radiation but was told specifically not to inform the workers under his supervision that they were in danger.

Miners' families often traveled with the miners and lived in housing established for them directly on the sites. The majority of the respondents worked only as miners; however, a small number worked as millworkers, processing raw uranium ore. Both those who mined and those who milled reported that they used water from the area for drinking, bathing, washing, and household uses. Children played on the tailings and mine wastes from the work sites, even using the mines as their play areas. Livestock grazed in these areas, drinking the water and huddling in abandoned mines for warmth during winter months.

A common characteristic evident in all the interviews was the lack of basic social service benefits or knowledge of how to gain access to social and legal services. Only twelve of the respondents (out of fifty-five experiencing radiation-related health effects) had filed lawsuits, and only eleven had filed workers' compensation claims. Prior to their illnesses, forty-one families reported that at no time had they received government assistance or social services. After their health problems were diagnosed, twenty-seven families reported receiving some form of governmental or social assistance.

Most families interviewed lived in rural, remote areas and often lacked transportation or the financial means to buy gasoline; they relied on relatives to assist them. Many respondents found social service and legal systems too complicated with bureaucratic entanglements, so they did not access them at all or gave up early on in the process. One respondent could not keep up with ongoing appointments to qualify for disability because she did not have transportation; she consequently discontinued her visits. Of the twenty-two individuals eligible for Social Security benefits, only five reported receiving this entitlement. One widow, when asked why she did not file for benefits, explained that she felt intimidated by the process because she was told she had to write letters. She had no stationery or stamps and could not write in English, so she decided against it. Thirty-nine respondents had not entered claims for workers' compensation, saying they did not think they were eligible.

Factors inhibiting the ability of Navajo uranium miners and their families to claim or gain compensation primarily involved, for one reason or another, lack of information about the dangers of uranium mining, the dangers of living in uranium-contaminated settings, the nature of illnesses resulting from radiation exposure, the existence of or eligibility for workers' compensation and social services, and the nature of grievance procedures—time limitations and requirements for victims to prove work-related injury created restrictive barriers.

Gaining entry into the bureaucratic maze of grievance procedures required (among other things) knowledge of their existence, knowledge of eligibility rules, and knowledge of the English language, as well as literacy skills and access to transportation. It is significant to note that informants indicated concern over the possibility that there may have been traditional families (workers or family members) on the reservation who were never apprised in comprehensible terms that their illnesses may have been caused by working in a radiation-related industry. This lack of information would preclude them from entering the grievance and compensation process.

MILLWORKERS STUDY

In 1990 Dawson presented the findings of the above study to a Senate committee meeting in Shiprock on the Navajo Nation. She gave testimony on the mental health impacts experienced by Navajo underground uranium miners and their families.[34] This hearing was held to gather testimony concerning proposed federal radiation compensation legislation. After Dawson testified, several Navajo uranium millers approached her. They requested that they also be studied, since at the time of the hearing, their millworker exposures and health issues were not reflected in the proposed

	Navajo	Non-Indian
Lived within one-half mile of uranium mine	34%	18%
Lived within one-half mile of uranium mill	76%	20%
Children played near a mine or mill	38%	12%
Brought uranium materials home	58%	47%

Figure 6.3

Proximity to uranium mines and material, adapted from table 4 in Madsen, Dawson, and Spykerman 1996.

compensation legislation. This request became the impetus for a millworkers study conducted by Dawson, Gary Madsen, and Bryan Spykerman during the fall of 1992 on the Navajo Nation and in the following year among non-Indians who worked in Utah and Colorado.

Data were gathered from eighty-three American Indians (almost all Navajo) and eighty-seven non-Indians through in-person interviews of millers or their survivors. Questions concerned millworking conditions, including perceived radiation exposures; self-reported health histories; psychosocial impacts; and environmental exposures to respondents and their families.[35]

The studies indicated that a vast majority of workers were never warned about the radiation hazards associated with millwork, experienced significant exposures to ore and yellowcake dust during their employment (the Nuclear Regulatory Commission in 1986 noted that uranium dust presented the most significant hazard for the workers), accumulated ore dust on their clothing, and took their clothing off the work site, allowing for possible exposures to both their families and the larger community.[36] Regarding the entire sample, the most frequently reported health problems were shortness of breath, persistent cough, lung cancer, emphysema, silicosis, pulmonary fibrosis, and pneumoconiosis. These symptoms and diagnosed diseases were consistent with the ore and yellowcake dust conditions experienced by the workers.

Differences between the Navajo respondents and the non-Indians were also found. The Navajo millers (82 percent) were more than twice as likely as the non-Indians (33 percent) to attribute their health problems to their millwork environment. Also, 60 percent of the Indians noted experiencing anxiety or depression that they related to their physical health problems, as compared to about 40 percent of the non-Indian respondents. The studies also identified larger environmental issues. Here, too, there were differences between Navajo and Anglo respondents (figure 6.3).[37]

Overall, these larger environmental exposures suggest that the Navajo millers and their families experienced greater risks than did the non-Indians. This finding is not surprising, given the significant time lag between government studies confirming significant health risks in 1951 and the implementation of basic occupational health and safety regulations in 1971. Workers developed lung cancer and other radiogenic illnesses—and these problems were predicted and studied by government scientists—yet, for many years, workers were not informed of their illnesses or treated.[38]

NAVAJO ACTIVISM

Due to the lengthy latency period between exposures and the development of health problems, it was not until people began to manifest illnesses and to die that the workers and their families began to question the health effects of their uranium employment. The Navajo, in particular, had unique obstacles related to the recognition of radiation-related problems, which were likely shared by other American Indian tribes. For example, the Navajo language lacked the terms to define and describe radiation and radiogenic effects. So unlike the Anglo population, the Navajo needed to develop a nuclear lexicon. It was especially difficult for workers early on to attribute their health problems to their uranium work. Many believed that their lung problems, for instance, were related to breaking a taboo in the natural world—for example, standing next to where lightning had struck. By not making the connection between their health problems and their work, the workers and their survivors could not apply for workers' compensation or other disability and survivors' benefits. In addition, for traditional Navajo people, it is taboo to talk about deceased people.[39]

Beginning in the early 1970s, with the appearance of deaths and health problems, a network of Navajo activists emerged. They included former workers, family members of workers, and health professionals. The latter were associated with the US Indian Health Service. They were at the forefront of educating Navajo workers and their families about radiation-related work exposures, health problems, and redress.[40]

We suggest that the way they approached these problems can provide others with a useful model for addressing the needs for environmental justice. The Navajo employed a variety of approaches including the following:

- Navajo health representatives identified uranium workers' illnesses initially through the Navajo Nation's Community Health Representatives program, a federally funded tribal health advocacy program.
- Four support groups—two for miners and two for millers—

provided a support base and dissemination of information. A fifth group was recently created to assist uranium workers' families in seeking redress for their perceived radiation-related health problems.

- One of the support groups evolved into the Navajo Office of Uranium Workers, which became an important registry for workers and their families for research and compensation.
- The Uranium Education Program at the Navajo Nation's Diné College was established, with funding provided by the National Institute of Environmental Health Sciences. An important component of the work involved translating nuclear technological terms into the Navajo language and dialects.
- Legislative lobbying for redress and compensation aided greatly in the passage of the Radiation Exposure Compensation Act of 1990 and the amendments of 2000.[41]

These programs were effective because many Navajo activists were involved in more than one of the above activities over a long period of time. The Navajo were highly successful in organizing and bringing about change for the Navajo workers and their families. They became a model for other workers off the reservation, providing them with tactics and techniques for organizing around nuclear issues.[42]

Perhaps the most profound remedial actions taken by members of the Navajo Nation and its government have involved collaborative and participatory efforts to document the effects of uranium mining. Federal and state efforts to identify hazards, come up with remedial plans, and implement those plans are conducted in partnership with the Navajo Nation. And when these efforts fail to provide meaningful and effective remedy, the Navajo Nation has taken additional steps on its own. The most powerful example of remedy is the April 29, 2005, resolution passed by the Navajo Tribal Council. With this act (the Diné Natural Resources Protection Act), the Navajo Nation has created the legal means to prohibit the resumption of uranium mining on Navajo lands, citing the severe health impacts Navajo workers have already incurred and concern that existing technologies do not provide sufficient safeguards to ensure the health and well-being of the people and their environs.[43]

BROADER CONSIDERATIONS

The legacy of Cold War–era uranium production on the Navajo Nation involves much more than a struggle over the health problems of individual workers, their families, or area residents exposed to hazardous conditions in days gone by. The wastes from mining and milling include long-lived radiogenic hazards that contaminate, and will continue to contaminate, the soil, water, and air for years to come. And new threats are multiplying. Large portions of the world's national budgets are now earmarked to cover military research, weapons development, expansion of armed forces, the costs of engagement, and measures to combat global warming, with the related costs of developing new sources of energy. These expenditures require or assume a ready supply of uranium. We have seen changing values for a pound of uranium oxide, sold in December 2000 for US$7, in 2006 for US$54, and in July 2008 for $91 per pound. In the Navajo Nation, as in the broader region, this rapid escalation in the price of uranium has translated into intense pressure to mine old tailings, reopen old mines, and develop new ones.

The harm to Navajo health, lives, and futures resonates with the experiences and suffering of communities around the world that have played or are playing host to uranium mining. Half of the world's production in 2006 came from Canada and Australia, but the escalating value of uranium ore has prompted expansion or recommissioning of existing mining and contracts for new ventures in the United States, Canada, Australia, Guatemala, Argentina, Brazil, India, Armenia, the Czech Republic, Slovakia, Finland, Russia, Ukraine, Kazakhstan, Kyrgyzstan, Mongolia, Uzbekistan, Pakistan, China, Saudi Arabia, Niger, Namibia, Malawi, Zambia, and South Africa.[44] The Swedish parliament's 1997 review of the social impacts of uranium mining found that some 70 percent of the world's mines were located in lands inhabited by indigenous peoples.[45] The Dene, Inuit, and Alogonquins and other First Nations of Canada; the Navajo Diné, Hopi, Zuni, Laguna and other Pueblo peoples, Ute and other North American tribes; Australian aboriginal groups; the Bihar in India; and Tuareg communities in Niger are just a few of the indigenous, ethnic, and other minority groups who have hosted uranium mining.

The US government has acknowledged limited culpability for the human health problems resulting from Navajo uranium exposure and has attempted very limited remediation. For most other uranium miners and resident peoples, in places where uranium mining is often unregulated, the environmental hazards of production are ignored, and mining is conducted by multinational corporations whose labor and environmental practices would be illegal at "home."

Around the world, local-level initiatives are responding to the failures of national governments to protect the health and safety of their peoples, such as the Navajo actions to ban new uranium mining. In Canada, the world's largest producer of uranium in 2007, a ban on uranium exploration in British Columbia was first established in 1998, and a new ban prohibiting mining companies from staking claims on deposits of uranium and thorium was imposed as of April 2008. Also in April 2008, the Nunatsiavut government established a three-year moratorium on the working, production, mining, and development of uranium on Labrador Inuit lands. Nova Scotia has had a moratorium on uranium exploration and mining since 1982. Denmark prohibits all uranium mining or prospecting on the island of Greenland. In Ireland, County Donegal has denied uranium prospecting licenses. And in Australia, state governments are resisting expansion of the uranium industry. Thus, at this writing, in Western Australia, Queensland, and New South Wales, uranium mining is prohibited by the state government, and the South Australia state government prohibits new uranium mining.

Nevertheless, powerful forces are at work pushing new nuclear power as the "green energy" alternative to combat global warming, as well as pushing for expanded uranium mining and milling. In 2007, following the United States' lead with its 2006 Advanced Energy Initiative and the Global Nuclear Energy Partnership, the European Union adopted legislation labeling nuclear power as an approved strategy for reducing greenhouse emissions. As countries around the world announce and implement their plans to build new uranium enrichment and nuclear power facilities, the Navajo and other communities that have hosted uranium mining and milling continue to seek ways to communicate their experiences and assert cautionary concerns. This history and their story continue to unfold.

Acknowledgments

This chapter is a reprint, with slight revision by Barbara Rose Johnston, from Johnston 2007:97–116. An earlier version of this work was also published as chapter 14, "Resource Use and Abuse on Native American Land: Uranium Mining in the American Southwest," by Barbara Rose Johnston and Susan Dawson in Johnston 1994. Revision of the 1994 essay was done with the financial support of the John T. and Catherine D. MacArthur Foundation through a research and writing grant, "Considering the Consequential Damages of Nuclear War Legacies," to the Center for Political Ecology (2004–2005), the School for Advanced Research, and the Weatherhead Foundation (2006–2007) and, in this current form, with support from The Christensen Fund. Special thanks are given to Barbara Rylko-Bauer for help in tracking down details concerning the use of slave labor in World War II and postwar uranium mining.

Notes

1. Laura Frank, "Deadly Denial: Navajo Miners Stand Ground in a Different Kind of Cold War," *Rocky Mountain News*, July 23, 2008.

2. F. J. Hahne, "Early Uranium Mining in the United States," 1989, http://www.world-nuclear.org/usumin.htm (accessed October 2006).

3. Raye C. Ringholz, "Uranium Frenzy: Boom and Bust on the Colorado Plateau," 1989, http://www.onlineutah.com/uraniumhistory.shtml (accessed February 2005).

4. Miller 1986; Preston 2006.

5. Gordon Edwards, "How Uranium from Great Bear Lake Ended Up in A-Bombs," 1997, http://www.ccnr.org/uranium_events (accessed October 2006); Chenoweth 1997; Fischer 1990; Roy E. Horton, "Out of (South) Africa: Pretoria's Nuclear Weapons Experience," 1999, http://www.usafa.af.mil/df/inss/OCP/ocp27.pdf (accessed October 2006).

6. Preston 2006:162–163. It is unclear from Preston's book what sources were used to support her account of slave labor in the uranium mines and processing plant. Christopher Simpson (1995:308) identifies the German firm Auerwerke as exploiting slave labor from the Sachsenhausen concentration camp. Jack Morrison (2000:208) documents the use of slave labor from the women's concentration camp Ravensbrück. Barbara Rylko-Bauer, an anthropologist, in interviewing her mother, a survivor of three Nazi concentration camps, reports:

> While my mother was interred at Ravensbrück, she underwent a selection conducted by an SS officer who had come from Oranienburg. She recalls his examining her teeth and gums, her hands, and then making a mark on her forehead with some sort of crayon. She was selected as part of a transport of women who were being sent to Oranienburg to work in some military-related plant. She later found out that this was considered almost like a death sentence because many prisoners got sick and even died and there was a high risk of some kind of poisoning. She thinks maybe lead poisoning. My mother was saved from this fate by a former medical school classmate of hers, named Dr. Adamska, who was working as a prisoner-assistant to the Nazi physician in Ravensbrück. When Adamska saw her in the long line of naked women waiting to be examined before their transfer, she convinced the Nazi doctor to declare my mother unfit for labor. So she was sent back to her barracks and did not join this other group that was sent off to Oranienburg. (Barbara Rylko-Bauer, personal communication August 25, 2006)

7. Dvořák 2006; Maremäe et al. 2003:17.

8. Speer 1971:304.

9. James B. Contant, A. H. Compton, and H. C. Urey, "Memorandum: United States Engineer Office, Manhattan District, Oak Ridge Tennessee, October 30, 1943," p. 2, http://mindfully.org/Nucs/Groves-Memo-Manhattan30Oct43a.htm (accessed October 2006).

10. Caufield 1989:75.

11. Brugge and Goble 2002; World Information Service on Energy (WISE), "Chronology of Uranium Tailings Dam Failures," 2004, http://www.wise-uranium.org/mdafu.html (accessed October 2006).

12. Brugge and Goble 2002; Caufield 1989; Utah Division of Indian Affairs, "Diné (Navajo Nation)," 2006, http://indian.utah.gov/utah_tribes_today/dine.html (accessed October 2006).

13. Doyle 1950:2.

14. Doyle 1950.

15. Allen 1989; Tso and Shields 1980:13.

16. Atomic Energy Commission (AEC) 1951 pamphlet, quoted in Caufield 1989:81–82.

17. Brugge and Goble 2002.

18. Hodge, Stannard, and Hursh 1973; Axelson 1995.

19. Cunningham and Saigo 1990.

20. Hueper 1942; Advisory Committee on Human Radiation Experiments (ACHRE) 1996:356.

21. Duncan Holaday, Letter, Duncan Holaday to Chief, Industrial Hygiene, 20 November 1950 (Radon and External Radiation Studies in Uranium Mines), ACHRE document IND091394-B; Department of Energy (DOE), "Shiprock Mill Site," 2005, http://www.eia.doe.gov/cneaf/nuclear/page/umtra/shiprock_title1.html (accessed February 2006).

22. Caufield 1989:78–79. For additional narrative detail, see Brugge, Benally, and Yazzie-Lewis 2007.

23. Caufield 1989:79.

24. *John Begay et al. v. United States* (1985), discussed in ACHRE 1996:254.

25. Saleem 2003.

26. Samet et al. 1984.

27. Shields et al. 1992.

28. Archer et al. 1965; Archer, Wagoner, and Lundin 1973; Pinkerton et al. 2004; Thun et al. 1985; Wagoner et al. 1964; Waxweiler et al. 1983.

29. Tso and Shields 1980:13; Brugge and Goble 2002.

30. World Information Service on Energy (WISE), "Chronology of Uranium Tailings Dam Failures," 2004, http://www.wise-uranium.org/mdafu.html (accessed October 2006); Environmental Protection Agency, "United Nuclear Corporation, McKinley County, New Mexico," 2005, http://www.epa.gov/earth1r6/6sf/pdffiles/0600819.pdf (accessed October 2006); Saleem 2003.

31. US Congress 1979.

32. Environmental Protection Agency, "United Nuclear Corporation, McKinley County, New Mexico," 2005, http://www.epa.gov/earth1r6/6sf/pdffiles/0600819.pdf (accessed October 2006); Vivian Craig, "Church Rock Uranium Monitoring Project," 2003, http://www. crcpd.org/radon/Nashville/100703-1400_craig.ppt (accessed October 2006).

33. Dawson 1992.

34. US Congress 1990.

35. Dawson and Madsen 1995; Dawson, Madsen, and Spykerman 1997; Madsen, Dawson, and Spykerman 1996.

36. McElroy and Brodsky 1986.

37. Dawson, Madsen, and Spykerman 1997; Madsen, Dawson, and Spykerman 1996.

38. For additional detail on the history of uranium production and atmospheric testing in the United States and their devastating environmental and health impacts on workers and communities in the American Southwest, with a critical look at government efforts to protect the health of workers and residential communities, see Dawson and Madsen 2007.

39. Charley et al. 2004; Dawson 1992; Dawson, Charley, and Harrison 1997.

40. Charley et al. 2004; Dawson, Charley, and Harrison 1997.

41. Charley et al. 2004.

42. As evidenced by their role in hosting the Second Indigenous World Uranium Summit, in November 2006. The declaration that emerged from this meeting notes:

> We, the Peoples gathered at the Indigenous World Uranium Summit, at this critical time of intensifying nuclear threats to Mother Earth and all life, demand a worldwide ban on uranium mining, processing, enrichment, fuel use, and weapons testing and deployment, and nuclear waste dumping on Native Lands.
>
> Past, present and future generations of Indigenous Peoples have been disproportionately affected by the international nuclear weapons and power industry. The nuclear fuel chain poisons our people, land, air and waters and threatens our very existence and our future generations. Nuclear power is not a solution to global warming. Uranium mining, nuclear energy development and international agreements (for example, the recent United States–India nuclear cooperation treaty) that foster the nuclear fuel chain violate our basic human rights and fundamental natural laws of Mother Earth, endangering our traditional cultures and spiritual well-being.
>
> We reaffirm the Declaration of the World Uranium Hearing in Salzburg, Austria, in 1992, that "uranium and other radioactive minerals must remain in their natural location." Further, we stand in solidarity with the Navajo Nation for enacting the Diné Natural Resources Protection Act of 2005, which bans uranium mining and processing and is based on the Fundamental Laws of the Diné. And we dedicate ourselves to a nuclear-free future.

> Indigenous Peoples are connected spiritually and culturally to our Mother, the Earth. Accordingly, we endorse and encourage development of renewable energy sources that sustain—not destroy—Indigenous lands and the Earth's ecosystems.
>
> In tribute to our ancestors, we continue centuries of resistance against colonialism. We recognize the work, courage, dedication and sacrifice of those individuals from Indigenous Nations and from Australia, Brazil, Canada, China, Germany, India, Japan, the United States, and Vanuatu, who participated in the Summit. (Declaration of the Indigenous World Uranium Summit, Window Rock, Navajo Nation, USA, December 2, 2006)

For World Indigenous Uranium Summit audio and video statements, see "Intercontinental cry for the people, the land, and the truth" Web site, http://intercontinentalcry.org/world-indigenous-uranium-summit-audio-and-video-statements/ (accessed September 2008).

43. Diné Natural Resources Protection Act, "An Act Relating to Resources, and Diné Fundamental Law; Enacting the Diné Natural Resource Protection Act of 2005; Amending Title 18 of the Navajo Nation Code," Resolution of the Navajo Nation Council, 20th Navajo Nation Council, Third Year, 2005, http://www.sric.org/uranium/DNRPA.pdf (accessed October 2006).

44. World Information Service on Energy (WISE), "Uranium Maps, 2006 Annual Production," 2006, http://www.wise-uranium.org/umaps.html (accessed September 2008).

45. Eva Göes, Birger Schlaug, Ragnhild Pohanka, Per Lager, and Elisa Abascal Reye, "Global Justice—Indigenous Peoples and Uranium Mining," 1997, http://www.wise-uranium.org/uip412.html (accessed July 2006).

7

Jobs and Sovereignty

Tribal Employment Rights and Energy Development in the Twentieth Century

Colleen O'Neill

Since the mid-twentieth century, tribal governments have asserted their sovereignty rights by expanding their control over natural resources on reservation land to negotiate better leasing terms with multinational corporations and protect sacred landscapes from industrial pollution. They have taken over the development of these resources for the benefit of tribal economies as well, creating jobs for Native peoples. Looking at the history of sovereignty and energy from the perspective of Indian workers complicates the story, both in how we assess the impact of energy industries on reservation land and in the ways that workers themselves have redefined the terms of this development. Through the efforts of Indian workers, the terms of sovereignty have been expanded to include control not only over natural resource rights but also over the jobs that such development creates.[1]

In assessing the impact of oil, coal, uranium, and natural gas development, we see mixed results. On one hand, energy industries provided important opportunities to tribal governments, offering some, such as the Navajos, significant royalty revenues that supplied much of the Navajo Nation's operating budget. On the other hand, scholars and activists argue, the negative effects of energy development clearly outweighed the gains from the revenue generated. Drilling, mining, processing, and storing those resources created a clear pattern of environmental racism. American Indians, who historically wielded little political leverage with states or the federal government and faced desperate economic choices, were saddled with the lion's share of the energy industry's toxic burden.[2] (See Powell and Long's chapter 10, this volume. Also, in chapter 6, Johnston, Dawson, and Madsen clearly outline the health problems Navajos faced as a result of working in uranium mines.) Tribal officials and Native workers performed a difficult balancing act characteristic of colonial economies, weighing jobs and royalties against their own health and sovereign power to control their own resources.[3] Examining the role of Indian workers in this context not only forces us to ask whether Indians benefited from the development of energy resources but also requires us to push the inquiry further and examine which members of Native communities gained and *who* was more likely to suffer as energy companies extracted and processed coal, oil, and uranium from their lands. American Indian workers might well fall into both categories, enjoying the wages they could earn in extractive industries yet suffering long-term health problems that were often a by-product of their work. Bringing Native workers into the story reveals their communities to be differentiated and complex, in which class interests mingle and sometimes contradict tribal loyalties.

In the mid to late twentieth century, capital-intensive energy development (coal, natural gas, oil, and uranium) brought the kinds of employment that had been unavailable in many Native communities: building and maintaining power plants and pipelines and mining the resources. These skilled, sometimes unionized, jobs paid better wages than many reservation residents made picking produce, maintaining railroad tracks, or herding livestock for relatives. These jobs also offered some Native workers an alternative to seasonal migrant work, a way to remain in their reservation communities for good.[4]

When Native workers fought for access to these skilled jobs, they began a multitribal grassroots movement that would expand the terms of sovereignty (see Glaser's chapter 8 and Needham's chapter 9, this volume). But these jobs and the energy they produced were not always open to American Indians, even though the work was located on reservation land. As Glaser's chapter demonstrates, despite Navajos' impressive coal resources, they found their access to electricity limited. They might supply coal to the massive power plants, but the fruits of such labor remained out of reach for many families, bypassing them overhead on power lines that supplied electricity to the cities beyond the reservation. Energy companies and construction firms often brought their own, non-Indian workers to build and maintain energy facilities. So energy development served as a catalyst for tribal employment rights activists, as well as emerging nationalist politics. When Native workers fought for access to these skilled jobs, they mobilized a multitribal grassroots movement that expanded the terms of sovereignty itself.

This chapter reconstructs the history of the Tribal Employment Rights Ordinance (TERO), the strategy that Native workers and their lawyers developed in the early 1970s to enforce Indian preference in hiring, agreements that already existed but had never been enforced adequately. Initially inspired by Navajo construction workers demanding jobs at the Navajo Generating Station and by Blackfeet activists who insisted on enforcement of Indian hiring preferences in the oil and gas industry, the ordinance quickly surpassed its initial intent.[5] Soon, tribes throughout the United States—even those without significant energy resources—were establishing TERO offices to enforce Indian hiring preferences in all kinds of companies doing business in Indian country. Since then, TERO officers have transformed their offices into hiring halls and served as advocates for Native workers facing racism in venues both on and off the reservation.[6]

THE NAVAJO CONSTRUCTION WORKERS ASSOCIATION AND THE NAVAJO GENERATING STATION

In early 1971 four Navajo construction workers walked into the Tuba City, Arizona, office of Diné be'iiná náhiilna' bee agha'diit'aahii (DNA), a legal services agency that represented Navajos in civil rights cases and other legal disputes.[7] The workers were there to complain about discrimination in hiring against Navajos at the Navajo Generating Station, a massive construction project in Page, Arizona, operated by Arizona Public Service, California Edison, and the Bechtel Corporation. The lease required the contractors building the plant to hire Navajo workers, but union hiring procedures had undermined this contractual obligation and no one had tried to enforce it. The construction workers unions hired members from their own established list of workers, and it was unlikely that Navajos, as a group, would gain priority. Moreover, union workers moving in from other construction jobs in the West often displaced Navajos who had managed to get work at the power plant. Along with three other activists, Kenneth White, a Navajo who was a member of the carpenters union and a shop steward at the plant, was ready to challenge the contractors' practices. The DNA staff quickly referred the four to Daniel Press, an attorney in the Fort Defiance office who had more experience with employment law.[8] The struggle that ensued between the Navajo Generating Station and the

Navajo workers brought resources and jobs together as two parts of the sovereignty issue. Press described it later: "They were building it on Navajo land and using Navajo water" but not using Navajo labor.[9]

A young, energetic attorney who had graduated from Yale Law School just three years earlier, Dan Press had developed his expertise in Indian employment issues by defending Navajo workers in various cases he filed against the Bureau of Indian Affairs (BIA), including a complaint against discrimination at the Gallup Supply Center Warehouse, a facility the BIA used to store commodity food and other agency supplies. According to Press, in 1970 the warehouse workforce was strictly organized along racial lines. Navajos performed the lowest-level work, Latinos served as their supervisors, and Anglos occupied the top management positions. Press explained, "There was clear discrimination that went down the ladder. They [the Navajos] were searched when they left the building to make sure they weren't stealing anything, and they were limited in all kinds of ways, bathroom breaks, etc."[10] Navajos also faced layoffs in the summer, but white supervisors remained on the payroll. When Press filed a lawsuit on the Navajo workers' behalf, BIA officials came out to Gallup to investigate. Six months later, the National Indian Youth Council (NIYC), a militant Red Power organization that got its start in Gallup, brought the case to national attention by picketing the facility.[11] In NIYC's biweekly newspaper, the organization described a bleak situation in which Indians were "only used as beast of burdens."[12] As a result, the BIA settled the case, although without admitting to systematic discrimination. The BIA transferred the offending senior officials to other operations and opened the way for Navajos to advance to supervisory roles. James Hena, assistant to the Commissioner of Indian Affairs, in a report of his investigation of the complaint, glossed over the reasons those officials were removed: "To term it simply, the Supervisors have lost their effectiveness to communicate with the employees, or their acceptance by the complainants is ended for all time."[13] Years later, when Dan Press came across the workers he had defended in this case, he noted that "life had gotten much better and some of the employees had been promoted off the bottom level." This effort, according to Press, "was probably some of the first activism in Indian country around employment rights."[14]

What happened next at the Navajo Generating Station, on the heels of the Gallup warehouse controversy, would have wide-ranging, long-term implications. The Navajo construction workers initiated a grassroots campaign that sowed the seeds for a national movement and broadened notions of sovereignty. Tribes were beginning to challenge the inequitable terms characteristic of mining leases. To the demands addressing unfair royalty rates, pollution, and a legacy of poor resource management, Native workers added a demand for access to the jobs that such development created.

A few weeks after the NIYC demonstration at the Gallup Supply Center Warehouse, the struggle at the power plant began to escalate. In June 1971 Dan Press and the Navajo workers he represented—Kenneth White, Sam Damon, Tom Lincoln, and Kenneth Cody—met with George Vallasis, the Navajo Nation's general counsel; representatives from the construction workers unions; and officials from the firms that were building the Navajo Generating Station (Bechtel and Morrison-Knudsen). Press and his clients left the meeting feeling disheartened because the hiring barriers set in place by the industry and the unions seemed insurmountable. After a bit of legal research, however, they discovered that the Navajo hiring preference clause included in the companies' contract with the Navajo Nation gave Press the opportunity to argue their case.[15] Consequently, Dan Press filed a lawsuit with the Equal Employment Opportunity Commission (EEOC) and the Office of Federal Contract Compliance.[16]

The construction workers knew that they had to mobilize the community in order to improve conditions at the power plant. They organized the Navajo Construction Workers Association and talked to their friends, family members, and neighbors at chapter house meetings and other gatherings. Slowly, momentum grew. At each meeting, their numbers increased. Dan Press remembers:

> Each time I'd go out...there would be a larger group of both people who were working there and from the community.... They lived right there in the shadow of the facility, the Page power plant. When they'd go to the office, they would be told they had to go to Flagstaff, to the union office. So these folks would scratch whatever couple of pennies they had together to pay for gas to go down there. It was a hundred miles away, and they'd go down there and they were told, "I'm sorry. All we can do is put you on the C list. We almost never hire off the C list."[17]

Soon they were attracting nearly four hundred people to each of their meetings and were making an impression on members of the Navajo Tribal Council, including Chairman Peter MacDonald. The tribe organized the Office of Navajo Labor Relations (ONLR) and hired Kenneth White as the initial contract compliance officer.[18] Press remembers one skeptic at the meeting who thought that the construction workers' efforts were futile.

Reportedly, in one of Kenneth White's favorite stories about the organizing efforts, this man said, "See those big red rocks out there. That's where the unions and Bechtel is. They're up there, and we are down here. We are never going to get up there." Later, as Dan Press tells it, when Kenneth White ran into the naysayer again, the man reported that "he was working, his grandson was working and his son-in-law was working." He turned to White and said, "I think I owe you an apology."[19]

INDIAN HIRING PREFERENCE

Indian hiring preference already existed in most federal contracts and private leasing agreements. In fact, as early as 1834 federal officials had established the precedent in Section 9 of the Act to Organize the Department of Indian Affairs by requiring that jobs such as interpreters, blacksmiths, and teachers be filled by "persons of Indian descent." According to historian Steve Novak, from the mid-nineteenth century through the 1930s, the BIA mainly employed Indians in lower-level, unskilled positions. Even though the percentage of Indians working in BIA jobs began to shrink with the advent of civil service reform and expansion of the agency, reformers and federal officials held out hope that hiring Indians would aid the assimilationist program.[20] New Deal legislation reconfirmed this hiring practice, giving preference to Indians to work on development and conservation projects throughout the West, including the Navajo reservation.[21] Although federal officials may have hoped that jobs would "prevent a return to the blanket," many American Indians saw working on BIA projects as a strategy to sustain their communities and cultures.[22] Indeed, wages were important for survival, but leaders also understood access to jobs in broader terms—as a treaty right. Historian Frank Rzeczkowski quoted a Crow leader making this connection at a ditch council meeting in 1895: "This land and this ditch money is ours, and we want to build our own ditches and get some of our money back."[23] Four years later, Crow headman Plenty Coups continued to demand these jobs when he protested the hiring of white workers on a federal irrigation project on the Crow reservation. Nearly seventy years later, title VII of the 1964 Civil Rights Act confirmed Indian preference in hiring.[24]

The problem came in the enforcement of such agreements. According to Dan Press, employers, including the BIA, completely ignored Indian preference clauses. "It was discretionary," Press explained. "They interpreted preference very narrowly."[25] In establishing the ONLR, the Navajo Nation took a bold step by developing a monitoring and enforcement body that was completely independent of any federal agency. It was not a program instituted by Congress or the BIA, nor was it simply an extension of a federal program, such as Housing and Urban Development (HUD) and the Indian New Deal. The Navajo Nation, by creating its own agency to regulate Navajo labor policies, strongly asserted its sovereignty rights to govern—regardless of federal oversight. Soon, other tribes followed the Navajo example.

In 1972 Dan Press moved to Washington, DC, but remained active in American Indian law. Inspired by the development of the ONLR, he worked with members of an Indian consulting firm, ACKCO (American Indian Professional Services), to develop a new program that encouraged tribes to establish agencies similar to the Navajos'. The result was an initiative funded by an EEOC grant and called the Tribal Employment Rights Ordinance (TERO).[26] Press and the ACKCO consultants produced a model ordinance and a handbook for tribal officials outlining the legal basis for Indian preference.[27] In April 1977 they gathered representatives from twelve tribes at Kenita Lodge on the Warm Springs reservation in central Oregon to discuss the idea. Kenneth White, the leader of the Navajo Construction Workers, was the keynote speaker.

THE TRIBAL EMPLOYMENT RIGHTS ORDINANCE

In White's inspirational address, he was quick to remind his audience of what had happened:

> We Native Americans must stand up for what is rightfully ours. Our once poor "reservations" are filled with large deposits of natural resources. Many private companies have come on our lands, and left the once-god-given, what we call "mother earth" scarred, useless, and dry. They have brought pollution, without caring about the land or the people, and many power plants, pipelines, coal mines, etc., have been built. Many more are sure to come.[28]

Despite the environmental damage wrought by those companies, White did not call for a ban on energy development. He avoided the trap that has often pitted environmentalists and labor activists against each other, particularly in battles over mining, oil drilling, and nuclear waste storage. Instead, he linked the importance of Native people controlling their own resources to the ending of discrimination in giving access to jobs and in hiring:

> We must stand up for our rights. Our people have been discriminated against in hiring and employment practices for long enough.... Indian preference programs aid the average grassroots Indian worker, and that is what we are striving for. Indian

> preference also makes the companies that take so much from our lands give a little back by providing us Indian people with much needed jobs.[29]

John Navarro, the human resources manager at Tohono O'odham in Arizona, and Conrad Edwards, the CETA director for the Colville Tribe near Spokane, Washington, were among the participants at the Warm Springs conference.[30] Like Kenneth White, both had been struggling with employment issues in their reservation communities. Edwards was embroiled in a dispute with a lumber mill. He recalled, "The facility was on the reservation, and they were processing tribal timber, yet we had all kinds of problems getting our people hired, keeping them hired, and moving them up the ladder."[31] John Navarro was fighting a similar battle on the Tohono O'odham reservation, trying to get tribal members construction jobs on a Housing and Urban Development (HUD) project.

Edwards and Navarro left the Tribal Employment Rights Conference emboldened with a model TERO ordinance and confident that Indian preference in hiring was a right that could indeed be enforced. "After we got together," John Navarro recalled, "we knew immediately that we would go back home, get the ordinance passed, start our TERO programs, and have some success."[32]

At first, enforcing Indian preference required great nerve, determination, and creativity. One of the original TERO activists, Carl Schildt, the Blackfeet Community Action Project director, was legendary. According to Dan Press, even before a TERO ordinance was put in place, Schildt would approach the foreman on a reservation construction site and tell him, "See that bulldozer over there? If there isn't an Indian on top it tomorrow, the bulldozer isn't going to be found."[33] The next day, there would be an Indian worker operating the equipment. With no precedents, no procedures in place, "Buckles" (as Schildt was called) was particularly resourceful in finding ways to ensure contractors' cooperation. Rodney "Fish" Gervais, a member of the Blackfeet Tribal Council and former TERO compliance officer, recalled that TERO was "just a concept" and that the laws were often made "kind of after the fact." When a particular contractor refused to comply, Schildt threatened him with a fine of $500 a day per violation, a figure he literally "pulled out of the sky."[34]

Reflecting on those early TERO officers, Press emphasized, "It took a lot of guts for those folks to just walk in to an employer and say, 'This is the law. You shall comply. It's going to change the way you hire.'"[35] John Navarro remembered just how confrontational those moments could be. He recalled resorting to a bit of theater in order to convince one HUD contractor to comply: "When I told him he had...to give tribal people preference, he became unfriendly and hostile and said, 'Who in the heck are you?' (He went beyond the 'heck' part, okay.)" Navarro had yet to secure support from the Tohono O'odham Tribal Council, but, luckily for him, the contractor was unaware of this. "So I went to the telephone and pretended to dial. I pretended I was speaking to the captain of the tribal police force and said, 'Well, he's not in right now? Tell him to call me at this the number.'" When the contractor asked him to explain, Navarro said, "I'm calling the police....I'm the person that's going to have you removed from this reservation if you don't leave immediately."[36] Navarro's ruse worked. After that, according to Navarro, those contractors were much less confrontational and even eager to learn how they could comply with the TERO ordinance.

Early TERO activists continued to chisel away at a wall of paternalistic attitudes and bureaucratic practices that had discouraged Native people from challenging employment discrimination in the past. Conrad Edwards remembered confronting the supervisor of a highway project on the Colville reservation. When Edwards was driving by the construction site, he was disappointed to see that few of the workers were Indians. When he pulled over to inform the contractor that this was in violation of the TERO ordinance, the contractor replied in a condescending tone, "Let me tell you something, chief. You see those ribbons tied in those trees over there? That's twenty-two-and-a-half feet off the centerline of this road. You see that little staple there that's got the same kind of ribbon on it? That's twenty-two-and-a-half feet on this side....We have a right of way because Indian preference begins on the other side of those ribbons." Feeling defeated, Edwards turned and walked away. "Since I didn't have my ordinance in hand or anything, I headed back to my car," Edwards recalled. "But the more I walked, the madder I got, so I turned around and walked back. I tapped him on the shoulder and said, 'Let me tell you something, sir. You see the ribbons on the tree by your pickup?...That's where this project is going to stop until we get a compliance agreement.'" Edwards recommended that the contractor have his attorney review the contract. Then Edwards warned, "I'm going to come back and remove all of this equipment off the reservation. I have the authority to do that." When Edwards returned the next day, the construction site was empty, and the supervisor was sitting in his truck outside the TERO office, waiting for him. The contractor had followed Edward's advice and talked with his attorney, who advised him, "Settle this right now."[37] After that, Edwards placed a few Native laborers and heavy equipment operators on the job.

Stories like those told by White, Navarro, Press, Edwards, and Gervais circulated widely among TERO activists. Retelling these tales seemed to firm up their resolve to keep up the fight. In a recent conversation, Conrad Edwards confessed, "There were so many times that I got frustrated and hit roadblocks and...was ready to chuck it all." But at those times, Edwards would find strength in the determination of his fellow TERO activists fighting similar battles throughout the country. "We were really impassioned about what we were doing. There were times when I would say, 'What would Kenny White do in a situation like this?' you know? These folks were all fighters." The legendary "Buckles," the Blackfeet TERO officer, was particularly inspiring when he directed the tribal police to seize $28,000,000 worth of mining equipment. These stories motivated Edwards to say, "Damn it! I'm going to go through with this."[38]

The result of such resolve was the development of tribal institutions responsible for regulating labor conditions on reservation land and protecting the access to jobs that otherwise would have remained beyond the reach of most Native workers. These men's efforts complement other initiatives, such as challenging coal and oil companies and insisting on equitable royalties, that emboldened tribal governments in the era of "self-determination."

In the ten years that followed, the number of tribes participating in TERO would expand significantly, as well as its original mission. Between 1977 and 1987 more than one hundred tribes initiated TERO programs. Since then, according to the Council for Tribal Employment Rights (CTER), the organization that emerged from the 1977 Warm Springs conference, this number has grown to more than three hundred tribes and Alaskan Native villages. These offices are no longer just watchdog operations, although they remain militant enforcers of Indian preference agreements. Some, such as the Sho-Ban (Shoshone-Bannock) office on the Fort Hall reservation in Idaho, serve as employment agencies and furnish employers with lists of qualified Indian workers.[39] The Cherokee Nation TERO office (like that of many other tribes) maintains a "skills bank," from which it refers qualified Indian workers to certified employers. Developing the employment referral arm was important if TERO officials were going to be able to enforce the ordinance. John Navarro explains: "Once we established that we did have the power to make the employer hire Indian people, many of us got caught with our pants down, if you will." When the employer agreed, according to Navarro, "his next comment was, 'Okay, I need ten workers tomorrow at seven o'clock in the morning.'" Pooling their experience and resources, Navarro and Edwards asked Larry Brown, a former union organizer from the Spokane Tribe, to help develop their skills banks, modeling these on union hiring halls. In fact, Navarro recalled, many American Indian workers would refer to TERO as a union: "They got confused, but we tried to take the best ideas we could find from many different sources. We were proactive in preventing problems."[40]

Some TERO offices remain focused on enforcing Indian hiring preference agreements and administering employment referrals to tribal members, but some activists have pushed the original objectives further. For example, Rodney "Fish" Gervais used his position as TERO director for the Blackfeet to raise broader issues of civil rights, border town racism, and unemployment. He was concerned about the disparity in unemployment between his community and Cut Bank, a small border town that suffered from the decline of the oil and gas industry yet maintained a higher standard of living than reservation residents enjoyed. Now a member of the Blackfeet Tribal Council, in April 2006 he was pivotal in organizing a border town racism conference out of which developed the Montana Indian Civil Rights Commission.[41]

More important, TERO was a new way for tribes to assert their sovereignty. According to one *Sho-Ban News* reporter, the Indians themselves initiated this effort: "There are no federal agencies telling tribes they must adopt such a program, or issuing regulations that impose requirements on how the tribes should run its [*sic*] program. Instead, each tribe has had the freedom to develop the TERO program only if it wants, at a pace and in a manner that meets its own special circumstances."[42] Assessing the past twenty-five years of TERO's history, Bobby Whitefeather, chairman of the Red Lake Band of Chippewa Indians of Minnesota, stated, "Indian preference [is] an important instrument of our sovereignty."[43]

TERO programs have dramatically improved Indian workers' opportunities. After the Blackfeet developed a TERO ordinance, the number of their tribal members working on reservation construction projects tripled. Tohono O'odham workers experienced a similar jump in employment at the copper mine on their reservation.[44] The percentage of Navajos employed in large-scale industrial jobs on their land increased from 10 percent to 60 percent. Kenneth White attributes the growing numbers of Diné workers employed in highly skilled jobs to the ONLR enforcement of Indian preference. Looking back at his own efforts, he said with pleasure:

> And after this, a lot of Indian craftsmen got jobs at Peabody Coal.

> We fought for them. And they trained a lot of people, heavy equipment operators and everything. I went over there and saw a lot of my people doing heavy equipment. Oh, that really made me happy! I stood up for that. I fought for that. There's a big generating station over here this side of Farmington. Right there, there's a lot of Navajos working there too. Craftsmen. They train them on the job. All over, all over the country, they know how now. That was through this act, through what we done for the rights, you know. That really made me happy.[45]

At first, trade unions opposed such programs. They were extremely reluctant to give up control over the hiring process. Unions such as Carpenters Local 1100 in Flagstaff, Arizona, had exercised this authority at the expense of American Indian workers. They were slow to realize that granting preference to Indians in union jobs would not destroy the unions. Gradually, they found out that replacing white workers with Indians did not undermine the union. Instead, it created Indian union members on Indian land.

Eventually, unions began working with the ONLR to include a Navajo preference clause in their collective bargaining agreements. These clauses were similar to those included in leasing agreements that were supposed to give Navajos priority access to jobs on the reservation.[46] The labor movement has become an important advocate for Navajo workers, wielding increasing power in Navajo tribal politics.[47] Unions such as the Carpenters, Laborers International, and Operating Engineers unions, which represent energy industry workers throughout the United States, have made significant efforts to work with the Council for Tribal Employment Rights (CTER), offering to train and recruit tribal members for jobs on and off reservation land. Those unions have even made major concessions to tribal governments, giving up "union shop" provisions, the cornerstone of unions' power, in exchange for tribal labor agreements.[48]

The TERO movement offers an interesting comparison with the Council of Energy Resource Tribes (CERT), the better-known, multitribal organization that emerged in this era. Although the approaches and functions of TERO and CERT have differed, each serves as an example of the institution-building initiatives that Native communities developed in this period of "decolonization." Both organizations challenged corporate development processes. CERT leaders demanded an end to leasing practices that undervalued tribal coal, oil, and other mineral reserves. They also questioned the companies' adherence to, and the federal enforcement of, environmental laws. The organization has been heavily criticized by Native activists as being a creation of the Department of Energy or as representing only the most powerful tribes and the interest of indigenous elites. Whatever CERT's limitations, according to journalist Marjane Ambler, its members successfully created an information clearinghouse on geology, mining, and energy markets, making them less dependent on federal bureaucracies for technical expertise. CERT also proved useful as an advocacy organization, representing tribal development interests in Washington, DC.[49]

TERO, by contrast, started through the initiative of Native workers rather than of tribal leaders.[50] Like CERT, it challenged the terms of development. But TERO activists added another layer to the sovereignty debate by advocating the rights of Native workers to the jobs in those energy industries. The economic dimension of the multifaceted sovereignty struggle would include workplace issues and access to jobs, in addition to control over the nature of energy development, leasing provisions, and royalty rates.

Over the years, the relationship between CERT and CTER has been quite close because many of CTER's members also belong to CERT. In fact, the two organizations have a history of cooperation. David Lester, who in 1982 became the president of CERT, helped Navarro and Edwards secure a grant from the Administration for Native Americans, a federal initiative founded in 1974 to aid economic development on Indian reservations. Since then, according to Navarro (figure 7.1), the two organizations have given "reciprocal respect and support for each other."[51] CERT has been helpful in explaining the need for Indian preference when negotiating with energy companies.

The TERO case demonstrates the distinctive experience of American Indian workers, compared with other workers of color. The collective strategies they employed, such as the TERO initiative, set them apart from Black, Asian, and Latino workers. Even though all faced discrimination in the workplace, American Indians found unions particularly unsympathetic to their concerns. Important Latino and Black leaders emerging from the labor movement mobilized workers around broader social justice and civil rights issues.[52] In American Indians' relationship with energy industries, however, a legacy of treaty obligations and leasing agreements, not constitutional promises, defined their relationship to US civil society. By challenging the employers' rights, Native Americans were redefining sovereignty around the issue of work, thereby renegotiating the terms of capitalist development itself.

FIGURE 7.1

John Navarro, retiring president of CTER, and his wife, Norma Navarro, at a National CTER convention in Tulalip in August 2008. Both are wearing gifts given to them by the Pacific Northwest TERO region. His Pendleton blanket coat was made by Martina Quaempts Gone of Pendleton, Oregon. Photo by John A. Barkley, Jr.

LABOR AND SOVEREIGNTY

During the thirty years since Kenneth White and others assembled at Warm Springs to discuss tribal employment rights, the labor and sovereignty debate has shifted away from non-Indian corporations operating on Indian land to tribal governments managing their own enterprises. With the phenomenal success of gaming, labor issues have grown even more complicated. In the 1970s the relationship between jobs and sovereignty was clear. Non-Indian corporations were obligated to employ Indian workers as a condition of developing and exploiting the natural resources on reservation land. But what happened when tribal governments became the employers and non-Indians became part of their workforce? Some tribal leaders have seen federal labor law as a threat to their rights to govern, rather than as legislation meant to protect all workers, Indians included.

On January 4, 2005, Arizona congressman J. D. Hayworth introduced legislation he claimed would demonstrate to Native people that the United States of America trusts a "sovereign tribal government to treat its employees fairly."[53] HR 16, The Tribal Labor Relations Restoration Act of 2005, was meant to override a 2004 National Labor Relations Board (NLRB) ruling that extended its jurisdiction to include Indian-owned and operated businesses on reservation lands. This decision reversed several legal precedents that had limited the scope of the NLRB's regulation of labor law on Indian land.[54] The legislation's title implied that a self-evident sovereignty right, one that protected a tribe's authority to regulate labor conditions, existed before the latest NLRB ruling. As a result, according to Rep. Hayworth, the legislation would set the record straight and "insert simple but necessary clarification" that tribally owned and operated businesses on reservation land were never meant to be governed under the National Labor Relations Act (NLRA).[55] Hayworth, however, did not see his legislation enacted, and he failed in his reelection bid in 2006.

The history of labor and sovereignty on reservation lands is much more complex than Hayworth inferred. Jurisdictional questions about whether federal labor law applies to Indian reservations have been raised since Congress passed the NLRA in 1935.[56] The problem of sorting out who controls the conditions of labor on reservation lands predates the recent development of large-scale Indian gaming operations and will undoubtedly take more than a simple revision of the NLRA.[57]

Recent battles over the extension of NLRB jurisdiction on reservation land, then, raise larger questions about the relationship between labor and sovereignty. American Indian activists and tribal leaders have generally defined sovereignty as a political, cultural, and economic right, one that enables them to determine tribal membership, to govern themselves and their land, and to control their own natural resources.[58] Labor complicates this issue, not only in expanding the definition of sovereignty to include jobs but also in defining the nature of employer–worker relationships. From the 1950s through the 1970s, when most of the employers were non-Indians, sovereignty issues seemed clear. As tribal leaders and employment rights activists asserted, neither off-reservation corporations nor labor unions dominated by non-Indians had the authority or the right to regulate tribal economies. But when the tribes become the employers and the workers are both Native and non-Native, as is the case in gaming establishments, the issues of labor and sovereignty become murky.

The NLRB, since its inception, has been inconsistent in its rulings on jurisdictional issues. In the 1950s and 1960s the NLRB thwarted the efforts of tribal governments to prohibit union organizing on reservation lands. With the development of corporate mining on the Fort Hall and Navajo reservations, for example, the labor board ruled that federal law superseded tribal ordinances. In both cases, tribal leaders argued that the development of unions would mean that non-Indians would replace Native workers in those jobs, regardless of the fact that most people signing union cards were Navajo and Shoshone-Bannock. In 1954 the Shoshone-Bannock Tribal Council made this connection explicit in a resolution that prohibited union organizing and required companies that leased reservation (or allotted) land to give hiring preference to Indian workers. The same year, the Navajo Tribal Council passed a law that banned unions from reservation land and threatened to void leases with companies that entered into collective bargaining agreements. Neither tribal government was successful in convincing federal authorities that sovereignty included controlling labor conditions on their land. Later (as I briefly discuss below), some tribal governments asserted their power by passing "right to work" ordinances.[59]

In the 1970s, as tribal governments began developing their own enterprises, they were faced with new challenges from organized labor. Mining and construction firms, largely unionized industries, dominated much of the postwar reservation economic development. In the 1950s and 1960s, tribal governments served as intermediaries, trying to balance the demands of companies leasing their lands and the needs of Indian workers. In some cases, they discouraged union activity in order to create a pro-business climate and attract off-reservation capital. Now, the tribes, as employers, consider federal laws regulating their operations a clear violation of their sovereignty, raising the sovereignty issue to new heights. In a 1976 precedent-setting case, the NLRB ruled that the White Mountain Apache could evict union organizers from its lumber mill because Indian-owned and Indian-operated enterprises were exempt from the NLRA. As governments, Indian tribes were prohibited from passing anti-labor laws, but as employers, they did not have to conform to provisions of the NLRA. Like states and territories, they would be treated as any other government employer. The *Ft. Apache Timber Company* ruling set the standard until 2004, when the NLRB again dramatically reversed its position, announcing in its

San Manuel Indian Bingo and Casino decision that federal labor law did have jurisdiction over tribal businesses.[60] Such dramatic interplay in the courts and executive regulatory bodies (such as the NLRB) demonstrates the vulnerability of sovereignty claims and the limits to tribal governing powers.

Many American Indian communities, including the leadership of the National Congress of American Indians (NCAI), joined Congressman Hayworth in denouncing the labor board's decision. Joe Garcia, NCAI president and governor of Ohkay Owingeh (San Juan) Pueblo, registered his support for HR 16 "solely because it confirms the sovereign governmental right of Indian tribes to make and live by their own labor policies based on the economic and social conditions existing on their lands."[61] He reminded the congressmen that a recent federal district court ruling involving his community affirmed those rights. This case, *NLRB v. Pueblo of San Juan*, established that the tribe did have the authority to enact a "right to work" ordinance, a measure enacted by the tribal government to protect itself from disruptive union activity such as strikes and to enforce Indian hiring preference.[62]

Garcia and others expressed concern that unions might exercise undue outside influence on tribal governing authority and threaten to control access to jobs in companies doing business on reservation land. From 1971 through 1996, for example, the Duke City Lumber Company operated a mill on land it leased from the San Juan Pueblo. The operation was a union shop, requiring all employees to become members of the Western Council of Industrial Workers. When Duke City sold its operation to the Idaho Timber Company, the tribe renegotiated its lease to stipulate that the company give preference to San Juan Pueblo members in hiring and refrain from entering into collective bargaining agreements. Soon the union filed an unfair labor practice with the NLRB. The tribe responded by passing Labor Organization Ordinance No. 96-63, a measure that prohibits union shops in businesses operating on reservation land. Upheld by the US 10th Circuit Court of Appeals, this "right to work" ordinance extends beyond the lumber mill or other non-Indian companies doing business at Ohkay Owingeh.[63]

Current labor law and new congressional initiatives seem to leave organized labor and tribal governments locked in an adversarial relationship. As a result, reservation workers are caught in a devastating conundrum. Under the latest NLRB ruling, they now enjoy the rights of other American workers: to form unions, to negotiate collective bargaining agreements, and to engage in collective actions—to strike—in order to gain concessions from their employers. They may also look to the NLRB for relief against unfair labor practices. But what price do they pay for this protection? Does the *San Manuel* ruling undermine the power of the workers' tribal governments? Or if more tribes develop "right to work" ordinances, will Native workers lose their rights as workers in the name of sovereignty? What about the fate of non-Indian workers employed in gaming establishments? Do their labor rights vanish when they venture onto reservation land? How does the experience of American Indian workers compare with that of other workers in the United States? How does their struggle for sovereignty, as well as their specific history as colonized peoples, set them apart?

These issues have complicated American Indians' involvement in unions since at least the 1930s. In an ambivalent relationship at best, Native workers and unions have struggled on many fronts to address significant cultural, political, and economic issues. American Indians have had to assert their collective needs as "workers" and "Indians" within a changing political landscape, one that often found unions at odds with emerging tribal governments. In the post-termination era, tribal governments tried to assert their sovereignty by rescinding federal labor law and resisting the lingering paternalism of the Bureau of Indian Affairs. As some Native labor activists discovered, fighting for sovereignty does not always translate into better working conditions. But American Indian workers have persisted. Navajo workers such as Kenneth White gained accommodations from employers, unions, and leaders and convinced the tribal government to create the Office of Navajo Labor Relations. Other Native workers White inspired, such as Conrad Edwards (figure 7.2) and other tribal employment rights activists, created Tribal Employment Rights offices throughout Indian Country, initiatives that encouraged tribes to craft their own labor laws and institutionalized workers' rights.[64]

The story of this movement raises important questions about the role of Native workers in post-termination sovereignty struggles. Certainly, economic issues, including those related to energy development, have been central to American Indian communities' sovereignty goals.[65] Many of the energy-rich tribes, such as the Navajo, the Blackfeet, and the Three Affiliated Tribes at Fort Berthold in North Dakota, asserted control over the development and regulation of their coal and oil reserves and struggled to improve the notoriously low royalty rates negotiated by the Bureau of Indian Affairs.[66] Examining this history in light of more contemporary conflicts between unions and tribal governments, their battles in the federal courts, and the grassroots campaigns initiated by Native workers reveals that the struggle toward sovereignty is a complex, multilayered journey. Sovereign nations did not result simply from a battle among federal,

FIGURE 7.2
Conrad Edwards, president of CTER, and Daniel Press, counsel for CTER, in 2007. Photo by Colleen O'Neill.

state, and tribal governments. Neither is the workers' contribution to this struggle for sovereignty merely a fight between tribal governments and unions. Decolonization involves all these parties, many of whom are locked in conflict over the power to regulate work and jobs on reservation land. The stories of Native workers asserting their rights with their unions, their employers, and federal officials compose a much more complicated history, one that acknowledges differences between and among Native communities.

Acknowledgments

Thanks to Ona Siporin, Lawrence Culver, Jennifer Duncan, David Kamper, Alexandra Harmon, and members of the Indians and Energy Symposium for their comments and research help on early versions of this chapter. Also, thanks to the Mountain West Center for Regional Studies at Utah State University for the faculty fellowship that supported my research on this project and to the Wenner Gren Foundation for Anthropological Research for funding the symposium "Indians, Labor, and Capitalist Culture: A Colloquium of Historians, Ethnohistorians, and Anthropologists," at the Newberry Library, during which ideas for this chapter started to take shape. And, most important, I would like to thank Kenneth White and the other activists who agreed to be interviewed for this chapter: Daniel Press, John Navarro, Conrad Edwards, Larry Ketcher, and Rodney "Fish" Gervais.

Notes

1. Coal and other types of mining and large-scale energy development projects provided Native workers with jobs off the reservation as well. Navajos migrated to the coal mines in Colorado for work as early as the 1920s. Yaqui and Apache men worked in the copper mines in southern Arizona (see Meeks 2007; O'Neill 2005; Rogge et al. 1995:143–149).

2. See Brugge, Benally, and Yazzie-Lewis 2007; Dawson 1992; Eichstaedt 1994; Ishiyama 2003; Lewis 2007; Brenda Norre, "Energy Genocide, Backlash Yield New Peoples' Movement in the Americas," *Indian Country Today*, July 24, 2006.

3. For a more in-depth discussion of American Indian history and colonialism, see O'Neill 2005:142–160; for the connection between colonialism and energy resource extraction, see Churchill and LaDuke 1992.

4. Littlefield and Knack 1996; O'Neill 2005.

5. Author interview with Rodney "Fish" Gervais, December 6, 2007 (tape and transcript in author's possession).

6. John McGill, "BBC Conference to Focus on Discrimination and Racial Profiling," *Glacier Reporter*, May 19, 2004, www.goldentrianglenews.com/articles/2004/05/19/glacier_reporter/news/news5.prt (accessed September 2006).

7. *Diné be'iiná náhiilna' bee agha'diit'aahii* means "attorneys who work for the revitalization of the people." See Iverson 2002a:238; DNA-People's Legal Services Web site, http://www.dnalegalservices.org/co.html (accessed March 2009).

8. O'Neill 2005:138.

9. Dan Press, interview with Sylvia Danovitch, History of the EEOC Oral History Project, May 26, 1994, p. 2 (edited transcript in author's possession).

10. Author interview with Dan Press, June 18, 2007 (tape and transcript in author's possession).

11. The Gallup Supply Warehouse stored supplies for distribution to BIA facilities on reservations in the Gallup area, such as Navajo and Zuni (see note 10; *ABC—Americans before Columbus, Newsletter of the National Indian Youth Council*, April–July 1970 [my thanks to Sterling Fluharty for bringing this source to my attention]; Shreve 2007; see also Fluharty 2003).

12. "Testimony of Gerald Wilkinson and Bill Pensoneau of the National Indian Youth Council before the National Council on Indian Opportunity, January 8, 1970,"

ABC—Americans before Columbus, Newsletter of the National Indian Youth Council, December 1969–January 1970.

13. James Hena, assistant to the Commissioner of Indian Affairs, to the Commissioner of Indian Affairs, August 7, 1970. National Archives I, Record Group 75, Bureau of Indian Affairs, Records of the Office of the Commissioner of Indian Affairs, Office Files of Commissioner Louis R. Bruce, 1969–1972, Entry #180-V, Box 11, Folder—Field Trips.

14. See note 10.

15. See note 10.

16. See note 9.

17. See note 10.

18. Robbins 1975:10.

19. See note 10.

20. Novak 1990; Prucha 1976:70.

21. Iverson 2002a; Novak 1990:642.

22. Hosmer 2004:294; Novak 1990:651. Also see the emerging historical literature that shows American Indians using wage work (in addition to working for the BIA) to sustain their cultures, instead of simply assimilating the values and behavior of the dominant society (Bauer 2006; Hosmer 1999; Littlefield and Knack 1996; Meeks 2003; O'Neill 2005; Raibmon 2005).

23. Unidentified Crow spokesman, quoted in Rzeczkowski 2003:260. Rzeczkowski points out that in 1895 another Crow leader, Cold Wind, was also concerned that non-Crow Indians would take their jobs.

24. In 1973 non-Indian BIA employees filed a class action lawsuit in the US District Court in New Mexico, charging that the Equal Employment Opportunities Act of 1972 nullified provisions that protected Indian preference in title VII of the 1964 Civil Rights Act. The legality of Indian preference was settled the following year by the US Supreme Court in *Morton v. Mancari.* In that landmark case, the court found that hiring preferences were specifically protected: "The purpose of these preferences, as variously expressed in the legislative history, has been to give Indians a greater participation in their own self-government; to further the Government's trust obligation toward the Indian tribes; and to reduce the negative effect of having non-Indians administer matters that affect Indian tribal life" (*Morton v. Mancari,* 417 US 535 [1974]). Legal scholars have interpreted this ruling as a precedent for viewing "Indian" as a political, instead of racial, category (Baca 2005:975).

25. See note 9.

26. *ACKCO* is spelled with the initials of this consulting firm's founders.

27. Press 1976; see Dan Press, interview with Sylvia Danovitch, History of the

EEOC Oral History Project, May 26, 1994, p. 7 (edited transcript in author's possession).

28. Kenneth White, keynote speech delivered at the first Indian Employment Rights Conference, Warm Springs, OR, April 1977; Press 1979:B-1.

29. White (see note 28).

30. CETA, the Comprehensive Employment and Training Act, was a federal program that funded various employment programs throughout the country for "disadvantaged" populations. John Navarro and Conrad Edwards went on to create the Council for Tribal Employment Rights (CTER). Navarro served as its president until 2007, when he retired and Conrad Edwards took over his responsibilities (see figures 7.1 and 7.2, respectively).

31. Author interview with Conrad Edwards, president, and John Navarro, founding president, Council for Tribal Employment Rights, December 6, 2007 (tape and transcript in author's possession).

32. Ibid.

33. See note 9.

34. See note 5.

35. See note 9.

36. See note 31.

37. Ibid.

38. Ibid.

39. "From One to 100: A Decade of TERO," *Sho-Ban News*, January 29, 1987.

40. See note 31.

41. See note 5. Also see "Civil Rights in Indian Country," http://www.indiancivilrights.org/ (accessed March 2008).

42. "TERO Promotes Tribal Self-Sufficiency," *Sho-Ban News*, September 3, 1987.

43. Quoted in John Kozlowicz, "TERO Celebrates 25 Years," *Hocak Worak, Newsletter of the Ho-Chunk Nation*, July 10, 2002, http://www.hocakworak.com/archive/2002/WL%202002%2007-10/HW-020710-02.htm (accessed March 2008).

44. "From One to 100: A Decade of TERO," *Sho-Ban News*, January 29, 1987.

45. Author interview with Kenneth White, April 4, 2003 (tape and transcript in author's possession).

46. Testimony of Thomas H. Brose, Hearing before the United States Commission on Civil Rights, Window Rock, AZ, October 22–24, 1973, vol. 1: Testimony (Washington, DC: Government Printing Office, 1973), 125.

47. Joe Shirley's appointment of Lawrence Oliver, former president of the United Mine Workers local in Window Rock and chairman of Naalnishí (the Navajo Labor Federation), to head the Division of Human Resources is indicative of the growing strength of organized labor in the Navajo Nation.

48. Presentation by representatives of Laborers International at the Council for Tribal Employment Rights 2006 Tribal Employment Law and Indian Preference Legal Update Conference, Las Vegas, NV, December 6–8.

49. For a detailed examination of CERT's beginnings and its critics, see Ambler 1990:73–117. Also see essays by Lynn Robbins, Winona LaDuke, and Marjane Ambler in Jorgensen 1984b; Fixico 1998.

50. Once established, TERO offices quickly became institutionalized within tribal governments.

51. See note 31. Also see the ANA Web site for more information about the scope of the program: http://www.acf.hhs.gov/programs/ana/about/about.html#mission (accessed July 2008).

52. A. Philip Randolph, president of the Brotherhood of Sleeping Car Porters, and Cesar Chavez, president of the United Farm Workers Union, were also important civil rights leaders.

53. Statement of Congressman J. D. Hayworth, Testimony on HR 16, Tribal Labor Relations Restoration Act of 2005, US House of Representatives, Committee on Education and the Workforce, Subcommittee on Employer–Employee Relations, Hearings, July 18, 2006, http://www.house.gov/ed_workforce/hearings/109th/eer/hr16/hayworth.htm (accessed August 2006).

54. *San Manuel Indian Bingo and Casino*, 341 NLRB 1055 (2004).

55. David Wilkins and K. Tsianina Lomawaima (2001:8) argue that "tribal rights are based in the doctrine of inherent sovereignty," as established through treaties, congressional action, and constitutional and federal case law that dates back to the early republic. It seems unlikely that Hayworth (see note 53) is referring to the same doctrine.

56. O'Neill 2005:120–121.

57. HR 16 is not J. D. Hayworth's first attempt at shielding Native communities from federal labor law. In October 1999 he introduced a bill, HR 2992, that would amend the Indian Gaming and Regulatory Act, exempting what he called "coerced labor agreements" in tribal/state gaming pacts. In 2001 he reintroduced this legislation as the Tribal Sovereignty Protection Act, renumbered as HR 103. Hayworth, whom the Center for Responsive Politics has listed as the second-highest recipient of individual campaign contributions from Jack Abramoff, lost his reelection bid in November 2006. With casino interests significantly featured on his list of financial backers, Hayworth was one of the few legislators refusing to return what many of his critics viewed as money tainted by its connection with the notorious lobbyist (Capital Eye: A Money-in-Politics Newsletter for the Center for Responsive Politics, http://www.capitaleye.org/abramoff_recips_full.asp [accessed August 2006]; "Hayworth Will Keep Tribal Gifts," *Arizona Republic*, December 23, 2005). It remains to be seen whether other

legislators will pick up where Hayworth left off and pursue a legislative override of *San Manuel*.

58. Sovereignty, as a legal doctrine, is quite complicated, based on tangled and competing jurisdictional conflicts involving federal, state, and tribal law (as well as executive order, congressional statute, and judicial ruling). The meaning of the term *sovereignty* has changed considerably over time, dependent on the shifting "uneven ground" of federal Indian policy. Here, I use the term more broadly, as a set of collective cultural, political, and economic rights central to decolonization and nation building. See Deloria and Lytle 1984; Mason 2000; Wilkins 1997; Wilkins and Lomawaima 2001:11–13.

59. *Simplot Company*, 107 NLRB 1211 (1954); *NLRB v. Pueblo of San Juan*, 276 F.3d 1186 (10th Cir. 2002). By the 1970s the anti-union climate had shifted on the Navajo reservation. In 1973 Thomas Brose, director of the Office of Navajo Labor Relations, explained that his staff rarely enforced the Navajo right-to-work law (O'Neill 2005:120–121, 132).

60. Press 1979:67. This is a manual prepared under a subcontract with ACKCO, Inc., pursuant to Contract #95-076, jointly funded and administered by the Administration on Native Americans and the Equal Employment Opportunity Commission. It can be found in the University of Idaho and University of New Mexico law libraries; see *Fort Apache Timber Company*, 226 NLRB 503 (1976); *Devil's Lake Sioux Manufacturing Corporation*, 243 NLRB 163 (1979); *Southern Indian Health Council*, 290 NLRB 436 (1988); *Sac & Fox Industries*, 307 NLRB 241 (1992); *San Manuel Indian Bingo and Casino*, 314 NLRB 138 (2004).

61. Statement of Joe Garcia, Testimony on HR 16, Tribal Labor Relations Restoration Act of 2005, US House of Representatives, Committee on Education and the Workforce, Subcommittee on Employer–Employee Relations, Hearings, July 18, 2006, http://www.house.gov/ed_workforce/hearings/109th/eer/hr16/hayworth.htm (accessed August 2006); see also Congressional Clarification of Treatment of Indian Tribes as Governments for Purpose of the National Labor Relations Act, The National Congress of American Indians, Resolution #MOH-04-028, http://www.ncai.org/ncai/data/resolution/midyear2004/04-28.pdf (accessed August 2006); *NLRB v. Pueblo of San Juan*, 276 F.3d 1186 (10th Cir. 2002) (en banc).

62. Garcia Testimony (see note 61).

63. The Indian gaming and tourist industry, in particular, is a growing battleground for unions such as the Hotel Employees and Restaurant Employees International Union (HERE), which has enjoyed measured success organizing workers in California. But the union's future remains murky because its legal battles are far from over. California's Indian Gaming Pact includes the Tribal Labor Relations

Ordinance, which allows for unions, but the pact prohibits picketing and restricts strikes (Erica Werner, "Indian Tribes Fight for Exemption from Federal Labor," *San Francisco Chronicle*, September 3, 2006, http://www.sfgate.com/cgi-bin/article.cgi?f=/n/a/2006/09/03/state/n084241D38.DTL&hw=San+Manuel&sn=001&sc=1000 [accessed September 2006]).

64. This is not to say that the Navajo Nation government is unabashedly pro-union. The tribal government's position on organized labor (like that of other governments) varies with the particular political climate. Recent organizing campaigns reveal tensions between tribal leaders and Navajo labor activists (see Kamper 2003). With the status of coal mining on the reservation in flux, United Mine Workers of America (UMWA) members sometimes find themselves in conflict with Navajo environmentalists (Jim Maniaci, "Black Mesa Worker Graymouth: Enviros Not Real Grassroots People," *Gallup Independent*, June 17, 2005, http://www.gallupindependent.com/2005/june/061705enviros.html [accessed September 2006]).

65. I am using the term *movement* here because those who created TERO offices did so with an activist strategy and passion. I observed members of the Council for Tribal Employment Rights use the term at their Legal Update meetings in Las Vegas, December 6–8, 2006, and December 5–7, 2007.

66. Ambler 1984:195; "Court Opens Window for Navajo Nation Trust Suit," October 27, 2003, http://www.indianz.com/News/archives/002205.asp (accessed March 2008); Barry Meier, "Navajo Lawsuits Contend US Government Failed the Tribe in Mining Royalty Deals," *New York Times*, July 18, 1999.

APPENDIX

Acronyms

ACKCO–American Indian Professional Services (founders' initials)
BIA–Bureau of Indian Affairs
CERT–Council of Energy Resource Tribes
CETA–Comprehensive Employment and Training Act
CTER–Council for Tribal Employment Rights
DNA–Diné be'iiná náhiilna' bee agha'diit'aahii
EEOC–Equal Employment Opportunity Commission
HUD–Department of Housing and Urban Development
NCAI–National Council of American Indians
NIYC–National Indian Youth Council
NLRA–National Labor Relations Act
NLRB–National Labor Relations Board
ONLR–Office of Navajo Labor Relations
TERO–Tribal Employment Rights Ordinance

8

"An Absolute Paragon of Paradoxes"

Native American Power and the Electrification of Arizona's Indian Reservations

Leah S. Glaser

In the year 2000, amidst California's energy crisis, Enron's spectacular collapse, and deregulation across the electrical industry, the US Department of Energy sponsored a report, far less publicized, revealing gross violations of democratic equality and distributive justice.[1] More than 14 percent of American Indian households located on reservations lacked electricity, compared with less than 1.5 percent of non-Indian Americans. Indians paid the highest electrical rates in proportion to their income and consumed the least amount of energy per household. The report revealed that Arizona's tribes experienced the greatest problems accessing electricity, even though hydroelectric dams, coal deposits, oil, and uranium mines made those reservations the centers of power production for the greater Southwest. Such startling statistics expose the colonial and elite power structures through which outside energy developers have historically victimized and exploited Native people, socially, environmentally, and economically.[2]

These statistics also mask the opportunities Indian people have sought, the actions they have taken, and the sovereignty tribes have exercised in accessing regional distribution systems to bring electricity to the reservation for domestic and industrial uses. Federal programs and assimilation

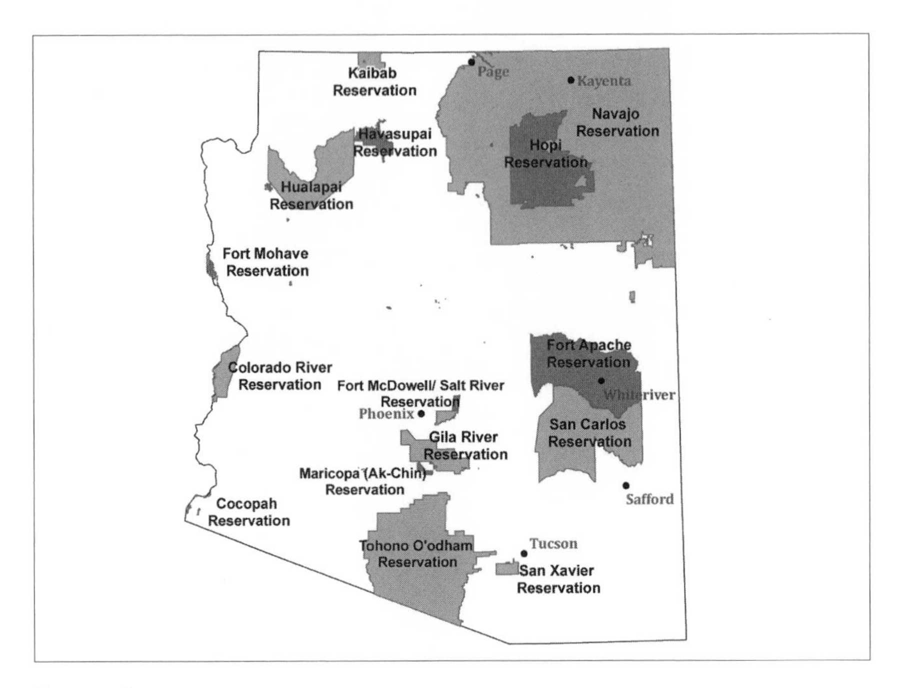

FIGURE 8.1A

Selected Native American tribes in Arizona. Map by Tracy DeGrazia.

policies in the twentieth century conditioned Indians to become consumers of electricity, as well as hosts for its production. After World War II, intensive resource development on tribal lands presented Indians with choices that seemed to create a "paragon of paradoxes": maintaining Indian identity and community by incorporating electrical technology into traditions, cultures, economies, and daily life.[3] Indians asserted their rights to join regional power grids and engage electricity as a vehicle for negotiating such decisions.

THE INDIAN AGENCY AS ELECTRICAL UTILITY

Indians living on certain reservations encountered electricity before many non-Indian rural people. Western Indian reservations were some of the earliest electrified rural areas in the country because of the Bureau of Indian Affairs (BIA), then called the Office of Indian Affairs. From the Civil War through World War I, non-Indian settlement in the West and the growth of government agencies and schools on reservations coincided with large-scale electrical generation and new long-distance transmission technologies. By World War II, the BIA's primary electric systems in Arizona

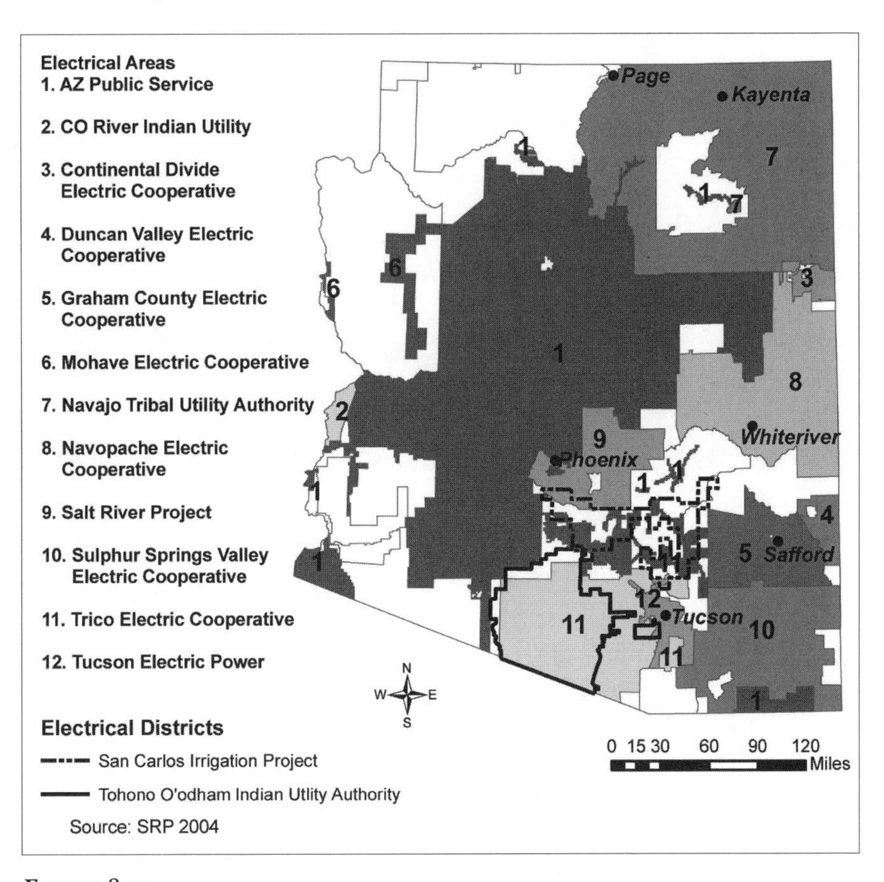

FIGURE 8.1B

Map showing electrical service areas in Arizona. Map by Tracy DeGrazia.

operated on the Fort Apache, San Carlos, Tohono O'Odham (then known as Papago), and Navajo reservations (figure 8.1a). In fact, Indian agencies often operated a region's largest and fastest-growing electric utilities, although they restricted service to their own buildings and employees. As the agencies' duties expanded, electrical power emerged as a tool for accomplishing their goal to assimilate American Indians culturally and economically (figure 8.1b).

The BIA office on the Fort Apache reservation exemplified the amount of electricity these agencies consumed. As early as 1903, a hydropower plant on the White River furnished the town of Whiteriver (figure 8.2) with lighting and pumping exclusively for agency use. Less than a decade later, the Whiteriver Indian Agency was requesting a larger plant to meet its needs. Agency superintendent Charles L. Davis claimed, "[Electrical] service for

FIGURE 8.2

Whiteriver Indian Agency, circa 1937. Courtesy of Nohwike' Bagowa, the White Mountain Apache Cultural Center and Museum, White Mountain Apache Tribe, Arizona. Photo by Wayne Truman Pratt.

the school and Agency will enter into almost every activity here," and he requested more power, beyond the agency's own domestic and irrigation pumping needs, to support the government's policies of assimilating Indians through farming.[4]

Consistent with the ideology of Progressive-era reformers, BIA administrators and engineers of the early twentieth century placed great faith in technology to solve the myriad industrial age problems, as well as to achieve the goals of assimilating Indians expressed through legislation such as the Dawes Allotment Act of 1887.[5] Invoking the values of Thomas Jefferson's agrarian ideal, reformers and, later, federal policy advocated permanent agricultural settlement as the only way in "which the civilization of the Apache [could] be accomplished." Electrical pumps would efficiently extract minerals and groundwater sources, even in arid Arizona. Irrigation would provide a steady livelihood and, to some extent, honor Native water rights. Justifying the agency's request for more power, one engineer explained, "The proposed plant...is one of the principal spokes in the great wheel of development and progress."[6]

The BIA's education of Indian children at boarding schools complemented its irrigation efforts in encouraging assimilation. Congress decommissioned Fort Apache as a military installation in 1922 and opened the Theodore Roosevelt Boarding School (figure 8.3). A boarding school in Whiteriver already had 265 Apache students, and the buildings and dormitories on the

Figure 8.3

Schoolboys at Theodore Roosevelt Boarding School at Fort Apache, Fort Apache reservation, with electrical power lines in the background, circa 1937. Courtesy of Nohwike' Bagowa, the White Mountain Apache Cultural Center and Museum, White Mountain Apache Tribe, Arizona. Photo by Wayne Truman Pratt.

Theodore Roosevelt campus at Fort Apache accommodated another 250 students, primarily Navajo. The new facilities dramatically increased the BIA's domestic power needs. In addition to a diesel plant, the new, education-centered Fort Apache community comprised administrative buildings, teachers' cottages, a laundry house, a blacksmith and carpenter shop, three trader's stores, a post office, a flour mill, an ice plant, a hospital, and storehouses.[7]

Boarding schools such as Theodore Roosevelt trained students to use the amenities of the industrial age. The curriculum promoted electrical consumption in accordance with Victorian-era gender roles. For example, the domestic work that home economics programs prescribed for Indian girls included using electrical appliances at home or "in the homes of others." Educators expected a female graduate to keep a house possessing the wooden floors, running water, modern kitchen appliances, and electrical lighting to which she had become accustomed. Social workers boasted that Indian households with schoolchildren were far cleaner and more orderly than those without.[8] Fort Apache's agency superintendent, William Donner, frustrated by what he interpreted as poor sanitation, even requested a field matron to come to the reservation and teach the management of a modern, industrial-era household to White Mountain Apache women as part of this program.[9]

Donner's ambitions for domestic use tripled Fort Apache's power requirements over the next decade. To achieve his goals, he consolidated the BIA's facilities to reduce costs, updated the electrical system, and ran a transmission line to the boarding school. Electrical operations resembled those of a small town utility throughout the 1920s and 1930s.[10] BIA employees and their families liberally consumed power for lighting, laundry, and cooking. Janet Lynn Wilson, the daughter of a Fort Apache Indian agent, claimed that electrical appliances filled her household.[11] The agency system struggled to accommodate personnel demands for refrigerators, washing machines, and irons. Another hydroelectric plant supplied the power to pump water to farmland, lawns, and gardens. Agency plants also delivered power to the area's sawmill, schools, hospitals, and local Christian missions. Exasperated and overwhelmed, Donner proclaimed, "It is a constant fight to hold down the current with no restrictions" on employee use of electricity.[12]

Because the load (the demand on a system's use) surpassed the agency's power capabilities, administrators continued to search for ways to conserve power throughout the 1930s and 1940s (figure 8.4). Plant operators restricted pumping to nighttime, when use tended to fall, and began charging the local missions a minimal rate. In at least one cost-saving decision, the superintendent considered the welfare of the reservation's Indian population. When someone raised the possibility of cutting off power to the independently owned, often non-Indian, stores, Donner objected to the adverse impact it would have on Indian customers.[13]

The BIA's Navajo Agency faced similar electrification challenges, further complicated by changes in federal Indian administration in the 1930s

Figure 8.4

Whiteriver Indian Agency office building, circa 1944. Courtesy of Cline Library, Northern Arizona University, Flagstaff. Photo by Tad Nichols.

(as exemplified by the Indian Reorganization Act; see Voggesser's chapter 4, this volume).[14] Under the new commissioner of Indian affairs, John Collier, the BIA consolidated five agencies that served fifty thousand Navajos living on more than 25,000 square miles of the reservation into one "capital" at Window Rock.[15] The restructuring required a new administration building, a council house, a power plant, a school, a warehouse, a machine shop and garage, a dispensary, employee quarters, and two community washhouses. One building superintendent boasted, "These buildings are of permanent type of construction conveniently arranged and equipped with modern conveniences," including electrical equipment.[16] A concrete building housed the diesel generator, and underground tunnels distributed electrical lines.

Employees compared the agency's electrical operations to the successful New Deal project that delivered affordable power and water to the depressed South. Building superintendent R. J. Tolson commented, "We do not operate exactly as the Tennessee Valley Authority, but under our new construction program, we are in hopes of developing much cheaper utilities."[17] With electrical demand exceeding supply, the new centralized Navajo Agency searched for ways to lower system costs. Area churches, stores, and trading posts could purchase electrical service from the closest Indian agency if they supplied a meter, equipment, and a service line. The

BIA, however, could (and sometimes did) refuse or negotiate service. When the Tuba City power plant overloaded, Navajo Daisy Albert accused agents of favoritism when they refused to deliver power to her father, Charlie Talawejei. Those same agents often leveraged the coveted service to promote the agency's assimilation goals. One official agreed to furnish free utilities to a public school in Shiprock, New Mexico, but only if the school admitted Indian children.[18]

Meanwhile, John Collier's new day school system promised the construction of several more modern facilities across reservations. A 1928 critique of the government's boarding school policy recommended bringing students back home to their communities for their education. Known as the Meriam Report, it did not specifically mention electricity but did inspire policy changes that would have long-term effects on electrification.[19] Collier promoted installation of diesel engines at the new schools as essential to children's health and training for the industrial world. In 1947 one unidentified Navajo agent agreed, in his report on the reservation's conditions: "[BIA schools] must be so designed and operated as to condition children to want better living, to want to go where resources and jobs are sufficient for decent living, and to be able to succeed by virtue of the training." He continued, "Much of this training must be a conditioning to modern living. This cannot be done in barracks or in dismal structures. It cannot be done in schools that are not equal to modern schools anywhere."[20] Classrooms, dormitories, and kitchens required heat, light, power, water, sewers, and garbage collection in order to operate. Furthermore, government officials believed that a reliable electric system ensured "the health and safety of Indian school children and Bureau personnel" by providing them with "comfortable living conditions."[21] Inspectors repeatedly recommended electric plants as safer and more efficient than wood, oil, or gas for heating and lighting.[22]

Several factors undermined the effectiveness of an industrial education. Some Indians resisted the schools' assimilative efforts by maintaining traditional practices in their home.[23] Most lived in scattered rural settlements and lacked access to electrical systems. Arizona's first high-voltage, long-distance transmission lines ran to populated agricultural and mining communities, delivering the electricity needed to produce two of the state's most valuable economic resources: cotton and copper. The rivers located near many reservations offered obvious opportunities to generate hydroelectric power, but neither the government nor private utility managers viewed Indian lands as desirable places to develop energy or Indian residents as electrical consumers. Instead, non-Indian economic goals consistently received preference in power delivery, even when federal reclamation activities challenged the Indian agency's monopoly on Arizona's power generation.[24]

POWER THROUGH RECLAMATION

Instead of the BIA, another federal agency offered an opportunity for Indians to access electrical service, through hydroelectric dams. On June 17, 1902, as BIA generators hummed and agency superintendents scrambled to meet power demands, Congress passed the National Reclamation Act to "reclaim" or irrigate arid western lands for farming through large water-storage projects constructed and funded by the government (see Colombi's chapter 5, this volume). The non-Indian farmers of the Salt River Valley Water Users' Association (SRVWUA) in central Arizona were among the first recipients of federal reclamation loans.[25] SRVWUA proposed the Salt River Project (SRP) to irrigate the desert valley by harnessing the Salt River behind a dam located 60 miles east of Phoenix in the Tonto Basin of the Superstition Mountains. After constructing a temporary power plant, federal engineers realized the site's enormous potential for hydroelectric power generation. Electricity could further irrigation goals by pumping groundwater. Commercial sales could help fund the dam's construction. Through an interagency contract, SRP might even fulfill some of the government's tribal trust responsibilities regarding water rights and agricultural development, by running a power line to a BIA-operated pumping plant to irrigate 10,000 acres of Pima Indian lands on the Gila River reservation at Sacaton. SRP entered into a non-irrigation power contract with the Sacaton Indian School, but costs, legal challenges over the merits of the Sacaton contract, fairness to the Pimas, and feasibility issues convinced Congress, instead, to address Pima water rights through the San Carlos Irrigation Project (SCIP), a landmark reclamation project operated by the Indian Irrigation Service.[26]

Approved by Congress in 1924, SCIP reinforced the BIA's role as a utility by authorizing the construction of Coolidge Dam to provide water to the Pima Indians on the Gila River reservation. Arguments over feasibility convinced federal officials to include a non-Indian irrigation district known as the San Carlos Irrigation and Drainage District (SCIDD) within SCIP's delivery scope. Thus, the enterprise would irrigate 100,000 acres of land equally divided between Indians and whites. But engineers found that a site on the San Carlos Apache reservation had the best foundation for the type of dam they had planned. When Congress authorized the development of hydropower at Coolidge in March 1928, reformer and future BIA commissioner John Collier advocated that the San Carlos Apaches receive power and proceeds from reservation power sites to offset the dam's flooding of four hundred Apache gravesites, roads, pumping plants, BIA buildings, and several Apache homes. The Federal Power Commission ruled that selling power to the tribe at a discounted rate served as adequate reimbursement. A single transmission line from the dam delivered only to the BIA agency at Rice, SCIP's primary power beneficiary on the San Carlos Apache reservation.[27]

Having complained about dangerous kerosene lamps for years, the San Carlos Agency eventually became heavily dependent upon SCIP electricity for its water, laundry equipment, kitchen and bakery equipment, hospital equipment, and entire lighting system. In the middle of the Great Depression, Superintendent James Kitch begged for a backup power plant for lighting, refrigeration, cooling and heating units, cooking, and irrigation pumping. A decade later, his successor, Ernest McCray, wrote, "There is scarcely a single building which does not require more power in addition to its lighting needs."[28] Nearby non-Indian towns such as Dudleyville also became SCIP power customers, but the BIA was often reluctant to serve any homes or communities that even private utility companies considered too remote to be cost effective. Few individual Apaches could take advantage of SCIP's hydropower, save those who relocated near the agency at Rice after the dam flooded their homes. Even then, the power failed to pump an adequate water supply for successful irrigation farming.[29]

RURAL INDIANS TAP RURAL ELECTRIFICATION

The Great Depression and a New Deal program aimed at non-Indian rural Americans living too far from power lines provided alternatives for reservations to access electrical distribution lines. When Congress passed the Rural Electrification Act in 1935, Indians were by no means its target beneficiaries. The legislation grew out of the Progressives' faith in technology as a social equalizer, as well as years of political battles about who—private enterprise or the public—should control electricity. Several tribes were ideally positioned, physically and politically, to benefit. Even when private utilities did serve rural areas, they delivered only to the most lucrative customers, that is, large population centers or irrigation districts.[30] Through the Rural Electrification Administration (REA), the government now lent money to local, rural organizations to build their own electrical delivery systems for their communities.

SRVWUA and SCIDD, non-Indian irrigation associations tied to Bureau of Reclamation and BIA projects (SRP and SCIP, respectively), wasted little time in applying for REA loans. The applications created jurisdictional tension between the agencies over the issue of funding electrical service to non-Indian and Indian constituencies. SCIDD hoped to expand irrigation pumping and domestic use but grew tired of waiting for the BIA's Indian Irrigation Service to provide electricity through SCIP.[31] Reclamation-sponsored SRVWUA worried that an extension of rural electric lines would allow the BIA to infringe upon its power markets with lower rates.[32] Arizona congresswoman Isabella Greenway introduced legislation in 1936 allowing SCIDD to borrow REA funds even though it fell within a BIA-operated project. Congress also approved a $145,000 REA loan to build 124 miles of distribution lines to almost five hundred farmers, including a hundred Pima Indians living on the Gila River reservation at Sacaton. The San Carlos Apaches, on whose land Coolidge Dam was located, turned to another REA project, unaffiliated with either the BIA or Bureau of Reclamation, to gain access to electricity.[33]

In 1943 the San Carlos Agency requested power from the REA-funded Sulphur Springs Valley Electrical Cooperative for its day school at Bylas (located 30 miles east of Coolidge Dam). The school superintendent indicated that many of the 750 Indians living nearby also desired service. Eventually, the newly formed Graham County Electric Cooperative (GCEC), hoping to build electrical use for its own system's sustainability, extended domestic service to them. GCEC's REA-sponsored survey reported that the Indian "cottage owners" intended to use electricity for purposes identical to non-Indians': lighting, a radio, an iron, a refrigerator, a washing machine.[34] By the 1950s, GCEC had constructed lines across the reservation to serve the trading posts and homes but, over time, could not accommodate the reservation's growing power needs.[35]

Most REA money targeted non-Indian farming associations engaged in agribusiness, but REA-funded electric cooperatives at least partially served many of the state's reservations, such as the San Carlos Apache. State agencies, such as the Arizona Corporation Commission, did not regulate the rates of government-owned utilities, so the REA was often a better deal than the BIA for an Indian consumer living within a cooperative's service area. Cursory studies have shown that because the REA's stated goal was total "area coverage," the REA often encouraged the inclusion of Indian reservations within proposed system boundaries, especially where it was economically feasible or necessary for building a viable system.[36] Over the years, REA service areas eventually encompassed portions of several reservations, including those of the Hualapai, Havasupai, Papago (Tohono O'odham), and Navajo.[37] REA appraisers credited education, relocation programs, and military service for introducing Indians to urban life and increasing their desire and demand for electrical service. The numbers of potential electrical consumers grew as more people moved into government housing concentrated around large population centers such as Bylas, allowing easier access to central power.[38] In the case of White Mountain Apache reservation, the local REA cooperative found Indian consumers not only desirable but also essential to system feasibility.

Before World War II, the REA rejected most of the loan requests from non-Indian communities in the White Mountains that it considered too small and financially infeasible.[39] Because the White Mountains counties encompassed Indian reservations, they were the poorest in the region. Barely half of the population could afford electrical power for normal household requirements. The number of farms increased throughout the 1940s, but their average size shrunk, a phenomenon that suggested an unstable agricultural economy. Almost 70 percent of farm operators were Indians, but their property was valued at a fraction of others in the state. Indian families maintained small 3-to-5-acre farms or gardens consisting of only a few crops.[40] In addition to the poor financial situation, large federal landholdings such as those of the Apache National Forest and the Fort Apache reservation, as well as the few railroad and highway systems, dictated sporadic settlement patterns. Low population density further hindered the economical construction of electrical systems.[41]

World War II home front activity brought economic changes that greatly improved the area's transportation infrastructure and potential rights-of-way for power lines. Incomes rose. Industrial and recreational development promised a stable, year-round power demand. REA organizers anticipated significantly more new homes, cottages, and resorts within and around the Apache National Forest. The promise of electricity encouraged the non-Indian towns of Lakeside and Woodruff to plan elaborate new churches, and Pinetop hoped to build an American Legion headquarters. The Apache village of Canyon Day anticipated future water systems and hoped to use electricity for pumping them.[42] All these factors suggested that the White Mountains could generate a large enough electrical load to construct an economically feasible system.

The failure of the region's previous applications indicated that a large and inclusive electric system would be critical to proving system feasibility and obtaining a loan. In 1946, organizers incorporated the Navopache Electric Cooperative (a name combining two counties, Navajo and Apache) to reflect a geographic scope that defied political boundaries. After the REA approved the application, Navopache began to build a regional power grid through line construction and system acquisition. But system reliability hinged on power generation. To supplement the small power plant in Lakeside, organizers eyed the large generators located on the Fort Apache reservation as valuable components in the region's emerging power system.[43]

Since the 1920s, power development on the Fort Apache reservation had extended beyond the Indian agency to the private lumber industry. The non-Indian–owned Southwest Lumber Company plant at McNary was the largest in the White Mountains. Burning sawdust and wood scraps fueled large turbines that provided electrical generation for milling. McNary Utilities charged its workers for domestic use but shut off their home lights at midnight to save power for the mill.[44] Southwest Lumber would provide Navopache with a large industrial consumer to meet the system load requirement, but more critically, Navopache needed to integrate the area's largest electrical generator into its system. In short, the commercial and agency generators on the Fort Apache reservation offered power, industrial and domestic customers, and access to miles of reservation land for extending power lines. Navopache acquired the McNary power plant soon afterwards, as well as the BIA's entire Whiteriver–Fort Apache power system by 1948. Both Southwest Lumber and the agency were eager to turn over the burden of utility responsibilities in favor of access to a more efficient and less expensive power source.[45]

The White Mountain Apache Tribe had been considering electrification for tribal use and investment since the Navopache cooperative sought right-of-way permission to extend its lines across the Fort Apache reservation in 1946. Encouraged by the BIA superintendent and the opportunity to extend electrical service not just across but also throughout the reservation, the tribal councilmen discussed the issue at length. They passed a resolution granting permission to survey a line from Lakeside to McNary in October 1946. The resolution included a 24,445-foot-long right-of-way allowing Navopache to construct, operate, and maintain a transmission line. It also stipulated financial compensation for any damages the line might cause to growing timber.[46] Last, the council allowed the cooperative to survey and build power lines to several reservation towns.[47] The actions absorbed the agency's existing customers as individual REA cooperative members. The tribal council, wielding control over tribal lands, ensured that the cooperative would hereafter have to recognize Indians as consumers.

Navopache worked to build a large enough Indian customer base to justify line construction costs over the reservation's mountainous and wooded terrain.[48] One of the first routes linesmen staked ran 25 miles through McNary, Whiteriver, and Fort Apache. Fifty Indian households in these communities qualified as potential power users. The cooperative picked up seven commercial customers in Whiteriver and fifteen Indian residences on the way to Fort Apache. Continued service to Canyon Day and the village of East Fork added about eighty more residential customers.[49]

Dependent on the tribe, its permissions, and its resources for power production, use, and rights-of-way agreements, Navopache often served as a political ally to the tribe, lobbying politicians on other aspects of industrialization, such as road building and career training. In turn, the tribe publicly supported funding legislation that strengthened the cooperative.[50] Apaches continued to join the cooperative directly as individual members as the White Mountain Apache Utility Authority gained more tribal control of water and sewage services. A BIA representative served on Navopache's board of directors for years, but in May 1975 the cooperative appointed thirty-year-old Apache Raymond Endfield Jr. to represent more than 66 percent of the reservation's REA member households (today, more than 90 percent).[51] Such political representation meant that the White Mountain Apache homes had to integrate physically into the region's power system.

ELECTRICITY AND THE "MODERN" HOME

Gaining access to power lines and consequently opportunities to consume electrical power required more than joining an REA cooperative. Individuals had to reconcile tradition with modernity, which forced tough decisions about how they lived. In *Technology as Freedom*, historian Ronald Tobey explained that New Deal philosophies equated household modernization with political (and physical) health and economic recovery.[52] That idea extended to Indians too. As a New Deal program, REA cooperatives pledged to deliver affordable electrical service rates to Indian families who had "permanent homes" and "who would desire electrical service." The term "permanent home," however, meant that only those who lived in houses of modern construction, rather than in traditional Indian structures, would receive power. REA evaluators predicted that those households would likely use enough electricity and its "companion conveniences" to "contribute materially to encouraging a higher standard of living and education among them."[53]

Before the war, traditional reservation structures, such as the Apache wickiup and the Navajo hogan (figure 8.5), outnumbered wood-framed houses that could be wired for lighting and multiple appliances.[54] Several factors contributed to a gradual shift to more permanent housing construction (figure 8.6). Certainly, a boarding school education, military

Figure 8.5
Navajo hogan. Courtesy of Cline Library, Northern Arizona University. Photo by Veronica Evaneshko.

Figure 8.6
Town of Navajo, circa 1950–1966. Courtesy of Cline Library, Northern Arizona University. Photo by Veronica Evaneshko.

service, and the relocation programs that sent thousands of Native Americans to the cities for work altered younger Apache expectations of their housing.[55] In October 1946, White Mountain Apache Charles Kitcheyan submitted a request for help to the tribal council when he wanted to wire his McNary home for electricity, and the BIA superintendent agreed to "try and have it done." Korean War veteran and Apache John Chissey wrote BIA officials to plead for his people, who, in his view, lived in miserable and unjust conditions: "I do know those Indians could have at least a house to live in: shower, bed, tables, chair, TV, radio, at least live like the rest of the people...those people there don't even know what life is."[56] The expectations of men such as Kitcheyan and Chissey resonated for some, but many Indians still lived far from population centers or power lines. Trade items had introduced industrial goods into many Navajo and Hopi communities, but tribal members maintained traditional, scattered living arrangements in remote areas throughout the 1950s and 1960s.

The civil rights era and the Cold War helped remove several obstacles to household modernization on the reservation. During this time, graduates of boarding, day, and missionary schools formed election slates urging a new kind of Navajo leader, one whose formal education encouraged an industrial lifestyle. Before World War II, electricity had been a by-product of federal Indian educational programs and agency activities, but a new generation of leaders saw electricity as a vehicle to bring industrialization back home for tribal use. Long-term and politically powerful council members Howard Gorman and Frank Bradley became the council's leading advocates for bringing technology to the reservation, but under tribal control.[57] Gorman expressed confidence: "After oil and gas wells have been exhausted, we will still be receiving the income from utilities." They had not only a smart business venture but also one that met the desires and needs of the people. "The Navajo family, whether they are living only in a summer shelter, in a hogan, or in a modern house, our people want to have the benefits of modern living with electricity in their homes," Gorman argued. "There is a great demand, and I would like to see natural gas and electricity in every hogan. People who have these facilities seem happier. They seem to have better health where they have these modern facilities."[58]

At the same time, Congress recognized the dire quality of life on southwestern reservations and passed legislation that continued to encourage (as Needham cites in chapter 9, this volume) an "American standard of living" for Native people through industrial infrastructure. Using the model of the Marshall Plan, which targeted its funds for rebuilding war-torn Europe, Congress passed the Navajo-Hopi Long Range Rehabilitation Act in 1950, granting $88 million for roads, communications, business enterprises, and other services. A portion of the bill offered low-cost, durable housing for Navajo families and tribal leaders. Council chairman Paul

Jones argued that it would help instill pride through home ownership.[59] (See Needham's chapter 9, this volume, for further discussion.)

Jones, who had lived in at least two major cities off the reservation, advocated this new type of "urban" living arrangement. He promoted clustered housing, instead of the traditional dispersed settlement pattern conducive to ranching and traditional stock raising. The chairman emphasized other community-oriented goals similar to village or urban life, such as stockpiling firewood and developing gas and power lines.[60]

In addition to Jones's leadership and the Rehabilitation Act, the Indian Extension Service branch of the BIA had promoted "better home conditions" and utilities such as water systems for improved health since the 1930s. According to the literature, the most important step to modern homemaking was to move Indians from their "primitive housing" into frame homes of wood or stone. Social workers praised tribal members when they used money for home improvements that included wiring and electrical hookups.[61] With the help of the Veterans Administration (a sponsor of the GI Bill, which helped thousands of returning soldiers nationwide purchase homes), the BIA established a carpentry school to teach construction skills for building wood frame homes prewired for electrical lighting. By 1952 one could find sewing machines, refrigerators, electric irons, and radios in many Indian households. Even if some American Indians technically qualified for loans, however, existing housing legislation required applicants to guarantee these with a property mortgage. This was a problem because the federal government held Indian lands in trust. Similarly, whereas non-Indians could tap funding sources such as the Farmers Home Administration to wire homes, the legal status of tribal members and tribal lands disqualified most reservation residents for such loans.[62] In the 1960s the War on Poverty publicly exposed living conditions on Indian reservations through several congressional hearings (including one in Tucson). New tribal and federal housing programs expanded opportunities for Indian-occupied or Indian-owned housing units offering electricity.[63]

ENERGY DEVELOPMENT, SELF-DETERMINATION, AND THE TRIBAL ENTERPRISE

As federal housing programs encouraged more Indians to become electrical consumers, the corporate development of mineral deposits and fossil fuels on the Colorado Plateau offered a new way for northeastern Arizona tribes to access electricity. Power plant construction, mining activities, and drilling projects on and around Navajo and Hopi lands became critical to regional energy development across the American Southwest (see Voggesser's chapter 4, O'Neill's chapter 7, and Needham's chapter 9, this volume). In addition, the Colorado Plateau's deep canyons offered the ideal conditions for large water-storage dams to produce significant amounts of hydroelectricity from the Colorado River (see Columbi's chapter 5, this volume). But planners targeted this power to expanding towns and cities located off the reservation, so tribes had to be assertive and resourceful in order to access the power generated within their own lands.

The Bureau of Reclamation's construction of Glen Canyon Dam near Page, Arizona, in the mid-1950s offered one of the first opportunities to harness Colorado River power for Indian use. Like the Navajo Agency, the Hopis' BIA agency had extended some power lines to places on the reservation before, but Keams Canyon Agency's steam plant had limited power to energize even its nearby schools and mission. The Arizona Public Service Company (APS) requested a franchise from the Hopi Tribal Council to run a power line carrying Glen Canyon power from Tuba City, located on the western end of the reservation, near the Hopi village of Moenkopi, to a uranium mill 10 miles east. In exchange for the franchise, APS agreed to deliver electrical service to Moenkopi, Old Oraibi, and New Oraibi, villages located along the same distribution lines that powered uranium and coal projects. APS purchased, rebuilt, and incorporated the system into a new power grid. In support of the agreement, the BIA superintendent argued that electricity was central to improving the Hopi economy by ensuring more attractive accommodations for tourism. Hopi tribal chairman Willard S. Sakiestewa Sr. looked forward to televisions and "modern electrical appliances" in Hopis' homes.[64]

The construction of Glen Canyon and the Hopis' agreement to a franchise sparked lively discussions in the neighboring Navajo Tribal Council over what member Paul Begay saw as the inevitability of electrification. "As time goes on," remarked Begay, "and communities continue to develop on the reservation, we will have more of these requests coming in from private utility companies which are in business to provide special services for which they will want to have authority to engage in utility activities on the reservation." As APS planned its service to the Hopis, the Navajo Tribal Council unanimously approved a resolution empowering the tribe with the same authority as off-reservation municipalities to issue franchises to similar private power companies. Previously, the BIA had granted such permission.[65]

The decision to assert control over the distribution of electrical energy produced on tribal lands was a response to new federal policy that historians refer to as "termination." Using the rhetoric of the emerging civil rights movement, termination advocates argued that Indians deserved the same opportunities and responsibilities as other American citizens. In practice, the policy reinforced earlier assimilation goals and dismissed Indian treaty rights, land claims, cultural values, and sovereignty. The government also failed to acknowledge that most tribes were not financially ready to cut off their federal relationship, not without enduring severe economic hardship. Although not slated for a termination, Navajo leaders responded to the threat of reduced funding by promoting economic independence and the doctrine of self-determination (see Voggesser's chapter 4, this volume). Rather than rely upon the trust relationship with the federal government for aid, the tribal council repeatedly asserted Navajo control over the industrialization of the reservation through communications and utility services, particularly electricity.

Navajo leaders addressed rising power needs that surpassed those of the BIA systems by the end of the 1950s, appropriating $5 million of the tribal budget to public works. In January 1959, after voicing cultural and economic concerns, the council unanimously approved the creation of an electric utility wholly owned and operated by the Navajos.[66] The Navajo Tribal Utility Authority (NTUA) began operations with 15,000 *potential* customers (only 250 actual), its mission being "to acquire, construct, operate, and maintain utility system properties throughout the entire Navajo reservation for the purpose of supplying electric, natural gas, water and sewer service to the inhabitants."[67] Consumers would largely bear delivery costs, but appropriations stemmed from the Resources Division of the Executive Branch, the BIA, and the tribal council. The board of directors set policy, spending plans, and rates, hired an REA-trained, non-Indian manager, and followed many REA practices and construction regulations. The manager hired a largely Navajo staff.[68] Tribal councilman Frank Bradley asserted, "The Navajo Tribal Utility Authority will extend every effort to bring utilities services to the Navajo people at reasonable and non-subsidized cost. We firmly believe that this enterprise of the Navajo Tribe will be only a self-sustaining one which will be of great ultimate benefit to the Navajo people."[69]

NTUA negotiated with the Farmington, New Mexico, electric utility to construct a transmission line from the eastern boundary of the reservation to Shiprock, New Mexico, and to install a substation there. NTUA took it over in 1961.[70] In 1963 the Navajo Tribe signed a contract with the Utah Construction Company, leasing 24,000 acres for strip-mining coal. The deal promised to bring electrical power closer to many Navajos, provide jobs, training, and housing improvements, and earn royalties for the tribe.[71] (See Needham's chapter 9, this volume, for more details on the ramifications of this deal.) Meanwhile, APS built a new coal-fired, steam electric power plant on Navajo lands near Fruitland, New Mexico. A high-powered transmission line hung along 80-foot-high towers, from the multimillion-dollar Four Corners Power Plant (figure 8.7) across Indian lands, in order to serve rapidly expanding Phoenix (as Needham's chapter 9, this volume, explains). Tribal lawyers negotiated a critical power agreement in which the Navajos received a significant supply of energy from the new plant. Although nearby residents could not take advantage of the high-voltage electric lines, NTUA received wholesale power rates for a thirty-year period. Tribal council members viewed this arrangement as an economical way to garner royalties, access electricity for domestic use, and promote economic development. Chairman Jones, Executive Secretary Maurice J. McCabe, and NTUA's lawyer Martin Bennett had long emphasized, "We need power, cheap power, as cheap as possible and lots of power if we are going to bring industry onto the reservation."[72]

NTUA built its tribal system by systematically acquiring existing or future systems. Attorneys warned against any outside interests engaging in retail power sales on the reservation, reserving these for a growing NTUA. Tribal lawyers included option-to-buy clauses in rights-of-way agreements while allowing power production and transportation rights. Likewise, the NTUA rejected an REA loan, fearing that federal agency involvement would undermine tribal sovereignty.[73] The insistence on protecting a future customer base for a reservation-wide, tribally controlled electrical system came at the expense of the neighboring Hopis. When APS requested a right-of-way from the Navajos to service the Hopi villages, the Navajo Tribal Council reserved the right to purchase the line at a later date. The negotiation delayed power delivery to Oraibi for almost a year.[74]

Amidst all the utility's activities, Navajo Tribal Council members expressed a variety of concerns. Was the tribe qualified for this highly complicated endeavor? How would the tribe educate tribal members about electricity? Council members Bradley and Gorman, as well as NTUA's non-Indian manager, Philip W. "Vance" Vanderhoof, promised advantages including heating and air conditioning, better health care, and better lighting to alleviate eye strain and encourage the rising numbers of day school children to study at home in the evening.[75] Ultimately, the council accepted the optimists' arguments and approved the APS plant because of its promises of reservation modernization, employment, and revenue. Tribal chairman Paul Jones's address at the groundbreaking ceremony for the Four Corners Power Plant on March 10, 1961, articulated the tribe's hopes for the plant:

FIGURE 8.7
This Navajo sheepherder and the Four Corners Power Plant occupy two distinct worlds separated by only a narrow strip of water. Courtesy of the National Archives, photo no. NWDNA 412-DA-1937.

> This is a great moment for the Navajo Tribe. The construction of a steam electric plant at this site brings to reality the results of many years of exploration and negotiation.
>
> The principal interest of the Navajo Tribe in projects such as this is to provide jobs for Navajos in construction and operation of the plant itself and a better way of life for all our people through the low cost power, which will be produced here. The electric energy will, we hope, attract many industries, thus creating additional employment opportunities throughout the area.
>
> I can visualize ultimately a grid of power lines throughout Navajoland, electric power in Navajo dwellings and, with the advent of such power, the acquisition of electrical appliances, including refrigeration, by the Navajos as a step toward bettering their standard of living....Financially, this power plant will be of great benefit to the Navajo Tribe. The Tribe will receive a percentage from the mining of coal and a fair wholesale rate on power. At the same time we shall enjoy the beneficial effect of electric energy wherever it is made available....We are entering a new era today—an era illuminated by electric power.[76]

Meanwhile the hydroelectric power source from Glen Canyon Dam continued to broaden service opportunities for the NTUA "to furnish electrical planning, development, operation, managing, and administration of all utilities for the Navajo Tribe." Tribal lawyers Walter Wolf and Leland Gardner (Navajo) successfully negotiated with the Bureau of Reclamation for a power delivery point at Kayenta, Arizona, as a condition of selling a right-of-way.[77] After workers completed a 100-mile line from Indian Wells to Kinlichee in 1962, Chairman Paul Jones threw the switch to energize the line amidst much pomp and circumstance. Councilmen Maurice McCabe and Howard Gorman presided over a ceremony in which NTUA workers presented an electric radio, a hot plate, and an iron to Mr. and Mrs. Henry Spake to celebrate the lighting of their remodeled hogan in Ganado, the first in the system. The *Navajo Times* boasted, "The availability of this electric power makes possible a better standard of living for thousands of Navajo peoples as well as making possible vast industrial expansion."[78]

Indeed, NTUA delivered electricity to industry and commercial entities first, but this industrialization encouraged wage work (see O'Neill's chapter 7, this volume), enabling more people to join the consumer market and purchase home appliances.[79] NTUA delivered to 2,282 customers by March 1964. The utility served thirty-five communities across three

Figure 8.8

The Navajo Generating Station occupies more than a thousand acres leased from the Navajo Indians and was the largest electric generation station in Arizona when completed, in 1974. Courtesy of the National Archives, photo no. NWDNA 412-DA-1639.

main areas, each boasting a branch office: Shiprock, Chinle/Kayenta, and Window Rock. Many individual homes located close to chapter houses (local/community chapters of the Navajo government), such as Lechee, just south of Page, received electricity and other services.[80]

The tribe continued to take steps to secure its own energy and expand its customer base to residents. In 1965 the Navajo Tribal Council leased property for electrical generation to the Western Energy Supply and Transmission Associates, a conglomeration of private western utilities that included SRP and APS. NTUA supplied the electrical power for the construction of the coal-fired Navajo Generating Station (NGS) (figure 8.8). By the early 1970s, Kayenta's substation powered Peabody Coal's mining activities at Black Mesa, which, in turn, powered NGS. Federal power agreements provided a large percentage of NTUA's electrical load.[81] The NTUA system boasted 7,303 customers (4,581 residential), 312 miles of transmission line, 1,130 miles of distribution lines, and 27 substations.[82]

About the same time, NTUA had become a more tribal enterprise as technically skilled and educated Navajos gradually took over daily operations of the tribal utility. Educated in the Ganado Mission School, Kayenta branch manager Malcolm P. "Mickey" Dalton learned the utility business on the job as an NTUA lineman. Edward McCabe Jr. had briefly served as the utility's first Navajo general manager. Dalton held the post for the next three decades. Attorney Lee Gardner became the first Navajo chairman of the board soon afterwards.[83]

As NTUA continued to expand, a range of factors inhibited the utility's mission to install "A Light in Every Hogan."[84] Over the years, land disputes, the non-Indian power industry, escalating costs, and energy shortages slowed system growth. Still, the development of a tribally owned, financially independent system symbolized and manifested the Navajo Tribe's determination to control its resources and technological future.

Other tribes followed the Navajo model. The REA-funded Trico Electric Cooperative in southern Arizona served part of the Papago (now called Tohono O'odham) reservation in the 1950s, but by 1970 Trico could afford to accommodate the needs of only sixteen out of forty communities on the reservation. The Tohono O'odham Tribal Council authorized $175,000 to develop a tribal utility and spent three and a half years negotiating various energy sources, supplies, and power contracts.[85] The tribe purchased all of Trico's facilities on the reservation, assuming its debt to REA, and then secured a loan from the REA under similar provisions as the Navajos'. By the 1980s, PTUA was serving 4,350 square miles and nearly 10,500 people.[86]

In sum, encouraged by assimilation policies to adopt the tools of industrial society, Arizona's Indians pursued a range of possibilities to access electrical power and guide its distribution to Indian consumers. The Apache tribes became members of local REA cooperatives, and the Hopis negotiated delivery from a private utility. The Navajos and Tohono O'odham created their own utilities to serve their specific needs.[87]

"A PARAGON OF PARADOXES": INDIANS AS ELECTRICAL CONSUMERS

The assumptions and values that accompanied widespread access to electricity challenged Indian societies to negotiate a way to live traditional Indian lives within an expanding modern industrial setting. Utilities always had to instruct new electrical users, but, as one non-Indian observed, on reservations they also had "to work around tradition, mythology, and everything else."[88] Reluctance to use electricity could stem from unaffordability, fear of physical or spiritual harm from an occasional short circuit, or generational differences. The Hopi experience perhaps offers the most dramatic manifestation of Indian resistance to electrification.[89]

On at least two occasions, in 1966 and 1968, a group of Hopi protesters in Hotevilla physically thwarted utility construction. These protesters were part of a coalition of Hopi leaders who had founded what they termed the "Hopi Traditionalist Movement" to identify a wide range of issues emphasizing dedication to Hopi culture, religion, and daily life. Although not against all industrial changes, they invoked public utilities as the vehicle through which outsiders aimed to destroy Hopi life. Digging holes for power poles would desecrate lands. Power line static could disturb the natural energy forces in sacred areas and scar the landscape. Electricity, specifically, would encourage dependence on a foreign culture. Their fear was that the power company would take away people's land if they failed to pay their bills. "We don't need water pipes or electric lights," one claimed. "These things are no good for the Hopi. We were instructed by the Spirit how to live."[90]

Other, often younger, Hopis voiced a different view in a local newsletter, *Hopi Action News*. Editorials argued that the improvements would combat the lure of the cities and ensure community survival. Eighth grader Fannie Kewan cited electricity, a sewage system, and better, government-built homes as a way of improving her community: "When we have electricity, our village might be a clean village." Classmate Cheryl Tenakhongva asked, "Must the younger generation wait for the older generation to die out before they modernize their homes?"[91]

In spite of these seemingly dichotomist sentiments, reconciling modernity with tradition seemed to dominate behavior on the reservation by the 1960s.[92] A *Hopi Action News* cartoon depicted a man placing an antenna atop a teepee. He turns to a neighbor and asks, "Whatta ya mean, I gotta have electricity first?"[93] Amidst a scene of intersecting roads and power lines (figure 8.9), a *Navajo Times* cartoon character commented, "What did that White Man say? If you can't beat 'em...just join them!" Another depicted two men rushing to leave or enter an electrified sweathouse in order to catch the Liston–Clay boxing match on television, the viewing of which connected Navajos to national popular culture (figure 8.10). In the White Mountains, the corporate paper *The Timberline* reported that more than four thousand Apaches led a life that "blended the old with the new." Sixty percent still lived in wickiups. The rest had moved into frame homes "that often boast[ed] TV antennas."[94] The *Navajo Times* printed one article that began like this: "Hogans and houses; sheep herds and electricity; ochre dyes and lipsticks; earthen jugs and TV antennas; emergence myth and typewriter, red man and white man; 'Yahteh' and 'howdy'; traditional and modern, old ways and new trails....This is Window Rock—an absolute paragon of paradoxes."[95]

FIGURE 8.9

"Join Them!" Courtesy of Navajo Times, *April 25, 1963.*

Although some electrical appliances (such as televisions) threatened vital traditions (such as storytelling), electricity often coalesced with traditional practices. Light bulbs replaced smoky fires to illuminate evening ceremonies, and microphones improved communication at community events.[96] Navajo rug weavers could practice their craft around the clock; as they increased productivity, they gained status. The commercial popularity of their product enabled them to afford appliances for their households. Inevitably, electricity influenced weaving as an art form, and some critics classified designs into "pre-electric" and "post-electric" categories.[97]

Furthermore, electricity supported tribal enterprises (beyond the NTUA) that altered the economy and the landscape. The Fort Apache Timber Company at Cibecue rivaled and eventually outlasted the Southwest Lumber Company at McNary. Moreover, electrical power encouraged recreational and tourism opportunities.[98] The White Mountain Apache Tribal Council repeatedly granted Navopache requests for rights-of-way to serve the reservations' new housing communities and recreational accommodations. These included the Sunrise Ski Resort and the Hon-Dah Casino.[99]

Figure 8.10

Liston–Clay fight. Courtesy of Navajo Times, *November 21, 1963.*

By the 1970s, power lines connected communities of 200 to larger centers of more than 3,300. Like non-Indians, many tribal members invested in electrical hookups and learned to use appliances and incorporate them into their rural lifestyles. The transformation of reservation life was not lost on the community. A cartoon featured in the *Fort Apache Scout* recognized how modern housing undermined the popular stereotype of the Indian. It pictured two homes sporting antennas in the background. In the foreground, an Apache man scolded a white woman in a car with New York license plates: "Lady, I don't care WHAT you saw on TV. This IS Fort Apache."[100]

A 1969 government report recognized that Indians needed to negotiate integration and separatism. "The way to achieve an intermediate position between the familiar culture and the dominant but alien one is not at all clear," the author concluded.[101] In reality, many tribes chose neither, preferring instead to walk the nuanced line between the traditional and the modern (figures 8.11 and 8.12). Harry Walters, curator of the museum at Navajo (now Diné) Community College, noted, "You often hear: 'All the old ways are gone.' In some ways, this is true. Yet, we are still Navajos. The language may be a little different, ceremonies a little different. We may use a pick-up instead of a horse to carry the ceremonial wand on the first day of Enemy way. Nevertheless we are still a unique people." Teacher Rex Lee Jim added, "Our adaptability is a tradition."[102]

FIGURE 8.11

Navajo family in Chinle Valley, circa 1968. Courtesy of the Navajo Nation Museum, Window Rock, Arizona, PRC (Public Relations Collection).

THE FUTURE OF THE ELECTRIFIED RESERVATION

Arizona's Indians have sought access to electrical lines and gradually taken control over electrical utilities and distribution systems while negotiating for more control over power production. At the end of the twentieth

Figure 8.12
Hopi village and TV antenna, 1972. Courtesy of the National Archives, photo no. NWDNS-412-DA-1924, by Terry Eiler

century, Congress proposed to "get the BIA out of the electric utility business in Arizona" definitively with the San Carlos Indian Irrigation Project Divestiture Act. Non-Indian customers had complained bitterly about poor service and high rates unregulated by the Arizona Corporation Commission (due to SCIP's affiliation with the federal government). The San Carlos Apaches accused the government of breaking its agreement to sell SCIP's inexpensive power to the Apaches in exchange for land flooded by Coolidge Dam. Both the Gila River Indian Community (Pima) and the San Carlos Apache Tribe supported legislation that would permit them to take control of their own electrical systems. Both tribes cited reasons of sovereignty, self-determination, and industrial development.[103]

Such divestment supported ongoing policies to decrease federal involvement in tribal affairs, as well as in regulating electrical utilities. Since 2000 the deregulation movement, as championed by Enron-esque energy companies, has proven to be a mixed bag for Arizona's tribes. Increased competition enabled utilities such as NTUA to negotiate cheap power, but, ironically, from sources generated well beyond the energy-rich borders of the Navajo reservation, such as Tucson. And even as Arizona began its own (never completed) deregulation process, many of the state's poorest communities, including the Tohono O'odham, felt the effects in neighboring California when power companies passed cost increases of up to 40 percent.[104]

Unfortunately, more Indian control over electrical distribution did not translate into universal access. Small community centers, such as Mexican Springs on the Navajo reservation and Santa Cruz on the Tohono O'odham reservation, still proved too remote to build electrical lines. Some communities still could not afford the construction and service fees.[105] In spite of attempts to secure electrical and political power, 28.6 percent of Hopis, 5.7 percent of the San Carlos reservation, 9.3 percent of the White Mountain Apache, 7.8 percent of the Tohono O'odham, and an astounding 36.8 percent of the Navajo Tribe still lacked access on the eve of the twenty-first century. These communities had the highest number of homes without electricity in the country. Several tribes have since secured federal hydropower (generated by Reclamation projects) from the Western Area Power Administration, an agency of the Department of Energy.[106]

During the late 1990s, former Secretary of Energy Bill Richardson urged tribal utilities toward renewable energy, including wind, solar, and geothermal. Many had already begun to develop additional "clean energy" and renewable power sources for reasons not just environmental (see Voggesser, chapter 5, and Powell and Long, chapter 10, this volume). In 2007, Arizona governor Janet Napolitano announced the Tribal Rural Electrification Program to serve as many as ten thousand Native American households not connected to or unable to connect to a power grid through solar power.[107] Rural electrification alternatives such as these avoid land exchanges and pollution from coal plants. But the Navajo government's decision to build the Desert Rock coal plant, to electrify twenty thousand more homes on the reservation, pitted economic development and modernity against environmental and health concerns (see Powell and Long, chapter 10, this volume).[108]

Even as many communities still await a dial tone and electrical power, the Internet is the most recent manifestation of using technology to maintain traditional values, ensure community cohesion, and enable self-sufficiency.[109] Wireless, cable, satellite, digital, and computer technologies have allowed rural populations as distant as rural Africa, India, and China to bypass power lines in order to gain urban information and services. Companies still favor profitable markets over need, however, so many reservation communities still lack access. During President Bill Clinton's visit to the Navajo reservation in 2000, he perpetuated the Progressive-era contention that equal access to technology would fuel and support a democratic society. He observed that Native Americans in the West had joined other poor and rural Americans separated by a "Digital Divide" and pledged to support this "key civil rights issue of the twenty-first century." NTUA considered offering the Internet as early as 1999, but in 2007 the tribe itself sponsored an initiative for Internet service to the reservation. The service has increased long-distance communication for greater safety networks, improved educational opportunities, helped preserve Native languages and culture, and supported entrepreneurialism. Yet, tribes and their advocates nationwide worry that too few Indians have access to traditional or wireless grids.[110]

For years, tribes have been resourceful in accessing regional power grids, despite economic feasibility and physical limitations. Having been introduced to (or forced into) an industrial lifestyle through government agencies, policies, and education over the past century, Indians identified local opportunities and obtained electrical power for Indians. Arizona's tribes, depending on their location and goals, claimed treaty obligations, took advantage of federal poverty programs, exploited the REA's mandate for area coverage and system feasibility, asserted sovereignty, and leveraged land bases to negotiate the distribution of the electricity generated in their own backyard, through public, private, and tribal agencies. The electrification process on reservations caused (and continues to cause) cultural and political divisions, but tribal communities have tapped in to long histories of challenge and adaptation. From replacing the horse with a pickup to preserving Native languages through computer software, Arizona's Indians have embraced modernity on their own terms. Likewise, they use and consume electricity, as tribes and as individuals.[111] As the country increasingly looks to produce more power from renewable energy sources, Indian people must be part of power generation *and* distribution decisions.

Acknowledgments

This article is based on material appearing in *Electrifying the Rural American West: Stories of Power, People, and Place* by Leah S. Glaser, fall 2009, from the University of Nebraska Press. Available wherever books are sold or from the University of Nebraska Press (800.755.1105) and on the Web at nebraskapress.unl.edu.

Notes

1. Distributive justice is a philosophical and sociological theory regarding the equitable allocation of resources in a society. For an argument promoting the integration of democracy, equality, and economic justice, see Zucker 2001.

2. Energy Information Administration, US Department of Energy, "Energy Consumption and Renewable Energy Development on Indian Lands," Washington, DC, March 2000, xiv. Scholars have referred to this phenomenon as *internal colonialism*. For more information on Indians' efforts to control this development, see Ambler 1990.

3. Maggie Wilson (an *Arizona Republic* reporter), "Opposing Cultures of Navajos Meet Head On," *Navajo Times*, August 1, 1962. For more on postwar consumerism outside Indian country, see Cohen 2003.

4. Embshoff to Olberg, May 12, 1915, Reed to Sells, August 9, 1915, Davis to Sells, October 18, 1920, July 15, 1921, Central Classified Files (CCF) 314, 1907–1956, C. A. Engle, "Power and Irrigation, White Mountain Reservation," November 1914, Irrigation Division, Reports and Related Records, Fort Apache Agency, RG 75, National Archives Building (NAB), Washington, DC.

5. The Dawes Allotment Act of 1887 advanced these goals by dividing reservations into Homestead Act–like parcels in order to encourage Indians to adopt the so-called American values of self-sufficiency through individual land tenure. The act was not applied to many of Arizona's reservations (including Fort Apache), but treaties such as that in 1868 with the Navajos had similarly encouraged the agrarian lifestyle on reservations. Treaty between the United States of America and the Navajo Tribe of Indians, August 12, 1868, in Kappler 1972:1015–1020. Also see Olberg to Sells, November 27, 1914, C. A. Engle, "Power and Irrigation, White Mountain Reservation," November 1914, Irrigation Division, Reports and Related Records, Arizona, RG 75, NAB; Charles Davis in "Indians of the United States: Investigations of the Field Service," Hearings by a Subcommittee of the Commission on Indian Affairs, vol. 3 (Washington, DC: Government Printing Office, 1920), 929–933.

6. Ironically, the plant's construction destroyed the existing irrigation system, and several Indians lost their farms. Schnauk to Reed, March 31, 1914, Peterson to Sells, August 15, 1914, Reed to Sells, August 9, 1915, Correspondence, CCF 341, 1907–1956, Fort Apache Agency, RG 75, NAB.

7. Fort Apache Information Sheet, Fort Apache Historic Park, Fort Apache, Arizona; Clotts and Brady, Description of Whiteriver Power and Irrigation Project, February 28, 1923; Burke to Reed, CCF 341, 1924, RG 75, NAB.

8. The junior high school curriculum specifically focused on the living conditions of the reservation home (the high school program emphasized off-reservation life). "Organization of Home Economics Classes," Navajo Agency, "The Unit Kitchen as a Factor in Home Economics Education," Fort Apache Agency, "Teaching and Training Home Economics," c. 1924, Box 104, San Carlos Agency, CCF 812, Max M. Drefkoff, "An Industrial Program for the Navajo Reservation, January 1948," Phoenix Area Office, Subject Files, Box 56, RG 75, National Archives and Records Administration (NARA)—Pacific Region (Laguna Niguel [LN]); Kluckhohn 1942:196, 197.

9. Donner to Commissioner, February 14, 1929, "Field Matron Work—Domestic Employment," CCF 970, Fort Apache Agency, Kitch to Commissioner, December 15, 1923, CCF 806.1, San Carlos Agency, RG 75, NARA—Pacific Region (LN).

10. "Six-Year Construction Plan, Circular No. 2943," "Schedule of Repairs and Improvements," CCF 403, Fort Apache Agency, RG 75, NARA—Pacific Region (LN).

11. Janet Lynn Wilson, interview questionnaire conducted by author, September 3, 2000.

12. Donner to Bradley, October 3, 1938, Donner to Collier, March 18, 1941, CCF 413.1, NARA—Pacific Region (LN).

13. Donner to Bradley, October 3, 1938, Donner to Collier, March 18, 1941, CCF 413.1, NARA—Pacific Region (LN).

14. The White Mountain Apache reorganized under the IRA, but the Navajos rejected much of it. Nevertheless, Collier reorganized and centralized the Navajo agencies under a single administration. See Iverson 1981:35–37, 2002a:155–157.

15. Iverson 1981:17.

16. Poynton to Bradley, December 7, 1938, Correspondence, 1933–1940, Box 61, Phoenix Area Office, RG 75, NARA—Pacific Region (LN).

17. Tolson to Green, November 10, 1947, Green to Lefler, October 20, 1947, CCF 284, 1946–1952, Box 114, Navajo Area Office, RG 75, NARA—Pacific Region (LN).

18. Fryer to Matchin, May 6, 1939, Lynn to Parry, May 27, 1939, Stenz to Garcia, February 16, 1940, Stewart to Albert, January 14, 1946, Stewart to Merrill, April 9, 1945, Hedquist to Cata, February 20, 1947, Fryer to McCurtain, August 5, 1938, CCF 284, Box 114, Navajo Area Office, RG 75, NARA—Pacific Region (LN).

19. Meriam et al. 1928.

20. Collier to Bradley, March 5, 1934, Collier to Fairbanks, April 28, 1934, Bradley to Collier, September 7, 1935, Construction Subject Files, Phoenix Area Office, "Report on Navajo Situation," p. 70, July 40, 1947, CCF 64, Box 39, Navajo Area Office, RG 75, NARA—Pacific Region (LN).

21. Quoted in Brigham 2001:87; John Carmody to Robert Tolson, August 4, 1947, Subject Files, CCF 423, "Heating and Lighting," 1945–1950, Navajo Area Office, RG 75, NARA—Pacific Region (LN).

22. Abstracts and Official Reports Concerning School Plants, Entry 739, RG 75, NAB, Washington, DC; McGinty to Aldrich, May 12, 1936, Federal Administration Division of Investigations, Public Works Administration, "Construction," Subject Files, 1933–1937, Phoenix Area Office, Box 62; "Contracts: Heat Light Power Gas and Water," CCF 284, "Heating and Lighting," CCF 423, 1937–1940, CCF 64, 1945–1952, Box 114, Navajo Agency, RG 75, NARA—Pacific Region (LN); Kluckhohn and Leighton 1958:94.

23. Iverson 2002a:174.

24. In 1910 the Apache Power Company proposed to build a power plant on the Fort Apache reservation to serve the mining town of Globe. The Indian Extension

Service's own superintendent of irrigation, Charles Real Olberg, observed that the potential power was of no benefit to the Indians because available arable land—even with pumping—was scarce. Olberg, Superintendent of Irrigation, to Reed, Chief Engineer, Indian Services, "Application for Power Site," April 10, 1913, Olberg to Reed, July 30, 1910, Report and Letters Relative to Application for Permit by Apache Power Company: San Carlos and Fort Apache Indian Reservation, Records of the Irrigation Division, RG 75, NARA—Pacific Region (LN); Brigham 2001:82.

25. The Newlands Reclamation Act, passed as a defining piece of Theodore Roosevelt's presidency, was the government's bold "solution" to the problems created by years of federal policies promoting agricultural settlement in the arid American West. Unfortunately, the government continued to promote agricultural settlement, in spite of repeated warnings in government-commissioned reports from notable explorers such as Stephen Long, Zebulon Pike, and John Wesley Powell that such settlement in the "Great American Desert" was not possible. The Reclamation Act reflected faith in technology and values of conservation promoted by Progressive reformers such as Roosevelt: technology would efficiently manage natural resources and realize the agrarian dream. The government usually hired a private contractor for construction projects and purportedly funded only economically viable projects, for which water users would repay the government over ten years. The loan period eventually expanded to accommodate borrowers' ability to pay. The government retained title, but the water users assumed project operations.

26. The Sacaton Project proved to be expensive, controversial, and unfair to the Pimas and their water claims, as revealed through several legal challenges. In addition, Pima refused groundwater, arguing that the poor water quality would ruin lands. SCIP also failed to accommodate Pima water rights equitably. To this day, the Gila River Tribe contests water rights to the Gila River through the courts. Newell 1905:62, 153, 156; Christine Pfaff, *San Carlos Irrigation Project*, National Park Service, Historic American Engineering Record, No. AZ-50, 1994, 13–15; David Introcaso, *Coolidge Dam*, National Park Service, Historic American Engineering Record, No. AZ-7, 1986, 39–49; Linenberger and Glaser 2002:111.

27. Southworth to Sears, August 15, 1935, Electrification, MS 311, Papers of Isabella Greenway, Arizona Historical Society, Tucson; Introcaso, *Coolidge Dam* (see note 26), 28–30, 50–55, 60–61; Rural Electrification Administration 1938:134–135.

28. Steckner to Commissioner, July 13, 1917, Box 63, CCF 423, Kitch to Commissioner, December 8, 1931, McCray to Southworth, September 9, 1942, CCF 510.221, Box 67, McCray to Poynton, November 3, 1929, CCF 806.2, Education, Box 102, San Carlos Agency, 1913–1952, RG 75, NARA—Pacific Region (LN).

29. McCray to Southworth, September 9, 1942, CCF 510, "School—Bylas Day

School," January 4, 1938, CCF 806.2, San Carlos Agency, RG75, NARA—Pacific Region (LN); Sears to Ross, March 10, 1936, Papers of Isabella Greenway; Introcaso, *Coolidge Dam* (see note 26), 60; Olberg to Reed, October 23, 1913, Phoenix Area Office, Irrigation Water Rights, Rights Protection Division, San Carlos, 1938–1940, NAB; *Arizona Trend* 1987:12.

30. C. H. Southworth, San Carlos Irrigation District, "Electrical Districts to Provide Medium for Rural Electrification: A Suggested Plan to Initiate and Administer Approved Projects for the Distribution of Electrical Energy," 1935, Papers of Isabella Greenway; Polk 1940:17.

31. Coxon to Greenway, April 28, 1936, Papers of Isabella Greenway; *Rural Electrification News*, May 1936, June 1936, and October 1936; Rural Electrification Administration 1938:134–135.

32. Orme to Greenway, May 12, 1936, H. D. Kochsmeier to Greenway, May 13, 1936, Papers of Isabella Greenway.

33. Coxon to Greenway, April 28, 1936, Southworth to Sears, REA, August 15, 1935, Papers of Isabella Greenway; *Rural Electrification News*, October 1936; Rural Electrification Administration 1937:9; Brigham 2001:84.

34. McCray to Bennett, July 12, 1943, CCF 510.221, Box 67, San Carlos Agency, 1913–1952, RG 75, NARA—Pacific Region (LN); Addenda to Appraisal of Arizona 17 Graham, Project Case Files of the Economic Analysis Section, 1937–1948, Applications and Loans Division, Divisional Records, RG 221, National Archives and Records Administration (NACP), College Park, MD; Stanford Research Institute, Mountain State Division, *The San Carlos Apache Reservation: A Resources Development Study*, Prepared for the San Carlos Apache Tribal Council, San Carlos, AZ (Stanford, CA: Stanford University, 1954), 10; Nelson Peck, Pima, Arizona, interview with author, August 7, 2000.

35. Stefan to Richter, "Traveler's Report," "Arizona 17 Graham," April 22, 1948, Field Activities Reports 1946–1951, Applications and Loans Division, Divisional Records, RG 221, NACP; Joint Hearing before the Select Committee on Indian Affairs, US Senate and the Committee on Interior and Insular Affairs, US House of Representatives, 102 Congress, S. 1869 and H.R. 1476, October 29, 1991.

36. Brigham 2001:85.

37. Files 11083, 19440, 20025, Application and Loan Division, Field Activities Reports, 1948–1949, New Mexico 22 McKinley; REA District Folder, "Arizona," revised January 1, 1948.

38. Walter Wolf, interview with author, April 23, 1998; New Mexico 25 McKinley, Field Activities Reports, 1948–1949, Applications and Loans Division, RG 221, NACP; File 6825-49, CCF 377, Navajo Agency, 1949, RG 75, NAB.

39. Correspondence and Agricultural Statistics, REA, May 21, 1937, "Arizona 13 Navajo," Project Case Files, Entry 3, RG 221, NACP.

40. Appraiser's Report, 14–16, 19, Addenda, "Arizona 13 Navajo," 1947, Records of Economic Analysis, Applications and Loans Division, Records of the Rural Electrification Administration, RG 221, NACP.

41. Appraiser's Report (see note 40), Addenda, 9, 11, 13, 27.

42. Appraiser's Report (see note 40), Addenda, 1–2; Tribal Relations, Acts of Tribal Councils, Fort Apache, July 1946–December 1946, R. D. Holtz, Superintendent to Commissioner of Indian Affairs; Max U. S. Colbert to R. D. Holtz, December 15, 1947, CCF, Fort Apache Agency, RG 75, NARA—Pacific Region (LN).

43. Minutes, 1950–1951, "Arizona 13 Navajo," Minutes of Meetings of Borrower Cooperatives 1943–1951, Cooperatives' Operations and Management Divisions, Divisional Records, RG 221, NACP; Tribal Relations, Acts of Tribal Councils, Fort Apache, July 1946–December 1946, CCF 54, Fort Apache Agency, RG 75, NARA—Pacific Region (LN).

44. See Matheny 1976; Campbell 1960:2–3; Vera Blake, interview by author, July 28, 2000.

45. C. J. Warren to Max Colbert, December 26, 1947, Appraiser's Report, Economic Analysis, "Arizona 13 Navajo," 1947, 9, 11, 126, RG 221, NACP; R. D. Holtz, Superintendent to W. A. Brophy, Commissioner of Indian Affairs, July 22 and December 31, 1946, Tribal Relations, Acts of Tribal Councils, Fort Apache, July 1946–December 1946; "Annual Report, 1952," CCF, 1940–1956, Phoenix Area Office, RG 75, NAB.

46. Minutes, October 14, 1946, "Arizona 13 Navajo," RG 221, NACP; Max Colbert to R. D. Holtz, Superintendent, Indian Agency, December 15, 1947, Addenda: Indians, Appraiser's Report, Economic Analysis, "Arizona 13 Navajo," RG 221, NACP.

47. Resolutions 162, 173, Fort Apache Indian Reservation Tribal Minutes, December 2, 1946, CCF 54, Fort Apache Agency, RG 75, NARA—Pacific Region (LN).

48. Ketchum to Hayden, January 25, 1955, Bell to Hayden, February 4, 1955, Wright to Hayden, August 5, 1957, Strong to Hayden, August 26, 1957, Walker to Hayden, July 19, 1960, Papers of Carl Hayden, Arizona Collections, University Libraries, Department of Archives and Manuscripts, Arizona State University, Tempe; Mac Eddy, interview by author, May 8, 1998; "Navopache on the Move," *Apache Scout*, October 1975.

49. "Arizona 13 Navajo," Field Activities Reports, 1946–1951, Applications and Loans Division, Divisional Records, April 3, 1948, December 6–9, 1948, RG 221, NACP.

50. Campbell 1960:4; Dewey Farr to Carl Hayden, August 23, 1955, Box 179, Folder 19, Papers of Carl Hayden; Correspondence between S. D. Gordom and Paul

Fannin, 1966–1967, 90th Congress, Box 32, Folder 12, Papers of Paul Fannin, Arizona Historical Foundation, Arizona State University.

51. "Raymond Endfield, Jr., Named to Navopache Board," *Fort Apache Scout,* May 1975; Reddy 1993:890; Raymond Endfield, interview by author, July 23, 2001.

52. Tobey 1996:6.

53. Colbert to Holtz, Superintendent, Indian Agency, December 15, 1947, Addenda: Indians, Appraiser's Report, Economic Analysis, "Arizona 13 Navajo," Box 4, RG 221, NACP.

54. Writers Program of the Works Projects Administration 1989:443; Newspaper Clippings, Box 12, Folder 21, Krause Collection, Arizona Historical Foundation, Tempe.

55. Clapps 1952:28–32; Bernstein 1991:131–158.

56. Fort Apache Indian Reservation, Tribal Minutes, October 14, 1946, CCF 54, Fort Apache Agency, RG 75, NARA—Pacific Region (LN); John Chissey, August 25, 1959, File 10591, CCF 620, Box 75, Fort Apache Agency, 1959, RG 75, NAB.

57. Iverson 1981:31; Peterson Zah, interview with the author, March 26, 2001; Bruce Gjeltema, personal communication May 5, 2001. Also see Iverson 2002a:180–226 and several documents in Iverson and Roessel 2002b that clarify the views of tribal leaders of the time (including Gorman and Bradley) regarding education, health, living conditions, and economic opportunity for Navajos.

58. Navajo Tribal Council Minutes, December 6, 1961, Navajo Agency Office, CCF 54, RG 75, NAB; Walter Wolf, interview with author, April 23, 1998; Young 1951–1961.

59. Iverson 1981:56–57; Walter Wolf, interview with author, April 23, 1998; B. H. Critchfield to Assistant to the Commissioner of Indian Affairs, March 8, 1950, District Director, Classified Files, Box 1, Phoenix Area Office, 1947–1949, RG 75, NARA—Pacific Region (LN); Navajo Tribal Council Minutes, November 29–December 2, 1949, CCF 64, Navajo Area Office, RG 75, NARA–Pacific Region (LN).

60. Paul Jones, Inaugural Address, Navajo Tribal Council, Series 84–88, Box 3, Folder 8, Barry Goldwater Papers, Arizona Historical Foundation, Arizona State University, Tempe; "Navajo Tribe Request Extension of Ten-Year Program," *Navajo Times,* November 1958; "$5 Million for Public Works Program," *Navajo Times,* November 1959; "New Road Construction on the Navajo Reservation," *Navajo Times,* December 1959; "Housing Program Assists Navajos," *Navajo Times,* September 1960; "Housing Plans on the Navajo Reservation," *Navajo Times,* January 3, 1962.

61. Annual Extension Report, 1951, Division of Extension and Industry, 1938–1947, CCF 919, Fort Apache Agency, RG 75 NARA—Pacific Region (LN); Marion P. Royer, Social Worker, Report, CCF 54, January 1963, RG 75, National Archives, Washington, DC.

62. Clapps 1952:32; Bernstein 1991:142–144.

63. "Housing Program Assists Navajos," *Navajo Times*, September 1960; "Self-Help Housing Program, 1963," File 9367, "White Mountain Apache Housing Authority," File 6627, Box 76, CCF 054, Fort Apache Agency, RG 75 NARA—Pacific Region (LN); Health, Education, and Welfare Committee, White Mountain Apache Office of Education, "Apache: Comprehensive Educational Plan White Mountain Apache Tribe," October 1978, 10; Bechtel Corporation, "Electric System Planning and NTUA Organizational Study," March 1964, copy at Records Management, Navajo Tribal Utility Authority (NTUA) Headquarters, Fort Defiance, AZ; National Advisory Commission 1967.

64. Bruce Kipp, "Navajos Block Utility from Bringing Electricity to Hopis," *The Phoenix Gazette*, April 15, 1960; Jim Cook, "Oldest Town Finally Gets Electricity," *Arizona Republican*, November 28, 1961; Nagata 1970:76–80.

65. Navajo Tribal Council Minutes, July 10, July 20, 1956, CCF 54, Navajo Agency, NAB.

66. Heyer 1962:50; "Journal of the Navajo Tribal Council," January 22, 1959, CCF 54, RG 75, NAB. For more on the discussions surrounding NTUA (Navajo Tribal Utility Authority), see Glaser 2009.

67. "Accomplishment Report for the Navajo Tribal Utility Authority," 1963, 7. Copy in Records Management, NTUA Headquarters, Fort Defiance, AZ.

68. Mac Eddy, interview by author, May 8, 1998.

69. "New Power System for Shiprock Area," *Navajo Times*, August 1960. Bradley would later serve as chairman of the utility's management board.

70. "Monthly Progress Report," *Navajo Times*, December 1960; "New Power System for Shiprock Area," *Navajo Times*, August 1960; Heyer 1962:50; "Journal of the Navajo Tribal Council," January 22, 1959, RG 75, NAB; Walter Wolf, interview with author, April 23, 1998; "Navajo Tribal Utility Report," *Navajo Times*, January 1961; "NTUA Is Negotiating for More Facilities," *Navajo Times*, July 30, 1964.

71. Sheridan 1995:301.

72. Navajo Tribal Council Minutes, August 18, 1960, 89, Navajo Agency, CCF 54, RG 75, NAB.

73. Navajo Tribal Council Minutes, August 18, 1960, 89, Navajo Agency, CCF 54, RG 75, NAB.

74. A land dispute between the tribes further delayed and complicated service to the Hopis. Bruce Kipp, "Navajos Block Utility from Bringing Electricity to Hopis," *Phoenix Gazette*, April 15, 1960.

75. Navajo Tribal Council Minutes, August 19, 1960, Navajo Agency, CCF 54, RG 75, NAB.

76. "The Fifteenth Annual Tribal Fair: The Era of Resource Development," Window Rock, AZ, September 7–10, 1961.

77. Young 1978:158–162; "New Power System for Shiprock Area" *Navajo Times,* August 1960; "Electric Power Soon in Town of Navajo," "Progress through Power," *Navajo Times,* June 7, 1961; Leland Gardner, Walter J. Wolf Retirement Banquet, Gallup, NM, May 4, 2001.

78. "Electric Power Comes to Tribe, Tribal Utility Authority Energizes Line System," *Navajo Times,* May 30, 1962; "Tribal Utility Authority Energizes Power Line System," "A Switch Is Pulled," "A Light Goes On," "Backbone Transmission Project Brings Light to Hogan," *Navajo Times,* June 13, 1962.

79. Peterson Zah, interview with the author, March 26, 2001. Also see O'Neill 2005.

80. "Accomplishment Report for the Navajo Tribal Utility Authority," 1963, 7, copy in Records Management, NTUA Headquarters, Fort Defiance, AZ.

81. Secretary of the Interior Stewart Udall submitted legislation for another coal-fired plant in 1967. The Peabody Coal Company had signed leases with the Navajo and Hopi tribes to strip-mine a site known as Black Mesa. The Peabody negotiations provided a boon to NTUA's Kayenta and Tuba City branches in terms of revenue, increased electrical requirements (load growth), and power supply. Part of the coal mined there (7 million tons a year) would be transported via electric railroad for 78 miles to power the Navajo Generating Station (NGS) at Page, Arizona, the boomtown created during the construction of Glen Canyon Dam. A portion of the Navajos' share of Colorado River water also powered the station. To electrify Los Angeles, the rest was combined into a slurry of coal and water to slide through an 18-inch-wide, 274-mile-long pipeline to the Mohave power plant on the Colorado River in southern Nevada. Pearson 2000; Callaway, Levy, and Henderson 1976:13; Annual Report of the Navajo Tribal Utility Authority, 1969, 1, 2, 1970, 1971; C. Mac Eddy to Management Board, June 8, 1969, General Manager's Files, 1960–1990, Records Management, NTUA-HQ.

82. Annual Report of the Navajo Tribal Utility Authority, 1969, 1–2, 1970, 1971; C. Mac Eddy to Management Board, June 8, 1969, General Manager's Files, 1960–1990, Records Management, NTUA-HQ.

83. Not every subsequent NTUA general manager was Indian, but Randall Medicine Bear served in the job through the 1990s and into the twenty-first century. C. Mac Eddy to Management Board, March 9, 1970, General Manager's Files, Records Management, NTUA-HQ; "A Century of Progress," *Navajo Times,* June 18, 1968; "40 Years of NTUA Employees," NTUA Annual Report, 40th Anniversary Edition, 1999, 18–26; Malcolm Dalton, interview with author, May 19, 2001.

84. "Power Supply Study," October 23, 1967, Roy Cleveland to Malcolm Dalton, September 11, 1987, General Manager's Files, Records Management, NTUA-HQ; "NTUA: A Light in Every Hogan," *Navajo Times,* September 5, 1962.

85. Willigen and Pancho to Fannin, August 28, 1968, Bicknell to Fannin, June 3, 1968, Papers of Paul Fannin, Arizona Historical Foundation, Hayden Library, Arizona State University, Tempe.

86. Testimony of Marvin L. Athey to Senate Select Committee on Indian Affairs, Joint Hearing before the Select Committee on Indian Affairs and House Committee on Interior and Insular Affairs on the San Carlos Indian Irrigation Project Divestiture Act of 1991, S. 1869 and H.R. 1476, 102nd Congress, 1st sess., October 29, 1991, p. 97.

87. NTUA does not serve the entire Navajo Nation. The Arizona Public Service Company still serves residents in the western portion of the reservation. The Continental Divide Electric Cooperative and Jemez Mountain Electric Cooperative serve residents in the east portion. Residents near Gallup and Farmington, New Mexico, receive city power. Rocky Mountain Electric also provides electric service to the reservation residents in southeastern Utah. Navajo Tribal Utility Authority, http://www.ntua.com/ (accessed January 2008).

88. Mac Eddy, interview by author, May 8, 1998.

89. Peterson Zah, "A Century of Progress," *Navajo Times,* June 18, 1968.

90. In 1966 the Traditionalist Movement added public utilities to the platform, for reasons more of dependence than opposition to change. Many owned cars and propane stoves and participated in wage labor. For a more nuanced examination of the movement, 1946–1977, see Clemens 1995:194, as well as the group's papers at the University of Arizona: Ralph Selina, Hopi, Folder 18, and Jolan Terez, "Hotevilla Wins," Folder 10, Hopi Traditionalist Movement Papers, 1949–1972, Special Collections, University of Arizona, Tucson; Editorial, *Hopi Action News,* August 5, 1966; "Construction of Road and Utility Line Causes Rift in Hotevilla," *Hopi Action News,* May 23, 1968; Winona La Duke, "Traditionalists Get Electricity without Objectionable Power Lines: Hopi Woman Is Solar Electrician for the Hopi Foundation," *News from Indian Country,* November 15, 1994; Mills 1997:12.

91. "Problems of My Community," *Hopi Action News,* November 18, 1966; "A Student's Viewpoint of Hotevilla," *Hopi Action News,* July 12, 1968.

92. Lewis 1991; Benedek 1993:25.

93. *Hopi Action News,* September 9, 1966.

94. "Energetic Apaches Give Up Warlike Roles," *The Timberline,* April 1961; "Are Your Records Safe?" Rural Lines, May 1959, 5:15–16.

95. Maggie Wilson (*Arizona Republic*), "Opposing Cultures of Navajos Meet Head On," *Navajo Times,* August 1, 1962.

96. Ancita Benally, interview with author, March 30, 2001.

97. Dockstader 1987:40; Andrew Nagen, "A Personal Look at Navajo Weavings," in *The Wingspread Collector's Guide to Santa Fe, Taos and Albuquerque*, http://www.collectorsguide.com/fa/fa085.shtml (accessed December 2009).

98. By 1959, resorts surpassed lumber as the leading business in the White Mountains. "Are Your Records Safe?" *Rural Lines*, May 1959, 5:15–16; Harry R. Kallender, forester, BIA, "McNary Town and the White Mountain Apache Forest on the Fort Apache Indian Reservation, Arizona," in The McNary Reunion Committee, *Reflections of McNary* (Show Low, AZ: The McNary Reunion Committee, 1989), 18.

99. Tribal Minutes, 1962–1969, CCF 54, Fort Apache Agency, Box 76, 89, RG 75, NAB.

100. *Fort Apache Scout*, September 1962.

101. Johnson 1969:i–ii, 2.

102. Trimble 1993:122, 126.

103. *Arizona Trend* 1987:12; Senate Select Committee on Indian Affairs, "San Carlos Indian Irrigation Project Divestiture Act," 102 Congress, 2nd sess., October 29, 1991, 60.

104. Max Jarman, "Electric Deregulation Hits Poor Arizona Areas Hard," *The Arizona Republic*, August 16, 2000.

105. "Mollie's TV," *Indian Arizona News*, August 1979; Ancita Benally, interview with author, March 30, 2001; Peterson Zah, interview with the author, March 26, 2001.

106. Malcolm Dalton, interview with author, May 19, 2001; Western Area Power Administration, "Native American Power Customers," http://www.wapa.gov/newsroom/FactSheets/factsnative.htm (accessed January 2008). The Diné Power Authority formed as a tribal enterprise to develop and control power generation on the reservation.

107. "Arizona Accelerates Solar Electricity Access for Tribes," *US States News*, August 28, 2007.

108. Felicity Barringer, "Navajos Hope for Millions a Year from Power Plant," *New York Times*, July 27, 2007.

109. Energy Information Administration (see note 2); Lisa Nurnberger, "Native American Phones," *All Things Considered*, National Public Radio, October 20, 1999; "Students in Tribe Go Online," *Tempe Tribune*, April 26, 1999; Kara Briggs, "Briggs: Communication Is the Key," *Indian Country Today*, December 17, 2008.

110. Essay contest winners Sheree Yazee, "Internet Will Provide Knowledge, Power for Navajos," and Sheldon Burnside, "NTUA Can Make a Splash by Helping Us Surf the Web," NTUA Annual Report, 40th Anniversary Edition, 1999, 17; Declan McCullagh, "Clinton Tackles Digital Divide," *Wired News*, February 22, 2000, http://www.wired.com/news/politics/0,1283,33002,00.html (accessed November

2001); Kathleen Ingley, "Rural Arizona Poverty Persists," *Arizona Republic*, November 22, 2000; "Students in Tribe Go Online," *Tempe Tribune*, April 26, 1999; Mary K. Preatt, "The Navajo Nation Connects Its People to the Internet," Computer-world, October 27, 2007; Felicia Fonseca, "Navajo Communities Still without Internet Access," *Indian Country Today*, April 20, 2008.

111. For more on the Navajo experience of change, adaptation, and incorporation, see O'Neill 2005; Iverson 2002a.

9

"A Piece of the Action"

Navajo Nationalism, Energy Development, and Metropolitan Inequality

Andrew Needham

Navajo tribal chairman Peter MacDonald's inaugural address in January 1971 culminated in a ringing call for self-determination. Standing before 7,500 people at the tribal fairgrounds, MacDonald laid out the three goals of his chairmanship: "First, what is rightfully ours, we must protect; what is rightfully due us, we must claim. Second, what we depend on from others, we must replace with the labor of our own hands and the skills of our own people. Third, what we do not have, we must create for ourselves."[1] One year later, in the early stages of the 1970s energy crisis, MacDonald told the National Governors Association of his plan to implement these goals. "The Navajo Nation has many of the ingredients to solve the energy crisis," he told the assembled governors, "[but] it must be clearly understood that it will no longer be accepted practice to sell the reservation off by the ton or by the barrel. From now on the Navajos want a piece of the action."[2] In MacDonald's mind, getting a "piece of the action" from energy development occurring on Navajo land would lead the tribe not only toward self-determination but also to greater political power within the Southwest and the nation.

MacDonald was hardly the only Navajo speaking about energy resources and self-determination in the late 1960s and early 1970s. During those years, Navajo tribal officials and activist groups such as the National Indian Youth Council, the American Indian Movement, Dineh for Justice, and the Committee for Navajo Liberation shared a political language, which I will term *Navajo nationalism*, that expressed as one of its central tenets the need for the Navajo Tribe to assert greater control over the energy development then transforming the Navajo landscape.

Evidence of this transformation ranged widely across the Colorado Plateau. In the east, near Farmington, New Mexico, Arizona Public Service's high-voltage transmission lines spread outward from Four Corners Power Plant to the growing cities of the Southwest. In the west, near Page, Arizona, the Salt River Project's survey stakes marked the land set aside for the Navajo Generating Station. And at the center of the Navajo Nation, Peabody Coal's giant drag lines tore coal from the strip mine located on Black Mesa. But the landscapes surrounding the Colorado Plateau are what revealed the breadth of the spatial inequalities that helped give voice to Navajo nationalism.[3] The power lines from the power plants located on or near Navajo land eventually marched forth onto the suburban landscapes of Phoenix, Los Angeles, and other southwestern metropolises.[4] For both tribal officials and Navajo activists, the political economy of energy development—in which residents of the metropolitan Southwest received inexpensive electricity while strip mines and air pollution damaged the Navajo landscape in return for minimal royalty payments—structured the Navajos' place in the Southwest. It represented the control that outside forces had over their land and lives. More broadly, it demonstrated to both tribal officials and activists that the southwestern economy was developed along neo-colonial lines, with development on Indian lands benefiting only the region's metropolitan areas.[5]

Tribal officials and youth activists may have agreed on this description of the Navajos' subordinate place within the Southwest, but they disagreed vehemently with each other on the meaning of "self-determination," "decolonization," and other key ideals of Navajo nationalism. Tribal officials such as MacDonald saw energy development as key to the formation of a Navajo state that would act as a regional power broker, and they sought to enter into partnerships with energy companies to give the Navajo Nation "a piece of the action." Younger activists saw the environmental damage and cultural change wrought by energy development as antithetical to Navajo culture. As Navajos struggled with one another and with those outside the Navajo Nation to give meaning to nationalism's ideals, energy development became the main issue informing their debates.

This chapter investigates these debates over nationalism and energy development. In doing so, it seeks to make connections between two political developments that have existed far apart in the minds of scholars: the nationalist movements among Indian peoples since the 1960s and the rapid growth of metropolitan America since World War II. It makes these connections with two primary arguments. First, it argues that the Navajo nationalism emerging in the late 1960s and early 1970s cannot be understood apart from the metropolitan demand for resources. Navajo nationalism was largely a response to the ongoing subordination of Navajos within the political economy of the wider Southwest. The dynamics of metropolitan growth gave new value to Navajo resources, both in the material value of power plants and transmission lines and in Navajos' new imaginations of the power to be gained by controlling those resources.[6] Metropolitan demand produced the notion that Navajos possessed massive mineral wealth. This notion allowed young activists to imagine the Navajo Nation as a space colonized by the greedy cities of the Southwest. It allowed Peter MacDonald to imagine the Navajo Nation as a mineral-rich "emerging" nation, powerful enough to control the distribution of power in the region. Moreover, all versions of Navajo nationalism recognized that metropolitan growth depended on the resources located on their land. The new nationalism attempted to manipulate this dependence to increase Navajo political power.

Second, the chapter stresses the centrality of Indian resources to metropolitan growth in the Southwest. Far too often, histories of metropolitan growth have ignored its far-reaching impact on the landscapes and peoples living beyond the suburban fringe.[7] Phoenix's modern landscape of subdivisions and high tech industry would have been impossible without the corresponding modern landscape of coal mines and power plants on the Colorado Plateau. Federal officials and metropolitan boosters worked to connect these two landscapes, bringing Navajo resources into the metropolitan orbit in the name of promoting growth and of "assimilating" the Navajo into the metropolitan economy. Given the failure of energy development to provide meaningful economic opportunity or political power to Navajos, Navajo nationalism was part of a larger criticism of the failings of the metropolitan political economy. Examining the importance of energy development to Navajo nationalism reveals not only the internal tensions of Navajo politics but also a broad connection between Indian nationalists and other groups in the United States critical of metropolitan inequality.[8]

GROWTH POLITICS AND ENERGY DEVELOPMENT IN THE SOUTHWEST

In the years following World War II, the metropolitan Southwest grew at a blistering pace. Between 1940 and 1970, Los Angeles grew from 1.5 million to 2.8 million residents, Albuquerque from 35,000 to 243,000, and Phoenix from 40,000 to 650,000.[9] Boosters held that people flocked to the Southwest because of the region's climate, frontier spirit, or modern lifestyles, but the growth reflected broader structural changes in the nation's political economy. The metropolitan Southwest benefited from the two most powerful of those changes. First, suburban home construction and national defense spending brought a flood of federal dollars to the Southwest.[10] Second, civic leaders shaped policy to attract this capital.[11] Civic leaders in Phoenix cut local property taxes and state manufacturing taxes, passed a stringent "right to work" law, and sent officials around the country to court business. The combination of federal spending and local boosterism created the metropolitan Southwest.[12]

These ideologies also changed the landscape beyond metropolitan borders. Both growth liberals and conservative boosters worked to bring Navajo labor and resources into the metropolitan orbit. The Navajo-Hopi Rehabilitation Act of 1950 attempted to develop consumer culture on the Navajo reservation and to begin relocating Navajos to urban areas.[13] Local boosters embraced relocation while promoting the leasing of Navajo mineral resources. Advocates of each ideology told Navajos that their efforts would lead to greater economic security. They also argued that Navajos must abandon tribalism and, in many cases, the reservation itself to achieve the "American standard of living." Although these policies proved markedly unsuccessful in redressing economic inequalities, they were successful in bringing Navajo energy resources into production for metropolitan consumers. The increasing use of energy resources and seemingly widening gap between the Navajo Nation and the metropolitan Southwest laid the basis for Navajo nationalism.

The Navajo-Hopi Long Range Rehabilitation Act of 1950 was the first important attempt to develop Navajo resources. Offering a combination of federal spending on road and communication infrastructure, resource surveys, and education, the act aimed, according to President Harry Truman's Assistant Secretary of the Interior William Warne, to get Navajo and Hopi peoples "out into the main swim of the economy and civilization down there in the Southwest."[14] The act displayed the postwar liberal faith in the potential of state-fueled growth and mass consumption to solve almost any social problem.[15] Navajo society, which faced dire health conditions and pitiful educational opportunities, represented both a challenge and a threat to American liberalism's high tide. If the federal government enabled Navajos "to overcome their difficulties and achieve a standard of living comparable with that of the nation as a whole," Secretary of the Interior Julius Krug insisted, the act would prove the transformative power of the "affluent society." It would also shore up the nation's Cold War reputation overseas by denying ammunition to what Warne termed "the anti-American foreign press" that used "the plight of the Navajos...to derogate the treatment received by minority groups in the United States."[16] Failure to bring Navajos up to the "American standard of living," then, threatened the nation's international prestige.[17]

While expressing faith in the ability of Navajos to achieve this standard of living, the bill's advocates also believed that Navajos required extensive instruction in modernity. Federal officials saw Navajos living in what they termed "a premodern state." William Warne testified to Congress: "The Navajos are passing through a stage of development that the rest of American society experienced fifty to one hundred years ago." He went on, "We must work to change their standard of living away from subsistence agriculture [or]...they cannot become part of the region in which they live."[18] Federal officials aimed simultaneously to modernize infrastructure on the reservation and educate Navajos in the way of the modern world. Navajos employed to build roads, schools, and telephone and electrical lines would attend intensive night classes in English literacy, economic management, and "all of the various...things that it [would] be advantageous...to know."[19] This education—proficiency in English, mechanical instruction, and capitalist work discipline—sought to create the basis of what Thomas Biolsi termed "modern individuality": "social persons who could fit into the American nation-state and the market system of metropolitan capitalism."[20]

Even with new roads and schools, which Navajo leaders welcomed, the act's primary legacy lay in its mineral surveys and in efforts to relocate Navajos away from the reservation. The mineral surveys, which reported substantial oil, natural gas, and coal reserves, stimulated interest among Arizona public utilities in coal resources on Navajo and Hopi land.[21] Relocation efforts—ranging from temporary off-reservation work programs to relocating nearly ten thousand Navajos to the abandoned Poston Internment Center on the Colorado River Indian reservation—reflected beliefs that Navajo ties to unproductive land stood in the way of Navajo modernization.[22] James Preston, Assistant Secretary of the Interior, testified that the Navajo country was "a picturesque and beautiful area" and said,

"They're starving, but they'll stay there unless something forces them to leave."[23] Warne and other highly placed officials told Navajos that they would find high-wage work in metropolitan centers, but the director of one off-reservation labor program told Congress a different story: "We have in that area been depending on imported labor, chiefly from Mexico.…Now, the Mexican Government has increased its safeguards…and it has been increasingly difficult for us to get Mexican nationals or white labor.… Therefore, there is a great deal of labor opportunity for Navajo Indians."[24] Navajos did, in fact, come to occupy a large percentage of the temporary agricultural workforce during the 1950s, the only sector of Arizona's economy in which they did so.[25] Even as officials argued that Navajos could rapidly achieve an "American standard of living," they steered them toward the lowest wage sectors of the southwestern economy. They asked Navajos to abandon their land to become a low-wage proletariat. Little wonder that most Navajos rejected relocation programs and demanded programs to draw jobs to the reservation.

As liberals in the Interior department pushed the Rehabilitation Act, metropolitan boosters in Phoenix sought to extend Arizona's control over Navajo land. These boosters represented a second growth ideology, which existed in concert and competition with the Rehabilitation Act's growth liberalism. Phoenix boosters welcomed growth liberal programs such as the Federal Housing Authority mortgages and social security payments—allowing suburban development and new retirement spending, respectively—but they eschewed liberalism's goal of broad-based growth. Instead, they pursued tax cuts and industrial promotion that would give Phoenix a comparative advantage over other metropolitan areas.[26] Phoenix's boosters gained new power with the 1953 appointment of Orme Lewis, a Phoenix lawyer, as assistant secretary of the Interior under President Dwight Eisenhower. Lewis worked to develop policies that would allow federal withdrawal from Indian affairs and would benefit Phoenix's growth. Upon taking his position, Lewis appointed Walter Bimson, a Phoenix banker (who later stated, "The growth of Phoenix was my paramount interest in all that I did"), to head a panel reviewing federal Indian policy. With a mandate to decrease federal spending, Bimson's panel recommended an expansion of relocation programs and leasing of Indian resources.[27] These proposals met the panel's policy mandates and also served to channel benefits toward Phoenix.

Nowhere was this clearer than in the case of mineral leasing. Already bolstered by the Rehabilitation Act's survey of mineral resources, Phoenix boosters' presence within the Interior department influenced Phoenix-based utilities' decision to explore the viability of Navajo resources. Like Lewis and Bimson, the chief executives of Phoenix's two electrical utilities, Walter Lucking of Arizona Public Service and R. J. McMullen of the Salt River Project, occupied prominent positions on Phoenix's Chamber of Commerce during the 1950s. As Phoenix and its electrical demand grew, Arizona's utilities required new energy resources. Given these connections, it is not surprising that the Eisenhower years saw a dramatic increase in leases, negotiated by federal officials, between the Navajo Tribe and Arizona's electrical utilities.[28]

Navajo leaders initially welcomed the interest of both utilities and mining companies. As Leah Glaser's chapter 8 (this volume) demonstrates, tribal officials promoted electrification through the Navajo Tribal Utility Authority as a means of creating new economic possibilities on Navajo land in the 1950s. Officials also welcomed the new revenues that energy development brought. In 1959, Paul Jones, Navajo tribal chairman, thanked the "divine Providence" that had brought "unexpected wealth from...natural resources." Jones referred mainly to the oil wells near Aneth, which brought $80 million to the tribe between 1955 and 1961. During those years, tribal officials expanded the social services provided for Navajos. The threat of termination led Jones and subsequent leaders to embrace energy development and to seek the expansion of tribal services. Jones declared, shortly after discovery of the oil in Aneth, "It has been stated in 1960 that there will be 120,000 Navajos. What are we going to do about it? We are not going to let our people starve. We will give them as decent a living as we can within our power. That is the reason for the various projects to get industry and drilling."[29] Jones viewed energy development as a means of providing a safety net should the federal government eliminate funding to the tribe. Although the Navajo Tribe never came close to facing a federal termination bill, the potential threat led leaders to embrace energy development as the only industry capable of protecting the tribe.

As coal mining became more prevalent in the 1960s, both energy development benefits and the attempts to establish the "American standard of living" appeared to be increasingly empty promises. Oil and natural gas continued to bring steady revenue, but large bonus payments from the initiation of operations ceased. Agreements to mine coal, signed at the historical nadir of coal prices, brought less money than did oil or gas leases. More important, although the tribe's leases with Utah International and Peabody Coal contained employment clauses giving hiring preferences to Navajos, these clauses imposed few penalties on the companies for not achieving the stated goals. Navajo people received few jobs above the level of "laborer" at either Utah International's Navajo Coal Mine or Peabody Coal's Black Mesa Mine, eventually sparking the labor mobilization that Colleen O'Neill's chapter 7 (this volume) details. Like the relocation programs, energy development incorporated Navajos at the lowest possible levels of employment while channeling the benefits of their labor toward the metropolitan centers.

The failure of 1950s federal and regional programs to incorporate Navajos into the regional economy sowed the seeds for Navajo nationalism. The programs had promised a trade-off: federal and local officials would dictate changes, and Navajos would gain economic security. The programs did indeed initiate dramatic changes to the Navajo world, but few Navajos saw economic benefits. Increasingly, many Navajos came to see the metropolitan Southwest not as a potential source of economic security, but as the main force exerting control over their land and their lives.

ENERGY DEVELOPMENT AND THE EMERGENCE OF NAVAJO NATIONALISM

Returning from a visit home in November 1970, Lena Dean, a student at Intermountain School in Brigham City, Utah, wrote a letter to the *Navajo Times*. She lamented seeing mining equipment travel past on the way to Black Mesa Mine and concluded with the following plea: "Let's not let the highways and new houses of Los Angeles spoil our beautiful home. It's time for the people and not the leaders to make decisions. Let Peabody go to Los Angeles and let's use our resources for our own good."[30] Dean's letter expresses the sentiments of many young Navajos, that energy development offered little to most Navajos and that the "American standard of living" reflected unhealthy values that endangered Navajo culture. Nowhere were those values more apparent than in the metropolitan Southwest's consumer culture, criticized by Douglas Dunlap in the *Navajo Times* as destroying Navajo land so that people could "use electric can openers and tooth brushes."[31] Dean and Dunlap were only two examples of a broader criticism, made by many young Navajos, that questioned the Navajos' incorporation into the regional economy. At the heart of this emerging Navajo nationalism were questions about the effects of energy development on Navajo culture and society.

These letters to the *Navajo Times* reflect the increasing militancy of some young Navajos in the late 1960s, partly resulting from pan-Indian organizing among young Navajos. The National Indian Youth Council (NIYC) had many Navajo members, some of whom, in 1969, established *Diné Baa-Hani*, a newspaper styled "the people's press" as an alternative to the tribally run *Navajo Times.*[32] Further, the American Indian Movement had attracted enough Navajos by 1974 to have a regular column in the *Navajo Times,* in which writers made similar arguments about energy development. Despite the influence of these pan-tribal organizations, identification as Navajo or Diné characterized most activism. Groups forming in the late 1960s almost always indicated their tribal status in their names: Dineh for Justice, the Coalition for Navajo Liberation, the Committee to Save Black Mesa. Specifically attuned to the status of Navajos within the Southwest, the rhetoric of these activist groups began cohering in the late 1960s to form a shared view of Navajos as a colonized people and the Navajo Nation as a colony of the metropolitan Southwest.[33]

In part, criticism of energy development grew in the late 1960s because it had become a greater material presence on the Navajo landscape. In the late 1950s and early 1960s, physical signs of energy development had been relatively contained—at the oil fields near Aneth, the gas wells near Teec Nos Pos, and the mine and power plant complex near the Four Corners. By the late 1960s, however, the infrastructure connecting Black Mesa Mine with the Mohave and the Navajo generating stations, as well as the power lines emanating from Four Corners, became increasingly visible across the reservation. This visibility prompted new questions about the relationship between Navajos and metropolitan consumers. *Diné Baa-Hani* explained, "The coal that fires their power plants to produce electricity for them will be returned to you in the air you breathe....They will make $750,000,000. They will give you 1.6% of this amount." The editors of *Diné Baa-Hani* went on to question the entire premise that incorporation into the regional economy would benefit Navajos: "They say the Indians must join the market economy, but they force us into a colonial economy. This is not economic development. This is economic termination!"[34]

Young activists blamed both the BIA and Navajo politicians for the negative impact of energy development. They attacked the BIA's advocacy of "modernization" plans as misrepresenting the Navajo economy as premodern. At least since the Rehabilitation Act, the BIA's model of economic development had been premised on the assumption that the Navajos were going through a transition from subsistence agriculture to a modern economy. According to this understanding, Navajo economic woes resulted from the mismatch between the tribe's "premodern" status and the surrounding modern industrial society. The Navajo economy, according to the BIA, was literally trapped in the past. In contrast, young activists blamed the BIA for subordinating Navajo interests to the demands of the regional economy for inexpensive electricity. Indeed, a 1975 GAO (US General

Accounting Office) study found that the BIA was woefully short of independent advisors on mineral leasing.[35] But the activists' criticism went beyond imputing that the BIA was ill-trained. In their minds, the BIA's economic development policies (and the liberal theories of growth on which these were based) made the fatal assumption that what benefited the regional economy would necessarily benefit Navajos.

The activists characterized tribal officials both as naïve dupes of the BIA who had given away valuable resources and as greedy parasites growing fat off energy contracts. The gentlest criticism of tribal officials implied that they acceded to the BIA's advice without gaining necessary information. In *Diné Baa-Hani,* Orville McKinney reported that the BIA had negotiated the contracts and told the tribal council to approve them without deliberation. McKinney concluded, "It is apparent that the Navajo tribal council signed the lease without a complete understanding of the ecological damage that these power plants could do....The pressure came through our favorite whipping boy—the BIA."[36] Judging from letters to the *Navajo Times,* many Navajos shared this conception of the tribal government as inept in the face of BIA pressure. Esther Patrick of Gallup wrote about the tribe's approval of the Navajo Generating Station: "Here we go again. The vultures of a non-Indian society are pulling the strings in Washington. The Four Corners Area is licking its chops to see where the stupid Indians can give in to some kind of political pressure."[37] Patrick stopped there, but others went further, charging that the tribal government had abandoned the people it represented. Caleb Johnson, a member of the Hopi Tribe, charged that both the Navajo and Hopi tribal councils had abandoned their public trust for financial gain: "The trend in these two tribal governments is for more and more profits at the expense of the land of all the people. But, I have yet to see in what way the Hopis and Navajos have been helped."[38]

Johnson's argument became common among those opposing energy developments. While residents of the affected areas experienced increased poverty, the tribal governments created "a self-supporting bureaucracy," failing to help "common people." The tribe had exchanged land resources, on which many tribal members relied, for financial resources that benefited only a growing tribal bureaucracy. Tribal leaders were to blame for agreeing to this exchange and for forcing it upon an unwilling people. These critics drew clear lines between the tribal government and the Navajo people. They viewed concern for Navajo people and Navajo culture as the essence of Navajo nationalism and viewed support for energy development as destroying Navajo culture. This version of nationalism saw nondevelopment as the key to preserving Navajo cultural identity. Leaders who supported energy development were the pawns of larger forces antithetical, and destructive, to Navajo culture.[39]

Nowhere was this more evident than in the depiction of Navajos living near energy development projects. The reportage in *Diné Baa-Hani* emphasized the distance of people on Black Mesa from the tribal government. Articles quoted people living on Black Mesa who stated that the mining had destroyed their land and livelihood and that they had been excluded from decisions about their own fates. The words of Many Mules' Daughter encapsulated these concerns: "Where they are mining now is my land. My father is buried there. His grave was torn up in the strip mining. I never approved of anything in the agreement to mine this area. I don't know of anybody who agreed to this contract."[40] The publishers of *Diné Baa-Hani* conceived their mission as protecting Diné living on Black Mesa from both the tribal government and energy companies.

The nationalists' defense of "traditional" people and culture should not be understood through reference to the dichotomy between traditionalism and progressivism often used to understand Native American politics. It did, however, signal the rejection of the integration of Navajos into the "American standard of living." Nationalists explicitly rejected the notion that the values of metropolitan consumer culture could produce Navajo equality within the wider society. Rather, they insisted that metropolitan America would never see Navajos as equal. Michael Benson wrote to the *Navajo Times* criticizing the Anglo editor's characterization of the "progressive Navajo" as sharing the values of his white classmates: "Having ceased to be Navajos so that we may travel this road you call 'Progress'...will you allow us the same heart trouble? Will you allow us to mow our lawns in the same suburbs? I think not. You will laugh in our faces as we try to find a place for ourselves in your society." Benson continued that following such a path would only cause Navajos to lose touch with their culture.[41] Young nationalists sought to craft an alternative notion of modernity that incorporated limited engagement with the wider world and the protection of Navajo culture. The manifesto of the group Dineh for Justice stated:

> We can easily point to some Navajos whom we consider "traditional" by their own definitions, yet who are secure in warm, modest homes with electricity....Just because someone drives a pickup, do not assume that he is a "progressive" Indian who

> abhors and disrespects his Navajo traditions! Yes, some of us have gone to college, but our education, if it was a good one, has pointed out to us that we do not want and will not live the life of an ulcerated white, middle-class Christian suburbanite....We do not want to hold back the times—we merely want to clarify that we are grateful to our elders for enriching us with a heritage, unique and secure, in this time of chaotic and rapid change.[42]

Or as Benson stated in his letter, "Tell me, am I traveling the 'Tradition' road or the 'Progress' road? How about building a new road for me? The Navajo road."[43]

At the heart of this search for a "Navajo road" was a rejection also of the broader growth politics underlying the "American" lifestyle. Young Navajo nationalists found American consumerism to be an abandonment of their culture, which did not value conspicuous consumption. They found themselves in a similar position as many in the counterculture, who engaged in a search for personal meaning that often turned to Indians as a source of authenticity.[44] (This similarity also brought criticism from some Navajos, such as Betty Boyd, who wrote to the *Navajo Times*, "Our leaders are turning out to be leaders in the world of the hippies, not the world of the Navajo.")[45] In protesting growth politics, however, nationalists went beyond most criticisms of American consumer culture. Advocates for growth politics, from Lyndon Johnson to Barry Goldwater, had contended that metropolitan growth would benefit the entire social spectrum, as a rising tide lifts all boats. For Navajo nationalists, the immediate reality of mining refuse, smokestacks, and power lines undermined these ideas. Instead of universally beneficial, growth seemed profoundly unequal and exploitative. The growth of suburban consumer landscapes in Phoenix and Los Angeles depended on Navajo energy development, but the returns from those developments did not find their way to Navajo pockets. Instead, profits went to energy companies, and perhaps a few corrupt Navajos, while the majority of Navajos lived in a landscape of poverty and ecological destruction.

Despite the sophistication of nationalists' criticisms, they offered few solutions to this exploitation. Although the leases were profoundly unequal, these did return needed revenue to the tribal government. Should the Navajo Tribe devise a way to block objectionable energy development projects, what would serve as the tribe's economic base? Upon election as tribal chairman in 1970, Peter MacDonald offered a plan to harness energy development to give Navajos new power within the metropolitan economy.

ENERGY DEVELOPMENT AS STATE BUILDING? PETER MACDONALD'S VISION

At first glance, Peter MacDonald seemed an unlikely figure to embrace Navajo nationalism. Born in 1928 near Teec Nos Pos, MacDonald left home in 1943 to enlist in the Marines. He would not permanently return for more than twenty years. Discharged in 1946, MacDonald moved to Oklahoma to attend Bacone High School and then the University of Oklahoma, earning a degree in electrical engineering in 1957. After graduation, MacDonald took a job as a project engineer with Hughes Aircraft in suburban Los Angeles. He returned to the Navajo Nation in 1963 to join the New Mexico state economic advisory board and to head the Navajo Nation's Management, Methods, and Procedures division. Two years later, he became head of the Office of Navajo Economic Opportunity, a Great Society project. In a way, MacDonald shared the professional and educational background—aerospace engineer, white collar employee, federal bureaucrat—of many of the white collar migrants who flocked to the Southwest during the postwar era.[46]

Despite this background, MacDonald echoed the militants' anticolonial rhetoric throughout his election campaign and his first two administrations. During the 1970 campaign, he repeatedly denounced his opponent, Raymond Nakai, for being remote from "the people" and caring more about securing money from energy companies than protecting the tribe's interests. He openly talked of the Navajo Nation as an American colony and referred to "the colonial relationship between the Navajo Nation and the cities of the Southwest." He displayed his difference from Nakai sartorially as well, conspicuously wearing ribbon and velvet shirts, cowboy hats, and silver and turquoise jewelry (Nakai wore suits while campaigning). Despite (or because of) his time away from the Navajo Nation, MacDonald emphasized his support for the "traditional" Navajos, having election photos taken with his family's sheep and near their hogans in Teec Nos Pos. The *Navajo Times* picked up on these differences: "[MacDonald] probably speaks more for the young people in the Navajo Nation" and "is more of a nationalist" than Nakai, who "is more of the voice of the establishment."[47]

Upon assuming office, MacDonald continued to emphasize the metropolitan Southwest's exploitation of Navajos. He aimed some of this rhetoric at political opponents off the reservation. After Barry Goldwater complained that MacDonald had endorsed Goldwater's opponent in the 1974 Senate race, MacDonald responded that Goldwater only liked Navajos who were content to remain centerfolds in *Arizona Highways*.[48]

MacDonald also used this polarizing rhetoric to point out the more systemic exploitation involved in energy development. He utilized several elements of the nationalist rhetoric developed by young Navajo militants. Speaking to the Phoenix Community Council, MacDonald stated, "Economically, our reservations are in a colonial relationship with the rest of the United States."[49] Energy development was not the only facet of this colonial relationship, but it was the most frequent referent in MacDonald's speeches. It allowed him to draw clear comparisons between the exploitation and deprivation of Navajo land and the consumer excesses of the surrounding cities. Speaking to officials from western states and power companies in Albuquerque, MacDonald stated, "For too long we have seen unfair contracts for the exploitation of our resources and our people. We have seen our land scarred by mine sites...so that the giant cities of our country can be too cool in summer and too warm in winter."[50] He evoked the residents of Black Mesa as the boldest case of southwestern inequality. Addressing the Rocky Mountain Mineral Law Foundation in Tucson, MacDonald denounced the current political economy's neglect of Navajo needs:

> It is obscene for energy to be produced on Indian lands and yet see our own people deprived of the very barest necessities of civilized life....Think for a minute about how it feels to be a Navajo shivering through a cold winter on Black Mesa...without electricity or gas or water, while at the same time you watch well-paid anglo workers assemble a ten or fifteen million dollar drag line only a few hundred yards from your front door.[51]

MacDonald, however, utilized this colonial critique for very different ends than did young militants. Whereas they sought to stop energy development and protect "traditional" Navajos, MacDonald advocated a new relationship with energy companies. He repeatedly addressed forums on the future of the Southwest that included business leaders and energy executives, along with government officials. In these speeches, he criticized existing power relationships but held back from directly criticizing energy companies for their role in creating inequalities. Young militants had pointed to the tribal government, energy companies, and the BIA as agents of colonialism. MacDonald focused only on the BIA. Unlike the militants, he did not denounce Peabody Coal or Arizona Public Service. The main goal of his speeches was not to repudiate energy development, but to protest the BIA-approved energy contracts that neglected the long-term needs of the Navajo Tribe.

In short, MacDonald believed that the BIA ignored the best interests of the tribe to satisfy the demands of the surrounding society for cheap power in the name of economic growth. He described energy development to Americans for Indian Opportunity: "The commodities, areas, terms, and timing were all determined by outside interests and the Navajo Tribe was always subjected to having to react to various proposals, usually without adequate preparation or background."[52] The terms MacDonald used in describing the role of the BIA—"subjected" and "determined by outside interests"—reflected his analysis that the BIA treated Navajos as colonial subjects. MacDonald also had financial objections to BIA activities. He felt that agency officials often endorsed contracts (such as the contracts with Peabody and Utah International) that gave the tribe a fixed return based on the volume of coal mined, rather than basing payments on coal's market value: "The Navajo people were told to accept this exploitation and be content with the royalties provided for them."[53] Such contracts, according to MacDonald, made the interests of the tribe antagonistic to those of the energy companies. MacDonald, then, critiqued the BIA for limiting the tribe's economic possibilities, leaving it a passive renter of energy resources instead of an active partner in their development. To rectify this situation, MacDonald sought to reduce BIA authority over economic development. Changes in Indian policy in the Nixon administration largely acceded to MacDonald's recommendations by delegating authority over economic devel-opment planning to the tribes. Armed with this new authority, MacDonald sought partnerships with energy companies.

MacDonald thus rejected younger nationalists' contention that energy companies were necessarily agents of colonialism. Rather, he came to view energy development as a potential source of self-determination. Free from the BIA's constraints, the tribe could make decisions about energy development with its people's interests in mind. This difference between MacDonald and young militants largely arose from separate definitions of "self-determination." For militants, self-determination primarily concerned cultural politics—the protection of cultural and religious traditions, as well as the landscapes central to these. MacDonald and his supporters viewed self-determination as a matter of tribal authority. MacDonald went so far as to say that not only would energy development become the major source of Navajo livelihood for the next fifty years but also Navajos would become powerful only through energy development. This belief intensified with the energy crisis of the early 1970s, which MacDonald believed represented the historical moment when the Navajo Nation could disrupt structures of inequality that subordinated Navajos to the metropolitan Southwest. By using the crises to garner "a piece of the action," MacDonald hoped to gain political and economic power that would place the Navajo Nation at least on equal footing with Phoenix and Los Angeles.

What constituted "a piece of the action"? Throughout MacDonald's speeches in the early 1970s, he posed the Navajo people as willing and able workers for energy industries: "They can and will transfer some of their talents to 20th century industry." The tribe itself, he insisted, was fiscally well positioned to assist in energy development: "The Navajo Nation presently enjoys a favorable borrowing potential, and under certain conditions, might use this and other entitlements in a manner beneficial to a joint venture."[55] This last phrase, "joint venture," reveals the influence of OPEC's rise to world power on MacDonald's thinking. OPEC gained significant power in 1973 and 1974 through oil embargoes that caused dramatic gasoline shortages and price increases. For MacDonald and other Indian leaders whose tribes owned mineral resources, these actions demonstrated how energy resources could give relatively powerless nation-states the ability to dictate to the nations that had once colonized them. Quickly, MacDonald and other Navajos began drawing comparisons between their own situation and that of the OPEC nations. "Navajos, Arab-Style, to Cash in on Resources," read the title of a 1974 editorial in the *Navajo Times*: "From now on the Navajos intend to use the same kind of tactics that oil-rich Arabs have employed. Our goal is the same: a bigger take from our desert Kingdom."[56] To gain power, however, new agreements with energy industries would be needed, agreements that promoted self-sufficiency and political power instead of economic dependence and exploitation.

With these economic goals in mind, MacDonald hoped to use "joint ventures" as a tool to transform Navajos' place in the Southwest. MacDonald envisioned joint ventures as partnerships between energy industries and the tribe that came with three main stipulations. First, Navajos must be business partners, not just passive suppliers of resources. Agreements must give Navajos the possibility of buying out their partners, in effect, nationalizing the industry. Second, tribal members must be employed as high-level managers. MacDonald stated, "Our people must...have the opportunity, if they choose, to become administrators in St. Louis," the site of Peabody's corporate headquarters. The goals of employment and nationalization thus came together in MacDonald's vision, with the non-Indian developer providing training that would enable Navajos to assume control of the business venture.[57] Third, energy companies must abide by tribal laws. MacDonald argued that tribal jurisdiction was a matter of equity: "If our laws and justice are good enough for our own people, then it has to be good enough for people who choose to do business on our lands. If companies don't want our laws, then they shouldn't want our minerals either."[58]

MacDonald did not reject the southwestern growth economy. The problem with that economy, in MacDonald's view, lay primarily in the unfair returns of existing leases and the paternalistic manner in which these had been negotiated. Joint ventures would enable the Navajo Nation to develop new expertise. Future joint ventures would bring economic development, self-sufficiency, and meaningful sovereignty to the Navajo Nation. Nationalism, for MacDonald, entailed strengthening the power of the tribe and reaping economic benefits from southwestern growth. The search for joint ventures, however, did little to address the objections of Navajos living on Black Mesa or their sympathizers writing in *Diné Baa-Hani.* They objected to the inequity of postwar growth policies, but they also objected to energy development itself, its changes to the landscape, and its displacement of "traditional" tribal members. Furthermore, as MacDonald explicated his nationalist vision, they objected to his philosophy, which valued tribal empowerment over the protection of individual Navajos. To them, any participation of the tribe in energy development contradicted the very idea of being Navajo. These disputes remained latent until the proposal of a new mine and plant at Burnham, New Mexico. Then they flared into the open, creating conflicts that continue to the present day, revealing the limited ability of the Navajo Tribe to transform the bonds of metropolitan inequality and the multiple positions that Navajos themselves took on energy development.

CONFLICTING VISIONS COME TO A HEAD: BURNHAM

Burnham was analogous to Black Mesa in many ways. It was a small community of between 1,200 and 3,500 Navajos, and its members relied mainly on raising sheep and migratory wage work. Other than generators used to power the local school and trading post, Burnham lacked electric power, as well as running water. In late 1971, Utah International and WESCO announced plans to build a coal gasification plant near Burnham. The following year, El Paso Natural Gas announced its own plans to build several similar plants. The plants were to process coal into a substitute form of natural gas, which would be shipped by pipeline to Phoenix and Los Angeles. The six plants and two new coal mines were to employ three thousand workers during construction, dropping to a thousand workers when operational. This would dramatically change the landscape of Burnham, bringing not only industrial construction but also new roads, power lines, and homes. Opponents of the plan cited a study estimating that the plants would bring sixty thousand new people to and through Burnham in the first fifteen years.[59]

Although MacDonald took a neutral public position on the plants, he clearly favored their construction. His statements of neutrality—"If the people do not want gasification, we will not have it"—were almost always followed by statements emphasizing the potential benefits of the plants: "We also seek new ideas, new influences, new opportunities. That is why we solicit industry. Industry to help reduce our rate of unemployment. Industry to help better our living standard. Industry to provide reservation employment that keeps our people here, at home."[60]

Furthermore, tribal officials repeatedly advocated for the plants. Mac Eddy, the tribe's director of program development, said that the plants would have "one of the greatest social and economic impacts that this region [would] ever experience." According to Eddy, the plants would provide the key engine to propel the Navajos out of colonial status: "The Navajo Nation has been a sleeping giant for many years, a nation within a nation, with a vast potential that has been exploited and often left with only the crumbs." But with the construction of the plants, he predicted a bright future: "The Navajo Nation can and will emerge as a model for others to respect and copy from, a nation with a balanced economy consisting of industry, commercial development, education, tradition, and employment factors that are *above* national standards."[61] These benefits, officials emphasized, would accrue to the entire Navajo Nation. Tribal officials largely portrayed the projects as necessary for the Nation's advancement. They argued that returns from current lease deals were declining—MacDonald claimed that these would drop 30 percent between 1975 and 1985—and that the projects would help the tribe's finances. El Paso's promise to renegotiate its existing coal lease would bring in $5.6 million immediately and an estimated $300 million over forty years. The WESCO deal, which would use coal from the Navajo Coal Mine, made "the best of a bad deal," bringing $200 million from increased coal development and additional revenue from leasing land for the plants.[62]

MacDonald argued that the proposed terms differed from the leases signed by previous administrations: the plants would bring jobs and increase sovereignty. Although the leases were not the joint venture that MacDonald had previously advocated, the companies did agree to mandate hiring targets. WESCO agreed to Navajo preference in hiring for the plants, accepting an initial quota of a 52 percent Navajo workforce and eventually 90 percent. Furthermore, WESCO agreed to institute a training program to introduce Navajo employees into skilled work and plant management. To ensure that Navajos would be eligible for construction jobs when the plants were built, the tribe entered into an agreement with the AFL-CIO to train Navajo apprentices in building trades unions. WESCO and El Paso agreed that the Navajo courts would have jurisdiction over disputes involving employment and workplace disputes, a concession that MacDonald portrayed as a major victory for the tribe's goals of sovereignty and self-determination.[63]

Finally, MacDonald attempted to convince tribal members that the new projects were consistent with Navajo tradition. MacDonald placed strategic planning as the central feature of a distinctive Navajo philosophy: "Traditionally, we have always followed a plan of strategy. We have never used force or acted rashly without applying our minds and our plans to the task." Drawing on key Navajo historical events, MacDonald constructed a narrative of Navajo tradition in which strategic engagement and negotiation with non-Navajos had allowed Navajos to control their own destiny: "Our past leaders have negotiated the release of our people from the bondage at Fort Sumner, and this is how our predecessors increased our land base...and this is how the livestock reduction was stopped. We have survived these great challenges, not because we are powerful, but because we have appealed to the rationality of men." Citing "economic strangulation, the forces of poverty, and the lack of education and training" as forces that endangered Navajos, MacDonald framed coal gasification as the necessary evil that would enable contemporary Navajos to surmount these challenges. In short, MacDonald fashioned a version of Navajo tradition in which wise leaders made prudent choices for the good of the people.[64]

In contrast, opponents of the projects focused only marginally on the "national" importance of the plants. When they did focus on arguments about the necessity of preserving the tribal treasury and tribal employment, they "hoisted" MacDonald on his joint venture "petard." With MacDonald's talk about the tribe acting as an equal partner in development, the new proposals, with payments on the royalty basis that MacDonald had previously criticized, seemed an abandonment of principle and another example of exploitation by energy companies. John Redhouse of the NIYC stated, "We should seek to develop our resources ourselves and receive a greater portion of their true value."[65] A new group of gasification opponents calling themselves the Committee for Navajo Development asked, in a full-page statement in the *Navajo Times,* why the proposals could not follow MacDonald's prescriptions for tribal development: "The gasification plants cannot be built without our coal and our land. Why can't the Navajo Tribe have controlling interest of the gasification plants?" To ensure that the point was not missed, the statement was headed with an illustration of a bulldozer advancing on a corral and hogan while power lines extended away toward Phoenix.[66]

The main focus of opponents, however, remained on the projects' effects on the community of Burnham, which came to stand for the Navajo people in opposition to the forces of exploitation. They contrasted the pro-growth agenda of the metropolitan Southwest and MacDonald himself with the supposedly eternal values of the Navajo people. One letter to the *Navajo Times* put it this way: "Our land is more valuable than your money. It will last forever. It will not even perish by the flames of fire. As long as the sun shines and the water flows, this land will be here to give life to man and animals—we cannot sell the lives of men and animals. Therefore we cannot sell this land."[67] Testifying before the Federal Power Commission, Richard Hughes, a Navajo lawyer representing Burnham residents, painted a portrait of destruction should the plants go through. Navajos in Burnham, he said, "stand to lose all they have, including the intangibles of a culture deeply rooted in the land...the proposed development will irreparably destroy the wild beauty of the land...the Navajo culture in large parts of northwestern New Mexico faces obliteration."[68]

These two versions of coal gasification's potential impact on the Navajo future confronted each other in the Burnham chapter house. In a marked difference from the Black Mesa lease ten years earlier, energy companies attempted to convince the community of Burnham of the projects' value. El Paso Natural Gas and WESCO hosted barbeques, informational sessions, and public meetings in Burnham while the leases were debated, between 1973 and 1976. They assured Burnham residents that they were different from Peabody Coal and Utah International. Unlike those companies, WESCO and El Paso promised Navajos employment and faced "substantially strong penalties" if they failed to do so. To demonstrate good faith, Bob Rudznik, general manager of WESCO, promised that enforcement would lie in the hands of Navajo regulators: "The tribe can take us to court if necessary. Individual Navajos who feel they haven't had a fair deal in hiring could appeal directly to the office of Navajo Labor Relations." To allay fears of environmental despoliation, the WESCO officials brought photos of South African coal gasification plants showing animals grazing nearby. They assured the audience that the company would pay residents for any land they needed: "We will pay a fair amount and in any way they want it."[69] Throughout the entire process, the companies appeared to solicit the concerns of residents and seek to find answers.

All of this was for naught as far as the residents of Burnham were concerned. Three times in 1973 and 1974, the Burnham chapter voted to reject coal gasification: the first two votes were unanimous, and the third tallied 114 no votes against 14 yes. Tribal officials appealed to the tribal loyalty of Burnham residents. Andrew Benally, director of the tribe's Department of Economic Development, urged the people of Burnham, "Accept your responsibility to add money to the tribal treasury as the residents of Black Mesa and the Aneth area have so willingly done." Ignoring Benally, the Burnham chapter sent a petition telling MacDonald to cease negotiations and ordering the tribal council to reject any coal gasification permits. Some officials blamed the chapter's overwhelming opposition on "outside agitators," but the votes demonstrated the increasing divide between MacDonald's supporters and the people in the local communities targeted for energy development, along with the young activists who supported them.[70]

MacDonald believed that the dynamics of metropolitan supply and demand could be manipulated to bring the Navajo Tribe into a position of influence, authority, and power. The residents of Burnham and the young activists saw the inequalities of the metropolitan economy as fixed and insurmountable. They saw their role as preventing further damage from metropolitan growth, both to the Navajo people and to the land. The flyer for the American Indian Movement's national convention in Farmington at the height of the coal gasification controversy expressed this belief. Ringed with images of energy development's consequences—smokestacks, coal shovels, and a figure in a gas mask—the flyer read, "Indian people must protect earth, air, and water for our children and children of the oppressors whose 'progress' has turned the earth into smoky ghettos."[71]

Opposition in Burnham made it impossible for MacDonald to support the proposals. The issue of Burnham damaged MacDonald politically among the supporters of "traditional" Navajos and helped to precipitate his defeat as chairman in 1981. The episode demonstrated the ability of concerted local opposition to block development, even if favored by the tribal government. This impasse led to policy changes by the tribal government. From 1977 onward, when Navajo politicians focused on their relations with energy companies, they no longer spoke of joint ventures or getting "a piece of the action." Instead, they focused on taxation, passing a business activities tax in 1978 that taxed "all goods produced, processed or extracted from the Navajo Nation" at 5 percent. Peabody Coal, Utah International, and Arizona Public Service began paying the tax in 1983 after the Supreme Court ruled in *Merrion v. Jicarilla Apache* that businesses operating on tribal land are subject to such taxation. The tax represented a repudiation of

MacDonald's ideas of economic development. The tribe would regulate and tax the activities of energy companies operating on Navajo land, but it would not, for the time being, seek their partnership. As Dana Powell and Dáilan Long's chapter 10 demonstrates, however, partnership with global energy producers remained a continued temptation to the Navajo Tribe. New offers arose in the early 2000s as rising energy prices and the Bush administration's loosened environmental regulation again made energy production at Burnham an attractive possibility to energy companies and tribal officials alike. And again, as Powell and Long detail, a coalition of local activists formed the major opposition.

Navajos' continued attraction and opposition to energy development reflect the structural inequalities created by energy development. The Navajo Tribe has proved unable to translate its mineral wealth into sustained prosperity for more than a small number of Navajo workers. In many ways, the tribe's most successful strategy has been taxation. In this, the tribe defended the sovereign power to regulate industry that operates on tribal land. At the same time, this strategy represented a capitulation to inequalities that the metropolitan economy had fixed in space. The tribal government could work around the margins of this geography; it could draw revenues from limited regulation of activities that occurred on tribal land. It could not, however, change the dynamic in which metropolitan demand for electricity transformed Navajo landscapes. By the time Navajo people came to view the strip mines, power plants, and power lines as dangerous, it was too late. Concerted political action could stop new development, but it could not reverse existing exploitative development.

From the late 1960s until the late 1970s, Navajo nationalists engaged in some of the earliest criticism of the environmental effects of energy development and also metropolitan economic inequality. Historians have only begun to take seriously the criticisms by various nationalist groups of the 1960s and 1970s. As Robert Self has illustrated, people of color utilizing the language of nationalism and community protection were among the first to call into question metropolitan inequality. Black and Chicano nationalists argued from positions in the hollowed-out urban center of the metropolis; Navajo nationalists argued from the exploited metropolitan periphery.[72] Yet, these groups experienced similar phenomena: the uneven development of metropolitan capitalism, which channeled benefits to suburban landscapes while fixing poverty and pollution within the "less desirable" landscapes of the inner city and the distant hinterland.

Notes

1. Peter MacDonald, "Text of MacDonald's Inaugural Address," *Navajo Times*, January 7, 1971.

2. "The Navajos and the National Energy Crunch," *Navajo Times*, February 17, 1972.

3. For the central place of uneven geographical development in modern capitalism, see Harvey 1997, 2006.

4. The best maps of energy development on the Navajo Nation can be found in Goodman 1987. The best illustration of the connections between the metropolitan Southwest and the Colorado Plateau forged by the electric utility industry can be found in federal reports from the early 1970s. See, especially, US Bureau of Reclamation 1971.

5. Scholars of postcolonialism have long stressed that metropolitan development and hinterland underdevelopment are interconnected and central to the creation of the modern global economy. See, for example, Coronil 1996:57–81. For an attempt to think about the connected histories of metropolitan and hinterland development in the United States, see Needham and Dieterich-Ward 2009.

6. I use *imagine* here deliberately, in order to evoke Benedict Anderson's argument (1983) that nations do not naturally come into being but are actively created. I later contend that MacDonald used the political imagining of the potential power of a Navajo state to attempt to win support for his program from Navajos and concessions from power companies.

7. This is true of urban histories and of most histories that have self-consciously adopted the label of "metropolitan history." "Urban histories" have been rightly criticized for stopping their inquiries at often arbitrary political boundaries. "Metropolitan histories," which, in the words of Matthew Lassiter (2006:7), aim to treat "cities and suburbs as part of the same narrative," have failed to go far enough abroad to reveal the scope of postwar metropolitan transformations. For critiques of the limited scope of urban history, see Needham and Dieterich-Ward 2009 and Mohl 1998.

8. For African American nationalist critiques of the inequalities between Oakland and the suburban East Bay, see Self 2003.

9. By "metropolitan Southwest," I refer to a new region that developed following World War II, with population centers characterized by suburban housing, light industrial manufacturing, and increasingly large commercial spaces. The reliance of all three of these components on ever-increasing amounts of electricity created the demand for energy resources on the Navajo Nation. In turn, the power lines that

reached from the Navajo Nation to all three metropolitan areas served to knit the new region together.

10. Scholars of postwar America have used the term *growth liberalism* to refer to a series of Keynesian federal policies, originating in the New Deal but utilized mainly after the war, that attempted to spur mass consumer demand as a means of producing economic growth that supposedly would have broad social benefits. These policies included the Federal Housing Administration's support for suburban home construction and ownership, social security, the Wagner Act, and most broadly, fiscal policy that favored the promotion of growth over concern for balanced budgets. See Brinkley 1995; Collins 2000; Cohen 2003. For an emphasis on military spending, sometimes referred to as "military Keynesianism," see Lotchkin 1992.

11. Harvey Molotch (1976) terms these local policies as the "growth machines" of local government. In my larger research, I stress that the various growth machines of postwar metropolitan development existed in competition with one another for investment capital and federal spending. Also see Molotch and Logan 1987.

12. For the details of this argument, see Needham 2006. For the intersection of local growth politics and federal spending in the South, see Schulman 1991.

13. The best treatment of the BIA's program to relocate Indian populations to urban areas is Fixico 1986.

14. William Warne, quoted in "Navajo and Hopi Rehabilitation," Hearings before the US House Committee on Public Lands, Subcommittee on Indian Affairs, 81st Congress, 1st sess., April 18, 19, 22, May 16–18, 1949, 29 (hereafter cited as *Navajo and Hopi Rehabilitation Hearings*).

15. Cohen 2003:chaps. 3–4.

16. Initial quotation from Krug in US Department of the Interior, *The Navajo: A Long-Term Plan for Navajo Rehabilitation,* Washington, DC, 1947, 9. Second quotation from Warne, Navajo and Hopi Rehabilitation Hearings (see note 14), 8.

17. For the influence of the Cold War on federal Indian policymakers, see Rosier 2006.

18. Warne, Navajo and Hopi Rehabilitation Hearings (see note 14), 25.

19. Ibid., 23.

20. Biolsi 1995:30. See also Biolsi 1992.

21. Federal officials had earlier recognized the presence of energy resources on Navajo land. As Peter Iverson (2002a:133–136) has argued, BIA officials directed the establishment of the Navajo Tribal Council in 1922 to enable the exploration of oil reserves on the reservation.

22. Located south of Parker Dam on the eastern bank of the Colorado River, the Colorado River Indian Reservation (CRIR) was home to two small groups of

Chemuhuevi and Mojave Indians. The construction of Parker Dam in 1942 had allowed the development of irrigated agriculture on the reservation. Estimating that those groups would use only 25,000 acres, the Bureau of Indian Affairs made the remainder available to "Indians of other tribes in the Colorado River watershed who [did] not have sufficient land for their own support," namely, members of the Navajo and Hopi tribes. The promotional material for the Navajo-Hopi Rehabilitation Act made clear the distinction between the modernity of the CRIR and the status of the Navajo Nation. The photos of the Navajo landscape showed deep arroyos, abandoned hogans and corrals, and little possibility for improvement. In contrast, the photos of the Colorado River reservation showed ordered fields full of crops harvested by tractor (US Department of the Interior [see note 16], 32–34). This report elided the federal government's role in creating economic pressures on the Navajo reservation. The federal government's stock reduction programs crippled the Navajo economy, as Richard White (1982) argues, to benefit Hoover Dam and the wider southwestern economy.

23. Preston, Navajo and Hopi Rehabilitation Hearings (see note 14), 73.

24. Navajo and Hopi Rehabilitation Hearings (see note 14), 172.

25. Meeks 2007.

26. Phoenix boosters, in their resistance to the national growth liberal consensus, exemplify the understudied power of localism as a force in the history of American development. In contrast to federal economists, who viewed growth through broad economic statistics such as gross domestic product, Phoenix boosters experienced growth as intense competition between metropolitan areas. See Sugrue 2004.

27. Bimson's quote in Dedera 1973:27. The report Bimson chaired is the *Survey Report of the Bureau of Indian Affairs* (House Committee on Interior and Insular Affairs, 1954).

28. For membership in the Chamber of Commerce, see Koenig 1982.

29. Both Jones quotations are from Iverson 2002b, pages 253 and 39, respectively.

30. Lena Dean, letter to the editor, *Navajo Times*, December 17, 1970.

31. Douglas Dunlap, letter to the editor, *Navajo Times*, November 5, 1970.

32. For more on NIYC organizing on the Navajo Nation, see Shreve 2007.

33. Charles Wilkinson (2005) makes the important point that nationalist organizing around tribal identity had a far greater impact in the Native American rights movement than did the pan-Indian organizing that has received the majority of scholarly attention.

34. "They're Just Saying That," *Diné Baa-Hani*, September 1970.

35. The report read, "At five of the six agency offices we visited that had been delegated authority for minerals management, BIA, by its own admission, does not have adequate minerals expertise. Minerals management is, generally, carried out by staff

without formal mineral training" (US General Accounting Office, *Indian Natural Resources, Part II: Coal, Oil, and Gas: Better Management Can Improve Development and Increase Indian Income and Employment,* Washington, DC, 1976, 11).

36. Orville McKinney, "Giant Powerplants Pose Threat to the Beauty of Navajoland," *Diné Baa-Hani,* September 1970.

37. Esther Patrick, letter to the editor, *Navajo Times,* September 3, 1970.

38. Caleb Johnson, letter to the editor, *Navajo Times,* October 22, 1969. In this letter, Johnson expresses some of the anger of traditional leaders who refused to recognize the authority of the Hopi Tribal Council. As Charles Wilkinson (1999) has demonstrated, the Hopi Tribal Council was virtually created by John Boyden, the Hopi Tribe's lawyer. Wilkinson has discovered that at the same time Boyden worked for the Hopi Tribe, he also worked for Peabody Coal, a staggering conflict of interest that Wilkinson has argued led to a lease unduly favorable toward Peabody. Part of the Peabody lease area was on land claimed by both the Navajo and Hopi tribes, a conflict that would lead to a long-running land dispute throughout the 1970s and 1980s.

39. This stark division on resource development was not typical of all tribes. As Wilkinson (2009:chap. 12) has argued, resource protection and management became a key area of Native nation–building.

40. Interviews of Black Mesa residents, *Diné Baa-Hani,* October 1970.

41. Michael Benson, letter to the editor, *Navajo Times,* March 28, 1968.

42. "Dineh for Justice Responds," *Navajo Times,* October 3, 1968.

43. Michael Benson, letter to the editor, *Navajo Times,* March 28, 1968.

44. For this argument, see Smith 2007:142–160.

45. Betty Boyd, letter to the editor, *Navajo Times,* September 10, 1970.

46. MacDonald was essentially an auxiliary member of the celebrated Code Talker regiment. He never actually served with the group but was still associated with it. For a brief biographical sketch of MacDonald, see Iverson 2002a:246. MacDonald's autobiography (1993) is useful for detailing his early life. The sections on his chairmanship, however, are excessively concerned with settling political scores and are difficult to follow.

47. "The Candidates for Chairman," *Navajo Times,* October 17, 1970. Ironically, MacDonald was borrowing much of this populist language from Nakai, whose 1963 campaign had established a new populist language for appealing to voters and who had begun insisting on the use of the term *Navajo Nation.* Described by Peter Iverson (2002a:228) as "the first modern Navajo politician" for his ability to use the media to forge a direct bond between himself and "Navajo," Nakai had argued that the tribal government in Window Rock had become remote from "the people" and that Navajo politicians relied too much on non-Navajo experts. Nakai framed the relationship

between the Navajo people and the tribal government in almost the same terms MacDonald would use eight years later. In his first inaugural address, Nakai proclaimed, "I will spend less money in my administration on monuments and white elephants and more for the direct and lasting benefit of the Navajos in the hogans.... I will seek advice from our non-Indian consultants, but not take orders from them.... I will engage economists to give economic advice, engineers to give engineering advice, and lawyers to give legal advice. For political advice, I will go to the people" (Iverson 2002a:228).

48. Iverson 2002a:249.

49. "Opposes Leasehold Tax: Pete Talks in Phoenix," *Navajo Times*, March 4, 1971.

50. "MacDonald Warns against Continued Exploitation of Indian Energy Resources," *Navajo Times*, January 6, 1975.

51. "Indian Tribes Must Get Fair Return for Resources," *Navajo Times*, April 22, 1976.

52. Ibid.

53. "In Washington Speech Chairman Outlines Resources Development Plan," *Navajo Times*, October 5, 1974.

54. "MacDonald Names Major Sources of Future Tribal Revenue," *Navajo Times*, July 18, 1974.

55. Ibid.

56. Jim Benally, "Navajos, Arab-Style, to Cash in on Resources," *Navajo Times*, March 13, 1974.

57. Ibid.

58. "MacDonald Announces CERT Terms," *Navajo Times*, December 12, 1975.

59. "Gasification: A Crucial Issue," *Navajo Times*, January 23, 1975.

60. "Big Potential Seen in Coal Gasification Plants," *Navajo Times*, February 15, 1973.

61. "Eddy Wants Plants," *Navajo Times*, February 25, 1975.

62. "MacDonald Discusses Tribe's Fiscal Status; Urges Economic Development," *Navajo Times*, July 1, 1976.

63. "Gasification" (see note 59); "MacDonald Gets Commitments prior to Energy Development," *Navajo Times*, March 16, 1976.

64. Peter MacDonald, "Navajo Tradition," *Navajo Times*, February 17, 1974.

65. Jerry Kammer, "Coal Gasification in Navajoland: A Question of Culture and Economics," *Navajo Times*, September 26, 1974.

66. Committee for Navajo Development, "Stop Coal Gasification and Support Navajo Development," *Navajo Times*, October 23, 1975.

67. Harold Foster, letter to the editor, *Navajo Times*, December 30, 1976.

68. "Coal Gasification" (see note 65).

69. Ibid.

70. "Burnham Votes on Gasification," *Navajo Times*, May 14, 1973; "Burnham Rejects Gasification," *Navajo Times*, May 28, 1973; "Benally Urges Burnham to Vote for Gasification," *Navajo Times*, October 19, 1975; "Burnham Rejects Gasification Again," *Navajo Times*, November 2, 1975.

71. AIM National Convention advertisement, *Navajo Times*, May 22, 1975.

72. Self 2003.

10

Landscapes of Power

Renewable Energy Activism in Diné Bikéyah

Dana E. Powell and Dáilan J. Long

The rough dirt road to Alice Gilmore's home twists through desert badlands of the northeastern Navajo (Diné) Nation, passing the Navajo Coal Mine, gray mountains of coal combustion waste (CCW) and coal seams glittering in the desert sun. These open-air piles of CCW are the left-over deposits from the Four Corners Power Plant, a 2,040-megawatt coal-fired plant twenty miles north on reservation land. As the springtime wind picks up, plumes of silvery ash billow and drift in the direction of Ms. Gilmore's home. This region is called Ram Springs, Burnham, Desert Rock, and Area Four of the Navajo Mine—depending on who is doing the naming. Local Diné people call it Deníststah bit'óh (Ram Springs) for the natural water springs that once nourished large flocks of sheep and goats, even families. Other places, such as Chíí'hagéédí (Place Where Red Sand Is Dug Out), overlap the area and are roots of kinship for local families. The tribal government and the State of New Mexico call the place Burnham, though the tribe recently redrew geopolitical boundaries, generating controversy over where the Burnham community ends and the Nenahnezad community begins. Advocates of a new 1,500-megawatt coal-fired power plant slated for a half mile west of Ms. Gilmore's home refer to this region as Desert Rock, evoking a desolate, uninhabited landscape, lifeless and undeveloped. Finally, the same location is also known as Area Four North, a territorial subdivision delineated by the US Office of Surface Mining in Denver. Looking across the vast desert, such demarcations of place and identity seem absurd. How different people, with their competing interests, have named and imagined this northeastern Navajo landscape is at the heart of an ongoing debate in Navajo land, drawing interest from well beyond the reservation's borders.

The dirt road turns sharply, cutting southwest of the mine and then climbing a small rise up to the Gilmore homestead, an assortment of old weathered structures perched on a hill, treeless and exposed beneath a typically cloudless, sun-soaked, cerulean sky. I pass an old corral made of hand-hewn, rough wooden posts, sheets of tin and discarded truck tires, and a roofless, crumbling house, its sagging sandstone bricks disintegrating back into the ground from which they originated. From this vantage point, the rocky spires of the Jurassic-era Shiprock formation are visible to the west, and the dry riverbeds and stark badlands stretch onward to the east as far as the eye can see. Sunlight reflects off aluminum rooftops of homes in the distance; as in most of the reservation, neighbors dwell far apart for grazing land purposes. Beneath our feet, the dry ground is littered with bones, scraps of plywood, curls of rusted barbwire, shards of broken glass polished smooth by time and the wind, and the glitter of stones: jasper, flakes of quartz and flint. I have come to Ram Springs to join local families and activists in meeting with a group of national journalists who have traveled here to learn about energy development projects affecting Navajo communities.

I arrive early with Mike, an environmental policy specialist, and we wait quietly, scanning the vast horizon, watching for the arrival of the activists and local elders. Soon, Dáilan pulls up in a shiny four-wheel-drive pickup truck; his mother and aunt ride with him in the truck's cab. Dáilan's family resides in Burnham, and they have been resisting the Desert Rock Energy Project since the tribe proposed it publicly in 2003. Dáilan's mother and aunt are here, along with other older women from the area, to greet the journalists and share their stories for opposing the project. Squinting into the bold midday sun, we unload several metal folding chairs from the truck bed, arrange them for the grandmothers to sit on, and stake the flimsy legs of a tripod flip-chart easel into the hard earth. Dáilan sketches diagrams to illustrate for his elders and the visiting journalists the latest happenings with the proposed Desert Rock project. His mother and aunt sit on the open tailgate and share a thermos of hot coffee. Ms. Gilmore (figure 10.1) welcomes

FIGURE 10.1

Alice Gilmore stops to rest at her young sister's gravesite. She has been told by the Diné Power Authority (DPA) that her father long ago signed over all the family's grazing permits to the strip mine. The DPA refuses to show her written records. Her family burial areas, home, and grazing lands will all be destroyed by the new strip mine. Caption and photo by Carlan Tapp.

everyone to her home, pulling her thin shawl around her shoulders against the wind, and her daughter translates her words into English: "I want the land to be like it was before, but I know it never will be. Sometimes I really grieve for it. I mourn for it." Softly, almost inaudibly, a mine blast rumbles in the background. Black smoke rises, the ground shudders, and it will be hours before the dust and ash settle.

THE EVERYDAY LIFE OF ENERGY DEVELOPMENT

This recent encounter at the Gilmore homestead is part of a much broader, ongoing public, academic, and policy debate over energy development in indigenous territories.[1] Such a debate is entangled in and informed by—as well as informs—national and transnational discussions on sustainability, sovereignty, and the livelihoods of rural communities worldwide. In this chapter, we take up the theme of "Indians and energy" from a perspective that offers a primarily ethnographic analysis of a complex contemporary conjuncture. We draw upon our empirical research and experiences of engagement with the indigenous environmental justice movement in North America as a non-Native ally/anthropologist and a Navajo (Diné) activist and resident of the area in question in this chapter.[2] The work presented here addresses a crucial issue facing indigenous communities across the Americas and beyond: the confluence of lands rich in mineral resources, often expansive rural land bases, economic marginalization, political disempowerment or repression, legacies of disproportionate impacts of fossil fuel development, and, increasingly, intimate experiences with the lived effects of global climate change.[3]

We argue that struggles over energy development taken up by indigenous environmental movements increasingly not only criticize and resist but also generate thoughtful alternatives to the status quo of energy production and extraction, which has been the prevailing mode of operation, in many Native territories. In the case of the complex negotiations that make up the Desert Rock Energy Project controversy, a productive public dialogue has emerged, invigorating debate over the future of energy development for the tribe and the region and producing concrete proposals for renewable energy projects as alternatives to coal-fired electrical power production. This case illustrates how rural, place-based Native communities are responding to the pressures of contemporary energy issues, climate change, fossil fuel extraction, and renewable energy technologies. The significance of these responses reverberates far beyond Navajo land. Renewable energy activism poses an opportunity for new directions in developing sustainable economies, livelihoods, and tribal sovereignty in many locales, with yet undetermined pathways, alliances, and outcomes.[4] Furthermore, we submit that this case demonstrates the intensity of community dialogue on energy issues (voices largely omitted from national and global debates), a discussion grounded in particular energy development proposals and the lives of tribal members at the front lines of these changes.[5]

THE CASE OF DESERT ROCK AND THE POWER OF ALTERNATIVES

Since the passing of the Indian Self-Determination and Education Act of 1975, American Indian tribes have exercised sovereignty by establishing and continually negotiating their own strategies of economic development. For the Navajo Nation, uranium and coal mining have been the primary sources of tribal revenue. After more than two decades of community-based critique and scholarly debates over the effects of uranium "yellowcake" extraction, radiation exposure, and other contaminants on the health of miners and the environment (see Johnston, Dawson, and Madsen, chapter 6, this volume), in 2005 the Navajo Nation passed the Diné Natural Resources Protection Act (DNRPA) to establish a moratorium on uranium mining on the reservation, based on Diné Fundamental Laws. Recently, Navajo Nation president Joe Shirley Jr. issued an official statement that condemned the "genocide" of Navajo people wrought by the Cold War race for nuclear weapons (which require uranium to produce the weapons' plutonium cores). He also endorsed the new book *The Navajo People and Uranium Mining*, which details the suffering and human costs exacted from families by this industry. In press statements and in a publication of his own, President Shirley stood strong against proposals to reopen uranium mines and stressed the need to protect Navajo people from renewing this destructive legacy, which largely serves outside interests of US industry and foreign policy.[6]

The same year that the Diné Natural Resources Protection Act banned uranium mining, the contested Mohave Generating Station in Nevada and its feeder mine on Navajo land, the Black Mesa Coal Mine (operated by Peabody Coal Company), closed under growing pressure from regional environmental groups, both Diné and non-Native. The groups expressed particular concern over the mine's depletion of the N-Aquifer, the primary groundwater source for humans and livestock in the Western Agency of the Navajo reservation. Many of the core groups that pushed for the Black Mesa mine closure have organized themselves into a Navajo-based alliance called the Just Transition Coalition.[7] They are requesting that the regulatory authority (California Public Utilities Commission) mandate the funds received by the utility Southern California Edison from sulfur allowance trading, because of the closure of the Mohave Generating Station, be redistributed directly into renewable energy projects that benefit the Navajo Nation and the Hopi Tribe. Their vision posits an alternative to returning to dependency on local coal resources for livelihoods and tribal revenue.[8] In sum, recent experiences of suffering from uranium extractions have become translated into tribal policy in the form of the DNRPA. And uranium, once the crucial raw material of development for national security, has now become a symbol of historical exploitation and environmental injustice against Navajo people. The moral ambiguity and uncertain investments in coal power, however, remain open and contested matters and serve as a catalyst for the formation of new coalitions and a growing number of proposals for solar and wind power development on tribal lands.[9]

These recent struggles over uranium and coal form an integral part of the background shaping the current politics and debates over the Desert

Rock Energy Project (DREP), the latest energy "exploitation" or "opportunity" to emerge on the political and environmental landscape of the Navajo Nation. A microcosm of global debates over climate change, tribal sovereignty, and energy development, DREP is a focal point for examining contemporary concerns over energy development in Indian Country. In 2003 the Houston-based energy company Sithe Global Power partnered with a tribal enterprise, Diné Power Authority, to propose DREP, a 1,500-megawatt, coal-fired power plant as the newest and most expedient means of tribal economic development. The Navajo Nation Council approved the project the same year, and other alliances were established with outside investment firms and entities. Construction of the plant is proposed alongside the tribally initiated Navajo Transmission Project, which would provide the transmission lines and other grid infrastructure necessary to transport electricity from Navajo land to out-of-state utilities, the presumed purchasers of this power. The power plant would cover 600 acres of Navajo land in Burnham (Ram Springs), New Mexico, and would require a 25-square-mile mine expansion of the BHP Billiton Navajo Coal Mine, which operates north of the proposed DREP location. The Four Corners Power Plant and the San Juan Generating Station, two nearby coal plants built in the 1960s, are already significant contributors to poor health and air quality in the Four Corners region.[10] The area is an intense industrial zone categorized as a "national sacrifice area" (along with southern Appalachia and parts of the Great Plains) by the Department of Energy and the Trilateral Commission; exporting power to southwestern cities overrides local public health concerns.[11]

The Desert Rock Energy Project Draft Environmental Impact Statement (DEIS), released in July 2007, notes that the clustering of existing industrial facilities and the necessary supporting infrastructure would "disproportionately impact" local communities.[12] The Desert Rock project would be a significant addition to a region already heavily dependent on coal development, and its projected emissions would amount to putting 2.8 million more vehicles on regional highways per year.[13] Its anticipated annual emissions of 12.7 million tons of carbon dioxide (CO^2), now widely recognized as a major contributor to global warming, are omitted in official discussions of the project. The project proponents' claims of "clean coal" technology coupled with sovereign immunity predominate, thus dismissing DREP's certain contribution to the overall pollution of the Four Corners region and the 15 percent increase in New Mexico's overall CO^2 emissions.[14] Yet, the Navajo Nation administration continues to promote the Desert Rock project as the central hope for tribal economic development,

FIGURE 10.2

Lucy A. Willie sits atop Red Mesa, a sacred eagle nesting area overlooking Chaco Wash and the location of the mine extension and Desert Rock Power Plant: "I have lived here for sixty-four years. I was born here. I wonder why they want the new power plant. No one comes to my house to tell me about it. The new mine and power plant will take my grazing permits, destroy my home, kill all the animals. It will all be destroyed. All these things will be gone. It is so sad. It really hurts. It is all about the money. What about us? What about the Navajo People?" Caption and photo by Carlan Tapp.

followed closely by the Nation's new Fire Rock Casino outside Gallup, New Mexico, and new tourist attractions in Monument Valley, Arizona. The Desert Rock controversy is unique, however, because its discourse articulates with current transnational debates on indigenous rights, self-governance, and global climate change (figure 10.2).

Within the Navajo community, the Desert Rock issue is internally complex and contested, imbued with the experiences of coal and other extractive-industry plant workers, some of whom are now tribal leaders.[15] Many anti-mine and anti-DREP activists have (or had) family members who worked for the Black Mesa Mine or the BHP Billiton Navajo Coal Mine, further complicating the internal dynamics of the movement. These imbrications of a particular family's employment in and resistance to extractive industries form a common theme across Navajo land. Given Dáilan's upbringing as the son and brother of power plant workers, the idea of an additional coal plant at first did not unsettle him and others who live near the two existing coal plants in the area. The environmental pollution of high-impact mining was thought of as "other people's problem," and scenic views of industrial operations were the norm. Many saw the jobs offered by large industries as economic angels, delivering benefits that far outweighed any problems—and the problems themselves were kept quiet, never making the local media. Resonating with events thirty years ago in Burnham (see Needham, chapter 9, this volume), community people had to take direct action, in the form of a blockade of the proposed site, for their opposition to be taken seriously.

Since the industry's arrival in Navajo land in the early twentieth century, coal mining has become an integral part of Navajo livelihoods and cultural practices, perhaps because extractive industry is systemically embedded in the tribe's economic map as a result of the historical formation of the tribal government. Shortly after oil was discovered on reservation land, federal agencies established the Navajo Nation tribal government in 1924 as a "business council" to enable mineral extraction on reservation lands held in federal trust. Modeled on the federal three-branch system, this new governing structure conflicted with and departed from customary practices of decentralized, regionally based self-governance (*Naach'id*) and functioned instead to accommodate an emerging US energy paradigm and its attending foreign policy interests.[16] This paradigm of fossil fuel–based extractive industries and uranium mining, in particular, ushered in decades of steady environmental devastation and significant health problems, especially among Navajo mineworkers and plant employees.[17] Such experiences have led many tribal members to mistrust and criticize what they see as a colonized tribal council and its decisions on further fossil-fuel development, given the many risks of coal investments.[18]

Like many struggles around development issues, the present controversy over Desert Rock has roots in the Burnham community at least as deep and compressed as the coal beds themselves. Andrew Needham (chapter 9, this volume) describes this complex history of energy activism in Burnham, which grew out of the American Indian Movement and a new moment of Navajo nationalism in the 1970s. Whereas Needham found 1970s resisters categorically rejecting energy development, however, we find that many contemporary critics, though rejecting coal development, are promoting alternative forms of energy production. But many tribal members are ambivalent about the unknown cultural and environmental effects of wind and solar installations, and others continue to support coal development primarily for the sake of on-reservation employment. Like the earlier coal gasification plants that were proposed (and eventually defeated through local opposition), the contemporary proponents of Desert Rock also promise employment that will keep Navajo kids "at home," as well as millions of dollars of tribal revenue, which would advance the reservation's standard of living and provide electricity for export to southwestern cities. Unlike the earlier Burnham proposals, however, DREP's advocates laud the possibility of at least partial tribal ownership of the power plant—a move that would realize a dream of former chairman of the Navajo Nation Peter MacDonald, sovereign technologies.[19] Once again, Burnham has become a site of contention over coal-fired power, and community members' 2003–2008 letters to the editor of the *Navajo Times* strike eerie chords of resonance with letters written thirty years before. Current and local expressions of resistance against DREP are part of this long-standing, enduring struggle and Burnham residents' identities as environmental and human rights activists.[20] And just as local opposition in Burnham eventually made pursuing the coal gasification plants in the 1970s "politically impossible" for that administration, current residents and their allies are working to do the same today. This is not a simple case of history repeating itself, however, because the outcomes are unpredictable, the alliances are new, and, more important, the locally based groups are going beyond criticism to propose and demonstrate the use of sun and wind resources as alternative methods of energy development.

The public's mistrust of the Desert Rock Energy Project was palpable and quantifiable at the ten public hearings on the Desert Rock DEIS that occurred on the reservation and in the greater region during the summer of 2007. Across all ten hearings, less than 5 percent of the speakers publicly supported the DREP proposal, and approximately 95 percent of speakers voiced unequivocal opposition. At the end of the DEIS comment period, 54,000 public comments were submitted to the Bureau of Indian Affairs. At one hearing on the reservation, a 74-year-old retired teacher walked purposively to the microphone at the front of the chapter house and expressed her thoughts in a brief statement she introduced as "The Sacrifice of the Glittering World," alluding to Diné philosophical teachings that the present is a fifth and "glittering" world. Questioning the 1,500 jobs promised by DREP proponents, she spoke of her many years of experience as an educator and warned, "Young people shouldn't be employed in these dangerous, low-level jobs. They need to be educated to think critically.... The Nation has chosen to make the Four Corners region a sacrifice area."[21] Subsequent speakers echoed her caution, especially in the discussion of the number and quality of jobs that the plant might provide, arguing that these would be a mere "drop in the bucket" toward improving the tribe's current rates of stifling unemployment and crushing poverty.[22] Furthermore, these speakers argued, the risk to human and animal health and the landscape does not make these few jobs worth pursuing.[23]

ROOTS OF RESISTANCE: COMMUNITY ORGANIZING, BODIES, AND GENDER

The public hearings on the Draft Environmental Impact Statement for the Desert Rock Energy Project garnered local and national media attention, much of which focused on overviews of environmental campaigns, policies, and economics. These stories attracted new allies to the movement but largely overlooked the voices of a diverse spectrum of tribal members and the ways in which specific historical experiences background the present opposition to Desert Rock. In rural communities throughout the Navajo Nation, we find that most individuals do not speak about DREP without referencing a history of injustices and environmental traumas brought on by energy development in recent decades. As part of a broader study, a Burnham resident conducted more than forty qualitative interviews (primarily in the Navajo language) with various project stakeholders, including many Diné people residing around the proposed power plant location.[24] The findings of this three-year ethnographic project demonstrate that the well-being of people and their livestock is the core concern of the local community members opposing DREP. Many of these testimonies point to deep attachments to place, through specific memories and stories, and describe a landscape very much animated and made meaningful by oral histories and place-based knowledge.[25] Many of the testimonies were from elderly area residents—primarily women—who retain the cultural authority in the Diné tradition to make decisions concerning land use and livestock. These elders have witnessed generations of change in their area, including the arrival of the two existing power plants in the 1960s, but remain unconvinced that DREP would satisfy their long-standing desires for household electricity and running water, quality employment for their children, and prosperity overall. Addressing the possibility of being relocated from her land to make way for the power plant, one resident stated:

> I do not wish to move elsewhere. I live right here. This is my birthplace, a place where my father raised us, a place where my father sang his blessing songs and said his prayers for us and his grandchildren. His livelihood still remains. The places he herded sheep are still alive with memories. My life remains here

> and on the farm where I also live.... I lost five of my female cows, and each of them was with an unborn calf during the winter from drinking contaminated water in the mining area. The energy company creates hopes and dreams it does not keep.[26]

Specific attachments to place and to tangible and intangible relationships are iterated with a sense of betrayal. Oral teachings, emplaced memories, and customary know-how become secondary to permits that now define and regulate land ownership.

This particular elder and the woman conducting the interview are part of a much longer history of Navajo women's leadership outside formal political structures, especially in matters related to the health of the land and people. The nonprofit organization Diné Citizens Against Ruining Our Environment (Diné CARE) has been central to much of this work on the reservation, from resisting toxic waste storage facilities to opposing timber harvesting in the reservation's pine, juniper, and piñon forests.[27] Diné CARE is a reservation-wide, decentralized network of Navajo activists that has been primarily women-led since its inception. In 1987 a toxic waste incinerator proposed for the Navajo chapter of Dilkon, Arizona, spurred this first Navajo grassroots organization to address environmental issues on the reservation. Families and community members mobilized to defeat the incinerator proposal, and their success story traveled, prompting other Native and non-Native communities to seek Diné CARE's support in countering industrial and extractive development projects in the 1990s. Operating as more of a network or web than as a single-site institution, Diné CARE has successfully tackled projects such as the timber harvesting in the Navajo sacred male deity, the Chuska Mountains, bringing about a moratorium on additional harvesting and helping spawn a new generation of activists. Additionally, working with regional and national groups, Diné CARE helped form a five-state coalition that in 2000 helped amend the 1990 Radiation Exposure Compensation Act (RECA), affecting thousands of Navajo (and non-Navajo) uranium miners.

In 2004 Burnham resident and community organizer Sarah Jane White joined with Diné CARE to expose the dangers of the proposed power plant. In response to the tribe's 2003 proposal for DREP, White formed the grassroots group Doodá Desert Rock (No Desert Rock) with the support of Diné CARE.[28] White and Diné CARE's campaign work is geared toward Navajo-centered education about cultural and environmental protection that encourages tribal members to make informed opinions and decisions about energy developments in their communities. White learned of the proposed Desert Rock power plant and translated the issue into the Navajo language for non-English speakers—often with much difficulty, because concepts such as "climate change" and even "coal-fired power plant" (expressed as "giant metal stove") do not translate smoothly or without complex explication. Drawing upon Navajo cultural philosophies and storytelling traditions, White relayed her message to families throughout the vast desert expanse of northwestern New Mexico, traveling door-to-door, following a method of *k'é* (building relations) and producing knowledge that had already proved central to the success of Diné CARE's campaigns in the 1980s and 1990s. By providing Navajo communities with the resources and support needed to organize at the grassroots level, Diné CARE advances the belief that Diné people are capable of nurturing a sustainable and healthy environment, if provided with solid financial, technical, and spiritual support.[29]

For many Navajo activists, their opposition finds roots in Navajo creation stories, which point to the primary role of women in shaping the lifeways and ethics of the Diné in their ancestral territory. Oral histories, which remain a core method of transmitting these values to new generations, are grounded in stories pertaining to specific locations within a landscape defined by the Diné's four sacred mountains, each one dense with a specific historical knowledge.[30] These four mountains mark the boundaries of Navajo land (Diné Bikeyah), which are not contiguous with the present-day political boundaries of the reservation. Asdzáá Náádlehe (Changing Woman) is the central Navajo deity, whose teachings and actions form the backbone of Navajo identity, ethics, and ritual. In the story of Navajo genesis, the Navajo people were created from balls of corn pollen and rubbings from the flesh of her own body.[31] Changing Woman formed land and sacred epidermal matter into new, human flesh. Many connect this intimate relationship with an imperative to protect the land against present threats: protection of the land is protection of the embodied self. As ecofeminists and many Native feminists argue, women's bodies are often the first and hardest hit by environmental pollution and ecological degradation, so "everywhere, women [are] the first to protest against environmental destruction."[32] The thickness of these connections between gender, sickness, and environmental activism exceeds the scope of this chapter. It is explored elsewhere in feminist arguments that the health of the environment is materially and metaphorically linked with women's bodies, which are also sites of inscription for racism, colonialism, and other forms of violence.[33]

Historically, Diné society has followed matrilineal kinship arrangements, and Navajo women have organized communities in a manner consistent with power dynamics inherent in a complex clan system first created by Asdzáá Náádlehe. Individuals identify foremost with the clan of their mother, then that of their father and grandparents in the Diné language. Customarily, Navajo elders identify younger generations as "grandchild," "son" or "daughter," "brother" or "sister," which designate clan relationships but do not correspond to the sanguine relations implied in English usage of these same terms. The manifestation of these relationships is essentially at work in Diné grassroots organizing and knowledge formation but is largely absent in the decision-making processes, bureaucratic systems, and planning models in place in tribal governance.[34] As we observed in our work and as many of our (activist and non-activist) consultants articulated, matriarchal patterns and practices are most evident in Navajo communities, whereas patriarchal systems dominate the political, social, and economic practices and agendas of the tribal council. This gendered friction around notions of authorized political leadership is displayed, and rendered more complex, in a recent *Navajo Times* political cartoon depicting US Senator Hillary Clinton (endorsed by the Navajo Nation president Joe Shirley Jr. in her 2008 Democratic Party nomination race against Barack Obama) being encouraged, despite criticism from "Traditionalists...[who feel] that a woman should not be a leader."[35] Such support for Clinton, however, contradicts the negative opinions surrounding a Navajo woman's recent bid for the Navajo presidency.

Male privilege, concentrated and reproduced through positions of power, often omits or ignores the ethical and everyday concerns of many Diné (and non-Diné) women about domestic and household economies and a healthful future for the environment and for their children. Many women opposing Desert Rock openly link government policies on energy development and their negative outcomes directly to effects experienced by communities, identifying male decision makers as primarily concerned with the welfare of the political and economic system. The Desert Rock struggle reveals these gendered differences in understanding, analyzing, and acting upon energy development issues, as evidenced by the public hearings, letters to the editor, grassroots leadership, and opinions of key actors involved in this debate.

TECHNOLOGIES OF ATONEMENT: NAVAJO GRASSROOTS PROPOSALS FOR RENEWABLE POWER

Navajo spiritual leaders understand the Diné lifeway to be a daily ceremonial cycle that begins with morning prayer to greet the dawn deities and Father Sun and to request holistic balance with Mother Earth throughout the day.[36] The physical manifestation of one's respect for elements considered natural and sacred is the most appropriate display of homage to the spiritual entities that exist in the Navajo environment—an "environment" that exceeds most conventional imaginaries of "nature." The concept of k'é (relations) is integral to the Diné understanding of "environment," and it is the justification of Navajo resistance to environmental degradation.[37] The Navajo environment is called Nahasdzáán dóó yádílhíl (Mother Earth and Father Sky) and implicitly carries with it an imperative and inherent responsibility to maintain *hozhó* (beauty and balance) by virtue of the *álch'i silá* concept (natural pairs face/relate to each other).[38] The epicenter of the bipolar (Earth and Sky) opposites, Nahasdzáán dóó yádílhíl, is tranquility of individual, community, and environment. In this context, toxic pollution violates the spiritual essence of sacred elements such as air and water, creating imbalances in Navajo social, economic, and spiritual life. These imbalances can lead to physical and psychological illnesses manifested in human bodies. Sickness can be healed, however, through atonements and specific ceremonies. As many elders argue, imbalances may be brought on by the violation of various taboos, including engagement with an energy paradigm that does not acknowledge the spiritual landscape central to Diné identities. The Diné environment, in its more expansive definition, has been the site of outside intervention and intrusion at least since the Navajo Long Walk of 1864, when the Diné were displaced from their original homelands through calculated acts of direct and structural violence. Now, through the various technologies of fossil fuel energy development and in collusion with the energy industry, the Navajo government violates its mandate to protect the people, instead participating firsthand in the displacement of constituents from their lands.

Most Diné CARE organizers do not consider themselves "environmentalists" as such, nor do many consider themselves "activists." These slippery categories of identification are used loosely yet are heavily laden, circulating and accruing meaning through a kind of abstract global environmentalism but often taking on specific meanings in particular historical or cultural locations.[39] As Kosek shows, in the cultural politics of nature in northern New Mexico, to be an "environmentalist" is often code for "white" or "outsider" or other specialized and racialized terms of exclusion in an ecologically distinct, ethnically diverse, and historically Native and Hispano region.[40] In this context, it comes as no surprise that many Diné citizens would reject the identification of "environmentalist," despite regional and national media coverage that represents them as such. Cutting across religious, employment, and geographic distinctions, many Diné consider a land-based ethic to be the driving force behind actively seeking to (re)balance many aspects of the Navajo economy and human–nonhuman relationships. In this sense, many activists see their work to protect the land and people as, at its core, work to preserve Navajo cultural identity and knowledge. Emphasizing the intimate links between cultural and environmental survival, Native feminist scholar Andrea Smith argues that "cultural genocide is the result when Native land bases are not protected."[41]

Because Navajo teachings emphasize that the Earth and its natural elements are sacred and active entities, violating certain ethical boundaries (such as removing uranium from the Earth's interior) brings serious repercussions, many of which are so serious as to defy any attempt at atonement. This philosophy is known as the Diné Fundamental Laws (DFL), ethical guidelines for the Diné lifeway, codified and adopted as law in 2005 by the Navajo Nation Council from polyvocal, unwritten transmission through oral histories. Although the Diné Natural Resources Protection Act (DNRPA) of 2005 drew upon the authority of Diné Fundamental Laws to pass a ban on uranium mining, the tribal council takes a contradictory stance on the DFL when discussing Desert Rock.[42] The Diné Policy Institute, a research and policy analysis center located at the tribal college in Tsaile, Arizona, has determined through its collective research that DREP does not comply with the DFL.[43] The application and implementation of these research findings and of the DFL itself, however, remain open and contested matters of intellectual and political debate.[44]

Diné CARE, along with many groups and individuals across the reservation, hopes that development decisions made by and for the Navajo Nation will follow the spirit of the DFL and the pathways of oral teachings that promote forward, critical thinking and planning (*nitsahakéés* and *nahat'a*, respectively). This pathway is navigable when all are held accountable to the core concepts of k'é and hozhó and the ethical principles rooted in Diné creation stories. For instance, Jóhonaa'éí, the Sun God, extended solar rays (*sháándíín*) that impregnated Asdzáá Náádlehe with the Hero Twins, Monster Slayer and Born-for-Water. These sun rays generated the energy needed for the continuation of life and all the Navajo generations and clans that have followed. Oral histories such as this, as well as related understandings of cultural mythologies, receive new meanings through contemporary energy issues and current discourse on sustainable development and climate change. The work to advance renewable energy projects on Navajo lands provides one example of such transformation of meanings. Navajo tribal members understand the controversial legacy of fossil fuel energy development on Navajo lands, but many also envision

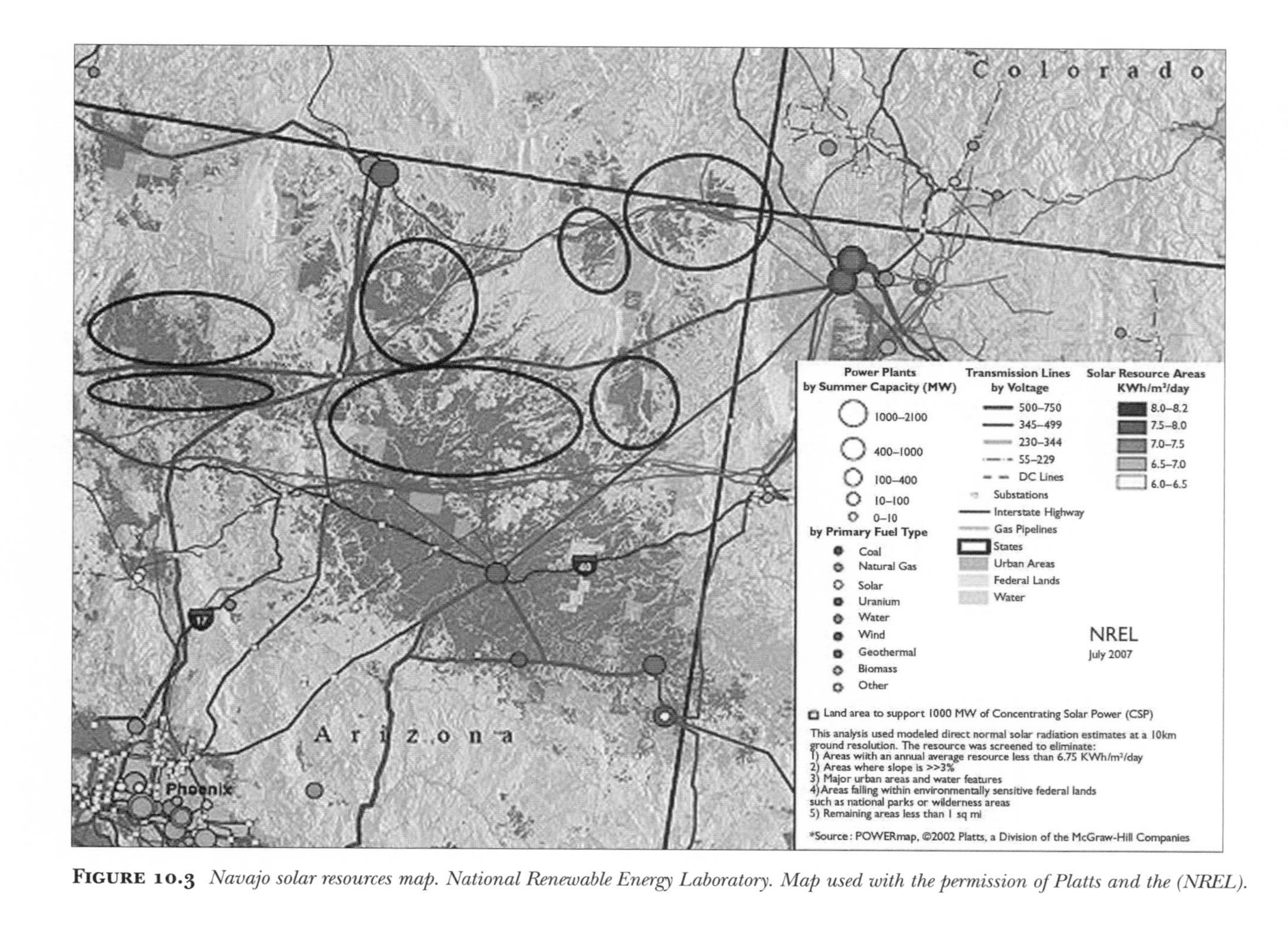

FIGURE 10.3 *Navajo solar resources map. National Renewable Energy Laboratory. Map used with the permission of Platts and the (NREL).*

more sustainable ways of development, ones that comport with the DFL. Wind and solar resources are plentiful on the reservation, as documented by Department of Energy and National Renewable Energy Laboratory research (figure 10.3).

Customary Diné epistemology teaches that the sun and the wind are sacred life-givers, supporting the healthy development of new life when revered and protected from contamination.

In January 2008, Diné CARE, in partnership with the environmental consulting group Ecos Consulting of Durango, Colorado, released a report in response to the Desert Rock proposal and its attending Draft Environmental Impact Statement. The report provides a prescriptive renewable-energy analysis and roadmap that conveys customary Navajo understandings of the environment and advances the applicability of such understandings to Navajo energy development. The report, *Energy and Economic Alternatives to Desert Rock,* is tangible proof of Diné tribal members' creative and viable solutions to contemporary problems facing the tribe. In particular, the Navajo Nation is geographically positioned to develop its solar capacity: "The Southwest has solar energy resources that are among the best in the world according to the Solar Energy Industries Association, presenting great opportunities for solar development in the area."[45] "The region's high quality solar resources are evident...these available resources are proximate to existing and proposed transmission lines and they dwarf the amount of energy available from excavating and burning Navajo coal over the coming century."[46]

The report reflects a cultural vision historically grounded in Navajo creation stories, philosophy, and DFL. It demonstrates that historic Navajo values are dynamic and flexible and can be applied to and reinvigorated by contemporary technologies. Parabolic troughs, solar dishes and engines, and solar power towers are three systems that would perform well on the Navajo Nation, depending on the materials that make up typical commercial photovoltaic cells. At the time of this writing, renewable energy projects are planned for many areas throughout the Southwest, on and off tribal lands. In March 2008 the German company Schott AG broke ground in Albuquerque, New Mexico, to manufacture solar technology equipment.[47] The Native-owned Sacred Power Corporation continues to install solar systems on both Navajo and Pueblo residential dwellings and on commercial and government buildings in New Mexico and Arizona. On March 14, 2008, the Navajo-Hopi Land Commission of the Navajo Nation asked the US Congress to appropriate funds for a large-scale solar energy project at Paragon Ranch in New Mexico, which would provide power for Navajo families and for export to off-reservation markets.[48]

Wind development is also viable on the Navajo Nation and in the greater Southwest. For example, in December 2007 Nambé Pueblo partnered with Green Energy Wind to build a 300-megawatt wind farm near Santa Fe, New Mexico.[49] In Diné philosophy, wind (*nílch'i*) is the breath of life, visible in the whorls on all people's fingertips. Its natural movement, harnessed by turbine technology, would produce electrical power on the Navajo Nation for Navajo families and institutions. The report details this research:

> Extensive research on windy lands, utilizing Geographic Information Systems (GIS) has been performed by Sustainable Energy Solutions at NAU (Northern Arizona University), including a report entitled *Navajo Wind Energy Development Exclusions: An Analysis of Land Suitable for Wind Energy Development on the Navajo Nation.* NAU has found potential Navajo Nation wind capacity within Arizona lands alone at a 70-meter hub height to be over 11,000 MW. Of this, 1,215 MW is particularly high-value Class 4 to Class 7 resource wind. This is total wind capacity on windy land that is *also* developable, meaning that the lands are not in parks, wetlands, slopes, canyons, etc.[50]

Additional examples of current viable wind projects are the proposed Grey Mountain Wind Farm project near Cameron, Arizona, in the southwestern corner of the Navajo Nation, where anemometers have been collecting wind data for more than a year; the Sunshine Wind Park in eastern Coconino County, Arizona; and the San Juan Mesa Wind Project in east-central New Mexico.

The *Energy and Economic Alternatives to Desert Rock* report found that energy services equivalent to those proposed from Desert Rock could be delivered by a mixture of wind and solar power and natural gas facilities constructed on the Navajo Nation. This, combined with continued growth in utility-funded, energy-efficiency programs in the target power markets of Nevada and Arizona, means that the overall cost of delivered energy would be less than that of Desert Rock. The report finds that renewable energy projects create 80 percent more construction jobs and five times as many long-term operations and maintenance jobs—increased and higher-quality employment being one of the central concerns of the community, non-governmental organizations, and tribal officials. Moreover, the report finds that solar and wind power can provide greater indirect job creation and more economic multipliers within the regional economy, making the net economic benefits of the renewable energy scenario approximately four times those proposed for Desert Rock.[51] Although the report was initially drafted as a concrete response to the Desert Rock Energy Project proposal during the Environmental Impact Statement process, its analysis is intended to be an energy plan and a vision for the future of the Navajo Nation and the greater region. The technical, traditional, and policy-related knowledge that went into this report is a tool for community-based education on energy development, climate change, and alternative economic possibilities. Culturally specific contextualization and translation into the Diné language make it possible for the report to speak not only to renewable energy experts but also to a wide range of concerned citizens, tribal leaders, larger nongovernmental organizations, and policy researchers.

NATIVE ENVIRONMENTAL JUSTICE: CATALYSTS AND CONNECTIONS

Contemporary debates on the Navajo Nation form a microcosm of struggles in Native communities across North America and around the world. Therefore, the controversy surrounding the Desert Rock Energy Project tells a global story with implications reaching far beyond the geopolitical boundaries of the Navajo Nation. Coal power versus (or in addition to) wind and solar power is an urgent and open question facing "energy-rich" tribes, primarily those western tribes whose lands contain subterranean minerals. Notably, this question is increasingly political in the context of global climate change, emerging global markets for carbon trading, and a growing pan-Indianism evidenced by the newly formed Indigenous Peoples' Caucus and the United Nations Seventh Permanent Forum on Indigenous Peoples. As Garrit Voggesser details in chapter 4 (this volume), recent changes in federal energy policy (especially since 2005) and new Department of Energy (DOE) funding sources have created the conditions for renewable energy projects to take hold in Indian Country more rapidly and at larger scales than ever before. In addition to federal funding, a network of grassroots and nonprofit funders are supporting leadership and piloting projects in tribal renewable energy projects.

Despite this complex interplay of enduring challenges, fresh opportunities, and emerging players, the experiences of Native peoples as they relate to the geopolitics of power production remain largely underexamined in environmental justice literature.[52] A full review of the history of environmental justice movements in the United States and related literatures is beyond the scope of this chapter but can be found in interdisciplinary works elsewhere.[53] At stake is the ability to perceive significant historical patterns: the 1987–1989 struggle over the proposed toxic waste dump on the Navajo Nation in Dilkon, Arizona, launched not only Diné CARE but also a national and transnational Native environmental justice movement through the formation of new organizations, new relationships, critical analyses, and energy development campaigns. In this movement, which continues to travel transnationally and articulate (in fact, create) indigenous communities worldwide, the burgeoning question of "green technologies" is not simply economic; it is also deeply cultural, political, spiritual, and social.

As mentioned briefly above, in the late 1980s in Dilkon, Arizona, on the Navajo Nation, the tribe proposed an economic development scheme to build a large-scale medical waste incinerator, treatment, and storage facility in the community. Confronting this proposal as "toxic" and "culturally insensitive" (because of customary Diné perspectives on death and the disposal of bodies), one activist describes how many in the community rejected this proposal. In particular, "the matriarchs in Dilkon came forward, and talked about life in its entirety."[54] News of the successful defeat of the toxic-waste treatment facility in the tiny community of Dilkon reached Native and non-Native communities across the country, and in 1990, local activists hosted a gathering called "Protecting Mother Earth." Supporters came from as far away as the Qualla Boundary (Cherokee, North Carolina) and Anishanaabe territory (Minnesota) to camp out for several days and share their experiences and critical analyses of human rights, social justice, and environmental issues in their homelands. This event helped create the Indigenous Environmental Network (IEN), which has continued to hold Protecting Mother Earth gatherings all across the country every other year since 1990. This encounter also spawned movements at multiple and overlapping scales: a reservation-wide/regional movement continues today in the form of community-based organizations from the east to the west of Navajo land, and a national/transnational movement continues today through the work of IEN and other affiliated Native environmental justice organizations. At all levels, these movements focus on the environmental, social, and cultural effects of energy development on Native territories.

At the same time, in the late 1980s an event occurred that implicated the federal government in human rights transgressions against Native communities and helped support the formation of these new, nongovernmental, Native environmental justice organizations. Greenpeace and other groups had been working on uncovering information related to radiation exposure experimentation that occurred during the Cold War period of advances in nuclear technology. In 1994 President Clinton's former energy secretary Hazel O'Leary released previously classified information confirming that the federal government knowingly removed contaminated soil from underground nuclear test sites on Western Shoshone territory (at the United States' Nevada Test Site for nuclear weapons) and buried the material in the rural northwestern Native Alaskan community of Point Hope, Alaska, without informing local residents of the risks.[55] This was part of the Atomic Energy Commission's experimental study of the impacts of radioactive fallout on the Arctic environment—and, by extension, on the Arctic's human and nonhuman inhabitants. The US government's intentional deception of the American public in a secret series of toxic experiments was later exposed. This event in Alaska became an organizing force and mobilized many Native and non-Native people to call on the Department of Energy for a cleanup of the Point Hope site. New exposure of nuclear contamination of US populations, the momentum of the antinuclear movement and environmental groups, and the toxic-waste treatment facility struggle on the Navajo Nation all helped launch national campaigns such as Honor the Earth and the Indigenous Environmental Network.

For the organization Honor the Earth, confronting and attempting to transform the current paradigm of energy development on tribal lands is about "energy sovereignty" and "energy justice," but of a different kind than has been seen before. This discourse is familiar in that assertions of sovereignty and justice were central to the 1980s mission of the Council of Energy Resource Tribes (CERT) in organizing tribes for greater control over the production and "prudent development" of their energy mineral resources. But Native environmental justice organizations such as Honor the Earth and IEN are distinct in their approaches to technology, calling specifically for investment in wind and solar power to position tribes to lead the country in "green, or at least greener, energy economies"[56]

> Reservations are communities, and the question is, how do you create a sustainable and self-sufficient community? At the same time that we're advocating for this tremendous potential for Native lands to be a hub for renewable energy development that could literally help power the Nation, we're trying to nurture community capacity, growing intellectual and technical skills, and demonstrating the viability of a new local energy economy. We are dealing on a grassroots level, going small turbine to small turbine and solar panel to solar panel and looking at the benefits of creating renewable energy systems that foster community.[57]

This vision is being implemented through pilot renewable-energy projects, community education, and youth and elder trainings, evidenced by Honor the Earth's half-dozen ongoing renewable-energy projects in diverse indigenous territories, ranging from a recently installed 65-kilowatt wind turbine powering the tribal radio station on the Pine Ridge Lakota reservation to solar heating panel installations for homes and community centers on the Northern Cheyenne reservation.[58]

Concurrent with this movement's work on alternative energy is work among tribal governments, energy entrepreneurs, and state agencies. Federal funding sources such as the Department of Energy's Tribal Energy Program have made more resources available to tribes for research, technical assistance, ongoing educational workshops, and hardware installations through a proposal and feasibility process.[59] In the private realm, companies such as the Hopi-based NativeSun and part-Diné-owned GeoTechnika continue to offer renewable energy workshops and hands-on instructional installations of small-scale systems on residential and community buildings. At a recent training conducted by two of these entrepreneurs (both women, one Diné) at a Navajo chapter house, the majority of the participants were middle-aged and elderly women from the community who wanted to find out how they could bring power out to their rural, off-grid homes and upgrade solar photovoltaic systems installed in the 1980s. Many of these participants expressed their frustration at having requested for years without success the extension of electrical power lines to their homes, despite the transmission lines stretching across their grazing territories within sight of their homes, carrying power to urban settlements.[60] Small companies such as these often work community by community, in tandem with tribal and state governments, installing individual systems and offering technical trainings.

The Navajo Nation is working to strengthen its own renewable energy projects, such as the solar photovoltaic systems installed on homes throughout the Navajo Nation by the tribally owned Navajo Tribal Utility Authority and the large-scale Paragon Ranch Solar Project recently announced by the Navajo-Hopi Land Commission. Such initiatives—which require collaboration among diverse tribal and nontribal entities—point to the complex networks and unlikely alliances produced through alternative energy development in Indian Country. The emphasis of this chapter is on the grassroots, Native environmental justice movements and their small-scale but big-vision projects, which sometimes (but not always) intersect with the interests of private entrepreneurs and governmental agencies involved in renewable energy. The intersections of these diverse networks require further research and elaboration elsewhere. It remains crucial, however, to situate the work of these social and environmental justice movements in the context of other initiatives occurring on tribal land. Their points of articulation and divergence offer an opportunity to rethink the conventional boundaries and expressions of political action and imagination. In this instance, we are witnessing the definition of natural resources expand from the subterranean to the atmospheric, and instead of a collision of the technological with the spiritual, as we might expect, we see new modes of integration.[61]

SACRED EPISTEMOLOGIES, GEOLOGIES, AND MODERN TECHNOLOGIES

As mentioned above in the discussion of Diné Fundamental Laws, Native environmental movements often have their roots in indigenous ontologies and epistemologies—recognitions of particular ways of being in and knowing the world. As Jennifer Nez Denetdale points out, these ways of being and knowing are largely transmitted and transformed through Diné oral history traditions, a practice of knowledge largely overlooked in Eurocentric or dominant narratives of US history.[62] In the Diné worldview, as one tribal employee put it, Native environmental justice is about a "holistic approach," which "involves looking beyond the human":

> We are the pollen of offerings made long ago, and so EJ [environmental justice] includes not just us, but it's about those who are yet to come. The root understanding of our notion of EJ is from the ancestors—their knowledge and teachings. It's from white shell, turquoise, abalone, and jet...it's about "the environment" in the context of all things....EJ is different in the Native context, first because the land, or "real estate," is valued differently as reservation and as federal trust land. Also, EJ is different because of the different, and deeper, connections to the land held by many Native people. The belief in Mother Earth and Father Sky and in sites that are sacred is part of this difference.[63]

Such reflections point to what may be considered an "ontology of difference" among many Native activists and organizations.[64] Distinct and historically particular relationships to the land and its dramatic geologic formations, to the past, and to nonhuman others are situated in the context of a neo-colonialism critique and a normative notion of social and environmental justice. This "ontology of difference" is evident at multiple scales of the movement, from the Indigenous Environmental Network's efforts at the climate change summit in Bali, Indonesia, and at ongoing intertribal gatherings, to Diné CARE's deployment of Diné Fundamental Laws in its renewable energy advocacy. But this is not a totalizing, complete, or essentialist difference, nor an antimodernist position. In fact, Native environmental justice movements overall are not essentially anticapitalist, nor do they take capitalism as a uniform, universal enemy (as do some of their peers in the global justice movement). They are using their critical difference to call for a novel approach to economic practices and profit-seeking ventures. In academic, activist, and governance arenas, many are interrogating the subtle and nuanced meanings of *alternative* and *development*:[65]

> The agenda in the US is towards pushing utility-scale, centralized renewable-energy systems such as wind and solar, based upon an exportation-orientated economic system that views energy production as a commodity. These systems are not sustainable. They only prolong large energy structures that view energy production to meet an industrial growth system. Without reevaluating what we mean as an "alternative energy system," I am concerned we will have wind and solar systems built on the same capitalist model that is depleting the abilities of Mother Earth to meet the needs of an industrialized world. I am an advocate for our Native Nations to develop wind and solar, but most of our tribes have traditional belief systems that must guide us in these forms of development. When we, as Native Nations, create massive wind-power projects, we must have ceremonies to obtain permission to utilize the sacred elements—to harness and process wind and sun into electricity that will be exported off our Native lands into these colonial grid systems that don't directly benefit our people. So how do we, as Diné, or Dakota, or any other Native tribes, reconcile the approach and model of energy development we engage in? We've only begun to ask these questions.[66]

As this suggests, many questions regarding the cultural aspects of energy development remain indeterminate and contested, including—perhaps especially—those concerning renewable energy technologies. The Native environmental justice movement is indeed taking up these difficult questions through its own research and analysis, publications, events, presentations, and organizing work. Diné CARE's *Economic and Energy Alternatives to Desert Rock* report addresses such concerns as it situates its call for renewable energy technologies within a broader cultural framework. But the shift from the Burnham-based coal power activism of the 1970s to the Burnham-based coal power activism of the early 2000s is that no longer does energy development equate to the enemy or a monster; no longer is resistance the reason for the existence of activist identities. Instead, a dynamic analysis and debate are emerging about which specific technologies might integrate (and at what scales) with Diné geologies, philosophies, ethics, and visions for the future.

CONCLUSIONS AND NEW DIRECTIONS

The Desert Rock debate has become a convergence point for concerns over governance, indigeneity, and sovereignty. We see clearly how the experiences of specific places shape how people understand the exploitations and opportunities of energy development. Interestingly, calls for renewable, decentralized power production parallel calls for greater decentralization and autonomy in tribal governance. This turn in Native environmental justice movements toward renewable energy technologies and new practices of democracy indicates a new moment of opportunity, though still precarious and unpredictable.

In Diné Bikeyah, landscapes damaged by uranium and coal mining are the same landscapes that offer possibilities for new forms of power and new partnerships among tribal governments, grassroots activists, federal agencies, energy entrepreneurs, and even industry. Andrew Needham (chapter 9, this volume) describes how 1970s activists categorically "objected to energy development itself" and felt that "any participation of the tribe in energy development contradicted the very idea of being Navajo." But nongovernmental organizations, young Diné activists, and tribal government leaders presently are working together on a different approach, seeing renewable energy and a broader "green economy" as hope for a transition toward a renewed reservation economy less dependent on extractive industry and "boom or bust" models. These partnerships are debating energy policies and technologies for the tribe and its local chapters with implications that go beyond local debates to join with academic and policy discussions on the human effects of climate change.[67] Old categories of "modern" and "traditional"—though still rhetorically salient—are insufficient for understanding the ways that cultural practices, Diné epistemologies, and twenty-first-century technoscience are intermingling to form new platforms for analysis and action. Being Navajo, for many of these advocates, is fully commensurate with these new technologies and is practiced through working to redirect "development" for the tribe as a whole. These debates—and the attending installations of large-scale, so-called "appropriate technologies"—remain unsettled. The contested nature of where, when, by whom, and by what means particular renewable-energy projects are established raises crucial questions about democracy and participation in any "development" agenda. Likewise, cosmological and ethical considerations of what it means to harness sacred elements such as the wind and sun, which transport energy and creation stories, remain unresolved. Ultimately at stake in these evolving energy-development debates are who controls science, technology, traditional knowledge, and geopolitical space and how this affects opportunities for increased tribal sovereignty in the twenty-first century.

Acknowledgments

With gratitude, we recognize the funding agencies that have supported our work, helping to make this research possible: Dana acknowledges support from The Wenner-Gren Foundation, the National Science Foundation (grant number 0715346), the Jacobs Fund of the Whatcom Museum, the Royster Society of Fellows, and the Graduate School at the University of North Carolina–Chapel Hill. Dáilan thanks the Tucker Foundation of Dartmouth College and the Olga-Lewin Krauss Fellowship. Both of us are thankful, as well, for the information gathered from the individuals and community-based organizations, which deeply inform this chapter, especially Diné Citizens Against Ruining Our Environment and the San Juan Citizens Alliance.

Notes

1. In discussions of "development" on indigenous lands, there is a tendency to overlook the experiences, feelings, memories, and creative responses of the people most intimately affected by extractive projects. As a corrective, this chapter aims to foreground the critiques and visions of those communities. At the same time, following recent work in indigenous studies, especially in anthropology, we aim to show how indigeneity in the twenty-first century is formulated in new, unexpected, and unpredictable ways, as shown in de la Cadena and Starn 2007 and Dombrowski 2001. In this case, we suggest that energy development itself is a nexus of changing expressions of indigeneity, in which "modern" technologies of development are not resisted outright but are sites of contestation and shifting cultural meanings.

2. The two authors, a Diné environmental activist and a non-Native cultural anthropologist, collaborated on this piece, each with an acute awareness of his or her own limited and partial position, different background, yet similar engagement, all of

which shape the perspectives informing this chapter. Our distinctly different experiences have been streamlined into a "we" voice for the purposes of this chapter, but each of us, in unique ways, is both insider and outsider to the communities and issues described here. Although we speak from our own work and research and not for anyone other than ourselves, we do speak with the voices and experiences of others in mind, others who have been generous enough to teach us.

3. Extensive research and activism across the social sciences document these complex struggles around the world. Some of the best work detailing intersections between indigenous movements and transnational forces, especially those related to extractive industry and activism, can be found in the following: Blaser, Feit, and McRae 2004; Cruikshank 2005; Dove 2006; Gedicks 2001; Grossman 2007; Hodgson 2002; LaDuke 1999, 2006; Nash 2001; Saywer 2004; Tsing 2005; Walsh 2004.

4. In the face of global climate change, as Zoltán Grossman (2007:7) shows, emerging projects such as renewable energy technologies may pose new opportunities for strengthening alliances between indigenous and local (nontribal) governments, grassroots movements, and other actors.

5. Our work enters into an ongoing interdisciplinary discussion, in science and technology studies, critical development studies, and globalization studies, in which new theories and practices of critiquing and rethinking "development" are being made, largely through the work of activism and social movements. See Escobar 2008; Hess 2007. See also the work of the Center for Integrating Research and Action (CIRA) at the University of North Carolina–Chapel Hill, (http://cira.unc.edu/ [accessed December 2009]).

6. Joe Shirley Jr., "Remembrance to Avoid an Unwanted Fate," statement released in support of the book *Navajos and Uranium Mining* (Brugge, Benally, and Yazzie-Lewis 2006), Navajo Nation, Window Rock, AZ, 2006; Shirley 2006.

7. At the time of this writing, the Environmental Impact Statement on the Black Mesa Mine has been reopened, raising the possibility that Peabody Coal Company may be permitted to resume mining at Black Mesa.

8. Enei Begaye of the Black Mesa Water Coalition, personal communication July 6, 2008. Spearheading this network of nongovernmental organizations are the Black Mesa Water Coalition, Sierra Club, Grand Canyon Trust, and To Nizhoni Ani. For more information, see http://www.blackmesawatercoalition.org/justTransition.html (accessed December 2009). For more background on energy development at Black Mesa, see Begaye 2006.

9. For examples of renewable energy work on tribal lands being done beyond Navajo territory, see the work of the Intertribal Council on Utility Policy, Honor the Earth, and the Sacred Power Corporation.

10. The air emissions of greatest concern are sulfates, nitrates, carbon monoxide, mercury, fine particulate matter, and large particulate matter, as detailed in the "Healthcare Costs" section of the report. Ecos Consulting, *Energy and Economic Alternatives to the Desert Rock Energy Project,* Report for Diné CARE, Durango, CO, January 12, 2008, pp. 12–21.

11. For more on the notion of "geographies of sacrifice," see Kuletz 1998; on the Trilateral Commission's decision, see Sklar 1980:243.

12. URS Corporation, *Draft Environmental Impact Statement on the Desert Rock Energy Project,* prepared for the US Department of the Interior and the US Bureau of Indian Affairs, 2007, chapter 5, p. 30.

13. Paul Sheldon, Senior Manager, Policy and Research Programs, Ecos Consulting, personal communication March 25, 2008.

14. Sue Major Holmes, "Richardson Questions Desert Rock," *The Durango Herald,* July 28, 2007.

15. We use *Navajo community* and *Navajo Tribe* as shorthand for this heterogeneous, diverse, and dynamic population. Far from being a bounded group of people, a singular or stable entity, the Navajo community is diasporic, globally networked, and internally differentiated in many ways.

16. David Wilkins (2003:84–85) writes, "The [Navajo Nation] council was largely a creature of the Secretary of the Interior and certainly not an organization organizing powers of self-government."

17. For further discussions of the impacts of uranium mining and the Navajo peoples' production to fuel the nuclear age, see Brugge, Benally, and Yazzie-Lewis 2006; Eichstaedt 1994.

18. Ward Churchill (1993:264) terms large numbers of uranium mines within reservation boundaries "radioactive colonization," stating that "90 percent of mining that occurred was on or adjacent to Indian lands."

19. The current proposal, at the time of this writing, stands at 10–25 percent tribal ownership of the plant.

20. Dorothy Holland addresses the complex intersection of historical, "enduring struggles" and contemporary formations of new activist identities in Holland and Lave 2001 and in Holland 2003.

21. Diné elder, DEIS public hearing, Shiprock Chapter House, Shiprock, New Mexico, July 12, 2007.

22. As detailed by Indian Country Extension, with data taken from the 2000 US Census, "according to the Navajo Nation's 2000–2001 Comprehensive Economic Development Strategy, the nation's unemployment rate is 44 percent, the median family income is $11,885, and the per capita income is $6,217. Over 56 percent of Navajos

live below the poverty level, the highest poverty rate in the U.S., even among American Indians" (http://www.indiancountryextension.org/extension.php?=6 [accessed December 2009]).

23. The full record of public comments such as these is on public record with the US Department of Interior, Bureau of Indian Affairs.

24. Sarah Jane White, personal communication September 24, 2007. Burnham Native and elder Sarah Jane White initiated grassroots resistance to the proposed Desert Rock Energy Project while still holding office as a chapter official in 2003–2004, shortly after the tribe proposed the plant. Over the course of three years (2005–2008), White went door-to-door in her own community to interview local residents. The findings of her research are included in Ecos Consulting (see note 10), appendix A.

25. For related discussions on the intersections among stories, oral histories, language, and place-based knowledge, see Basso 1996; Escobar 1998, 2001. Specific to the Navajo context, see Kelley and Francis 1994.

26. Ecos Consulting (see note 10), appendix A, Stakeholder #1.

27. In this chapter, we focus on the work of Diné CARE because it has been the primary locus of the research and practice informing our collaborative project. Other grassroots initiatives in Navajo land are also working on the Desert Rock issue, focusing more broadly on environmental, social justice, and energy development issues (see, for instance, the work of Doodá Desert Rock, the Black Mesa Water Coalition, To Nizhoni Ani, and C Aquifer for Diné).

28. For additional background on the early stages of Navajo grassroots resistance to the Desert Rock Energy Project, as well as related gender dynamics, see Long 2007.

29. For a more detailed discussion on the background, campaigns, philosophies, and experiences of Diné CARE from the 1980s through mid-1990s, especially pertaining to the campaign against the timber industry in the reservation's Chuska Mountains, see Sherry 2002:24.

30. For more on this notion of storied landscapes and the dynamism of nonhuman others in shaping Native identities, knowledges, and histories, see Cruikshank 2005.

31. Scarberry 1981.

32. Mies and Shiva 1993:2–3.

33. The Hóózhójí (Blessing Way Ceremony) was performed on Asdzáá Náádlehe, and this ceremony is the backbone of all Diné ceremonies.

34. See Krauss 1994:257.

35. Ahasteen cartoon, *Navajo Times*, February 14, 2008.

36. There are multiple and diverging religious and spiritual practices and orientations among Navajo people, including "traditionalists" (or the Corn Pollen Way), the

Native American Church and Roadmen, Catholicism, various strains of Protestantism, and, more recently, charismatic fundamentalist Christianity practiced in summer tent revivals and new churches. Medicine men and women are the "Navajo spiritual leaders" overtly referred to in this discussion because many Diné people consider them to be the locus of "Navajo culture and tradition," even if the same people engage in other religious practices. Many spiritual leaders in the newer traditions, however, may share similar principles relating to the "environment." More research is necessary to explore the current conjuncture of religious diversity and environmental ethics.

37. The concept of k'é is used not only by activists to ground their work but also by Diné policy analysts and researchers working on similar concerns. See the recent working papers of the Diné Policy Institute, including Curley 2007.

38. Roger Begay, Bicultural Training Manager, Peace Making Program, Judicial Branch of the Navajo Nation, offered this concept to explain the Diné offerings, ceremonies, and prayers to rectify human "wrongdoings" to the environment. Begay notes that the Navajo deities did not give the Diné "knowledge to mine uranium, coal, and oil"; therefore, proper conduct ("putting things in place") and accordance with Fundamental Laws will help "put things into perspective within the universe" (Roger Begay, personal communication December 13, 2007).

39. For more on the transnational circulation of environmental identities, especially as these pertain to indigenous groups in Asia, see Tsing 2005.

40. Kosek 2006.

41. Smith 2005:122.

42. Moreover, there is a dissonance in the council's codified use of DFL and Navajo popular understanding of DFL based on k'é. As previously mentioned, orality of DFL in Navajo communities shapes popular knowledge formation and is understood to be articulated in the context of decision making, accountability, and the future to come. The council, however, uses DFL to defend its prior decisions on coal development.

43. For the full DPI report, see Benally and Curley 2007.

44. Alex et al. 2008.

45. Dr. Frederick H. Morse, "Central Station Solar Electricity: Concentrating Solar Power," cited in Ecos Consulting (see note 10 above), 50.

46. Ibid.

47. Associated Press, "Albuquerque Attracts German Solar Plant," *Santa Fe New Mexican,* March 3, 2008.

48. "Navajo Hopi Land Commission Asks Congress to Fund Proposed Solar Energy Initiative at Paragon Ranch," press release, Navajo Nation Washington Office, March 14, 2008.

49. Staci Matlock, "Nambé Pueblo Plans Wind Farm, Proposed Facility Would Be

State's Largest," *Santa Fe New Mexican*, December 19, 2007, http://www.santafenewmexican.com/Local%20News/Pueblo_plans_wind_farm (accessed December 2009).

50. Ecos Consulting (see note 10), 47.

51. Ibid., Executive Summary.

52. Here, we follow the argument set forth in Hooks and Smith 2004.

53. See, for instance, Bullard 1990; Doretta E. Taylor, *Race, Class, Gender, and American Environmentalism*, US Department of Agriculture, Forest Service, Pacific Northwest Research Station PNW-GTR-534, 2002.

54. Earl Tulley, Diné CARE founding member, personal communication February 15, 2008.

55. See Peschek 1997.

56. Staff member of a leading national Native environmental organization, personal communication March 4, 2008.

57. Ibid.

58. Honor the Earth has partnered with engineers and nonprofit organizations such as the Intertribal Council on Utility Policy, as well as tribal governments, on numerous other projects: for example, the first Native-owned-and-operated wind turbine in the United States, installed on the Rosebud Lakota reservation in South Dakota; solar photovoltaic installations on the reservation of the Skull Valley Band of Goshutes in Utah; and solar power on the Dann Ranch in Western Shoshone territory in Nevada. Additional collaborative projects with Southwest tribes are underway.

59. See the US Department of Energy's Web site, http://apps1.eere.energy.gov/tribalenergy/ (accessed December 2009).

60. The Navajo Tribal Utility Authority recognizes the ongoing challenges and costs of rural electrification, noting that it costs approximately $20,000–$25,000 per mile (and more, depending on the terrain) to bring transmission lines to rural homesteads (NTUA employee, personal communication June 17, 2008).

61. Much of the "resistance theory" literature posits indigenous communities as inherently resistant to technology or to "development" as such. We are working around this reductive polarity, highlighting instead the more complex and subtler considerations at work among tribal governments and communities, who face particularly difficult dilemmas of balancing economic well-being with environmental and public health.

62. See Denetdale's (2007:17–50) critique of conventional renditions of Diné history and her advancement of a methodology for decolonizing narratives of the past.

63. Earl Tulley, personal communication March 18, 2008.

64. For a discussion of this "ontology of difference" as expressed through Navajo environmental activism, see Powell and Curley 2009.

65. For a more extensive deconstruction of capitalism as a unifying global force, coming from community-based movements working on establishing alternative economic practices and new economic subjectivities, see Gibson-Graham 2006.

66. Tom Goldtooth, Director, Indigenous Environmental Network, personal communication June 12, 2006.

67. We argue that this work is both a form of producing knowledge and a form of politics that exceed conventional definitions of political action often set forth in political science and social movements studies. As argued elsewhere, this creates a kind of intellectual and political "knowledge-practice" that engages, mobilizes, and informs university-based knowledge production. For further discussion of this concept of "knowledge-practice" in social movements, see Casas-Cortés, Osterweil, and Powell 2008.

11

Cultural Sovereignty and Tribal Energy Development

Creating a Land Ethic for the Twenty-first Century

Rebecca Tsosie

Speaking at a conference on cultural sovereignty at the Arizona State University College of Law, the late Claudeen Bates Arthur, a Navajo attorney and justice of the Navajo Nation's Supreme Court, cautioned Native peoples to distinguish their "internal self-images from those images that come from outside" and to identify the "images [they] have adopted from the past, which have come in from the outside to influence who [they] are now."[1] There have been, of course, many influences from the outside that have contributed to how Native peoples understand themselves today, including education, federal law and policy, and federal court decisions articulating the limits of Native sovereignty. The process is compounded by stereotypes generated from the outside that either romanticize Native peoples as pre-industrial, primitive peoples living in harmony with nature without the benefits of civilization or technology (the "noble savage") or vilify Native peoples as rapacious commercial entrepreneurs, marketing gaming and cigarettes—and natural resources—to non-Indian consumers and seeking to evade state regulatory law in the process. Some outsiders wonder, as did Donald Trump, are the "gaming tribes" even "real Indians"?[2] And what does it mean, to be a "real Indian" in the twenty-first century?

According to Claudeen Bates Arthur, Native people must ask themselves "whether or not the present cultural identity [they] are trying to preserve is who [they] really are and who [they] want to be."[3] Native people must ask themselves what they want for future generations. They must acknowledge that past policies have influenced them, often "without any affirmative choice" on [their] part, yet also take responsibility for future choices. Only Indian nations can "decide for themselves what is important for their survival as tribal people."[4] For the Navajo people, she said, the future must be articulated with reference to "the fundamental philosophy and laws ordained by the Holy People, which are those concepts that remain unchanged despite intrusions from outside and those things that were there when we came to our homeland between the four sacred mountains and that will distinguish us as *Diné* ('the People') forever."[5]

What does it mean to draw on the "fundamental philosophy and laws of the Holy People"? Does this notion have any utility for other cultures or peoples? Claudeen Bates Arthur related the norms in relation to the cultural sovereignty of the Diné people, but the lesson for other peoples is clear. Without an ethical framework to guide future decisions, we are all victims of our past patterns, conditioning, and internalized conceptions of "who we are." We will repeat the past because we lack a conception of how to initiate new frameworks to guide the future. Within Navajo epistemology, she explained,

> all begins to the east. Whatever you are going to do in your life, making life decisions...the process is the same. Over here on the east side you put some thought into the matter, *Nitsa'ha'kees.* After giving the matter some thought, you come over to the south side and you make plans for what you need to do, *Nahat'ah.* If you do those two well, think and plan, over here on the west side is *Ilina* and that is life, living. If you think, plan, and live, in a good way, with the right prayers and motivation, then over here on the north side is *Siihasin*...hope, faith, restoration—a state of harmony, maybe the ultimate perfection.[6]

The chapters in this volume reveal the complicated history of energy development on Indian lands in the Southwest. The lessons of this history will be instructive as the tribal, state, and federal governments create environmental policies and make decisions for the future, particularly given the challenges of climate change. The ethical framework we develop will determine our collective destiny on the lands that sustain us.

THE ETHICS OF ENERGY PRODUCTION IN AN ERA OF CLIMATE CHANGE

This is the moment in time for nations and societies across the globe to reevaluate their energy production policies using a comprehensive framework of thought and "right action." The question is not "whether" we will experience climate change in the future. The question is how we are going to deal with the potentially catastrophic effects of climate change. The 2007 Synthesis Report on Climate Change, generated by the Intergovernmental Panel on Climate Change (IPCC), composed of noted climate scientists throughout the world, found an 80 percent growth in carbon dioxide emissions between 1970 and 2004.[7] Carbon dioxide is a major component of the greenhouse gas (GHG) emissions responsible for global warming. Although climate change models vary, the report projects a 25–90 percent increase of GHG emissions between 2000 and 2030. The projected consequences are stunning. Scientists estimate that global warming and glacial melt will result in the loss of all glaciers in Glacier National Park within the next twenty years. The melting glaciers of the planet will lead to increasingly rapid rises in ocean levels that will submerge many island states and portions of the Arctic, necessitating mass relocation of human populations. The world will experience the loss of 20–30 percent of species through extinction. Weather disasters, such as severe storms and hurricanes, droughts and floods, will cause billions of dollars in damage and will also require relocation of communities. Agricultural patterns of production will shift as large areas of land become unproductive because of water stress. The IPCC report is a "consensus document" that reflects a conservative estimate of the potential harms due to climate change. Other climate scientists have used models that predict much more extensive and catastrophic harms.

Given this grim reality, how should we prepare for the future? The debates over climate change policy reference the need for "adaptation" policies and query whether "mitigation" is even possible at this juncture.[8] Most nations have signed the Kyoto Protocol as a way to inspire global consensus on the need to reduce GHG emissions. But the United States continues to resist this action, blaming the problem on developing countries such as India and China and neglecting its own role as the leading producer of GHG emissions in the world. To some extent, Indian nations are lumped into the US global policy on climate change, again through no choice of their own but mainly because they lack standing as independent nations to agree to or dissent from the Kyoto Protocol. Does this mean, however, that Indian nations cannot plan for the future independently of the United States? Claudeen Bates Arthur's conception of cultural sovereignty means that Indian nations *must* plan for the future independently of the United States. In so doing, Native people must start at the "beginning," at the level of thought: who are we, and who do we want to be in the twenty-first century in terms of energy policy? This is the essence of "self-determination" and a sacred responsibility to the land and to future generations.

UNDERSTANDING THE LESSONS OF THE PAST

As tribes engage the process of self-determination, the lessons of the past will be quite illuminating. The chapters in this volume provide much valuable data for the process of defining tribal energy policies for the twenty-first century. In the introduction, Sherry Smith and Brian Frehner ask whether energy development on Native lands in the Southwest has been a story of "exploitation" or "opportunity." They find ample data for both. Citing journalist Marjane Ambler, Smith and Frehner write in chapter 1, "Native Americans represent 1 percent of the US population but hold 10 percent of the nation's energy reserves." They point out the successful economic development of the Southern Ute Tribe as an example of tribal self-determination and autonomy over energy resource production on tribal lands. Indeed, self-determination is a pervasive theme throughout the volume, represented well by Garrit Voggesser's chapter 4 account of the Jicarilla Apache Tribe's development of tribal oil and gas reserves and Andrew Needham's chapter 9 discussion of the Navajo nationalism that led to tribal control over coal production and generation of power on the Navajo reservation. Through these multiple accounts, it becomes absolutely clear that energy development has promoted tribal economic development and increased the political strength of Indian nations holding large reserves of energy resources. Furthermore, tribal energy development has led to the institutional development of tribal governments, resulting, for example, in tribal control over the labor market that serves energy resource production, as documented in Colleen O'Neill's chapter 7. It has also motivated the creation of intertribal structures such as the Council of Energy Resource Tribes, intended to facilitate Native control over energy development on tribal lands within the national and global markets.

The multiple accounts presented in this volume offer a fascinating exploration of the Native response to federal policy: to adapt and then to re-create structures that support a robust sense of tribal sovereignty and autonomy over tribal lands and resources. This is particularly clear in Leah

Glaser's chapter 8 discussion of the electrification of Arizona's Indian reservations, which describes how the federal government promoted electricity as a tool for assimilation. After World War II, tribal leaders enlisted electrical power to gain greater control over what they perceived as inevitable industrial changes to come, economically and domestically. Glaser observes the adaptability of Indian nations as they incorporated capitalization and modernization on their own terms, "as tribes and as individuals." Initially forced to adopt an industrial lifestyle, Indian nations subsequently identified opportunities to access electrical power for their own members and used public, private, and tribal agencies to negotiate the delivery of that service on the reservation.

The various chapters in this volume attest to the incredible endurance of Indian nations and to their undying commitment to survive as separate governments exercising sovereignty over their land, people, and resources. These are not stories of pre-industrial, uncivilized "victims" of modernization. Rather, these are stories of brilliant and charismatic leadership, of the ability to see into the future, to plan and take action at the right time. These are stories that reflect the unceasing commitment of individual Native people and tribal governments to a vision of Native autonomy that will provide for the future generations. The stories inspire, they motivate, they represent an accurate picture of Native agency in the energy production wars that have been going on since the nineteenth century. But are these stories the basis for right thought and right action in the twenty-first century? In part, they are. But the full story must include the stories of exploitation described in other chapters in this volume. The theme of "exploitation" is the counterweight to the theme of "opportunity" in these historical accounts.

Perhaps the most chilling story of exploitation is the story of the legacy of uranium mining and milling on the Navajo Nation presented in chapter 6 by Johnston, Dawson, and Madsen. This chapter discusses the federal policies and practices that promoted uranium production for the use of the US military—the classified survey of the Colorado Plateau in the 1940s that led to the secret harvesting of uranium oxide for the Manhattan Project from tailings piles on the Navajo Nation, the Atomic Energy Commission's policy of offering discovery bonuses for uranium prospecting, which gave a financial incentive for Native Americans to locate uranium sources for the US government. The chapter reveals how Navajo miners and their families were exposed to toxic levels of radioactive dust and waste, were unprotected by even the most rudimentary forms of technology available to mitigate those harms—ventilation shafts or fans in the mines, protective clothing—and then were covertly studied by the US Public Health Service to document the health impacts. Johnston relates how the US Public Health Service studies commenced in 1949, after the toxic effects of uranium mining were well documented, without any disclosure of information to the miners of potential health hazards and, indeed, with the intention to conceal from miners and families any suggestion that their diseases were radiation related.

One might ask how this history is different at all from the US Public Health Service's notorious "Tuskegee experiment" on African Americans in the South, which lasted for some forty years until it was made public in the 1970s.[9] The US Public Health Service covertly monitored African American men in a study of "bad blood" to document the progressive and fatal course of syphillis, long after a cure was discovered, placing countless individuals and families at risk of death. The men were not told that they had the disease, nor were they offered therapeutic interventions. Instead, the Public Health Service studied the "natural progression of the disease." Indeed, in terms of exploitation and the notion that people of color are "expendable" in the service of "scientific research" for the good of society, the two case studies are quite analogous. And perhaps it is no accident that both cases resulted in lawsuits and in eventual federal legislative action "apologizing" for the harms and offering nominal monetary compensation to individuals and surviving spouses who could "prove" their harms within the relevant legal standard.

What is the legacy of uranium mining on the Navajo Nation and other reservations where it took place? Johnston, Dawson, and Madsen's chapter 6 is clear that the effects of radioactive exposure are long-term, continuing into the present. Despite efforts to clean up the waste, the tailings piles still exist on many reservations, and the contamination of land and water is well documented and enduring. The Church Rock disaster, which resulted from the breach of a mill tailings pond and release of 93 million gallons of water into the community's only water source, with widespread exposure of human beings and livestock, is a profound example of the negligence by energy companies and the acquiescence of federal policymakers to the exploitation of Native peoples. The poisoned livestock were ingested by the people. The radioactive water seeped into the soil. It defies common sense to understand why there are no long-term health studies of Native populations to monitor the effects of uranium mining. The statistics on birth defects and cancer rates are presented as merely "anecdotal" incidents, although many tribal members believe that these are directly attributable to past policies.

At least for the Navajo Nation, however, the story ends with an act of self-determination. The Navajo Nation Tribal Council enacted the Diné Natural Resources Act in 2005 in order to prohibit the resumption of uranium mining on Navajo lands, because of the health hazards and the lack of adequate technology to address those hazards.[10] The 2005 statute was premised, in part, on a finding that uranium mining is not consistent with the fundamental laws of the Navajo Nation, which are codified in the Navajo Nation Code. As Dana Powell and Dáilan Long observe in chapter 10, the Navajo Nation Tribal Council did not take a similar position on the morality of coal mining, thereby leading to the current controversy over the planned Desert Rock power plant, which is the latest coal-fired power plant to be sited on the Navajo Nation. Ironically, the power plant will be located within the community of Burnham, which successfully resisted tribal development of coal gasification plants in the late 1970s through a proposed partnership with El Paso Natural Gas Co. on the grounds that this would irreparably harm the community's air, water, and land resources. As Andrew Needham's chapter 9 explains, Burnham's resistance to the coal gasification plant was a classic demonstration of cultural sovereignty. The community expressed its own values in relation to the lands that have always sustained it, even though these appeared to contradict the values of the Navajo Nation, as expressed through then-chairman Peter MacDonald. Cultural sovereignty is related to political sovereignty, but it is also quite distinctive, rooted in the "moral vision that has always guided Indian nations in their collective existence as distinctive peoples."[11] Will history repeat itself in the context of the dispute over Desert Rock? Or has "sovereignty" already been exercised in the Navajo Nation's approval of the latest coal-fired power plant on its reservation, within a region already identified as a "national sacrifice area" by the Department of Energy because of the severe and cumulative environmental impacts of the several power plants and coal mines that already exist within this area?

CREATING A SUSTAINABLE FUTURE

In addition to probing the lessons of the past, the chapters in this volume explore how our understanding of past patterns can guide future policies and decisions—state, federal, tribal, corporate, individual. Chapter 10, by Powell and Long, offers an appropriate starting place to imagine the future of tribal energy policy in the twenty-first century. The authors describe energy development as "a nexus of changing expressions of indigeneity, in which 'modern' technologies of development are not resisted outright but are sites of contestation and shifting cultural meanings." The dispute over Desert Rock, for example, evokes the earlier contested notions of "self-determination" that Needham (chapter 9) describes in emerging tribal energy policies in the 1970s. According to Needham, younger activists on the Navajo Nation employed the term to resist exploitive forms of energy development premised on Western forms of colonial thinking and to enforce the traditional, community, and land-based values of their ancestors. The same term was employed by Chairman MacDonald and other tribal leaders to promote tribal energy development and control over the commercial value of tribal natural resources within a competitive global marketplace serving the expanding metropolitan centers in the Southwest, such as Los Angeles, Las Vegas, and Phoenix. The very concept of "self-determination," in reference to energy development, is dependent upon a normative conception of what is appropriate within the cultural landscape that governs tribal lands.

Powell and Long conclude that Navajo self-determination in the area of energy production must engage the particular values of sustainability, health, sovereignty, and respect for land as these relate to Diné understandings of the world. It is time to evaluate the ethical basis for energy development as reflected in US domestic policy and international policy and to examine where indigenous values can be used to guide tribal energy policy. Within the United States and most Western nations, environmental policy is the product of the combined influences of environmental ethics, science, and economics. Tribal environmental policy, in contrast, "must be responsive to the interacting forces of traditional ecological knowledge, Western science, economics, and tribal systems of ethics."[12] Indian nations must be able to distinguish energy policies driven by Anglo American norms from those that correspond to tribal norms. This is part of the process of distinguishing "external" and "internal" influences that Claudeen Bates Arthur referred to. We, as human beings, must have some notion of our relationship to our natural environment that guides and structures our "environmental policies," that is, our notion of what conduct is appropriate in developing land and resources. This relationship, however, manifests differently for Native peoples, as the original, land-based cultures of this land, than it does for the dominant society. These traditional ethical norms become the basis for tribal cultural sovereignty over energy development, leading to potential conflicts between local communities, such as Burnham, and the tribal government, which may be operating according to a different ethical norm. Conflicting land ethics are a major factor in intratribal disputes over energy production on tribal lands.

The predominant "land ethic" that has shaped environmental policy in the United States is an "ethic of opportunity," based on the utilitarian model of property rights, first advocated by philosophers such as Jeremy Bentham and now reflected in the contemporary work of theorists such as Richard Posner. In the utilitarian view, "right conduct" is modeled in terms of economic efficiency: what will serve the greatest number of people, what will maximize the value of the resource, what will promote the highest and best use of resources in the open marketplace. In the contemporary debates over climate change, economists use scientific data to model optimal behavior, finding that the most "efficient" approach to adaptation may require nations to wait fifty years to assess the "actual" impacts of climate change and then craft adaptation strategies (which would be too expensive to develop without sufficient data proving the harm), in the meantime using other projections to maintain a competitive edge in an era of climate change. In this view, there are actually "climate change winners"—nations and commercial entities that capitalize on the need for adaptation, gaining the competitive edge in this process. Conveniently, the existing scientific models indicate that the United States and Western European nations are ideally situated to be climate change winners. The "losers" will predominantly be located in the southern hemisphere, in Africa and portions of Asia.

What do we do about species that cannot adapt? What about human populations that lose their lands, homes, and livelihoods? In short, what happens to the climate change losers? Again, using the efficiency model, the responsibility of other nations is limited only to their actual role as causal agents. Causation is difficult to prove in the area of climate change because GHG concentrations are the result of multiple emissions across the globe and are cumulative over time. Thus, climate change is a "global problem" without an easy solution. If it is cost-effective to relocate a community or "save" a species, then this fits within the ethical model of what "should" be done. If not, either species extinction is the unfortunate outcome of "natural selection" and the organism's inability to adapt or, in the case of human populations, the global community must decide whether to offer charitable and humanitarian assistance. In the case of the Native people in the rapidly melting Arctic, it is entirely possible that relocating the villages, as groups, to a defined land base will not be economically feasible. Under current projections, it is entirely possible that relocating individuals to urban centers, thereby destroying their ability to live as distinctive peoples upon their traditional lands, will be more cost-effective.

Is this acceptable? For those who endorse the efficiency model, it is. If the human, spiritual, and cultural costs are unacceptable, however, we must articulate an ethical model promoting a different structure of thought. Human rights law offers a capacity to evaluate the intercultural dimensions of the "rights" that human beings have, as individuals and as collectives. The Declaration on the Rights of Indigenous Peoples was adopted by the United Nations General Assembly in October 2007. The declaration's preamble recognizes an "urgent need to respect and promote the inherent rights of indigenous peoples which derive from their political, economic and social structures and from their cultures, spiritual traditions, histories and philosophies, especially their rights to their lands, territories and resources."[13] The declaration promulgates a list of forty-six articles that detail those rights, including the right of indigenous peoples to be free from forced relocation and their right, under Article 25, to "maintain and strengthen their distinctive spiritual relationship with their traditionally owned or otherwise occupied and used lands, territories, waters and coastal seas and other resources and to uphold their responsibilities to future generations in this regard."[14]

What does the declaration imply for the Inuit and other Arctic peoples? The document attests to an "ethic of place" that guides the relationship of indigenous peoples to their lands and suggests that Native people have a right to environmental self-determination sufficient to protect that relationship. This is as much a cultural right as a political right. It should not depend on the recognition of the group's "sovereignty" as a legal or jurisdictional matter. Rather, the right should be sufficient to impose a duty upon nation-states to mitigate the harms to the Native peoples from climate change on their traditional lands. This is the core of the case for applying human rights principles to contemporary cases of environmental injustice, in which the harms of economic development disproportionately fall upon vulnerable communities. To evaluate the issue on a different level, we could examine Benedict Colombi's chapter 5, describing the effects of large dams on the traditional lifeways of the Cocopa people, who have been split by the international border between the United States and Mexico. The Cocopa Indians who exist as a federally recognized entity in the United States had an opportunity to benefit from their status and position within the internal structure of the United States, but this was not available to their relatives in Mexico. Although the development of dams along the Colorado River has negatively affected the US Cocopa's traditional lifestyle, the federally recognized group has the opportunity to engage in adaptive economic development and participate in the market economy. The Cocopa Indians in Mexico do not enjoy this benefit. Colombi finds that the destruction of their fishery resource has resulted in massive "poverty and criminalization" for the Cocopa Indians who relied on this resource. The ecological catastrophe reflects a human catastrophe: the respective policies of two national governments, Mexico and the United States, ignore the human rights of the collective "Cocopah Nation."

The same disproportionate dynamic is likely to accompany the harms of climate change. Some tribes, such as the Navajo Nation, will be climate change winners because they will benefit from the political power of the United States and its global position. By not signing the Kyoto Protocol, the United States can choose to participate in global efforts to reduce GHG emissions—or not. The Navajo Nation has the same freedom. According to Powell and Long (chapter 10), the Desert Rock power plant is projected to release 12.7 million tons of carbon dioxide per year (the equivalent of 2.8 million new vehicles on the highway [see citation in chapter 10, note 13]). The Navajo Nation's sovereignty entitles it to make the decision about whether Desert Rock will "benefit" the Navajo Nation, but how should it measure those benefits? Jobs will be created, lease revenue will be generated, tax revenues will be generated. The economic indicators seem beneficial. But how do we measure the harms? First, how do we measure the harms to the Navajo Nation? Some Burnham residents will be deprived of grazing or homesite leases. This is fully within the discretion of the Navajo Nation, however, and can be compensated with alternative lands. Many Navajos will suffer from the further degradation of land, air, and water caused by the direct output of the plant's emissions and by the toxic sludge generated by the technology that "removes" a percentage of pollutants such as mercury and sulfur before they are released into the air. Non-Native residents on state land will be similarly affected. Should the Navajo Nation care about harms to those communities? Currently, the US Environmental Protection Agency has the authority to determine the permissible level of pollution. If the air permit is issued and the facility operates in compliance with the permit, then there will be federal "approval" of any harms caused by pollution.

But what about the harms to the climate change losers of the world? Desert Rock will be a substantial contributor to global GHG emissions and concomitant global warming. This is fact and not speculation. Some of those harmed will be other Native groups, federally recognized groups in Alaska and non-federally recognized Inuit groups in Canada, Greenland, and other areas of the Arctic. Should the Navajo Nation factor in the harms to them? Should the United States? Tribal leaders from around the country advocated for support of federal climate legislation in 2009, in part because of the documented severe consequences of climate change for Alaska Native villages and tribes in the Pacific Northwest. Tribal leaders have noted the human rights implications of climate change for indigenous peoples and have also advocated for federal legislation that recognizes Indian nations as "sovereign partners in addressing the problems of climate change." Indian nations should engage the debate with full knowledge that some tribes will be climate change winners and some will be climate change losers. Federal and tribal policy will have to determine what respective duties and responsibilities each set of "sovereign partners" has to the other.

Using the classic Western lens of economic efficiency, the equation is simple. The Navajo Nation should calculate the economic benefits to the tribe and weigh those against the direct costs to the tribe and its members. If the Navajo Nation can sustain the harms of an additional power plant to tribal members, then the development makes sense. The Navajo Nation has no legal obligation to worry about what happens to Alaska Native villages, polar bears, or even citizens outside the Navajo Nation, so long as the Nation is in compliance with EPA standards, which are very much premised on efficiency and risk assessment predictions made upon the available science. Nor is the Navajo Nation required to think about harm to future generations. Climate science calls for periodic reports, and policymakers are encouraged to wait for substantial scientific evidence before making any substantial changes in revising pollutant standards or risk assessments.

It may be that under the Fundamental Laws of the Navajo Nation, the Nation's ethical inquiry is much more profound. The fundamental laws speak to the interrelatedness of all living things. The laws offer an ethical framework to guide the actions of the Navajo Nation and its members according to the instructions of the Holy People at the time of creation. The fundamental laws speak of the four sacred mountains that surround the Navajo Nation as living entities, with qualities and characteristics that sustain the Navajo people and that, in turn, must be cared for by the Navajo People. Indeed, the Navajo Nation's duty to protect the San Francisco Peaks, one of the four sacred mountains, formed the basis for its opposition to the Forest Service's decision to allow the manufacture of artificial snow on the San Francisco Peaks using billions of gallons of treated sewage effluent. In *Navajo Nation v. United States Forest Service,* a coalition of tribes, composed of political and spiritual leaders from several Indian nations in the Southwest, protested the desecration of the mountain and described the mountain as a living entity that had always given life to and sustained the various Indian nations that consider the mountain a sacred site.[15] After a negative decision by the ninth circuit Court of Appeals, sitting en banc, the Navajo Nation and other plaintiffs have vowed not to give up. Unlike Western cultures, which limit the concept of the "sacred" to religious uses, the traditional laws of the Diné and many other Native people describe a universe that *is* sacred, imposing stringent duties upon human beings to manage their interactions with other peoples and with the natural world using a set of ethics premised on respect, reciprocity, balance, and concepts of kinship or relationship. Under this system, one must consider the effects of one's actions on the natural world and other beings, not to mention the future generations. In seven generations, what will the "national sacrifice areas" of the United States—namely, the Four Corners region and Appalachia—look like? Who will live there, and how will they live?

The ethical quandary is not purely a "Native" issue. The discharge of sewage effluent on the San Francisco Peaks caused major concern to a number of Indian nations and also various environmental and health groups, demonstrating the intercultural dimensions of ethical land use policy. Indeed, the Dalai Lama advocates "an approach to ethics based on universal rather than religious values."[16] He finds that human beings are more similar than they are different, in that all living beings seek to maximize happiness and minimize suffering. He states that "both science and the law can help us forecast the likely consequences of our actions" yet neither can "tell us how we ought to act in a moral sense."[17] Only an ethical framework can do this. Furthermore, the Dalai Lama advises us not to reject a spiritual foundation for our system of ethics. He counsels us to distinguish "religion" from "spirituality" and declares that spirituality embraces the qualities of the human spirit that lead to happiness and well-being: love, compassion, patience, a sense of harmony, a sense of responsibility. In particular, the "ethic of compassion" is what allows human beings to empathize with the suffering of others and to avoid selfish conduct that promotes one's own well-being at the expense of others: "If we reserve ethical conduct for those whom we feel close to, the danger is that we will neglect our responsibilities to those outside this circle."[18] This lesson is reflected in the Court's opinion in *Navajo Nation v. United States Forest Service*, which describes the Native Nation's fight to prevent desecration of a sacred mountain as merely a "religious preference" of a small minority group, which cannot possibly dictate the government's conduct on "its own land."

Donald Fixico offers a luminous account of the central dilemma that has confronted Native people as they exercise self-determination over their natural resources. Fixico's chapter 2 relates important traditional narratives about the earth and the appropriate relationships between Native peoples and the earth in describing the relevant values comprised within an "ethic of place." Traditional indigenous knowledge is real and present in those narratives, and it is deeply embedded in the psyche of individuals and groups that are heirs to this knowledge. These systems of knowledge, however, can come into conflict with the realities of daily physical survival on the reservation, giving rise to the central dilemma identified by Dr. Fixico. There is, on the one hand, a profound struggle for physical survival, and both tribal and individual decisions to develop tribal natural resources serve this need by bringing revenue and jobs to the reservation. Tribal economic development also leads to political power, which represents a different form of survival, also vitally important to Native people. On the other hand, there is the tragic realization that sometimes the cost of development is the loss of traditional philosophies and values that connect tribal peoples to the earth. This is the result of development both on and off tribal lands that implicates sacred places and the health and well-being of communities on their traditional lands. Traditional philosophies and values reflect the essence of indigeneity, and there is speculation that cultural survival enables the physical and political survival of Native peoples, rather than the other way around. If Native peoples lose the "core" of their identity, what will they become? The psychological, spiritual, and emotional consequences are profound.

For this reason, some commentators believe that tribal economic development is necessarily at odds with cultural preservation and that the respective values guiding each endeavor are hopelessly in conflict. This appraisal, however, is simplistic. It ignores the need of Native Nations to engage simultaneously in economic development *and* cultural preservation. As the chapters in this volume acknowledge, there are difficult choices to be made, but individual tribal members, tribal governments, and Native communities are up to the task. Self-determination, whether at an individual or tribal level, starts with a process of thinking and a willingness to use appropriate values to make decisions along the way. As Dr. Wilson Aronilth, a Diné philosopher and educator, notes, "the Corn Pollen Road of Life" depends upon adherence to the set of values that are present at birth and expressed in one's clan identity and the cultural practices that connect an individual to other parts of the community and natural world.[19] If one knows these values and expresses them through choice and action, then one is successful in the life journey.

Which tribal members are exercising "self-determination" and "sovereignty" when there are divisions within the tribe? As chapter 9 by Needham and chapter 10 by Powell and Long show, political sovereignty may be exercised by the tribal council, acting on behalf of the Navajo Nation. Cultural sovereignty, however, is the domain of all constituencies on the reservation, the elders and traditional people, the activists, the communities that will be directly affected, and "nongovernmental organizations," such as Diné CARE, that are committed to exercising the traditional role of Navajo women to protect the land. At one time, commentators attributed these grassroots efforts to the influence of non-Indian activists in the environmental justice movement seeking to deploy romantic stereotypes about "real Indians" to halt tribal economic development. Needham (chapter 9) and Powell and Long (chapter 10), however, explain the nuanced character of tribal cultural sovereignty. These indigenous grassroots movements are efforts to define a Native land ethic that can guide development in accordance with the set of values that was given to the group at its inception. The decision about tribal energy policy must ultimately be made at the tribal level. The process leading up to this decision, however, is unquestionably tied to the cultural norms of the Native Nation. Chapter 4 by Voggesser and Powell and Long's chapter 10 point out that development of renewable energy, such as wind and solar power, offers tribes an alternative option for economic growth and perhaps even a greater capacity to create jobs and sustainable growth of communities on the reservation.

The future of tribal energy policy is dependent upon the robust expression of cultural sovereignty within Native Nations and in tribal communities. The lesson from Brian Frehner's chapter 3 examination of Angie Debo's work on oil exploitation and the Oklahoma tribes is quite telling: cultural "outsiders" should not attempt to characterize Native peoples as "victims of exploitation" and then tell them what they *should* do. This approach is paternalistic, insulting, and potentially quite harmful. Self-determination is the process of autonomous decision making, and it must be expressed through the multiple sets of values and perspectives that characterize contemporary tribal societies. As Powell and Long (chapter 10) observe, "landscapes damaged by uranium and coal mining are the same landscapes that offer possibilities for new forms of power and new partnerships among tribal governments, grassroots activists, federal agencies, energy entrepreneurs, and even industry." This is a holistic process that focuses on the legacy of the past as much as the potential of the future. The process depends upon dialogue and engagement and on the willingness of Native communities to determine which aspects of themselves are the result of "external" forces and which aspects are truly "internal" to the people as they have always been, attached to certain lands and guided by "sacred epistemologies." Binary, categorical judgments will only obscure the multiple possibilities in the future. This is perhaps best illustrated by what transpired at a meeting of the United Nations General Assembly on December 11, 1992. Oren Lyons, Faithkeeper of the Six Nations of the Iroquois Confederacy, and Thomas Banyaca, a traditional elder from the Hopi Nation, held up a depiction of an ancient rock drawing located on the Hopi reservation. Mr. Banyaca explained:

> This rock drawing shows part of the Hopi prophecy. There are two paths. The first with technology but separate from natural and spiritual law leads to these jagged lines representing chaos. The lower path is one that remains in harmony with natural law. Here we see a line that represents a choice like a bridge joining the paths. If we return to spiritual harmony and live from our hearts, we can experience a paradise in this world. If we continue only on this upper path, we will come to destruction.[20]

The lesson in Mr. Banyaca's cultural narrative is telling: energy production has economic, political, and social consequences. But it also has cultural and spiritual consequences. The consequences are profound for Native communities, but these are not limited to Native communities. Because of their enduring epistemologies, however, Native Nations may be the only governmental entities that can bring these multiple aspects of development into the ethical calculation of what is appropriate energy policy for the twenty-first century. Native land ethics are part of the cultural sovereignty of the Native Nations, but they can also be used to illuminate the human rights consequences of domestic and international energy policy.

Notes

1. Arthur 2002:21.

2. Light and Rand 2005:109, quoting Trump's comment about the Pequots, a successful gaming tribe: "[They] don't look like Indians to me and they don't look like Indians to Indians."

3. Arthur 2002:23.

4. Ibid.

5. Ibid.

6. Ibid.

7. Intergovernmental Panel on Climate Change, "Climate Change 2007: Synthesis Report and Summary for Policymakers," IPCC Plenary XXVII, Valencia, Spain, November 12–17, 2007 (summarizing the IPCC's Fourth Assessment Report).

8. Tsosie 2007:1625, 1659.

9. Palmer 1977:604.

10. 18 Navajo Nation Code, section 1303, 2005.

11. Coffey and Tsosie 2001:191.

12. Tsosie 1996:225, 226.

13. United Nations Declaration on the Rights of Indigenous Peoples, A/RES/61/295, Sixty-first Session, 2007.

14. Ibid.

15. *Navajo Nation v. United States Forest Service*, No. 06-15371, 9th Circuit Court of Appeals, en banc, August 8, 2008.

16. His Holiness The Dalai Lama 1999:xii.

17. Ibid., 11–12.

18. Ibid., 125.

19. Aronilth 1980.

20. The Hopi Message to the United Nations General Assembly, submitted by Thomas Banyaca, Kykotsmovi, Arizona, December 11, 1992.

LEGISLATIVE AND LEGAL TIMELINE FOR INDIAN ENERGY RESOURCE DEVELOPMENT

1887—(Dawes) General Allotment Act

1891—Act of 1891 (the first legislation for leasing tribal minerals)

1924—Act of 1924

1926—Act of 1926

1927—Act of 1927

1934—Indian Reorganization Act (IRA)

1938—Indian Mineral Leasing Act (IMLA)

1966—National Historic Preservation Act (NHPA)

1969—National Environmental Policy Act (NEPA)

1974—Founding of the Native American Natural Resources Development Federation

1975—Founding of the Council of Energy Resource Tribes

1976—*Jicarilla v. Andrus*

1976—Creation of the American Indian Policy Review Commission

1981—Appointment of the Linowes Commission

1982—*Merrion v. Jicarilla Apache Tribe*

1982—Indian Mineral Development Act (IMDA)

1982—Creation of Minerals Management Service

1983—Federal Oil and Gas Royalty Management Act (FOGRMA)

1989—*Cotton Petroleum v. New Mexico*

1992—Indian Energy Resources Act (IERA)

2003—Energy Policy Act of 2003

2005—Energy Policy Act of 2005

2005—Indian Tribal Energy Development and Self-Determination Act

References

Advisory Committee on Human Radiation Experiments (ACHRE)

1996 Final Report of the Advisory Committee on Human Radiation Experiments. New York: Oxford University Press.

Alex, Nikki, Moroni Benally, Andrew Curley, Amber Crotty, and James Singer

2008 Navajo Nation Constitutional Feasibility and Government Reform Project. White Paper. Tsaile, AZ: Diné Policy Institute.

Ali, Saleem H.

2003 Mining, the Environment, and Indigenous Development Conflicts. Tucson: University of Arizona Press.

Allen, Mark

1989 North American Control of Tribal Resource Development in the Context of Federal Trust and Self-Determination. Boston College Environmental Affairs Law Review 16:857–895.

Alvord, Lori Arviso, and Elizabeth Cohen Van Pelt

1999 The Scalpel and the Silver Bear. New York: Bantam Books.

Ambler, Marjane

1984a Uncertainty in CERT. *In* Native Americans and Energy Development, vol. II. Joseph G. Jorgensen, ed. Pp. 71–77. Boston: Anthropology Resource Center / Seventh Generation Fund.

1984b The Three Affiliated Tribes at Fort Berthold—Mandan, Hidatsa, Arikara—Seek to Control Their Energy Resources. *In* Native Americans and Energy Development, vol. II. Joseph G. Jorgensen, ed. Pp. 194–199. Boston: Anthropology Resource Center / Seventh Generation Fund.

1990 Breaking the Iron Bonds: Indian Control of Energy Development. Lawrence: University Press of Kansas.

2005 Building Green Campuses for the Seventh Generation. Tribal College Journal 17:8–9.

References

Anaya, S. James, and Robert A. Williams Jr.

2001 The Protection of Indigenous Peoples' Rights over Lands and Natural Resources under the Inter-American Human Rights System. Harvard Human Rights Journal 14:33–86.

Anderson, Benedict

1983 Imagined Communities: Reflections on the Origins and Spread of Nationalism. London and New York: Verso.

Archer, Victor E., S. E. Miller, Duncan A. Holaday, and Henry N. Doyle

1956 Health Protection of Uranium Miners and Millers. AMA Archives of Industrial Health 14:48–55.

Archer, Victor E., Joseph K. Wagoner, and Frank E. Lundin

1973 Cancer Mortality among Uranium Mill Workers. Journal of Occupational Medicine 15:11–14.

Arizona Trend

1987 Lights Dim for BIA Power Business. Arizona Trend: Magazine of Business and Finance 1:12.

Aronilth, Wilson, Jr.

1994[1980] Dine Bi Bee Ohoo'aah Ba Sila: An Introduction to Navajo Philosophy. Tsaile, AZ: Navajo Community College Press.

Arthur, Claudeen Bates

2002 The Role of the Tribal Attorney. Arizona State Law Journal 34:21–26.

Atomic Energy Commission (AEC)

1951 Prospecting for Uranium. Washington, DC: US Government Printing Office (GPO).

Axelson, Olaf

1995 Cancer Risks from Exposure to Radon in Houses. Environmental Health Perspectives 103, Suppl. no. 2:37–43.

Babcock, Frederic

1928 Curtis's Oil Hands. Nation 127(September 26).

Baca, Lawrence R.

2005 American Indians, the Racial Surprise in the 1964 Civil Rights Act: They May, More Correctly, Perhaps, Be Denominated a Political Group. Howard Law Journal 48:971–998.

Bahre, Conrad Joseph

1967 The Reduction of Seri Indian Range and Residence in the State of Sonora, Mexico (1536–Present). MA thesis, University of Arizona.

Barnett, Tim, Robert Malone, William Pennell, Detlet Stammer, Bert Semtner, and Warren Washington

2004 The Effects of Climate Change on Water Resources in the West: Introduction and Overview. Climatic Change 62:1–11.

Barnett, Tim P., David W. Pierce, Hugo G. Hidalgo, Celine Bonfils, Benjamin D. Santer, Tapash Das, Govindasamy Bala, Andrew W. Wood, Toru Nozawa, Arthur A. Mirin, Daniel R. Cayan, and Michael D. Dettinger

2008 Human-Induced Changes in the Hydrology of the Western United States. Science 319:1080–1083.

Basso, Keith

1996 Wisdom Sits in Places: Landscape and Language among the Western Apache. Albuquerque: University of New Mexico Press.

Bauer, William J.

2006 "We Were All Migrant Workers Here": Round Valley Indian Labor in Northern California, 1850–1929. Western Historical Quarterly 37:43–64.

Begaye, Enei

2006 The Black Mesa Controversy. Cultural Survival Quarterly 29:29–31.

Benally, Moroni, and Andrew Curley

2007 Comments on the Desert Rock Energy Project, Draft Environmental Impact Statement. July. Tsaile, AZ: Diné Policy Institute.

Benedek, Emily

1993 The Wind Don't Know Me: A History of the Navajo–Hopi Land Dispute. New York: Vintage Books.

Bernstein, Alison R.

1991 American Indians and World War II: Toward a New Era in Indian Affairs. Norman: University of Oklahoma Press.

Biolsi, Thomas

1992 Organizing the Lakota: The Political Economy of the New Deal on the Pine Ridge and Rosebud Reservations. Tucson: University of Arizona Press.

1995 The Birth of the Reservation: Making the Modern Individual among the Lakota. American Ethnologist 22:28–53.

Blaser, Mario, Harvey A. Feit, and Glenn McRae

2004 Introduction. *In* In the Way of Development: Indigenous Peoples, Life Projects and Globalization. London: Zed Books.

Brigham, Jay

2001 Lighting the Reservation: The Impact of the Rural Electrification Administration on Native Lands. Journal of the West 40:81–88.

Brinkley, Alan

1995 The End of Reform: New Deal Liberalism in Recession and War. New York: Alfred A. Knopf.

Brugge, Doug, Timothy Benally, and Esther Yazzie-Lewis, eds.

2007 The Navajo People and Uranium Mining. Albuquerque: University of New Mexico Press.

Brugge, Doug, and Rob Goble

2002 The History of Uranium Mining and the Navajo People. American Journal of Public Health 92:1410–1419.

2006 A Documentary History of Uranium Mining and the Navajo People. *In* The Navajo People and Uranium Mining. Doug Brugge, Timothy Bennally, and Esther Yazzie-Lewis, eds. Pp. 25–43. Albuquerque: University of New Mexico Press.

Bullard, Robert D.

1990 Dumping in Dixie: Race, Class, and Environmental Quality. Boulder, CO: Westview.

Callaway, D. G., J. E. Levy, and E. B. Henderson

1976 The Effects of Power Production and Strip Mining on Local Navajo Populations. Lake Powell Research Project Bulletin, no. 22. Los Angeles: Institute of Geophysics and Planetary Physics, University of California.

Campbell, Mona

1960 McNary: Company Town. Tempe: Arizona Historical Foundation, Hayden Library, Arizona State University.

Casas-Cortés, Maribel, Michal Osterweil, and Dana E. Powell

2008 Blurring Boundaries: Knowledge-Practices in Contemporary Social Movements. Anthropological Quarterly 81:17–58.

Castetter, Edward F., and Willis H. Bell

1951 Yuman Indian Agriculture: Primitive Subsistence on the Lower Colorado and Gila Rivers. Albuquerque: University of New Mexico Press.

Caufield, Catherine

1989 Multiple Exposures: Chronicles of the Radiation Age. Toronto: Stoddart.

Caylor, Ann

2000 "A Promise Long Deferred": Federal Reclamation on the Colorado River Indian Reservation. The Pacific Historical Review 69:193–215.

Chambers, Reid Peyton, and Monroe E. Price

1973–1974 Regulating Sovereignty: Discretion and the Leasing of Indian Lands. Stanford Law Review 26:1061–1096.

Charley, Perry H., Susan E. Dawson, Gary E. Madsen, and Bryan R. Spykerman

2004 Navajo Uranium Education Programs: The Search for Environmental Justice. Journal of Applied Environmental Education Communication 3:101–108.

Chenoweth, W. L.

1997 Raw Materials Activities of the Manhattan Project on the Colorado Plateau. Nonrenewable Resources 6:33–41.

Chernow, Ron

1998 Titan: The Life of John D. Rockefeller, Sr. New York: Vintage Books.

Churchill, Ward

1993 Struggle for the Land: Indigenous Resistance to Genocide, Ecocide, and Expropriation in Contemporary North America. Monroe, ME: Common Courage.

Churchill, Ward, and Winona LaDuke
1992 Native North America: The Political Economy of Radioactive Colonization. *In* The State of Native America: Genocide, Colonization and Resistance. M. Annette Jaimes, ed. Pp. 241–266. Boston: South End Press.

Clapps, Inez H.
1952 Social Change among the White Mountain Apache Indians from 1800s to the Present. MA thesis, Montana State University.

Clemens, Richard
1995 Roads in the Sky: The Hopi Indian in a Century of Change. Boulder, CO: Westview.

Coffer, William E.
1982 Sipapu: The Story of the Indians of Arizona and New Mexico. New York, Cincinnati, Toronto, London, and Melbourne: Van Nostrand Reinhold.

Coffey, Wallace, and Rebecca Tsosie
2001 Rethinking the Tribal Sovereignty Doctrine: Cultural Sovereignty and the Collective Future of Indian Nations. Stanford Law and Policy Review 12:191–221.

Cohen, Felix S.
2005 Cohen's Handbook of Federal Indian Law. Newark, NJ: Lexis Nexis.

Cohen, Lizabeth
2003 A Consumer's Republic: The Politics of Mass Consumption in Postwar America. New York: Alfred A. Knopf.

Collins, Robert
2000 More: The Politics of Economic Growth in Postwar America. New York: Oxford University Press.

Commission on Fiscal Accountability of the Nation's Energy Resources (Linowes Report)
1982 Fiscal Accountability of the Nation's Energy Resources. Washington, DC: GPO.

Coronil, Fernando
1996 Beyond Occidentalism: Toward Nonimperial Geohistorical Categories. Cultural Anthropology 11:57–81.

Courlander, Harold
1971 The Fourth World of the Hopis: The Epic Story of the Hopi Indians as Preserved in Their Legends and Traditions. Albuquerque: University of New Mexico Press.

Craig, J. A.
1926 A New Fishery in Mexico. California Fish and Game 12:166–169.

Crapanzano, Vincent
2003[1972] The Fifth World of Forester Bennett: Portrait of a Navajo. Lincoln and London: University of Nebraska Press.

Cruikshank, Julie
2005 Do Glaciers Listen? Local Knowledge, Colonial Encounters, and Social Imagination. Vancouver: UBC Press.

Cunningham, William P., and Barbara Woodworth Saigo
1990 Environmental Science: A Global Concern. Dubuque, IA: Wm. C. Brown.

Curley, Andrew
2007 Uranium, Coal and the Logic for Non-withdrawal: The Use of Traditional Principles in Natural Resource Policy and Governance on the Navajo Nation. Tsaile, AZ: Diné Policy Institute.

Dawson, Susan E.
1992 Navajo Uranium Mining Workers and the Effects of Occupational Illnesses: A Case Study. Human Organization 51:389–397.

Dawson, Susan E., Perry H. Charley, and Phillip Harrison Jr.
1997 Advocacy and Social Action among Navajo Uranium Workers and Their Families. *In* Social Work in Health Settings: Practice in Context. Toba Schwaber Kerson, ed. Pp. 391–407. New York: Haworth.
2006 Advocacy and Social Action among Navajo People: Uranium Workers and Their Families, 1988–1995. *In* The Navajo People and Uranium Mining. Doug Brugge, Timothy Bennally, and Esther Yazzie-Lewis, eds. Pp. 58–75. Albuquerque: University of New Mexico Press.

Dawson, Susan E., and Gary E. Madsen
1995 American Indian Uranium Millworkers: The Perceived Effects of Chronic Occupational Exposure. Journal of Health and Social Policy 7:19–31.
2007 Uranium Mine Workers, Atomic Downwinders, and the Radiation Exposure Compensation Act (RECA): The Nuclear Legacy. *In* Half-Lives and Half-Truths: Confronting the Radioactive Legacies of the Cold War. Barbara Rose Johnston, ed. Pp. 117–143. Santa Fe, NM: School for Advanced Research Press.

Dawson, Susan E., Gary E. Madsen, and Bryan R. Spykerman
1997 Public Health Issues Concerning American Indian and Non-Indian Uranium Millworkers. Journal of Health and Social Policy 8:41–56.

Debo, Angie
1949 Oklahoma, Foot-Loose and Fancy-Free. Norman: University of Oklahoma Press.
1968[1940] And Still the Waters Run: The Betrayal of the Five Civilized Tribes. Princeton, NJ: Princeton University Press.
1976 To Establish Justice. Western Historical Quarterly 7:405-412.
1985 Prairie City: The Story of an American Community. Tulsa, OK: Council Oak Books, Ltd. First published 1944 by Alfred A. Knopf.
1988 Angie Debo: An Autobiographical Sketch, Eulogy, and Bibliography. Stillwater: Oklahoma State University College of Arts and Sciences and Department of History.

Dedera, Don

1973 Walter Reed Bimson: Arizona's Indispensable Man. Arizona Highways 49:22–26.

de la Cadena, Marisol, and Orin Starn, eds.

2007 Indigenous Experience Today. Oxford and New York: Berg.

Deloria, Philip J.

2004 Indians in Unexpected Places. Lawrence: University Press of Kansas.

Deloria, Vine, Jr., and Clifford Lytle

1984 The Nations Within: The Past and Future of American Indian Sovereignty. New York: Pantheon Books.

Denetdale, Jennifer Nez

2007 Reclaiming Diné History: The Legacies of Navajo Chief Manuelito and Juanita. Albuquerque: University of New Mexico Press.

Dockstader, Frederick J.

1987 Tradition Updated: Contemporary Navajo Weavers Have Experimented Boldly, Developing New Forms and Even New Techniques. American Craft 47:40.

Dombrowski, Kirk

2001 Against Culture: Development, Politics, and Religion in Indian Alaska. Lincoln and London: University of Nebraska Press.

Dove, Michael R.

2006 Indigenous People and Environmental Politics. Annual Review of Anthropology 35:191–208.

Doyle, Henry H.

1950 Survey of Uranium Mines on Navajo Reservation, November 14–17, 1949, January 11–12, 1950. Classified memorandum, US Public Health Service, Salt Lake City, Utah.

Driver, Harold

1957 Estimation of Intensity of Land Use from Ethnobiology: Applied to the Yuma Indians. Ethnohistory 4:174–197.

Dvořák, Tomás

2006 Uranium Mining versus the "Purging" of the Borderlands: German Labour in the Jáchymov Mines in the Late 1940s and Early 1950s. Soudobé deˇjiny 12:627–671.

Eichstaedt, Peter

1994 If You Poison Us: Uranium and Native Americans. Santa Fe, NM: Red Crane Books.

Ellis, William Donohue

1993 Out of the Osage: The Foster Story. Oklahoma City: Western Heritage Books for the Oklahoma Heritage Association.

Escobar, Arturo

1998 Whose Knowledge, Whose Nature? Biodiversity, Conservation, and the Political Ecology of Social Movements. Journal of Political Ecology 5:53–82.

2001 Culture Sits in Places: Reflections on Globalism and Subaltern Strategies of Localization. Political Geography 20:139–174.

2008 Places and Regions in the Age of Globality: Social Movements and Biodiversity Conservation in the Colombian Pacific. Durham, NC: Duke University Press.

Fischer, David

1990 South Africa: As a Nuclear Supplier. *In* International Nuclear Trade and Nonproliferation: The Challenge of the Emerging Suppliers. W. C. Potter, ed. Pp. 273–286. Lexington, MA: Lexington Books.

Fixico, Donald L.

1986 Termination and Relocation: Federal Indian Policy, 1945–1961. Albuquerque: University of New Mexico Press.

1998 The Invasion of Indian Country in the Twentieth Century: American Capitalism and Tribal Natural Resources. Niwot: University Press of Colorado.

2003 The American Indian Mind in a Linear World: American Indian Studies and Traditional Knowledge. New York: Routledge.

Fluharty, Sterling

2003 "For a Greater Indian America": The Origins of the National Indian Youth Council. MA thesis, University of Oklahoma.

Fontana, Bernard L.

1963 The Hopi-Navajo Colony on the Lower Colorado River: A Problem in Ethnohistorical Interpretation. Ethnohistory 10:162–182.

Fox, Maggie

1982 An Historical, Statutory and Regulatory Review of Oil and Gas Leasing on Indian Lands and the Proposed Changes: "Better Late Than Never." Unpublished MS, Native American Rights Fund, National Indian Law Library, Boulder, CO.

Franks, Kenny A., and Paul F. Lambert

1985 Early California Oil: A Photographic History, 1865–1940. College Station: Texas A&M University Press.

Gedicks, Al

2001 Resource Rebels: Native Challenges to Mining and Oil Corporations. Cambridge, MA: South End Press.

Gibson-Graham, J. K.

2006 A Postcapitalist Politics. Minneapolis: University of Minnesota Press.

Glaser, Leah S.

2009 Electrifying the Rural American West: Stories of Power, People, and Place. Lincoln: University of Nebraska Press.

Glenn, Edward P., Christopher Lee, Richard Felger, and Scott Zengels

1995 Effects of Water Management on the Wetlands of the Colorado River Delta, Mexico. Conservation Biology 10:1175–1186.

Glennon, Robert J., and Peter W. Culp

2001 The Last Green Lagoon: How and Why the Bush Administration Should Save the Colorado River Delta. Ecology Law Quarterly 28:912–936.

Goodman, James

1987 The Navajo Atlas: Environments, Resources, Peoples, and History of the Diné Bikeyah. Norman: University of Oklahoma Press.

Gough, Robert

2001a Energy, Indians, and Environmental Justice. Native Americas 18:22.

2001b Restoring a Balance: Wind Power on the Great Plains. Native Americas 18:18.

2002 Indigenous Peoples and Renewable Energy: Thinking Locally, Acting Globally—A Modest Native Proposal for Climate Justice from the Northern Great Plains. Second National People of Color Environmental Leadership Summit—Summit II, Resource Paper Series. Washington, DC: Summit II National Office.

Greenberg, Henry, and Georgia Greenberg

1996 Power of a Navajo: Carl Gorman: The Man and His Life. Santa Fe, NM: Clear Light.

Greenberg, James B.

1998 The Tragedy of Commoditization: Political Ecology of the Colorado River Delta's Destruction. Research in Economic Anthropology 19:133–149.

Gross, Winifred T.

1981 Tribal Resources: Federal Trust Responsibility: United States Energy Development versus Trust Responsibilities to Indian Tribes. American Indian Law Review 9:309–343.

Grossman, Zoltán

2007 Possible Climate Change Responses for a United League of Indigenous Nations. Report of the Northwest Indian Applied Research Institute. Olympia, WA: The Evergreen State College.

Hanna, Jonathan M.

2007 Native Communities and Climate Change: Protecting Tribal Resources as Part of National Climate Policy. Boulder: Natural Resources Law Center, University of Colorado Law School / Western Water Assessment at the University of Colorado.

Harmon, Alexandra

1995 Lines in the Sand: Shifting Boundaries between Indians and Non-Indians in the Puget Sound Region. Western Historical Quarterly 26:429–453.

2001 Tribal Enrollment Councils: Lessons on Law and Indian Identity. Western Historical Quarterly 32:176–177.

2003 American Indians and Land Monopolies in the Gilded Age. Journal of American History 90:106–109.

Harris, Fred, and LaDonna Harris

1974 Indians, Coal, and the Big Sky. The Progressive 38:22–26.

The Harvard Project on American Indian Economic Development

2008 The State of the Native Nations: Conditions under US Policies of Self-Determination. New York: Oxford University Press.

Harvey, David

1997 Justice, Nature, and the Geography of Difference. London: Blackwell.

2006 Spaces of Global Capitalism: A Theory of Uneven Geographical Development. London: Verso.

Hawpetoss, Menomin

2007 Students Tackle Global Warming, Reducing Waste. Tribal College Journal 18:42–43.

Hess, David J.

2007 Alternative Pathways in Science and Industry: Activism, Innovation, and the Environment in an Era of Globalization. Cambridge, MA: The MIT Press.

Heyer, Jo

1962 Progress through Power: Electrical Training for the Navajo Tribe. Santa Fe, NM: Reynolds Electrical and Engineering Company.

His Holiness The Dalai Lama

1999 Ethics for a New Millenium. New York: Riverhead Books.

Hodge, H. C., J. N. Stannard, and J. B. Hursh

1973 Handbook of Experimental Pharmacology. Berlin: Springer-Verlag.

Hodgson, Dorothy L.

2002 Introduction: Comparative Perspectives on the Indigenous Rights Movement in Africa and the Americas. American Anthropologist 104:1037–1049.

Holland, Dorothy

2003 Multiple Identities in Practice: On the Dilemmas of Being a Hunter and an Environmentalist in the USA. Focaal—European Journal of Anthropology 42:23–41.

Holland, Dorothy, and Jean Lave

2001 Introduction. *In* History in Person: Enduring Struggles, Contentious Practice, Intimate Identities. Dorothy Holland and Jean Lave, eds. Santa Fe, NM: School of American Research Press.

Hooks, Gregory, and Chad L. Smith

2004 The Treadmill of Destruction: National Sacrifice Areas and Native Americans. American Sociological Review 69:558–575.

Hosmer, Brian

1999 American Indians in the Marketplace: Persistence and Innovation among the Menominees and Metlakatlans, 1870–1920. Lawrence: University Press of Kansas.

2004 "Dollar a Day and Glad to Have It": Work Relief on the Wind River Indian

Reservation as Memory. *In* Native Pathways: American Indian Culture and Economic Development in the Twentieth Century. Brian Hosmer and Colleen O'Neill, eds. Pp. 281–305. Boulder: University Press of Colorado.

Hosmer, Brian, and Colleen O'Neill, eds.

2004 Native Pathways: American Indian Culture and Economic Development in the Twentieth Century. Boulder: University Press of Colorado.

House Committee on Interior and Insular Affairs

1954 Survey Report of the Bureau of Indian Affairs, Committee Print 14, January 26, 1954. Washington, DC: GPO.

Hueper, William C.

1942 Occupational Tumors and Allied Diseases. Springfield, IL: C. C. Thomas.

Hurtado, Albert L.

2001 Romancing the West in the Twentieth Century: The Politics of History in a Contested Region. Western Historical Quarterly 32:417–435

Ishiyama, Noriko

2003 Environmental Justice and American Indian Tribal Sovereignty: Case Study of a Land-Use Conflict in Skull Valley, Utah. Antipode 35:119–139.

Israel, Daniel H.

1976 The Reemergence of Tribal Nationalism and Its Impact on Reservation Resource Development. University of Colorado Law Review 47:617–631.

Iverson, Peter

1981 The Navajo Nation. Westport, CT: Greenwood.

2002a Diné: A History of the Navajos. Albuquerque: University of New Mexico Press.

Iverson, Peter, and Monty Roessel, eds.

2002b For Our Navajo People: Diné Letters, Speeches and Petitions, 1900–1960. Albuquerque: University of New Mexico Press.

Jicarilla Apache Nation

2006 Jicarilla Apache Nation Code. Cincinnati, OH: American Legal Publishing Corporation (held by NARF).

Johnson, Helen W.

1969 Rural Indian Americans in Poverty. Washington, DC: Economic Research Service, US Department of Agriculture.

Johnston, Barbara Rose, and Susan Dawson

1994 Resource Use and Abuse on Native American Land: Uranium Mining in the American Southwest. *In* Who Pays the Price? The Sociocultural Context of Environmental Crisis. Barbara Rose Johnston, ed. Pp. 142–153. Washington, DC: Island Press.

Johnston, Barbara Rose, Susan Dawson, and Gary E. Madsen

2007 Uranium Mining and Milling: Navajo Experiences in the American Southwest, *In* Half-Lives and Half-Truths: Confronting the Radioactive Legacies of the Cold War. Barbara Rose Johnston, ed. Pp. 117–143. Santa Fe, NM: School for Advanced Research Press.

Jorgensen, Joseph G.

1984a The Political Economy of the Native American Energy Business. *In* Native Americans and Energy Development II. Joseph G. Jorgensen, ed. Pp. 10–51. Boston: Anthropology Resource Center / Seventh Generation Fund.

Jorgensen, Joseph G., ed.

1984b Native Americans and Energy Development II. Boston: Anthropology Resource Center / Seventh Generation Fund.

Kahn, Annie

1990 White Shell Woman: Beloved of the Navajo. *In* Native American Prophecies: Examining the History, Wisdom and Startling Predictions of Visionary Native Americans. Scott Peterson, ed. Pp. 127–158. St. Paul, MN: Paragon House.

Kamper, David

2003 The Politics and Poetics of Organizing Navajo Laborers. PhD dissertation, University of California, Los Angeles.

Kappler, Charles J., ed.

1972 Indian Treaties, 1778–1883. New York: Interland.

Katchongva, Dan

1992 Hopi, "He Will Use Any Means to Get What He Wants." *In* Native American Testimony: A Chronicle of Indian–White Relations from Prophecy to the Present, 1491–1992. Peter Nabokov, ed. Pp. 6–7. New York: Penguin Books.

Kelley, Klara Bonsack, and Harris Francis

1994 Navajo Sacred Places. Bloomington and Indianapolis: Indiana University Press.

Kelly, William H.

1944 A Preliminary Study of the Cocopa Indians of Mexico with an Analysis of the Influence of Geographic Position and Physical Environment on Certain Aspects of Their Culture. PhD dissertation, Harvard University.

1977 Cocopa Ethnography. Anthropological Papers of the University of Arizona, 29. Tucson: University of Arizona Press.

Kluckhohn, Clyde

1942 The Navahos in the Machine Age: How a Primitive People through Unusual Capacity for Adaptation Have Prospered in Technological Times. The Technology Review (February):196–197.

Kluckhohn, Clyde, and Dorothea Leighton

1958 The Navaho. Cambridge, MA: Harvard University Press.

Kniffen, Fred B.

1931 Lower California Studies, III: The Primitive Cultural Landscape of the Colorado Delta. University of California Publications in Geography 5:43–66.

Koenig, Michael

1982 Toward Metropolitan Status: Charter Government and the Rise of Phoenix, Arizona. PhD dissertation, Arizona State University.

Kosek, Jake

2006 Understories: The Political Life of Forests in Northern New Mexico. Durham, NC: Duke University Press.

Krauss, Celene

1996 Women of Color on the Front Line. *In* Unequal Protection: Environmental Justice and Communities of Color. Robert D. Bullard, ed. Pp. 256–271. San Francisco: Sierra Club Books. First published 1994 by Random House.

Kreith, Marcia

1991 Water Inputs in California Food Production. Sacramento, CA: Water Education Foundation.

Kroeber, Alfred Louis

1920 Yuman Tribes of the Lower Colorado. University of California Publications in American Archaeology and Ethnology, vol. 16, no. 8, pp. 475–485. Berkeley: University of California Press.

1925 Handbook of the Indians of California. Washington, DC: Bureau of American Ethnology of the Smithsonian Institution.

Kuletz, Valerie

1998 The Tainted Desert: Environmental and Social Ruin in the American West. New York: Routledge.

LaDuke, Winona

1984 The Council of Energy Resource Tribes. *In* Native Americans and Energy Development, vol. II. Joseph G. Jorgensen, ed. Pp. 58–70. Boston: Anthropology Resource Center / Seventh Generation Fund.

1999 All Our Relations: Native Struggles for Land and Life. Cambridge, MA: South End Press.

2006 Recovering the Sacred. Cambridge, MA: South End Press.

LaFarge, Oliver

1929 Laughing Boy. New York: New American Library.

Lassiter, Matthew

2006 The Silent Majority: Suburban Politics in the Sunbelt South. Princeton, NJ: Princeton University Press.

Leckie, Shirley A.

2000 Angie Debo, Pioneering Historian. Norman: University of Oklahoma Press.

Lee, George P.

1987 Silent Courage, an Indian Story: The Autobiography of George P. Lee, a Navajo. Salt Lake City, UT: Deseret Book Company.

Leopold, Aldo

1949 A Sand County Almanac, and Sketches Here and There. London: Oxford University Press.

Lewis, David Rich

1991 Reservation Leadership and the Progressive–Traditional Dichotomy: William Wash and the Northern Utes, 1865–1928. Ethnohistory 38:124–148.

2007 Skull Valley Goshutes and the Politics of Nuclear Waste: Environment, Economic Development, and Tribal Sovereignty. *In* Native Americans and the Environment: Perspectives on the Ecological Indian. Michael E. Harkin and David Rich Lewis, eds. Pp. 304–342. Lincoln: University of Nebraska Press.

Light, Steven Andrew, and R. L. Kathryn Rand

2005 Indian Gaming and Tribal Sovereignty: The Casino Compromise. Lawrence: University of Kansas Press.

Linenberger, Toni, and Leah S. Glaser

2002 Dams, Dynamos, and Development: The Bureau of Reclamation's Power Program and Electrification of the West. Bureau of Reclamation, US Department of the Interior. Washington, DC: GPO.

Linowes Report (*see* Commission on Fiscal Accountability of the Nation's Energy Resources)

Littlefield, Alice, and Martha Knack, eds.

1996 Native Americans and Wage Labor: Ethnohistorical Perspectives. Norman: University of Oklahoma Press.

Long, Dáilan J.

2007 Diyin Nohookáá Diné nihi'doo'nii: We Are Called the Holy Earth-Surface-People; Navajo Resistance to Cultural Genocide, Environmental Injustice, and the Desert Rock Energy Project. Master's thesis, Dartmouth College.

Lotchkin, Roger

1992 Fortress California, 1910–1965: From Warfare to Welfare. New York: Oxford University Press.

Lovins, Amory B.

1977 Soft Energy Paths: Toward a Durable Peace. Cambridge, MA: Ballinger.

MacDonald, Peter

1976 An Indian View of Minerals Development on Indian Lands. *In* Institute on Indian Land Development—Oil, Gas, Coal and Other Minerals. Pp. 1–5. Tucson, AZ: Rocky Mountain Mineral Law Foundation.

MacDonald, Peter, with Ted Schwarz

1993 The Last Warrior: Peter MacDonald and the Navajo Nation. New York: Orion Books.

MacDougal, Daniel Trembly

1906 The Delta of the Rio Colorado. Bulletin of the American Geographical Society 38:1–16.

Madsen, Gary E., Susan E. Dawson, and Bryan R. Spykerman

1996 Perceived Occupational and Environmental Exposures: A Case Study of Former Uranium Millworkers. Environment and Behavior 28:571–590.

Maremäe, Ello, Hain Tankler, Henno Putnik, and Ilge Maalmann, eds.

2003 Historical Survey of Nuclear Non-proliferation in Estonia, 1946–1995. Report prepared for the International Atomic Energy Agency. Tallinn, Estonia: Estonia Radiation Protection Centre / Swedish Nuclear Power Inspectorate.

Mason, Dale W.

2000 Indian Gaming: Tribal Sovereignty and American Politics. Norman: University of Oklahoma Press.

Matheny, Robert L.

1976 Lumbering in the White Mountains of Arizona, 1919–1942. Arizona and the West 33:237–256.

Matthews, Washington

1984 Creation of First Man and First Woman. *In* American Indian Myths and Legends. Richard Erodes and Alfonso Ortiz, eds. Pp. 39–41. New York: Pantheon Books.

McDonnell, Janet A.

1991 The Dispossession of the American Indian, 1887–1934. Bloomington: Indiana University Press.

McElroy, N., and A. Brodsky

1986 Training Manual for Uranium Mill Workers on Health Protection from Uranium. Washington, DC: Nuclear Regulatory Commission.

McIntosh, Kenneth

1988 Geronimo's Friend: Angie Debo and the New History. Chronicles of Oklahoma 66:164–177.

McNichols, Charles L.

1944 Crazy Weather. New York: Editions for the Armed Services.

Meeks, Eric V.

2003 The Tohono O'odham, Wage Labor, and Resistant Adaptation, 1900–1930. Western Historical Quarterly 34:469–490.

2007 Border Citizens: The Making of Indians, Mexicans, and Anglos in Arizona. Austin: University of Texas Press.

Meriam, Lewis, Ray A. Brown, Henry Roe Cloud, Edward Everett Dale, Emma Duke, Herbert R. Edwards, Fayette Avery McKenzie, Mary Louise Mark, W. Carson Ryan Jr., and William J. Spillman

1928 The Problem of Indian Administration, Summary of Findings and Recommendations. Washington, DC: Institute for Government Research.

Mies, Maria, and Vandana Shiva

1993 Ecofeminism. London and New York: Zed Books.

Miles, Andrea S.

2005–2006 Tribal Energy Resource Agreements: Tools for Achieving Energy Development and Tribal Self-Sufficiency or an Abdication of Federal Environmental and Trust Responsiblities? American Indian Law Review 30:461–476.

Miller, Richard L.

1986 Under the Cloud: The Decades of Nuclear Testing. New York: Free Press.

Mills, Thomas E.
1997 The Hopi Survival Kit. New York: Stewart, Tabori, and Chang.

Miner, H. Craig
1976 The Corporation and the Indian: Tribal Sovereignty and Industrial Civilization in Indian Territory, 1865–1907. Norman and London: University of Oklahoma Press.

Mohl, Raymond
1998 City and Region: The Missing Dimension in US Urban History. Journal of Urban History 25:3–21.

Molotch, Harvey
1976 The City as a Growth Machine. American Journal of Sociology 82:309–332.

Molotch, Harvey, and John Logan
1987 Urban Fortunes: Toward a Political Economy of Place. Berkeley: University of California Press.

Morrison, Jack G.
2000 Ravensbrück: Everyday Life in a Women's Concentration Camp, 1939–1945. Princeton, NJ: Markus Wiener.

Muehlmann, Shaylih
2009 How Do Real Indians Fish? Neoliberal Multiculturalism and Contested Indigeneities in the Colorado Delta. American Anthropologist 111:468–479.

Murphy, M. Maureen
1990 Indian Tribal Government Civil Jurisdiction: Emerging Jurisprudence, Congressional Research Service, January 31. Report no. CRS-1990-AML-0035.

Nagata, Shuichi
1970 Modern Transformations of Moenkopi Pueblo. Urbana: University of Illinois Press.

National Advisory Commission
1967 Rural Poverty: Hearings before the National Advisory Commission on Rural Poverty, Tucson, Arizona, January 26 and 27, 1967. Washington, DC: GPO.

Nash, June C.
2001 Mayan Visions: The Quest for Autonomy in an Age of Globalization. New York: Routledge.

Natural Resources Defense Council (NRDC)
2005 Indian Energy: What Happens Now? Washington, DC: NRDC.

Needham, Andrew, and Allen Dieterich-Ward
2009 Beyond the Metropolis: Metropolitan Growth and Regional Transformation in Postwar America. Journal of Urban History 36:943–969.

Needham, Todd Andrew
2006 Power Lines: Urban Space, Energy Development, and the Making of the Modern Southwest. PhD dissertation, University of Michigan.

Newell, F. H.
1905 Third Annual Report of Reclamation Service 1903–1904. Washington, DC: GPO.

Novak, Steven J.
1990 The Real Takeover of the BIA: The Preferential Hiring of Indians. Journal of Economic History 50:639–654.

O'Neill, Colleen
2005 Working the Navajo Way: Labor and Culture in the Twentieth Century. Lawrence: University Press of Kansas.

Palmer, Larry
1977 Paying for Suffering: The Problem of Human Experimentation. Maryland Law Review 56:604–623.

Pearson, Byron E.
2000 "We Have Almost Forgotten How to Hope": The Hualupai, the Navajo, and the Fight for the Central Arizona Project, 1944–1968. Western Historical Quarterly 31:297–316.

Perdue, Theda
2003 "Mixed Blood" Indians: Racial Construction in the Early South. Athens: University of Georgia Press.

Peschek, Joseph
1997 National Security Tales and the End of the Cold War. *In* Tales of the State: Narrative in Contemporary US Politics and Public Policy. Sanford F. Schram and Philip T. Neisser, eds. Pp. 212–222. New York: Rowman and Littlefield.

Pinkerton, Lynne E., Thomas F. Bloom, M. J. Hein, and Elizabeth M. Ward
2004 Mortality among a Cohort of Uranium Mill Workers: An Update. Occupational and Environmental Medicine 61:57–64.

Pisani, Donald J.
2002 Water and American Government: The Reclamation Bureau, National Water Policy, and the West, 1902–1935. Berkeley: University of California Press.

Pitt, Jennifer, Daniel F. Luecke, Michael J. Cohen, Edward P. Glenn, and Carlos Valdes-Casillas
2000 Two Nations, One River: Managing Ecosystem Conservation in the Colorado River Delta. Theme issue, "Water Issues in the US-Mexico Borderlands," Natural Resources Journal 40:819–864.

Polk, Orval H.
1940 An Economic Electric Power Survey of Arizona. PhD dissertation, University of Colorado.

Powell, Dana E., and Andrew Curley
2009 K'é, Hozhó, and Non-governmental Politics on the Navajo Nation: Ontologies of Difference Manifest in Environmental Activism. E-Journal of the World Anthropologies Network (January):4.

Presidential Commission on Indian Reservation Economies
1984 Report and Recommendations to the President of the United States. Washington, DC: Executive Office of the President.

Press, Dan
1979 Labor Law, Unions and Indian Self-Determination: The Powers and Options of Indian Tribes and Indian Workers under the National Labor Relations Act. Boulder, CO: ACKCO (American Indian Professional Services).

Press, Dan, ed.
1976 Indian Employment Rights: A Guide to Tribal Action. Boulder, CO: ACKCO (American Indian Professional Services).

Preston, Diana
2006 Before the Fallout: From Marie Curie to Hiroshima. New York: Berkeley Books.

Prucha, Francis Paul
1984 The Great Father: The United States Government and the American Indians. Lincoln: University of Nebraska Press.

Prucha, Frances Paul, ed.
1976 Documents of United States Indian Policy. Lincoln: University of Nebraska Press.

Raibmon, Paige
2005 Authentic Indians: Episodes of Encounter from the Late-Nineteenth-Century Northwest Coast. Durham, NC: Duke University Press.

Reddy, Marlita A.
1993 Statistical Record of Native North America. Detroit, MI: Gale Research.

Reichard, Gladys A.
1963 Navaho Religion, a Study of Symbolism. New York: Bollingen Foundation.

Rister, Carl Coke
1949 Oil! Titan of the Southwest. Norman: University of Oklahoma Press.

Robbins, Lynn
1975 Navajo Participation in Labor Unions. Lake Powell Research Project Bulletin, December. Los Angeles: University of California, Los Angeles, Institute of Geophysics and Planetary Physics.

Rogge, A. E., D. Lorn McWatters, Melissa Keanne, and Richard P. Emanuel
1995 Raising Arizona's Dams: Daily Life, Danger and Discrimination in the Dam Construction Camps of Central Arizona, 1890s–1940s. Tucson: University of Arizona Press.

Rosier, Paul
2006 "They Are Ancestral Homelands": Race, Place, and Politics in Cold War Native America. Journal of American History 92:1300–1326.

Royster, Judith V.
1997 Oil and Water in Indian Country. Natural Resources Journal 37:457–490.

Rural Electrification Administration

1937 Annual Report. Washington, DC: GPO.

1938 Annual Report. Washington, DC: GPO.

Rzeczkowski, Frank

2003 Reimagining Community: Intertribal Relations on the Northern Plains, 1885–1925. PhD dissertation, Northwestern University.

Saleem, H. Ali

2003 Mining, the Environment, and Indigenous Development Conflicts. Tucson: University of Arizona Press.

Samet, J. M., D. M. Kutvirt, R. J. Waxweiler, and C. R. Key

1984 Uranium Mining and Lung Cancer among Navajo Men. New England Journal of Medicine 310:1481–1484.

Saywer, Susana

2004 Crude Chronicles: Indigenous Politics, Multinational Oil, and Neoliberalism in Ecuador. Durham, NC: Duke University Press.

Scarberry, Susan J.

1981 Land into Flesh: Images of Intimacy. Frontiers: A Journal of Women Studies 6:26.

Schulman, Bruce

1991 From Cotton Belt to Sun Belt: Federal Policy, Economic Development, and the Transformation of the South, 1938–1980. New York: Oxford University Press.

Self, Robert

2003 American Babylon: Race and the Struggle for Postwar Oakland. Princeton, NJ: Princeton University Press.

Senate Select Committee on Indian Affairs

1980 Oil and Gas Leases on Indian Lands, Part 3. 97th Cong. 1st Sess., June 1, 1981. *In* American Indian Natural Resources: Oil and Gas, by Thomas Luebben. Pp. 1–247. Washington, DC: Institute for the Development of Indian Law.

Shepard, Paul

1978 Thinking Animals. New York: Viking Press.

Shepardson, Mary

1995 The Gender Status of Navajo Women. *In* Women and Power in Native North America. Laura F. Klein and Lillian A. Ackerman, eds. Pp. 159–176. Norman: University of Oklahoma Press.

Sheridan, Thomas

1995 Arizona: A History. Tucson: University of Arizona Press.

Sherry, John W.

2002 Land, Wind, and Hard Words: A Story of Navajo Activism. Albuquerque: University of New Mexico Press.

Shields, L. M., W. H. Wiese, B. J. Skipper, B. Charley, and L. Benally

1992 Navajo Birth Outcomes in the Shiprock Uranium Mining Area. Health Physics 63:542–551.

Shipps, Thomas H.

1992 Oil and Gas Lease Operations and Royalty Valuation on Indian Lands: What Is the Difference in Federal and Indian Leases? Indian Law Support Center Reporter 15:1–22.

2007 Tribal Energy Resource Agreements: Commentary on the Proposed Regulations. Native American Resources Newsletter 4:3.

Shirley, Joe, Jr.

2006 Remembrance to Avoid an Unwanted Fate. Navajo Nation Press Release. Window Rock, AZ.

Shreve, Bradley Glenn

2007 Red Power Rising: The National Indian Youth Council and the Origins of Intertribal Activism. PhD dissertation, University of New Mexico.

Silko, Leslie

1977 Ceremony. New York: New American Library.

Simpson, Christopher

1995 The Splendid Blond Beast: Money, Law, and Genocide in the Twentieth Century. Monroe, ME: Common Courage.

Sklar, Holly

1980 Trilateralism: The Trilateral Commission and Elite Planning for World Management. Boston: South End Press.

Smith, Andrea

2005 Conquest: Sexual Violence and American Indian Genocide. Cambridge, MA: South End Press.

Smith, Sherry

2007 Indians, the Counterculture, and the New Left. *In* Beyond Red Power: American Indian Politics and Activism since 1900. Daniel M. Cobb and Loretta Fowler, eds. Pp. 142–160. Santa Fe, NM: School for Advanced Research Press.

Speer, Albert

1971 Inside the Third Reich. New York: Avon Books.

Spicer, Edward H.

1962 Cycles of Conquest: The Impact of Spain, Mexico, and the United States on the Indians of the Southwest, 1533–1960. Tucson: University of Arizona Press.

Spiegel, Carolin

2005 International Water Law: The Contributions of Western United States Water Law to the United Nations Convention on the Law of the Non-navigable Uses of International Watercourses. Duke Journal of Comparative and International Law 15:333–361.

Stevenson, Gelvin

2005 The Future Is Green: Tribal Colleges Saving Water, Electricity—and Money. Tribal College Journal 17:10–15.

Stewart, Kenneth M.

1983 Mohave. *In* Southwest. Handbook of North American Indians, vol. 10. Alfonso Ortiz, ed. Pp. 55–70. Washington, DC: Smithsonian Institution.

Sturm, Circe

2002 Blood Politics: Race, Culture, and Identity in the Cherokee Nation of Oklahoma. Berkeley: University of California Press.

Suagee, Dean B.

1992 Self-Determination for Indigenous Peoples at the Dawn of the Solar Age. University of Michigan Journal of Law Reform 25:671–749.

1998 Renewable Energy in Indian Country: Options for Tribal Governments. Issue Brief 10. Renewable Energy Policy Project. Washington, DC: Center for Renewable Energy and Sustainable Technology.

Sugrue, Thomas

2004 All Politics Is Local: The Persistence of Localism in Twentieth-Century America. *In* The Democratic Experiment: New Directions in American Political History. Meg Jacobs, William Novak, and Julian Zelizer, eds. Pp. 301–326. Princeton, NJ: Princeton University Press.

Swimmer, Margaret

1981–1982 Indian Tribes: Self-Determination through Effective Management of Natural Resources. Tulsa Law Journal 17:507–533.

Sykes, Godfrey

1937 The Colorado Delta. American Geographical Society Special Publication, 19. Washington, DC: Carnegie Institution of Washington / American Geographical Society of New York.

Tapahonso, Luci

1997 Blue Horses Rush In: Poems and Stories. Tucson: University of Arizona Press.

1993 Sáanii Dahataal: The Women Are Singing. Tucson: University of Arizona Press.

Tarbell, Ida

1939 All in the Day's Work: An Autobiography. New York: Macmillan.

Task Force Seven

1976 Reservation and Resource Development and Protection. US American Indian Policy Review Commission Report. Washington, DC: GPO.

Thorne, Tanis C.

2003 The World's Richest Indian: The Scandal over Jackson Barnet's Oil Fortune. Oxford: Oxford University Press.

Thun, Michael J., Dean B. Baker, Kyle Steenland, Alexander B. Smith, William Halperin, and Thomas Berl

1985 Renal Toxicity in Uranium Mill Workers. Scandinavian Journal of Work and Environmental Health 11:83–90.

Tisdale, Shelby Jo-Anne

1997 Cocopah Identity and Cultural Survival: Indian Gaming and the Political Ecology of the Lower Colorado River Delta, 1850–1996. PhD dissertation, University of Arizona.

Tobey, Ronald

1996 Technology as Freedom: The New Deal and the Electrical Modernization of the American Home. Berkeley: University of California Press.

Tribal College Journal

2004 On Campus: Blackfeet Students Involved in Research. Tribal College Journal 16:36.

2005a CIT, NASA Explore Alternative Energy. Tribal College Journal 17:41–42.

2005b Students See Renewable Power Potential at SIPI. Tribal College Journal 17:35.

Trimble, Stephen

1993 The People: Indians of the American Southwest. Santa Fe, NM: School of American Research Press.

Tsing, Anna L.

2005 Friction: An Ethnography of Global Connection. Princeton, NJ, and Oxford: Princeton University Press.

Tso, Harold, and Lora Magnum Shields

1980 Navajo Mining Operations: Early Hazards and Recent Interventions. New Mexico Journal of Science 20:11–17.

Tsosie, Rebecca

1996–1997 Tribal Environmental Policy in an Era of Self-Determination: The Role of Ethics, Economics, and Traditional Ecological Knowledge. Vermont Law Review 21:225–333.

2007 Indigenous People and Environmental Justice: The Impact of Climate Change. University of Colorado Law Review 78:1625–1677.

Unrau, William E.

1989 Mixed-Bloods and Tribal Dissolution: Charles Curtis and the Quest for Indian Identity. Lawrence: University Press of Kansas.

US American Indian Policy Review Commission (AIPRC)

1977 Final Report Submitted to Congress, May 7, 1977. Washington, DC: GPO.

US Bureau of Reclamation

1971 Southwest Energy Study. Washington, DC: US GPO.

US Congress

1979 Mill Tailings Dam Break at Church Rock, New Mexico (Church Rock hearings), 96th Cong., 1st sess., October 22, House of Representatives, Committee on Interior and Insular Affairs, Subcommittee on Energy and the Environment.

1990 Testimony of Earl Mettler on Impacts of Past Uranium Mining Practices, 101st Cong., 2d sess., March 13, 1990, Senate, Committee on Energy and Natural Resources, Mineral Resources Development and Production Subcommittee, field hearing (101-0683) held in Shiprock, NM.

US Department of Energy (DOE), National Renewable Energy Laboratory

2006 Renewable Energy Development on Tribal Lands. Washington, DC: DOE.

US Department of the Interior

1972 Hearings before the Secretary of the Interior on Leasing of Oil Lands and Natural Gas Wells in Indian Territory and Territory of Oklahoma. May 8, 24, 25, 29 and June 7 and 19, 1906. New York: Arno Press.

US General Accounting Office (GAO)

1976 Indian Natural Resources, Part II: Coal, Oil, and Gas, Better Management Can Improve Development and Increase Indian Income and Employment. Report to the Senate Select Committee on Interior and Insular Affairs. Washington, DC: General Accounting Office.

US Senate

1974 New Mexico Indian Oversight Hearings, Part 2: The Problem and Program Needs of Urban Indians. Hearings before the Subcommittee on Indian Affairs of the Committee on Interior and Insular Affairs, 93rd Congress, 1st sess. Washington, DC: GPO.

1980 Department of the Interior and Related Agencies Appropriations for Fiscal Year 1980. Hearings before the Subcommittee of the Committee on Appropriations, 96th Congress, 1st sess. Washington, DC: GPO.

Velarde Tiller, Veronica E., ed.

1996 American Indian Reservations and Indian Trust Areas. Washington, DC: Economic Development Administration, US Department of Commerce.

Wagoner, Joseph K., Victor E. Archer, Benjamin E. Carroll, Duncan A. Holaday, and Pope A. Lawrence

1964 Cancer Mortality Patterns among US Uranium Miners and Millers, 1950 through 1962. Journal of the National Cancer Institute 32:787–801.

Walsh, Catherine

2004 The (Re)Articulation of Political Subjectivities and Colonial Difference in Ecuador: Reflections on Capitalism and the Geopolitics of Knowledge. Nepantla: Views from the South 3:61–97.

Waxweiler, Richard J., Victor E. Archer, Robert J. Roscoe, Arthur Watanabe, and Michael J. Thun

1983 Mortality Patterns among a Retrospective Cohort of Uranium Mill Workers. Proceedings of the Sixteenth Midyear Topical Meeting of the Health Physics Society. Albuquerque, NM: Health Physics Society.

White, Richard

1982 The Roots of Dependency: Environment and Social Change among the Choctaw, Pawnee, and Navajo. Lincoln: University of Nebraska Press.

Wilkins, David E.

1997 American Indian Sovereignty and the US Supreme Court: The Masking of Justice. Austin: University of Texas Press.

2003 The Navajo Political Experience. Lanham, MD: Rowman and Littlefield.

Wilkins, David E., and K. Tsianina Lomawaima

2001 Uneven Ground: American Indian Sovereignty and Federal Law. Norman: University of Oklahoma Press.

Wilkinson, Charles

1999 Fire on the Plateau. Washington, DC: Island Press.

2005 Blood Struggle: The Rise of Modern Indian Nations. New York: W. W. Norton.

Wilson, H. Clyde, and Leo J. Wolfe

1961 The Relationship between Unearned Income and Individual Productive Effort on the Jicarilla Apache Indian Reservation. Economic Development and Cultural Change 9:589–597.

Wolf, Eric R.

1982 Europe and the People without History. Berkeley: University of California Press.

Writers Program of the Works Projects Administration

1989 The WPA Guide to 1930s Arizona. Tucson: University of Arizona Press.

Yergin, Daniel

1991 The Prize: The Epic Quest for Oil, Money, and Power. New York: Simon and Schuster.

Young, Robert W.

1951–1961 A Decade of Progress: The Navajo Yearbook Report, no. viiii. Window Rock, AZ: Navajo Agency.

1978 A Political History of the Navajo Tribe. Tsaile, AZ: Navajo Community College Press.

Young Bear, Severt, and R. D. Theisz

1994 Standing in the Light: A Lakota Way of Seeing. Lincoln and London: University of Nebraska Press.

Zah, Peterson

2001 Foreword. *In* In the Fifth World: Portrait of the Navajo Nation. Adriel Heisey and Kenji Kawano, eds. Pp. 1–2. Tucson, AZ: Rio Nuevo.

Zucker, Ross

2001 Democratic Distributive Justice. New York: Cambridge University Press.

Index

School for Advanced Research Advanced Seminar Series

Published by SAR Press

Chaco & Hohokam: Prehistoric Regional Systems in the American Southwest
Patricia L. Crown & W. James Judge, eds.

Recapturing Anthropology: Working in the Present
Richard G. Fox, ed.

War in the Tribal Zone: Expanding States and Indigenous Warfare
R. Brian Ferguson & Neil L. Whitehead, eds.

Ideology and Pre-Columbian Civilizations
Arthur A. Demarest & Geoffrey W. Conrad, eds.

Dreaming: Anthropological and Psychological Interpretations
Barbara Tedlock, ed.

Historical Ecology: Cultural Knowledge and Changing Landscapes
Carole L. Crumley, ed.

Themes in Southwest Prehistory
George J. Gumerman, ed.

Memory, History, and Opposition under State Socialism
Rubie S. Watson, ed.

Other Intentions: Cultural Contexts and the Attribution of Inner States
Lawrence Rosen, ed.

Last Hunters–First Farmers: New Perspectives on the Prehistoric Transition to Agriculture
T. Douglas Price & Anne Birgitte Gebauer, eds.

Making Alternative Histories: The Practice of Archaeology and History in Non-Western Settings
Peter R. Schmidt & Thomas C. Patterson, eds.

Cyborgs & Citadels: Anthropological Interventions in Emerging Sciences and Technologies
Gary Lee Downey & Joseph Dumit, eds.

Senses of Place
Steven Feld & Keith H. Basso, eds.

The Origins of Language: What Nonhuman Primates Can Tell Us
Barbara J. King, ed.

Critical Anthropology Now: Unexpected Contexts, Shifting Constituencies, Changing Agendas
George E. Marcus, ed.

Archaic States
Gary M. Feinman & Joyce Marcus, eds.

Regimes of Language: Ideologies, Polities, and Identities
Paul V. Kroskrity, ed.

Biology, Brains, and Behavior: The Evolution of Human Development
Sue Taylor Parker, Jonas Langer, & Michael L. McKinney, eds.

Women & Men in the Prehispanic Southwest: Labor, Power, & Prestige
Patricia L. Crown, ed.

History in Person: Enduring Struggles, Contentious Practice, Intimate Identities
Dorothy Holland & Jean Lave, eds.

The Empire of Things: Regimes of Value and Material Culture
Fred R. Myers, ed.

Catastrophe & Culture: The Anthropology of Disaster
Susanna M. Hoffman & Anthony Oliver-Smith, eds.

Uruk Mesopotamia & Its Neighbors: Cross-Cultural Interactions in the Era of State Formation
Mitchell S. Rothman, ed.

Remaking Life & Death: Toward an Anthropology of the Biosciences
Sarah Franklin & Margaret Lock, eds.

Tikal: Dynasties, Foreigners, & Affairs of State: Advancing Maya Archaeology
Jeremy A. Sabloff, ed.

Published by SAR Press

Gray Areas: Ethnographic Encounters with Nursing Home Culture
Philip B. Stafford, ed.

Pluralizing Ethnography: Comparison and Representation in Maya Cultures, Histories, and Identities
John M. Watanabe & Edward F. Fischer, eds.

American Arrivals: Anthropology Engages the New Immigration
Nancy Foner, ed.

Violence
Neil L. Whitehead, ed.

Law & Empire in the Pacific: Fiji and Hawai'i
Sally Engle Merry & Donald Brenneis, eds.

Anthropology in the Margins of the State
Veena Das & Deborah Poole, eds.

The Archaeology of Colonial Encounters: Comparative Perspectives
Gil J. Stein, ed.

Globalization, Water, & Health: Resource Management in Times of Scarcity
Linda Whiteford & Scott Whiteford, eds.

A Catalyst for Ideas: Anthropological Archaeology and the Legacy of Douglas W. Schwartz
Vernon L. Scarborough, ed.

The Archaeology of Chaco Canyon: An Eleventh-Century Pueblo Regional Center
Stephen H. Lekson, ed.

Community Building in the Twenty-First Century
Stanley E. Hyland, ed.

Afro-Atlantic Dialogues: Anthropology in the Diaspora
Kevin A. Yelvington, ed.

Copán: The History of an Ancient Maya Kingdom
E. Wyllys Andrews & William L. Fash, eds.

The Evolution of Human Life History
Kristen Hawkes & Richard R. Paine, eds.

The Seductions of Community: Emancipations, Oppressions, Quandaries
Gerald W. Creed, ed.

The Gender of Globalization: Women Navigating Cultural and Economic Marginalities
Nandini Gunewardena & Ann Kingsolver, eds.

New Landscapes of Inequality: Neoliberalism and the Erosion of Democracy in America
Jane L. Collins, Micaela di Leonardo, & Brett Williams, eds.

Imperial Formations
Ann Laura Stoler, Carole McGranahan, & Peter C. Perdue, eds.

Opening Archaeology: Repatriation's Impact on Contemporary Research and Practice
Thomas W. Killion, ed.

Small Worlds: Method, Meaning, & Narrative in Microhistory
James F. Brooks, Christopher R. N. DeCorse, & John Walton, eds.

Memory Work: Archaeologies of Material Practices
Barbara J. Mills & William H. Walker, eds.

Figuring the Future: Globalization and the Temporalities of Children and Youth
Jennifer Cole & Deborah Durham, eds.

Timely Assets: The Politics of Resources and Their Temporalities
Elizabeth Emma Ferry & Mandana E. Limbert, eds.

Democracy: Anthropological Approaches
Julia Paley, ed.

Confronting Cancer: Metaphors, Inequality, and Advocacy
Juliet McMullin & Diane Weiner, eds.

Published by SAR Press

Development & Dispossession: The Crisis of Forced Displacement and Resettlement
Anthony Oliver-Smith, ed.

Global Health in Times of Violence
Barbara Rylko-Bauer, Linda Whiteford, & Paul Farmer, eds.

The Evolution of Leadership: Transitions in Decision Making from Small-Scale to Middle-Range Societies
Kevin J. Vaughn, Jelmer W. Eerkins, & John Kantner, eds.

Archaeology & Cultural Resource Management: Visions for the Future
Lynne Sebastian & William D. Lipe, eds.

Archaic State Interaction: The Eastern Mediterranean in the Bronze Age
William A. Parkinson & Michael L. Galaty, eds.

Roots of Conflict: Soils, Agriculture, and Sociopolitical Complexity in Ancient Hawai'i
Patrick V. Kirch, ed.

Indians & Energy: Exploitation and Opportunity in the American Southwest
Sherry L. Smith & Brian Frehner, eds.

Published by Cambridge University Press

The Anasazi in a Changing Environment
George J. Gumerman, ed.

Regional Perspectives on the Olmec
Robert J. Sharer & David C. Grove, eds.

The Chemistry of Prehistoric Human Bone
T. Douglas Price, ed.

The Emergence of Modern Humans: Biocultural Adaptations in the Later Pleistocene
Erik Trinkaus, ed.

The Anthropology of War
Jonathan Haas, ed.

The Evolution of Political Systems
Steadman Upham, ed.

Classic Maya Political History: Hieroglyphic and Archaeological Evidence
T. Patrick Culbert, ed.

Turko-Persia in Historical Perspective
Robert L. Canfield, ed.

Chiefdoms: Power, Economy, and Ideology
Timothy Earle, ed.

Reconstructing Prehistoric Pueblo Societies
William A. Longacre, ed.

Published by University of New Mexico Press

New Perspectives on the Pueblos
Alfonso Ortiz, ed.

Structure and Process in Latin America
Arnold Strickon & Sidney M. Greenfield, eds.

The Classic Maya Collapse
T. Patrick Culbert, ed.

Methods and Theories of Anthropological Genetics
M. H. Crawford & P. L. Workman, eds.

Sixteenth-Century Mexico: The Work of Sahagun
Munro S. Edmonson, ed.

Ancient Civilization and Trade
Jeremy A. Sabloff & C. C. Lamberg-Karlovsky, eds.

Photography in Archaeological Research
Elmer Harp, Jr., ed.

Meaning in Anthropology
Keith H. Basso & Henry A. Selby, eds.

The Valley of Mexico: Studies in Pre-Hispanic Ecology and Society
Eric R. Wolf, ed.

Demographic Anthropology: Quantitative Approaches
Ezra B. W. Zubrow, ed.

The Origins of Maya Civilization
Richard E. W. Adams, ed.

Explanation of Prehistoric Change
James N. Hill, ed.

Explorations in Ethnoarchaeology
Richard A. Gould, ed.

Entrepreneurs in Cultural Context
Sidney M. Greenfield, Arnold Strickon, & Robert T. Aubey, eds.

The Dying Community
Art Gallaher, Jr. & Harlan Padfield, eds.

Southwestern Indian Ritual Drama
Charlotte J. Frisbie, ed.

Lowland Maya Settlement Patterns
Wendy Ashmore, ed.

Simulations in Archaeology
Jeremy A. Sabloff, ed.

Chan Chan: Andean Desert City
Michael E. Moseley & Kent C. Day, eds.

Shipwreck Anthropology
Richard A. Gould, ed.

Elites: Ethnographic Issues
George E. Marcus, ed.

The Archaeology of Lower Central America
Frederick W. Lange & Doris Z. Stone, eds.

Late Lowland Maya Civilization: Classic to Postclassic
Jeremy A. Sabloff & E. Wyllys Andrews V, eds.

Published by University of California Press

Writing Culture: The Poetics and Politics of Ethnography
James Clifford & George E. Marcus, eds.

Published by University of Arizona Press

The Collapse of Ancient States and Civilizations
Norman Yoffee & George L. Cowgill, eds.

Participants in the School for Advanced Research short seminar "Energy Development in Indian Country," Santa Fe, New Mexico, September 27–30, 2007. *Standing, from left*: Colleen O'Neill, Donald L. Fixico, Andrea Boardman, Garrit Voggesser, Andrew Needham, Benedict J. Colombi, Rebecca Tsosie, Dana E. Powell, Leah S. Glaser; *seated, from left*: Sherry L. Smith, Brian Frehner. Photograph by Jason S. Ordaz.